WOMEN AND WORK

An Annual Review

volume 3

Women and Work: An Annual Review

The Sage series **Women and Work: An Annual Review** brings together research, critical analysis, and proposals for change in a dynamic and developing field—the world of women and work. Cutting across traditional academic boundaries, the series approaches subjects from a multidisciplinary perspective. Historians, anthropologists, economists, sociologists, managers, psychologists, educators, policymakers, and legal scholars share insights and findings—giving readers access to a scattered literature in a single comprehensive yearly volume.

Women and Work will examine differences among women—as well as differences between men and women—related to nationality, ethnicity, social class, and sexual preference. The series will explore demographic and legal trends, international and multinational comparisons, and theoretical and methodological developments.

WOMEN AND WORK

An Annual Review
volume 3

EDITORS

Barbara A. Gutek
Ann H. Stromberg
Laurie Larwood

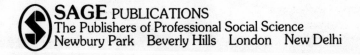
SAGE PUBLICATIONS
The Publishers of Professional Social Science
Newbury Park   Beverly Hills   London   New Delhi

Copyright © 1988 by Sage Publications, Inc.

For information address:

SAGE Publications, Inc.
2111 West Hillcrest Drive
Newbury Park, California 91320

SAGE Publications Inc.
275 South Beverly Drive
Beverly Hills
California 90212

SAGE Publications Ltd.
28 Banner Street
London EC1Y 8QE
England

SAGE PUBLICATIONS India Pvt. Ltd.
M-32 Market
Greater Kailash I
New Delhi 110 048 India

Printed in the United States of America

Library of Congress Cataloging-in-Publication Data

Library of Congress: 85-64 2613
International Standard Book Number: 0-8039-3252-9
International Standard Series Number: 0882-0910

FIRST PRINTING 1988

CONTENTS

ACKNOWLEDGMENTS

We gratefully acknowledge the assistance of the many people who worked with us on this volume. We thank B. J. Reich for all her efforts, and Jane Gray and Carole Becker for their many kindnesses. We and the authors also appreciate the valuable reviews of chapters provided by our editorial board members.

At this time, we particularly remember Eleanor Leacock, founding member of our Editorial Board, who died as we were preparing this volume.

SERIES EDITORS' INTRODUCTION

This is the third volume of *Women and Work: An Annual Review*, a series that brings together research, critical analyses, and review articles on the topic of working women. Based on the concept that a publication should be available to bring together research from all the disciplines that study women and work, the *Annual* is interdisciplinary in nature and intent. The purposes of the series are to spotlight the importance and variety of women's paid and unpaid work in our society and in other societies, to stimulate further research on women and work, and to provide a forum to which historians, anthropologists, economists, sociologists, psychologists, and management, educational, policy, and legal researchers, among others, can contribute.

Some research topics—such as women and work—are so wide ranging that they are not the exclusive province of any one discipline. Researchers studying multidisciplinary topics such as women and work often advance knowledge most when they intentionally cross traditionally distinct disciplinary boundaries. However, most scholars usually have a difficult time just keeping up with journals in their own fields, much less journals from other disciplines that might have occasional articles of relevance to them. *Women and Work* was created to overcome this problem, by bringing together important concepts, findings, and paradigms from the many disciplines engaged in the study of women and work. In this way, we hope to help to develop the field of women and work and to replace myths about working women and women's work with realities.

As with the first two volumes, each chapter in Volume 3 was invited and then reviewed by two members of the editorial board (one person within the author's discipline and one outside) as well as by the three series editors. The purpose of having reviewers from both the author's discipline and outside the author's discipline is to ensure that the articles are both current and accurate within the author's discipline and intelligible and accessible to readers outside the author's discipline.

In each volume of *Women and Work*, we present a symposium on a timely topic regarding women and work, generally by authors from several disciplines and, in some cases, with different points of view. This volume features a six-chapter symposium called "An International Perspective: Widening Our Horizons."

SYMPOSIUM: AN INTERNATIONAL PERSPECTIVE

In the United States some of the disciplines that study women and work, such as anthropology, have always transcended national borders; others have generally limited their study to women in this country. Further, sometimes because of the legitimate domain of the discipline (for example, management researchers tend to focus on women in U.S. management) and sometimes because of bias, researchers have particularly advanced our knowledge of women's employment in the United States with regard to elite professional and executive women. This trend toward focusing a disproportionate share of the research on a small proportion of employed women has been noted by many authors (see Stromberg & Harkess, 1988).

While research in the United States has proceeded rapidly in many areas concerning women and work, researchers in many disciplines in this country tend to be uninformed about theory and research carried out by scholars in other countries. Many European journals routinely publish in English in an effort to reach English-speaking researchers who are unlikely to notice work written in another language. Some European researchers have expressed disappointment that scholars in the United States still do not read or cite their research, even when it is in English. An international perspective is likely to reduce the isolation of our scholarship and to result in more collaborative and better-informed endeavors.

Somewhat belatedly, the various social sciences have discovered that the world is shrinking psychologically and that global economic interdependence is a reality. The situation in other countries has an effect on the United States as well as vice versa. In recognition of these trends, several of the social science disciplines have recently adopted international themes. For example, in 1987 the Academy of Management had as its theme an international perspective, and in 1988 the American Psychological Association has psychology in developing countries as its focus. The area of women and work, too, is affected by global interdependence. The kinds of jobs that women in the United States today get and reject depend in part on the paid and unpaid work of women in other countries. As manufacturing is increasingly a global process, with components made throughout the world, products are assembled in some distant location or in multiple locations to be shipped to various parts of the world. The labor of women and men in many countries and organizations is likely to have gone into the appliances used in your home, for example.

Similarly, national and corporate policies and regulations often take on an international perspective as multinational companies are introduced into host countries. For example, policies on maternity leave or sexual harassment, which may differ dramatically from location to location and are nonexistent in many parts of the world, can be introduced through multinational organizations.

Volume 3 of *Women and Work: An Annual Review* focuses on the global perspective on working women in order to call attention to the interdependence of working women throughout the world as well as to highlight similarities and differences in women's employment across countries. In putting together a symposium, we might have chosen a tightly knit set of articles representing one particular international perspective. We opted instead for a smorgasbord of articles in an attempt to "broaden our horizons." The six chapters in the symposium represent three ways in which we attempted to broaden our horizons. Three of them represent the growing research on comparative international development or the global economy. Researchers using the perspective of the global economy study economic interdependencies among countries as well as the effects of such interdependencies on various countries and within them, for example, on women. (For researchers who are unfamiliar with this field and wish to know more, there are several excellent volumes available; (see, for example, Beneria & Rolden, 1987; Nash & Fernández Kelly, 1983; Portes & Walton, 1981). One chapter on the global economy (Ward) represents an overview and the author's view of the field, and two other articles (Fernández Kelly and García; Nash) consist of specific research findings in the field. Fernández Kelly and García examine the effect of the global economy on Hispanic women's employment in Southern California, while Nash examines the effect of the global economy on women in Bolivia. A second type of chapter in the symposium is a specific analysis of working women in another culture from the perspective of an American researcher (Lapidus). The third type of chapter in the symposium represents the research of scholars outside the United States (Haavio-Mannila, Kauppinen-Toropainen, and Kandolin; Lewis and Cooper).

The first chapter in the symposium, "Women in the Global Economy," by Kathryn Ward, a sociologist, presents a provocative overview of the changes in paid labor brought about by a global economy, especially as it affects women in Third World countries. Ward argues that women's economic status has stagnated due to underdevelopment in Third World countries. She contends that women tend to be relegated to subsistence agriculture, transient employment by transnational companies, or jobs in the informal economy. According to Ward, capitalism, combined with patriarchy, accounts for differing effects of the global economy on men and women.

The next two chapters in the symposium detail particular situations of women and work. Anthropologists María Patricia Fernández Kelly and Anna M. García focus on the effect of the global economy on Hispanic women in the United States. They demonstrate that global economic and political processes affect employees in advanced industrial nations as well as Third World workers. More specifically, they examine two industries in Southern California, the garment industry and electronics, both of which employ many Hispanic women. Women are affected similarly by industrial restructuring in both industries in that they have similar hiring practices and wage levels, and both rely on various modes of subcontracting. Especially in the garment industry, however, more women are becoming small-scale entrepreneurs. There may be distinct advantages both for the companies where the women formerly worked and for the women entrepreneurs. Still, these women also tend to "live perilously on the edge of bankruptcy."

In her chapter, "The Mobilization of Women in the Bolivian Debt Crisis," June Nash provides another example of research on the way the global economy affects women's paid and unpaid work. The response of Latin American countries to the current debt crisis is affected by the policies of international agencies such as the International Monetary Fund, policies that in turn affect all aspects of life in the debtor countries. Nash illustrates the impacts of the debt on women and women's work in Bolivia. She focuses on women's strategies for economic survival in three regions of Bolivia: a mining area, an agricultural and trucking center, and an agrobusiness area.

In her chapter, political scientist Gail Lapidus focuses on one country, the Soviet Union. She examines the interaction of women's work and family roles in the U.S.S.R. Unlike the United States, the Soviet Union has specific policies about women's employment. Women are well integrated into the labor force and in fact constitute the majority (51%) of it. Yet there are problems. Occupations in the Soviet Union, as in most other countries, tend to be sex segregated, with women clustered into lower-paying and lower-prestige jobs. Work and family linkages are also problematic because, despite the widespread availability of child-care facilities in the Soviet Union, women shoulder the responsibility for maintaining household and family. Western policymakers and researchers have much to learn from the way the Soviet people grapple with these issues and from the reasons they have not been able to solve the problems faced by Soviet working women.

Finnish researchers Elina Haavio-Mannila, Kaisa Kauppinen-Toropainen, and Irja Kandolin report on their ongoing research on friendship, romance, and sex at work in the next chapter in the symposium. Finland is another country in which most women spend a significant portion of their adult lives in the labor force (Kauppinen-Toropainen, Haavio-Mannila, & Kandolin, 1984). Haavio-Mannila and her colleagues examine the extent to which the workplace contributes to cross-sex friendships, romance, and sexual harassment. They are particularly interested in the effect of sex composition of the work environment on friendship, romance, and sexual harassment because jobs in Finland, as in most other countries, are generally sex segregated. Are women's experiences different when they are in nontraditional jobs in which most of the other workers are men versus traditionally female jobs, in which women predominate?

The last chapter in the symposium is by two researchers in England, Suzan N.C. Lewis and Gary L. Cooper. They review the literature on stress in dual-earner couples. Their survey covers the range of English-speaking journals, and, although they rely heavily on U.S. data, they also include a section on the situation in the United Kingdom. Lewis and Cooper discuss sources of stress in dual-earner couples as well as the impact of stressors on their well-being. They accord a central role to sex-role ideology and conclude that the potential for stress in dual-earner couples is largely the product of internalized and institutionalized sex-role expectations. They also find that despite the intrusion of stress-producing sex-role expectations and, at least in the United Kingdom, policies based on stereotypical views of maternal responsibility, most couples cope well and are quite satisfied with their lifestyles. Not surprisingly, they find differences between husbands and wives, with women more likely than men to experience guilt and conflict between parental and work roles and men more likely than women to experience discomfort when their "major provider" role is threatened by their wives' success at work.

Together the six chapters in the symposium are intended to sensitize women and work scholars to the variety of experiences of women workers and the variety of research currently under way. Our aim in featuring a symposium on an international perspective is to widen our horizons.

CHAPTERS ON SELECTED TOPICS
REGARDING WOMEN AND WORK

In addition to the symposium, Volume 3 of Women and Work features five chapters about women and work on other selected topics: a chapter examining the hypothesis that women's relatively low wages are due to their intermittent employment history (Gwartney-Gibbs); a review of the literature on women's relationships with women in the workplace (O'Leary); an examination of the way women union stewards manage job and family responsibilities (Roby and Uttal); an examination of the development of commitment to work and family domains (Bielby and Bielby); and an explanation and test of a rational bias theory of discrimination in organizations (Larwood, Szwajkowski, and Rose). Two of the chapters in the symposium (Lapidus; Lewis and Cooper) and another two covering selected topics (Roby and Uttal; Bielby and Bielby) come under the broad topic of work and family. The prevalence of theory and research concerned with the interaction between work and family lends support to the contention that work-family linkages constitute a major research focus and a major issue for employed women, both in the United States and elsewhere.

In the first of the selected topics articles, sociologist Patricia A. Gwartney-Gibbs examines one common hypothesis frequently given for women's lower wages relative to men's: rusty skills. According to the rusty skills hypothesis, women's traditional household, childbearing, and child-care responsibilities lead to intermittency in employment; it is intermittency defined as "discontinuity of work experience" that accounts for women's lower wages. According to this argument, during the time a woman spends out of the labor force, her skills atrophy and thereby her human capital and subsequent earnings are lowered. Gwartney-Gibbs provides a careful analysis of the rusty skills hypothesis by disentangling several aspects of labor force discontinuity. She measures both characteristics of lifetime work experience (including duration with employers) and length of work experience (both time spent out of the labor force and intermittency defined as multiple labor force entries or exits). Her results challenge the argument that employment discontinuity should result in lower earnings. In fact, she contends that intermittency is a rational strategy for maintaining skills, rather than a mechanism by which skills become rusty.

Psychologist Virginia O'Leary reviews a generally understudied topic in her chapter, "Women's Relationships with Women in the Workplace." Pulling together literature from psychology, sociology, and popular sources, O'Leary examines what we know about women working for and with women. Because there is relatively little field research on the topic, many of the findings are based on laboratory studies or anecdotal accounts. Combining these disparate literatures, O'Leary comes to conclusions that are contrary to popular stereotypes—that working *for* a woman is problematic and working *with* women is difficult. Instead, she finds generally positive relationships between women at work, whether those are vertical, boss-subordinate relationships, or horizontal, co-worker relationships. However, her review of the literature shows that generally people still prefer to work for a man rather than a woman, if they express a preference, and many people believe that women are not wholly accepted in business.

Whereas O'Leary reviews an understudied topic, Pamela Roby and Lynet Uttal examine an understudied population: working women who are trade union stewards. Much has been written about the role conflict and role overload faced by women who combine paid employment with spouse and mother roles. Women who are union stewards add yet another role to their repertoire. Roby and Uttal consider how women handle all these roles and find some interesting, but not unexpected, differences between men and women union stewards, for example, in the kind of support they get from their spouses for their steward work.

Denise Bielby and William Bielby also review an area related to work and family. They focus on the concept of commitment, noting that "how adults form and distribute subjective attachments" across work and family roles has received little theoretical or research attention. The popular, "commonsense" notion is that men are more strongly committed than women to work, whereas women are more strongly committed than men to family. Synthesizing extant literature, Bielby and Bielby identify three alternative researchable perspectives on the commitment process in order to account for the way individuals develop preferences for a particular balance of paid work and family activities.

The final chapter in this volume, by Laurie Larwood, Eugene Szwajkowski, and Suzanna Rose, addresses "rational" discrimination. The authors test Larwood's rational bias theory of discrimination. According to rational bias theory, discrimination is a consequence of managers making personnel decisions concerning subordinates based on their own self-interest rather than on the abilities or capabilities of the subordinates. The chapter reviews the theory and reports results from a program of research on the topic. In three separate studies, Larwood, Szwajkowski, and Rose find support for rational bias in organizations and suggest that such bias helps to explain why discrimination in the workplace has proven difficult to eradicate.

—Barbara A. Gutek
Ann H. Stromberg
Laurie Larwood

REFERENCES

Beneria, L. & Rolden, M. (1987). *The Crossroads of Class and Gender.* Chicago: University of Chicago Press.

Kauppinen-Toropainen, K., Haavio-Mannila, E., & Kandolin, I. (1984). Women at work in Finland. In M. J. Davidson & C. L. Cooper (Eds.), *Working Women: An International Survey.* Chichester: John Wiley.

Nash, J., & Fernández-Kelly, M. P. (1983) *Women, Men, and the New International Division of Labor.* Albany: State University of New York Press.

Portes, A., & Walton, J. (1981) *Labor, Class, and the International System.* New York: Academic Press.

Stromberg, A. H., & Harkess, S. (1988) *Women Working* (2nd ed.). Mountain View, CA: Mayfield.

1

Women in the Global Economy

KATHRYN B. WARD

This article surveys the growing literature on women's economic status in the global economy. Using a world-system perspective, I argue that women's economic status has stagnated due to the processes of underdevelopment. Women are relegated to subsistence agriculture or enter the service or informal sectors. Women are excluded from industrial employment until the arrival of transnational corporations in light industries. This latter employment is transient and many women are once again displaced into service or informal economic sectors. To evaluate the effects of underdevelopment on women's status, we need to look at the degree of long-term independence and/or empowerment acquired by women through their contact with the global economy.

This article provides a synthesis of recent literature on women in development and research on the world-system or the global economy. A growing body of

AUTHOR'S NOTE: Some of the ideas in this chapter were formulated in papers presented at the Southwest Social Science Association meetings in San Antonio, Texas, in March 1985; Women in International Development Working Paper no. 120 (1986), Michigan State University; and in a keynote lecture at the Women and Work Conference at Purdue University, West Lafayette, Indiana, October 1986. I thank Rachel Rosenfeld for her integrative ideas; Linda Grant, Michael Timberlake, Paula England, Beth Hartung, Cindy Truelove, Davita Silfen Glasberg, the editors of this volume, and Marianne Ferber for their perceptive comments; Laura Whistle Cates for her patient word-processing; last, but not least, I acknowledge the inspiration of the late Jane Alison Weiss. Of course, I bear the ultimate responsibility for the contents.

macro and micro research has documented that, during development, women's economic status relative to men's has stagnated, particularly in currently developing countries or countries in the periphery of the capitalist world-system. Over time, the women's position has continued to decline (Boserup, 1970; Silvard, 1985; Tiano, 1987; United Nations, 1980; Ward, 1984). I propose that the world-system perspective (Bornschier & Chase-Dunn, 1985; Wallerstein, 1974) is more inclusive than previous modernization theories and hence more useful for explaining women's declining or stagnated status during development (for a review of other theories, see Inkeles & Smith, 1975; Todaro, 1985). The global economy shapes the overall context in which women work and live.

I argue that women's status has been directly and indirectly shaped by the emergence of the global capitalist economy, in particular, by three overlapping and sequential processes of trade dependency, dependent development, and debt dependency. As a consequence of the global economy, the peripheral regions in this global economy or capitalist world-system have experienced socioeconomic dependence on core nations along with *underdevelopment* or diminished relative rates of economic growth compared to core countries, structural distortion of their economies, heightened income inequality, and the lowered status of women (Bornschier, Chase-Dunn, & Rubinson, 1978; Ward, 1984). Here the diminished growth rates refer to the lower levels of economic growth for countries in the periphery compared to countries in the core. Structural distortion of the economy occurs when the periphery has an outward economic orientation toward the core trading partner and/or has experienced extraordinary growth of service sectors without first increasing industrial labor forces. Finally, inequality increases as core nations reap the benefits of their exploitation of peripheral countries; local periphery elites also benefit from their relationship with the core. Elites in the core (industrialized) and the periphery (developing) nations have controlled the flow and distribution of capital in the periphery.

The world-system emerged during the sixteenth century (Wallerstein, 1974) and now has incorporated three groups of regions/countries: core (industrialized), semiperiphery (nations in transition between core/periphery or socialist nations), and the periphery (currently developing countries). With the rise of socialism, socialist nations have occupied a competitive semiperiphery position. The world-system has encompassed the entire globe thereby leading to the seemingly anomalous situation of socialist nations and feudal societies competing in a capitalist world-economy (see Chase-Dunn, 1982).

Gender inequality increases when the processes of the capitalist world-system and underdevelopment interact with local forms of male dominance over women. This discussion assumes that in general capitalism is gender blind, but in interaction with patriarchy or male dominance, the resulting system—capitalist patriarchy—uses gender as a basic category in the economic system (for further elaboration of this perspective, see Hartmann, 1976; Mies, 1986; Sokoloff, 1980; Ward, 1984). In using the world-system perspective, I will gloss over cultural and religious differences by focusing on how the broader economic relationships of the core versus the semiperiphery and periphery affect the position of women (for discussion of the effects of religion, culture, and ideology, see, for example, Asfar, 1987; Austrin, 1987; Huntington, 1975; Ong, 1987). I argue, however, that the economic structure is the major determinant of the position of women.

Women as a group have had a lower proportion of the economic resources introduced by the world-system. As discussed below, with the arrival of the monetary economy via the world-system, women in subsistence economies found they had limited access to cash or monetary resources. Meanwhile, colonial officials gave indigenous men access to cash crops. Further, Western-sponsored development programs have targeted men. Thus women are often doubly disadvantaged by the world-system, as inhabitants of the periphery and as women.

I trace the deleterious effects of the global economy on women's status, defined here as women's access (relative to men's) to valued resources. My primary focus is on women's work both in the formal (paid) and in the informal (unpaid) economies in the developing or peripheral countries. *Informal economies* refer to the poorly paid labor with no social security in subsistence agriculture, domestic industries, food preparation, small-scale trading, and labor within the home (Portes, 1985; Portes & Sassen-Koob, 1987; Ward, 1984). I derive my synthesis through research using macro cross-national data and micro case studies. First, I examine how a process of the global economy, classical dependency, and pursuant underdevelopment affect women's socio-economic position in agriculture and trade. Second, I discuss the processes of dependent development or reliance on foreign investment and its effects through underdevelopment on women's position in industrial, service, and informal sectors. Third, I present a statistical overview of women's share of the total labor force and economic sectors (agriculture, industry, service) by position in the world-system and by geographic region. Fourth, I examine debt dependency and the potential impact of international debt crisis and underdevelopment on women's economic independence. Finally, I discuss two criteria for evaluating the effects of underdevelopment on women and directions for future research.

THE PROCESSES OF THE
GLOBAL ECONOMY

To analyze the role of women in the global economy, researchers often had to develop their own theories, because the early works on development rarely mentioned women other than as "breeders and feeders" (Boulding, 1977). Previous research assumed that, to bring about development, peripheral countries merely needed to follow the example of core countries. As development occurred, the socioeconomic benefits would automatically "trickle-down" to families and then to women. The peripheral countries soon found that following the example of core countries failed to bring about development.[1] Instead, underdevelopment occurred (lower rates of economic growth compared to the core, distortion of their economies, and heightened inequality). At the same time, the position of women relative to men has stagnated. Until recently, however, various theories of development have focused on the family and have often ignored the position of women as a group.

Classical Dependency

Bornschier and Chase-Dunn (1985) have argued that we can examine the initial effects of the world economy on underdevelopment through the process of classical dependency. *Classical dependency* refers to unequal socioeconomic relationships between the core and the periphery characterized by the extraction of raw materials and cash crops from the periphery for processing or consumption by the core. Periphery economies experienced commodity and trade partner concentration when they produced only a limited number of crops and/or minerals while trading with only one or two core nation partners (Galtung, 1971). In turn, the core regions provided the periphery with processed goods and the needed infrastructures for extraction of raw materials or crops. This pattern of trading relationships failed to generate autonomous economic growth and development in the periphery. Under such relationships, capital flowed to core and peripheral elites and was not reinvested for development efforts in the periphery. Peripheral regions became dependent on dominant core partners. Although the core was dependent on the periphery for raw materials, the core still controlled its peripheral trading partners through military force and dictating favorable terms for the core in its trading relationships. Thus, through this process, the periphery experienced the first characteristic of underdevelopment: lower relative rates of economic growth.

The peripheral regions experienced structural distortion of their economies because they were outwardly oriented toward the core regions rather than their own autonomous development (Galtung, 1971). Infrastructures such as business and transportation centers were established in the urban areas primarily to serve the international trade introduced by the world-system. Limited development of local production facilities occurred because the core provided the processing facilities and the finished goods. Concurrently, core countries tried to prevent competition with young core industries by discouraging industries in the economies of the periphery. For example, in India, Britain destroyed the emerging textile industries to protect British cotton mills (Griffin, 1979).

Hence only limited numbers of industrial or manufacturing jobs were created in peripheral regions, leading in part to the extraordinary growth of the tertiary or service sector compared to the growth of manufacturing *and* eventually the service sector in the core (Evans & Timberlake, 1980; London, 1987; Timberlake & Kentor, 1983). Thus agricultural workers displaced by mechanization could only find jobs in the service sector rather than in the industrial sector. Peripheral nations failed to develop their own industrial facilities for processing raw materials. Therefore, the peripheral nations experienced structural distortion of their economies through their outward dependence on the core for industrial goods and the extraordinary size of the less productive service sector.

Additionally, inequality increased between the core and the periphery as resources and capital flowed out of the periphery to the core because of the unequal exchange between the core and the periphery. Within the periphery, the privileged trading positions held by the elites increased income inequality because they used these connections with core elites to acquire more income and control the distribution of resources introduced by the world-system (Bornschier & Chase-Dunn, 1985; Rubinson, 1976). At the same time, gender inequality increased. Women in the periphery experienced the effects of both underdevelopment and limited access (relative to men's) to the new economic resources introduced by the arrival of the global economy (Ward, 1984).

Women and Underdevelopment

Researchers have defined the status of women in many ways (see Dixon, 1975; Mason, 1984; Rosaldo, 1980). I define the status of women as women's access to economic resources, relative to men's (Blumberg, 1981; Sanday, 1974; Tiano, 1987; Ward, 1984, 1985a; Ward & Pampel, 1985). Other components of women's status are women's relative share of educational, political, and organizational resources (Dixon, 1975; Seager & Olson, 1986; Silvard, 1985; Ward, 1984). Most researchers, however, argue that the economic component determines women's access to other resources. Space considerations limit my discussion to women's economic status.

Sanday (1974, 1981) has developed one of the more influential theories of women's status. She argues that men gained control over valued resources when changes were introduced by external influences such as war and colonial officials. Extending this argument, I propose that the arrival of the world capitalist system and commodity production in the peripheral areas resulted in an external sphere of control that enabled men to retain dominance over the valued economic resources introduced by the world-system and other resources such as schools or governments. Given the prevailing patriarchal relations (male dominance) of the core and the periphery, men were the group most likely to control the distribution of the new economic resources (for the elaboration of this argument, see Ward, 1984). In the next few sections, I use this perspective to examine women's access to agriculture and trade during classical dependency. Then I explore women's access to industrial, service, and informal economic sectors during the next process of dependent development.

Women and Agriculture

In many parts of the world, women have been the primary agricultural producers, providing up to 70% of the food supply (Blumberg, 1981; Boserup, 1970; United Nations, 1980). The colonial officials automatically assumed that men were the agricultural producers, because, in England and other core countries, men controlled agriculture (Boserup, 1970; Seidman, 1981; Tinker,

1976). Further, the arrival of land reform often meant the displacement of women from the land. The colonial officials gave the ownership of property and land to men instead of the women who were working the land (Blumberg, 1981; Boserup, 1970). Even though women have produced most of the food, men controlled the distribution of the food or the profits from selling/trading the food (Blumberg, 1981; Sanday, 1974, 1981). Thus because of the patriarchal structures and their interaction with the world-system, women once again had little control over the products of their agricultural labor.

With the arrival of colonial officials in Africa, and the institution of cash crop trading relationships, women became relegated to subsistence agricultural production without access to cash that was necessary for survival in the new economic system. African women have worked the fields by themselves when men have been conscripted to work in raw mineral extraction, for example, in South Africa and Lesotho (Mueller, 1977). In Latin America, the growing capital intensity of agriculture has further removed women from agricultural production (Deere, Humphries, & deLeal, 1982). At the same time, in Peru and Colombia, women are being recruited into agriculture when the men are recruited for factory jobs (Deere & deLeal, 1981). This agricultural work still is viewed by men as an extension of women's domestic work. Other women have been hired as strawberry workers in Mexico with their families to work on plantations for cash cropping or alternatively in agricultural businesses run by transnational corporations (Arizpe, 1977) or as agricultural workers in South and Southeast Asia (Blumberg, 1981; Boserup, 1970).

From the 1950s to the present, the importation of new agricultural technology and cultivation practices has often only reached men (Blumberg, 1981; Boserup, 1970; Charlton, 1984; Scott & Carr, 1985). For example, a group of development officials attempted to organize men in a village for education about new rice farming techniques. The men dutifully attended class, while women continued to work the rice fields, unaware of the new techniques (Tinker, 1976). Frequently, women have had only minimal access to credit, fertilizers, and other important resources needed to increase yields to feed ever growing populations. Finally, the Green Revolution in Central America and Asia, oriented toward elite farmers, has not only bypassed many male farmers, but has also been unavailable to most women farmers (Charlton, 1984; Sen, 1982).

Women also have participated in food processing, which consists of food preservation, processing, and storage. Over time, the arrival of new technology from the core has displaced women from processing employment (Chaney & Schmink, 1980; International Center for Research on Women [ICRW], 1980a; Jahan, 1979). The introduction of rubber rice rollers from Japan created unemployment among women as only men were hired to operate the rollers (Tinker, 1976). Women fish traders in West Africa were denied access to refrigeration (Robertson, 1976). Even though women might have provided cheaper labor, patriarchal relations restricted women's access to new technology and employment. These patriarchal relations also restricted women's trading activities.

Women and Trade

In Africa, the Caribbean, and parts of Asia, women traditionally have been the major traders (Boserup, 1970; Dixon; 1982). With the advent of the world-system and the arrival of the colonial administrations and trading companies, men gained access to and control over the international and national trading routes. Meanwhile, colonial officials, who ignored women's long-standing roles in trade, restricted women to regional and urban enclaves (Boserup, 1970; Mintz, 1971; Papanek, 1979; Simms & Dumor, 1976-1977). For example, after colonization, African women provided a cheap distributional network for international trading relationships via the urban areas where women distributed goods from urban ports to the interior or regional routes (Simms & Dumor, 1976-1977; Sudarkasa, 1977; Ward, 1985b). In other parts of the world, women traders contended with supermarkets being built on their traditional market-places. Further, they often have been unable to compete with men's mechanized businesses selling the same products (Mintz, 1971). The effects of the arrival of the world-system on women traders has been their increasing dependence on men for licenses and capital, even where men expected women's socioeconomic independence (Jules-Rosette, 1982). Thus, by the time of the arrival of foreign investment and dependent development, women in the peripheral regions were already excluded from capitalist production introduced by the global economy.

According to these case studies, cash cropping and the introduction of new processing technology had negative effects on women's access to economic resources. Macro cross-national research using multiple regression analyses on 105 countries also supports these findings (Ward, 1984, 1985a).[2] Trade dependency and dependence on foreign investment had negative effects on women's share of the total labor force and their share of the agricultural sectors in 1975, controlling for economic development, changes in the size of the labor force, and women's share of tertiary education. The mix of raw and processed imports and exports—that is, the diversity of trade—had a positive effect on women's employment. The more balanced the trade structure of the country, and the less economically dependent, the greater women's access to employment. State-controlled economies had a positive effect on women's share of the total labor force and share of agricultural employment. State-controlled economies can mediate some of the negative effects of the world-system on women's access to employment (Ward, 1984, 1985a). Thus classical dependency and under-development introduced by the world-system, for the most part, had negative effects on women's share of the overall labor force and agricultural sector. The actual size of negative effects on women's share of agriculture may be understated, because we lack reliable data on women's agricultural participation (Dixon, 1982).

Dependent Development

From the 1950s until the early 1970s, many peripheral nations sought to generate development through import substitution strategies. They built their own heavy industrial plants to remedy their poor balance of payments generated by past unequal trading relationships with core nations. For most peripheral countries, cash crops and raw minerals often failed to provide the needed capital to pay for the industrial plants. Because of their continued dependence on the core, the peripheral nations were forced to turn once again to the core and core corporations for investments to build production facilities. Meanwhile, world financial institutions such as the World Bank and the United Nations were interested in promoting investment in peripheral areas. As a result of these foreign capital flows, the periphery exhibited some short-term economic growth (see, for example, Cardoso & Faletto, 1979; Evans, 1979).

Over time, however, signs of underdevelopment reemerged. Bornschier and Chase-Dunn (1985) found that development generated by foreign investment eventually led to underdevelopment. Initially, economic growth occurred because foreign capital flowed into the country, thereby raising the level of the gross national product. In the long run, however, much of the profits and capital from the new industrial plants flowed overseas to the core nations, to the headquarters of the investing transnational corporations (TNCs), to local elites, or to all of the above. For example, Muller (1979, p. 164) found that not only did the TNCs use and tie up *local* capital, but they also repatriated 79% of their profits during 1960 through 1968. For TNC subsidiaries, 52% of the profits left peripheral countries. Thus profits often were not reinvested in local development efforts, and local capital left the country.

Further, structural distortion of the economy in the periphery occurred with the extraordinary growth of the service sector relative to the industrial sector (Evans & Timberlake, 1980; Timberlake, 1985). In the experience of the core nations, the agricultural labor force, displaced by mechanization, moved into labor-intensive factories. Much later, workers moved into the service sector as capitalism progressed and industries utilized more capital-intensive facilities. In contrast, the TNCs and core nations provided the latest in industrial technology for their plants in the peripheral areas (i.e., capital-intensive technology rather than labor-intensive technology). As a result, fewer jobs were created relative to the amount of investment. Agricultural workers displaced by the mechanization of agriculture by core corporations and local elites competed for a limited number of industrial positions. Hence many workers have moved directly into the less productive and low-wage service sector.

Underdevelopment was thereby regenerated because unemployed and displaced workers in peripheral nations who faced minimal growth in industrial employment bypassed industrial jobs and went into the less productive service sector. Further, although the initial *flows* of capital from foreign investment led to economic growth, in the long run, the cumulative *stocks* of capital from high levels of foreign investment relative to local investment led to capital outflow to core corporations and banks and the structural distortion of the economy. Thus the flows and stocks of capital are important components of the latest forms of dependent development and, as will be discussed later, debt dependency.

The poor economic position of women continued under import substitution policies. This precarious position was reinforced by the arrival of capital-intensive and heavy industries that reinforced occupational segregation. With the limited industrial job market in many peripheral nations, men were given job preference (Chaney & Schmink, 1980; Mazumdar, 1979).

Although women might provide cheaper labor, once again, patriarchal relations intervened to provide men with control over the new jobs (see Hartmann, 1976; Mies, 1986; for a more extensive discussion of capitalist patriarchy and men's control over women's productive and reproductive roles). This pattern points to a contradiction in capitalist patriarchy: Sometimes women are not hired as men seek to control female labor; yet, at other times, women are hired because employers can maximize profits by paying them lower wages than men. Hossfeld (1986) calls the use of these contradictions by employers and men "gender tactics." Pyle (1986) has documented how the Irish government managed foreign investment to exclude women industrial workers.

Protective legislation was another mechanism for precluding women's employment because employers wanted to avoid maternity costs that raised the cost of female labor. For example, in Peru during the late 1950s, no new women workers were hired in factories (Chaney & Schmink, 1980). Many of the plants replaced women's traditional cottage industries, but women were not hired in the new plants (Dixon, 1982). More women compared to men found jobs only in the service or the informal sectors, where they worked as domestic servants, food vendors, hawkers of single cigarettes, traders, laundresses, and seamstresses— all occupations unprotected by social security benefits (Portes & Sassen-Koob, 1987). As will be discussed below, this marginalization of women from industrial or paid employment has contributed to the growth and feminization of the informal sector (Chaney & Schmink, 1980; Sassen-Koob, 1984; Ward, 1985b). Now most women around the world are located in the agricultural, service, or informal sectors.

During the late 1960s and into the 1970s, some women have become the new favored workers in the next stage of development strategies: export processing or light labor-intensive industries in the global assembly line. Export processing yields products for exports rather than for local consumption. This shift toward women workers is a remarkable turnabout by TNCs on the desirability of women workers compared with hiring practices during import substitution. Although export processing has constituted a smaller proportion of overall manufacturing investment than import substitution (Bornschier & Chase-Dunn, 1985), export processing has had a higher proportion of women workers relative to men workers. As I also discuss below, international financial institutions such as the World Bank and other development agencies now tout export processing as the best new strategy for generating development and repaying loans.

Export Processing and the
Global Assembly Line

In their search for profits during the 1960s and 1970s, many core corporations sought cheaper labor costs to raise profits and to remain competitive. To do so required lowering labor costs either through cheaper labor or automation. At the same time, the TNCs were unable to raise prices to maintain profits. For example, a growing number of technological breakthroughs and industry competition lowered the selling prices of an integrated circuit from $50 in 1966 to $2.35 in 1976 (North American Congress on Latin America [NACLA], 1977, p. 7). Hence the reduction of labor costs was one solution. For example, the average daily wage (U.S. dollars, 1976) in U.S. electronics plants ranged from $28 to $37. In contrast, the Mexican daily wage was $7, and in Taiwan, it was $2 (NACLA, 1977, p. 15).

TNCs transformed their production to take advantage of cheap capital costs in the core by beginning capital-intensive production steps in the core. Then the TNCs used the cheap female labor of the periphery for assembly or finishing work. Through this arrangement, the periphery could ideally avoid its problems of expensive capital and employ its abundant labor supply to generate development. These steps have led to a *new* international division of labor that is highly complex, with each step in production divided among workers in different parts of the world (Fuentes & Ehrenreich, 1983; NACLA, 1977).

This new division of labor differs from the one used by the core countries during their development processes. First, during their development, the core countries and their industries maintained control over their products and limited competition for their products. Second, their industries produced for local consumption in the core rather than for large-scale export. Third, the industries in peripheral countries now compete with industries in other peripheral countries. As a result of this competition, these industries produce limited returns to be used for development compared with the past experiences of the core. Finally, in the global assembly line, production is broken up into steps. Peripheral countries have limited control over the overall production process when plants in their countries are merely one stop in the assembly process.

The TNC strategies were encouraged by the world financial institutions and core nations (primarily the World Bank, International Monetary Fund, and the United States). They provided loans, mandated export processing projects, and promoted the establishment of export processing zones (EPZs). These zones and periphery governments provided the TNCs with special industrial areas that had minimal or no taxes, no unions, and a supply of docile workers as an incentive to locate their plants in a particular country. In turn, the international financial institutions expected export processing to provide a source of income for loan payments (Fuentes & Ehrenreich, 1983).

Within the core nations, the TNCs moved textile, garment, and electronics plants to economically disadvantaged areas in the core where they could hire indigenous female populations at very low wages (Hossfeld, 1986; Robert, 1983; Safa, 1981). Meanwhile, the TNCs also sought the labor of women of color and recent immigrants, including illegal immigrants in core economies (Sassen-Koob, 1983, 1985). Finally, seeking cheap labor in the competitive world market, the export-oriented TNCs in light industries (electronics, textiles, garments, pharmaceuticals, and toys) went overseas to peripheral areas. There the TNCs could take advantage of the marginalized female labor force displaced or excluded from paid jobs during underdevelopment generated by classical dependency and dependent development. In this manner, TNCs could maintain their profits in ultracompetitive markets. The previously unexploited labor of women was a central variable of this new strategy.

The labor intensive elements of the TNCs' light industrial production have moved overseas from the United States and other core countries. The capital-intensive elements of production, planning, and research and development have remained in the hands of semiskilled U.S. workers (Ehrenreich & Fuentes, 1981; Green, 1983; Grossman, 1979-1980; Snow, 1983). While many of the electronics jobs have been occupied by either women or minorities, this proportion has changed. Snow (1983) found that most of the jobs that have gone overseas were women's positions. Most of the newly created jobs in electronics remaining in the United States have been men's jobs. Thus women workers in the core economies have lost electronic jobs. Similar trends have occurred in the textiles and garment industries (Chapkis & Enloe, 1983).

The core nations also supported the investment efforts of TNCs by introducing favorable tariff laws for core corporations investing in peripheral nations. Relying on favorable tariff schedules that provided an important margin of profit, many core companies transferred their production to the global assembly line. Under the U.S. Tariff code 807, the TNCs were charged tariffs only on value added abroad (defined value added to the product by the overseas assembly, not as the final product). For example, an electronics firm ships a partially assembled television worth $150 to an assembly plant in the periphery. Workers in that plant complete more assembly worth $50. The television is now worth $200, but the TNC only pays a tariff on the $50 of value added abroad. By 1977, over 596 electronics plants had run away to other countries to take advantage of these tariffs and many assembly workers in the core had lost their jobs (NACLA, 1977).

The peripheral nations perceived that TNC investment in export processing would provide much needed capital for investment in development efforts. Their workers would acquire job training and valuable skills, and the newly created jobs would alleviate some of their unemployment problems. The governments sought to establish export processing zones and to compete actively with one another for TNC investments (Grossman, 1979-1980; Siegel, 1979-1980).

Initially, the textile, garment, and electronics industries moved to Central America and the Caribbean in the 1960s (NACLA, 1977). After unionization drives, demands for higher wages by workers in Central America and the Caribbean, and extensive advertising campaigns by Southeast Asian countries (extolling the virtues of their workers and the types of relocation incentives), the plants moved to South Korea, Taiwan, and Singapore. After the mobilization of women workers to demand higher wages and better working conditions in these plants, the TNCs moved to the Philippines, Indonesia, Malaysia, and China. Now some of the plants are moving to the utterly impoverished areas, such as Bangladesh (Lim, 1983a). Given the relationship between TNCs and underdevelopment and the TNCs history of geographical mobility, I argue that the TNCs' investments in light industries eventually may have mixed consequences for women workers. In the following section, I will be developing the argument that, in the short run, such investments provide some women with jobs. In the long run, however, these women face job instability and potentially greater economic dependence on their families and TNCs. While the male-dominated design and production jobs stay in the core, women workers across core and periphery nations may find themselves competing more intensively with one another when the female assembly jobs are moving overseas. As Safa (1981) has noted, however, people in the core can do something about this competition. For example, West German unions now stipulate the wage rates of German TNC subsidiaries in the periphery.

Women in the Global Assembly Line

Women in the global assembly line are affected by the intersection of capitalism and patriarchal forces that shape women's productive and reproductive roles. TNCs use this intersection to pay the lowest possible wages. These patterns were first seen in the core countries. Social and economic institutions defined textile work as an extension of women's labor in the home. Factory owners recruited women workers in the core. With the unionization of some women workers in the core light industries, and their demands for higher wages, however, the TNCs sought female labor overseas at wages of up to 50% less than men's wages (Elson & Pearson, 1981a).

Overseas, the TNCs found many unemployed female and male workers in Central America, the Caribbean, and South and Southeast Asia. Although women workers in TNCs have been only a small proportion of all women workers, they now constitute a rapidly growing proportion of women workers, particularly in Southeast Asia. Lim (1985, p. 7) estimates that women compose at least 28% of *all* TNC employment. Of the light industries, women composed a majority of the assembly workers. The TNCs' target workers for the electronics plants, however, were young educated women who had no previous labor force experience. In the textile trades, TNCs often were able to hire single parents or older married women whose husbands or partners were unemployed. Other women workers include women agricultural workers who are seasonally unemployed. These workers have been found, for instance, in the Mexico border area or in Colombia (Fernández Kelly, 1983). Meanwhile, the general level of unemployment remained high around the industrial areas (Fernández Kelly, 1983; Tiano, 1984).

Economic Liberation?

Some researchers have argued that TNC employment provides economic opportunities for women and leads to the liberation of women from their economic marginalization and local patriarchal constraints (Lim, 1983a, 1983b, 1985; Tinker, 1976). For example, Lim (1983a, 1985) argues that women TNC workers receive better wages and working conditions than those found in local factories and other occupations. These wages enable women to acquire life experience, possessions, and status outside of the family. Women delay marriage and childbearing. Those women who work outside the home after marriage may have greater decision-making power within their families than women who do not work outside of the home (Lim, 1985).

Economic Subjugation?

Other researchers have argued that instead of liberating women, such employment only intensifies and reiterates women's subordinate position in their society (Elson, 1983; Elson & Pearson, 1981a; Fuentes & Ehrenreich, 1983; Young, 1984). Governments and TNC factories selectively manipulate women's reproductive *and* productive roles to meet the demand for female workers. For example, when employers in Puerto Rico became concerned about the supply of nonpregnant female labor, investments in sterilization and birth control programs increased dramatically (Enloe, 1984). Now over one-third of all Puerto Rican women have been sterilized.

Obviously, this relationship between TNC investment and family planning and sterilization programs needs further investigation (see Ward, 1984, for a discussion of the relationship between underdevelopment, family planning, the status of women, and fertility). For example, there are important differences between family planning and population control programs. Family planning programs involve an element of choice, while population control programs are coercive. If sterilization is a condition for continued employment, then this sterilization is population control. In Puerto Rico, women workers have only limited choice in family planning.

Another interesting example of government manipulation of women's family roles occurred in a semiperipheral country, Ireland, where the government feared that availability of industrial employment for women would threaten the family. The government then selectively recruited foreign investment that would provide men with jobs while using state policy to limit women's employment (Pyle, 1986). Last but not least, during World War II, the U.S. government used Rosie the Riveter propaganda plus provision of day-care facilities to encourage women's labor force participation. After the war, these incentives suddenly decreased and the government emphasized women's childbearing rather than paid employment roles.

Likewise, men and TNCs manipulate women's productive capabilities. I propose that women's economic dependence on these plants, men, and their families is recomposed and perpetuated through low wages, limited job stability, and untransferable training. Young women move from the control of their family and fathers to TNC plants that replicate the patriarchal control. These plants have male managers and hierarchical forms of organization that allow limited opportunities for advancement of women (Fernández Kelly, 1983; Grossman, 1979-1980; Ong, 1987; Pena, 1985). For example, the TNCs have tried to instill passive female behavior with tactics such as company-sponsored beauty pageants that promote core countries' standards of femininity and docility instead of paying women wages adequate for their own country (Grossman, 1979-1980). Meanwhile, men work as supervisors and technicians, where they receive higher wages and have greater opportunities for advancement than women (Fernández Kelly, 1983; Hossfeld, 1986).

Regarding wages, the women receive wages 50% lower than men's wages (Elson & Pearson, 1981a). In electronics during the late 1960s and early 1970s, women's wages ranged from 17 cents an hour in Indonesia to $1.20 an hour in Singapore (Grossman, 1979-1980). For the garment industry, the International Ladies Garment Workers Union has noted that women's wages "can run to 16 cents an hour for China, 57 cents an hour in Taiwan and over $1 an hour in Hong Kong" (Serrin, 1984, p. 5). In a program advised by the World Bank, Sri Lanka garment workers earn $5 for a long workweek (Fuentes & Ehrenreich, 1983, p. 38). Women's wages are $5 an hour or more for the same job in the United States. In many factories, if women become too proficient at their work, they lose their jobs before their accumulated work experience would make them eligible for higher wages. Employers argue that experienced women workers are too expensive compared to inexperienced workers.

These wages are low relative to subsistence costs. As Grossman (1979-1980, p. 10) found in Indonesia, monthly wages for a starting worker are $19 while monthly expenses are $26. After two years of employment, the worker can expect to make $29. Expenses are for a room shared with four or more roommates, transportation, and food. Fuentes and Ehrenreich (1983a, p. 17) note the relative prices and minutes that women have to work to buy an egg, one kilogram of rice, and a T-shirt; for example, some of the approximate times are listed by country and item: Sri Lanka—29, 161, and 3287 minutes; Korea—7, 119, and 312 minutes; Malaysia—14, 75, and 897 minutes; Philippines—20, 70, and 611 minutes. Clearly, even with the low prices in the periphery, women's worker wages are barely at the subsistence level. In fact, they have to work long hours just to purchase basic items.

Many women also turn over their wages to their families and can keep only small amounts for themselves. Sometimes the wages are so low that the families have subsidized the female workers. Wolf (1986) found, in rural Java, women's wages were so low, that families provided economic subsidies to their daughters. Thus TNCs were able to keep their wages low while maintaining their profit levels.

Rapid labor turnover, hazardous working conditions, threats by TNCs to run away, and downturns in the international economy threaten job stability in these factories. Also, if women workers become pregnant, they lose their jobs. In the electronics plants, women must peer through microscopes for many consecutive hours. Eventually, they lose the perfect eyesight needed for employment. Hazardous chemicals or dust in the textiles and garment plants also cause health problems (Ehrenreich & Fuentes, 1981; Grossman, 1979-1980; Jackson, 1983). Further, if the women workers attempt to organize into unions or struggle for higher wages, the companies may respond by threatening to close the plants, by firing women organizers, or by the use of violent thugs (Fuentes & Ehrenreich, 1983; Grossman, 1979-1980). Alternatively, women may find that, at the request of the TNCs, any prior protective legislation regarding health and safety regulations has disappeared (Grossman, 1979-1980).

Finally, the women's employment becomes tied to the vagaries of both the international and the local economies, where women's jobs are subject to recession-generated layoffs, particularly in the electronics industries. Training is minimal for the workers. Often when TNCs lay them off, the women find themselves with nontransferable job skills. Once the export processing zone incentives cease (e.g., with the imposition of taxes and tariffs), TNCs leave and women are unemployed. This has occurred in Jamaica and Puerto Rico (Bolles, 1983; Fuentes & Ehrenreich, 1983). Meanwhile, these displaced workers, who depend on the TNC jobs for their livelihood, must find new sources of income. Given the high overall unemployment rate in the periphery and women's earlier displacement from paid employment (both due to underdevelopment), these women then must seek work as service or informal sector workers, or as prostitutes, or they return home (Barry, 1979; Neumann, 1979-1980; Sassen-Koob, 1984). With these job stability problems, the number of women going through the TNC plants has grown over time. Ehrenreich and Fuentes (1981) have estimated that more than nine million women have passed in and out of the TNC plants. Thus, during economic crises of the global economy and faced with the loss of their jobs, women are potentially more dependent on men, their families, and the TNCs for survival.

In summary, in the short run, TNC employment enhances some women's job and wage opportunities, especially compared with the limited opportunities in other sectors. In the long run, however, many women who have TNC employment opportunities receive subsistence wages, work under the control of male managers, receive nontransferable training, and experience the instability of such employment when TNCs move to other countries. Finally, unemployed factory workers have limited access to other jobs due to high rates of unemployment in peripheral economies. Instead of liberating women, the long-run effects of this employment are to reshape women's subordination. Thus such investment and employment reintensifies and recomposes women's subordination. This pattern of short- and long-run effects follows the positive short-run and negative long-run effects of investment on development found by Bornschier and Chase-Dunn.

Macro-level research provides some support for these arguments. Bornschier and Chase-Dunn (1985) found that, in the long run, for a sample of 90 peripheral nations, higher levels of foreign investment in manufacturing had negative effects on economic growth and increased income inequality compared with countries with control over and/or limited foreign investment. Over time, foreign investment leads to continued underdevelopment because countries lose control over the type of investment, and profits are frequently repatriated to the core and not reinvested for development.

Similar negative effects of dependency have also been found for women. In her regression analyses on 105 countries, Ward (1984, 1985a) found that foreign investment and TNC investment in manufacturing in 1967 had negative effects on women's share of industrial employment in 1975. Trade dependency also affected women's industrial share. TNC investment in agriculture and a decrease in commodity concentration of exports decreased women's share of industrial jobs. The diversity of the foreign trade structure or the relative balance of raw and processed goods increased women's share. Finally, one consequence of underdevelopment, income inequality, also lowered women's industrial employment. Unfortunately, data that distinguish between the levels of investment in import substitution versus export processing were unavailable. Further, the effects of the export processing on women and development may take place over a longer time frame than between 1967 and 1975.

Women and Service Employment

Underdevelopment plays an important role in allocating women to the service sector through the extraordinary growth of the overall service sector. The most common job for women in the service sector is personal service or domestic work. This type of job is particularly prevalent among rural to urban female migrants (Buvinic, Youssef, & Von Elm, 1978; Jelin, 1977, 1980; Ward, 1985b). Other occupations include laundry, seamstressing, trading, and food-related jobs (Boserup, 1970; Dixon, 1982).

Once again, women are disadvantaged vis-à-vis men in the service sector. The women's jobs provide minimal wages and limited mobility to more lucrative positions in the service sector and other parts of the economy. Capitalist elites often view women's service employment as an extension of women's unpaid homework and pay accordingly (for an alternative view, see Smith, 1984). For example, women domestic workers often receive only room and board. At the same time, men have gained control over the higher-paying jobs in the service sector and those jobs that require more education (Papanek, 1979). Thus women in the service sector often face similar economic barriers to those confronting women in agriculture and industry.

Women and Informal Employment

After underdevelopment displaces women from other sectors in the economy, they often seek work in the informal sector, which is labor unprotected by social benefits in subsistence agriculture, domestic industries, food preparation, small-scale trading, and unpaid labor within the home (Portes, 1985; Portes & Sassen-Koob, 1987; Ward, 1984). Women's participation in the informal sector of urban areas is quite extensive. Out of all urban workers, approximately 53% to 69% of them are in the informal sector. Out of this informal sector in the periphery, 46% to 70% of the workers are female (ICRW, 1980a).

Saffiotti (1978) has argued that the world-system requires the informal sector for its survival and profits. This sector plays an important role in keeping wages depressed because the TNCs and employers assume that the informal sector labors of women and children can narrow disparities between subsistence needs and men's wages (see also Deere, Humphries, & deLeal, 1982; Jelin, 1977; Portes, 1985; Smith, 1984). As a consequence, employers may pay wages lower than the subsistence level.[3]

The conditions of underdevelopment and the informal sector place women in a significant socioeconomic bind. This sector provides minimal opportunities for women-headed households, who are the poorest of the poor (Buvinic, Youssef, & Von Elm, 1978). As noted earlier, women head one-fourth to one-third of all households around the world (Silvard, 1985). This percentage is increasing. Furthermore, informal sector activities are compatible with child rearing, thereby stymying potential socioeconomic pressures toward lower fertility. Women in this sector are more likely to end their breast-feeding earlier, thereby, in the absence of contraception, shortening the birth interval and raising fertility (Standing, 1983).

Hence, another related and emerging area of concern is the relationship between women's economic status and their fertility behavior during under-development (Ward, 1984). I argue that women should have control over their reproductive choice as well as access to economic resources. This is the difference between family planning and population control programs. Likewise, poor female heads of households must have access to economic resources, yet they are often denied access to jobs and training programs (Youssef & Hetler, 1983). Past research by Coale (1973) on the use of family planning indicates that people use family planning when three conditions are met: when family planning is a conscious choice, when family planning is socially and economically advantageous, and when birth control is available. For female-headed households, the informal labor of women and children can provide up to 50% of the household income (ICRW, 1980b). Thus these women perceive an economic advantage for children.

At the same time, if women have access to economic resources, then fertility often takes care of itself. The problem with underdevelopment is that women are economically marginalized into the service and informal sectors, where childbearing is economically advantageous (Ward, 1984). Therefore, Youssef (1979) advocates the provision of income-generation projects for women and not merely family planning programs as a means to deal with the problems of female-headed households in poverty and population growth.

CONTEMPORARY TRENDS IN WOMEN'S FORMAL EMPLOYMENT

Meanwhile, the consequences of women's marginal economic status during underdevelopment are clear even in official labor force statistics. Tables 1.1 and 1.2 provide a statistical overview of women's position in the official paid labor force by location in the world-system and by geographical region. These statistics are incomplete because many of women's economic activities are excluded in labor force statistics (Dixon, 1982; Newland, 1980). Further, these statistics do not include women's unpaid and informal sector activities that are a major source of subsistence for families around the world (ICRW, 1980b). Nonetheless, these data reveal distinct labor force patterns by position in the world economy and by region (see also the discussion in Ward, 1984).

Table 1.1 reveals that, in every region, core, semiperiphery, or periphery, women have a lower share of the labor force and of all economic sectors relative to men. (Here *semiperiphery* refers to countries between the core and periphery in economic power, for example, socialist nations or countries in transition between core and periphery status.) According to Table 1.1, women in the periphery lag behind their sisters in the core and semiperiphery in every category over time. Additionally, increases in women's share of the labor force and the various sectors have been negligible for women in the periphery. Most of the increases in women's share of the labor force have come through increases in women's share of the service sector.

Table 1.2 illustrates the geographical differences in women's share of the labor force and various sectors. Most African women are agricultural workers and have high rates of labor force participation. Yet their share of the labor force has not increased from 1960 to 1975. Grouping all African countries together also obscures the extremely low traditional rates of formal participation by Northern African women. In other regions of the world, we find high labor force participation rates for women in Europe along with a greater female share of the labor force and service sector. Women in the Americas have a low rate of participation in the overall labor force and in the agricultural and industrial

TABLE 1.1

Women's Share of the Labor Force, Participation Rate,
and Share of Agricultural, Industrial, and Service Sectors
in World-System, 1960 and 1975

Position	N^a	PWLF 1960 %	PWLF 1975 %	WLFP 1960 %	WLFP 1975 %	PWAG 1960 %	PWAG 1975 %	PWIND 1960 %	PWIND 1975 %	PWSER 1960 %	PWSER 1975 %
Core	18	31	35	39	46	22	24	20	23	42	45
Semiperiphery	30	28	31	37	41	27	28	20	22	32	37
Periphery	78	28	29	40	40	26	26	17	19	27	30

SOURCE: ILO (1977). Table 1.1 is from Ward, K. 1985b. "Women and Urbanization in the World-System." In *Urbanization and the World-Economy*, edited by M. Timberlake. Orlando: Academic, p. 319. Reprinted by permission.
NOTE: PWLF—women's share of labor force relative to men's; WLFP—women's participation rate; PWAG, PWIND, PWSER—women's share of agricultural, industrial, and service sectors, respectively, relative to men's. The share variables are computed by dividing the female labor force aged 15 to 64 (total or by sector) by the overall labor force aged 15 to 64 or employment in each sector. The participation variable is computed by dividing the total female labor force by the total female population aged 15 to 64.
a. Number of countries in each group.

TABLE 1.2

Women's Share of the Labor Force, Participation Rate,
and Share of Agricultural, Manufacturing, and Service Sector
by Geographic Region, 1960 and 1975

Geographic Region	N^a	PWLF 1960 %	PWLF 1975 %	WLFP 1960 %	WLFP 1975 %	PWAG 1960 %	PWAG 1975 %	PWIND 1960 %	PWIND 1975 %	PWSER 1960 %	PWSER 1975 %
Africa	41	31	31	47	45	31	32	15	17	24	26
Americas	27	23	25	28	29	11	10	20	19	43	43
Asia	31	25	28	36	38	27	29	18	22	20	26
Europe	27	33	35	43	48	30	32	22	24	40	44

SOURCE: ILO (1977). Table 1.2 is from Ward, K. 1985b. "Women and Urbanization in the World-System." In *Urbanization and the World-Economy*, edited by M. Timberlake. Orlando: Academic, p. 320. Reprinted by permission.
NOTE: PWLF—women's share of labor force relative to men's; WLFP—women's participation rate; PWAG, PWIND, PWSER—women's share of agricultural, industrial, and service sectors, respectively, relative to men's. The share variables are computed by dividing the female labor force aged 15 to 64 (total or by sector) by the overall labor force aged 15 to 64 or employment in each sector. The participation variable is computed by dividing the total female labor force by the total female population aged 15 to 64.
a. Number of countries in each group; there are 126 countries total.

sectors. At the same time, women constitute nearly half of the service sector. Meanwhile, Asian women have somewhat higher levels of participation and have slightly higher shares of agricultural and industrial employment. Thus women over time are still disadvantaged relative to men in their share of formal labor force and sectoral employment. They are also segregated into either the agriculture or the service sectors. These disparities exist across world-system and regional positions. I predict these differences will continue with the escalation of global debt crises.

Debt Dependency

Researchers have studied the third process of the world-system, debt dependency (Debt Crisis Network, 1985; Glasberg & Ward, 1985, 1986; Nash, this volume; Ward & Glasberg, 1986; Wood, 1985). Glasberg and Ward (1985, 1986) argue that trade dependency and transnational corporation investment have paved the way for the arrival of international finance capital or multinational banks in the periphery. Consistent with earlier research of Bornschier and Chase-Dunn (1985), they argue that, initially, the capital flows of the multinational banks and international loans will generate development. In the long run, however, problems with loan repayments will lead to underdevelopment, especially with the imposition of austerity programs. The stocks of debt will have similar negative effects on the development like the earlier effects of foreign investment stocks on development.

Since 1975, development efforts in peripheral regions have become increasingly burdened with high debts and interest payments to international financial institutions and private banks. The high price of oil set by OPEC has only compounded these problems. Additionally, the international financial institutions increasingly have dictated the restructuring of the ailing peripheral economies (Nash, this volume; Wood, 1985). This intervention has taken the form of mandatory austerity programs imposed by the International Monetary Fund and the World Bank, among others.[4] These programs have sought to restore "free market" policies and often have meant the demise of social and redistributional programs. Increasing proportions of national economies now service debt rather than development efforts. Potential development capital thereby flows out of the country to core financial institutions. At the same time, TNCs and international financial institutions encourage or mandate increased investment in export processing (Wood, 1985).

Debt dependency only perpetuates the disadvantaged economic status of women relative to men. In an economy with high unemployment, men receive preference for most jobs owing to patriarchal assumptions about men's provider roles (for an example of this in Ireland, see Pyle, 1986). This preference remains even though, during underdevelopment, dramatic increases in the number of female-headed households mean that more women must support their families (Buvinic, Youssef, & Von Elm, 1978). Repression of labor unions by TNCs and local governments hurts women workers who are already struggling for higher wages and who often bear the brunt of violence when governments and TNCs attempt to break unions (Chapkis & Enloe, 1983; Grossman, 1979-1980). Denationalization of plants diminishes government control over the wages and working conditions for women as well as the flight of the industries to other countries. The devaluation of currency and pursuant inflation that are supposed to improve the competitiveness of exports in turn raise the costs of imported parts for assembly in TNCs. Then these export plants close down and leave newly employed women out of work (Bolles, 1983). The cuts in social welfare programs mean that the national economy is being balanced on the backs of women. Finally, the commitment of the country's export earnings to the national debt rather than to development means that women subsistence farmers and other agricultural workers in the rural areas will fail to receive any new capital inputs to maintain or improve levels of agricultural production. Thus women's economic position has continued to stagnate during debt dependency. Additional case studies such as Nash's (this volume) documenting the effects of debt dependency on women are important given the growing debt crises around the world.

DISCUSSION

Because 1985 marked the end of the International Women's Decade, some speculation on the future trends in the world-system for women of the periphery and core as well as directions for future research are appropriate. By examining underdevelopment and marginalization of women at the micro and macro levels, we can evaluate the effects of underdevelopment on women's status. I would argue that two criteria are important: changes in the level of long-term development (underdevelopment) and the degree of long-term independence and/or empowerment acquired by women through their contact with the global economy (Bunch, 1974; Leghorn & Parker, 1981; for a human rights approach, see Young, 1984). In the long run, we need to question whether women's employment "makes survival easier for women, increases women's access to resources, or gives women more tools to fight with, more self-respect, or opportunities to get together and build networks" (Leghorn & Parker, 1981, p. 226). Given the negative effects on women's economic status during their contact with the world economy, I question the prospects for improvement in socioeconomic status of women if they participate in the capitalist system without structural changes in dependency or patriarchal relations.

Changes in Underdevelopment

After examining progress toward eliminating underdevelopment in the nations experiencing classical dependency, dependent development, and debt dependency, I would argue that, since the 1950s, the level of underdevelopment has remained relatively the same. Lower relative levels of economic development and growth compared to core nations for some of the earlier recipients of classical dependency and TNC investment are all too common (for example, countries in the Caribbean such as Puerto Rico and Jamaica). First, during underdevelopment, export processing fails to generate products for local consumption. For example, the Mexican government planned that the TNCs would use Mexican supplies and products for servicing their plants. Instead, the TNCs imported the supplies from their subsidiaries in other countries (Fernández Kelly, 1983). Second, the TNCs often consume local investment capital instead of bringing in capital from abroad (Muller, 1979). Third, by bargaining away taxes and tariffs in the export processing zones, the governments lose revenues and control over the TNCs' investments. Finally, these countries also have experienced increased debt dependence on the International Monetary Fund (IMF) and the World Bank. Debt dependency has led to austerity programs and capital flight in the afflicted nations (Bolles, 1983; Debt Crisis Network, 1985; Glasberg & Ward, 1985, 1986; Ward & Glasberg, 1986; Wood, 1985).

Likewise, the economies of the nations experiencing TNC investment have remained distorted in their orientation toward the core nations. Export processing fails to provide longterm employment for previously unemployed workers. So-called development money builds new airports and tourist facilities to woo TNC investments rather than to aid development efforts (Wood, 1985). Meanwhile, the unemployment problem remains unsolved as the plants frequently bring a new category of workers into the labor force. Other previously unemployed women and men remain without jobs. The unemployment situation is aggravated further when the TNCs lay off the new workers. Hence many peripheral nations are finding that the TNCs perpetuate underdevelopment. Yet many of these countries' development packages require export-oriented investment as a condition for continued loans from the International Monetary Fund and World Bank (Debt Crisis Network, 1985; Wood, 1985).

Inequality remains high in the peripheral countries as profits accrue to the local elites and the TNCs. If we include authoritarian states in examining socioeconomic equality, then many of the export processing countries have particularly poor records, for example, the Philippines, Indonesia, and South Korea (Enloe, 1982, 1983). The recent departure of the Marcos family from the Philippines and the fight over their vast fortune (generated by foreign aid) illustrate how elites prosper from underdevelopment. The high levels of U.S. military aid to countries in Southeast Asia and Central America, and a growing militarization of their societies, means less freedom for workers to organize for indigenous development and for a share of the profits from their labors. Thus, in the long run, underdevelopment is only reinforced in these countries.

Empowerment of Women?

Meanwhile, around the capitalist world-system, many women's socioeconomic position is becoming more dependent on men. As Stallard et al. (1983) have argued, without husbands and access to the cash economy, most women

and their children will be in poverty. Given the negative effects of underdevelopment on women's economic status, increasing numbers of women around the
world must support themselves and their families without the assistance of
husbands (Ward, 1987). As a consequence, women need access to their own
income-generation projects (Charlton, 1984; Dixon, 1978; Youssef, 1979).
Project planners should formulate these programs with some understanding of
how the global economy affects women's access to valued resources. Solutions
that merely call for women's access to jobs and some income may perpetuate
existing conditions that enable men to manipulate the productive and reproductive roles of women.

At the same time, the transition to socialism does not always liberate women
unless there is also change in patterns of patriarchal relations. Socialist or
state-inspired strategies for increasing women's access to economic and other
resources also need to deal with the relations of male domination inherent in
society for thousands of years (Von werlhof, 1984). Thus researchers and
policymakers would do well to keep in mind Sokoloff's (1980) dialectic between
home- and market work. Or, alternatively, in a dialectic between capital and
gender, patriarchal relations are transformed into new forms within each mode
of production (Elson & Pearson, 1981b). Here men somehow maintain an
external sphere of control that enables them to continue their control over
women.

Other researchers have argued that incorporation into the world-system
helps women (Lim, 1983a, 1983b) or at least places them into subjugated
positions where they can acquire radical consciousness about their positions.
While these assertions may be true, I argue that this perspective is only a
short-run approach and the long-term consequences of women's contact with
the world-system and TNCs are the continued though transformed subjugation
of women. Such conditions—for example, exploitation of women workers
through below subsistence wages in export processing plants—might raise
women's consciousness. In the long run, however, these conditions have a way of
becoming embedded in the emerging socioeconomic institutions in developing
countries. An analogous situation would be the argument that inequality is
necessary for a period of time to bring about development. Unfortunately, that
initial inequality has a way of becoming a permanent fixture of the economy.

The implications of this discussion are that researchers need to integrate
research carefully from both world-system *and* women in development perspectives at the macro *and* micro levels. The world-system theorists need to consider
women as a central group that is affected by and participates in the processes of
the world-system, for example, in urbanization, migration, and service sector
growth (Koo & Smith, 1983; Timberlake & Kentor, 1983; Ward, 1985b).
Likewise, researchers studying women in development need to examine how the
global economy or macro context has had a role in the declining status of women
during underdevelopment (see, for example, the critiques of past women in
development research by Nash, 1983). They need to address how the global

economy continues to play a role in women's subordination and economic dependence in diverse yet interdependent locations, for example, from subsistence agriculture in Africa to the TNC plants in Mexico and the Philippines. The major contribution of the world-system perspective is first that women in these countries are linked together. Second, while the various processes of underdevelopment may have initial positive effects on developing countries' economies, in the long run, continued underdevelopment and women's subordination occurs.

Solutions to the problems of underdevelopment and women's position lie in peripheral countries controlling the types and nature of investments. This can be difficult because, when governments attempt to control investment, the investors may withdraw and local investors may refuse to invest. Chase-Dunn (1982) points out that governments need to counter these events by controlling foreign investment while providing incentives for local investors and locally oriented development. The International Center for Research on Women (1980a), as discussed by Ward (1984), proposes that governments oversee TNC employment, provide alternative training for women, and enforce protective regulations on health and safety issues. Governments also should work with other nations to avoid the bargaining that leads to runaway plants. Further, labor-intensive plants that produce for local consumption should be encouraged so that capital stays in the country. Women workers should have access to equal employment opportunity, the right to organize, and opportunities for managerial experience.

Dixon (1978, 1982) advocates the establishment of rural labor-intensive industries. In promoting such industries, governments and development agencies should first note that women are in need of income generation. Second, they should note the existing economic activities of the targeted women along with their resources and skills. Third, women workers should be organized in groups and not as single or solo workers. This facilitates education and planning. Fourth, industries run by women should receive credit and technical assistance. Fifth, women workers should have access to labor-saving technology for their domestic work to avoid the exhausting double day. Finally, women should be given control over their money and property (Dixon, 1982).

Of course, attempting to locate and improve the position of women in the global economy is a massive undertaking. Rather than drawing definitive conclusions, this analysis raises many questions that cannot be examined in this space. The world-system perspective paints a broad picture that does not always account for all the variations between and among countries. Much work remains to be done. What are the direct and indirect links between the world economy and the various socioeconomic locations of women? Given the quality of data on women's economic activities, most cross-national studies probably reflect the experiences of only a small proportion of women. Regional differences may also affect women's status (Marshall, 1985), although some regional differences may reflect the timing of the regions' incorporation into the world-system or the origins of colonial administrations. Finally, a growing body of research has indicated that class often mediates the effects of development on women's status and fertility. For example, elite women may hire domestic servants. As a consequence, they may have greater opportunities for jobs or bear fewer children than women without servants (Hull, 1977; Jelin, 1977, 1980). Further, how do patriarchal relations interact with class differences? As we begin to answer some of these questions, then we can more fully specify the processes of the world-system and the position of women. After all, as the Chinese women have told us, women do hold up half the sky.

NOTES

1. Of course, many researchers and policy officials point to the economic miracle countries of Singapore, Taiwan, South Korea, and Malaysia, which invested heavily in export-oriented light industries and have experienced phenomenal economic growth. Research by Bornschier and Chase-Dunn (1985) would argue that these are merely short-run economic effects. In the long run, they would predict the reemergence of underdevelopment owing to the high levels of debt and the eventual flows of capital from the countries. The economies of these countries are beginning to slow down with the latest global recession. Furthermore, economic growth has been generated at the price of democracy and economic equality in most of these countries.

2. For more details on variable measurement and other regression models, see Ward (1984). Basically, I used a cross section of 105 countries with the independent variables lagged for a period of five to ten years. Regression analyses provide estimates of the direction and relative strength of the effects for each of the independent variables while controlling for the effects of the other independent variables. Data from 1975 were used because these data covered the widest range of countries (International Labor Office, 1977).

3. Some people would disagree with this position by arguing that employers pay only what the market requires or just enough to ensure a healthy labor force. I think this occurs only in an ideal or core setting with a tight labor market. In the periphery, high levels of unemployment mediate the power of workers to negotiate for subsistence-level wages. Studies from the periphery have demonstrated the existence of this low-wage strategy on the part of employers. This strategy has also been used in the United States. As Milkman (1976) has documented, during the 1930s Depression, employers assumed that women could make up the difference between wages and subsistence by intensifying their use production or informal sector activities. For example, women were expected to make their own clothes, process and prepare all their food, and so forth.

4. Financial institutions can only dictate terms to debtor nations if these nations are playing the game. Increasingly, these nations are not playing along with the banks. For example, in 1986, Peru linked its payments to its export earnings. In early 1987, Brazil and Ecuador announced the cessation of interest payments. Many countries, however, are still playing the game because they desperately need loans just to cover interest payments on old loans.

REFERENCES

Anker, R., Buvinic, M., & Youssef, N. (1982). *Women's roles and population trends in third world development.* London: ILO.

Arizpe, L. (1977). Women in the informal labor sector: The case of Mexico City. *Signs,* *3*(1), 25-37.

Asfar, H. (1987). *Women, state, and ideologies.* Albany: SUNY Press.

Austrin, N. (1987). *Modernization, legal reforms, and the place of women in Muslim countries.* Unpublished doctoral dissertation, Southern Illinois University.

Ballmer-Cao, T., Scheiddegger, J., Bornschier, T., & Heintz, P. (1979). *Compendium of data for world-system analyses.* Zurich: Soziologisches Institut der Universität Zurich.

Barry, K. (1979). *Female sexual slavery.* New York: New York University Press.

Blake, J. (1974, December). The changing status of women in developing countries. *Scientific American, 231,* 137-147.

Blumberg, R. L. (1981). Females, farming, and food. In B. Lewis (Ed.), *Invisible farmers: Women and the crisis in agriculture* (pp. 24-84). Washington, DC: Agency for International Development.

Bolles, L. (1983). Kitchens hit by priorities: Employed working-class Jamaican women confront the IMF. In J. Nash & M. Fernández Kelly (Eds.), *Women, men and the international division of labor* (pp. 138-160). Albany: SUNY Press.

Bornschier, V., & Ballmer-Cao, T. (1979). Income inequality: A cross-national study. *American Sociological Review, 44,* 487-506.

Bornschier, V., & Chase-Dunn, C. (1985). *Transnational corporations and underdevelopment.* New York: Praeger.

Bornschier, V., Chase-Dunn, C., & Rubinson, R. (1978). Cross-national evidence of the effects of foreign investment and aid on economic growth and inequality: A survey of the findings and a reanalysis. *American Journal of Sociology, 84,* 651-683.

Boserup, E. (1970). *Woman's role in economic development.* New York: St. Martin.

Boulding, E. (1977). *Women in the twentieth century world.* New York: Halstead.

Braverman, H. (1974). *Labor and monopoly capital.* New York: Monthly Review.

Bunch, C. (1974). The reform tool kit. *Quest, 1*(1), 37-51.

Buvinic, M., Youssef, N., & Von Elm, B. (1978). *Women-headed households: The ignored factor in development planning.* Washington, DC: International Center for Research on Women.

Cardoso, F., & Faletto, E. (1979). *Dependency and development in Latin America* (M. Urquidi, Trans.). Berkeley: University of California Press.

Chaney, E., & Schmink, M. (1980). Women and modernization: Access to tools. In J. Nash & H. Safa (Eds.), *Sex and class in Latin America* (pp. 160-82). New York: Bergin.

Chapkis, W., & Enloe, C. (1983). *Of common cloth.* Amsterdam: Transnational Institute.

Charlton, S. E. (1984). *Women in Third World development.* Boulder, CO: Westview.

Chase-Dunn, C. (1975). Dependence, development and inequality. *American Sociological Review, 40,* 720-738.

Chase-Dunn, C. (1982). The uses of formal comparative research on dependency theory and the world-system perspective. In H. Makler, A. Martinelli, & N. Smelser (Eds.), *The new international economy* (pp. 117-140). London: Sage.

Cho, S. K. (1985, August). *Feminization of labor movement in South Korea, 1970-1980.* Paper presented at the meetings of the American Sociological Association, Washington, DC.

Cho, U., & Koo, P. (1983). *Capital accumulation, women's work, and informal economies in Korea* (Working Papers on Women in International Development no. 21). East Lansing: Michigan State University, Office of Women in International Development.

Coale, A. (1973). The demographic transition reconsidered. *International Population Conference* (Vol. 1). Liege, Belgium: International Union for Scientific Study of Population.

Collver, A., & Langlois, E. (1962). The female labor force in metropolitan areas: An international comparison. *Economic Development and Cultural Change, 10*, 367-385.

Debt Crisis Network. (1985). *From debt to development.* Washington, DC: IPS.

Deere, C., & deLeal, M. L. (1981). Peasant production, proletarianization, and the sexual division of labor in the Andes. *Signs, 7*(2), 338-360.

Deere, C., Humphries, J., & deLeal, M. L. (1982). Class and historical analysis for the study of women and economic change. In R. Anker, M. Buvinic, & N. Youssef (Eds.), *Women's roles and population trends in the third world* (pp. 87-116). London: ILO.

Dixon, R. (1975). *Women's rights and fertility* (Reports on Population/Family Planning no. 17). New York: Population Council.

Dixon, R. (1978). *Rural women at work.* Baltimore: Johns Hopkins University Press.

Dixon, R. (1982). Women in agriculture: Counting the labor force in developing countries. *Population and Development Review, 8*(3), 539-566.

Ehrenreich, B., & Fuentes, A. (1981). Life on the global assembly line. *Ms., 9*(7), 52-59, 71.

Elson, D. (1983). Nimble fingers and other tables. In W. Chapkis & C. Enloe (Eds.), *Of common cloth* (pp. 5-14). Amsterdam: Transnational Institute.

Elson, D., & Pearson, R. (1981a, Spring). Nimble fingers make cheap workers: An analysis of women's employment in Third World export manufacturing. *Feminist Review*, pp. 87-107.

Elson, D., & Pearson, R. (1981b). The subordination of women and the internationalisation of factory production. In K. Young, C. Wolkowitz, & R. McCullagh (Eds.), *Of marriage and the market: Women's subordination in international perspective* (pp. 144-66). London: CSE.

Enloe, C. (1982). Women textile workers in the militarization of Southeast Asia. In J. Barr (Ed.), *Perspectives on power* (pp. 73-86) (Occasional Paper 13). Durham, NC: Duke University, Center for International Studies.

Enloe, C. (1983). Women textile workers in the militarization of Southeast Asia. In J. Nash & M. Fernández Kelly (Eds.), *Women, men, and the international division of labor* (pp. 407-425). Albany: SUNY Press.

Enloe, C. (1984). Third World women in factories. *Cultural Survival Quarterly, 8*(2), 54-56.

Evans, P. (1979). *Dependent development.* Princeton, NJ: Princeton University Press.

Evans, P., & Timberlake, M. (1980). Dependence, inequality, and growth in less developed countries. *American Sociological Review, 45*(4), 531-552.

Fernández Kelly, M. (1983). *For we are sold: I and my people: Women and industry in Mexico's frontier.* Albany: SUNY Press.

Fiala, R. (1983). Inequality and the service sector in less developed countries. *American Sociological Review, 48*, 421-427.

Fuentes, A., & Ehrenreich, B. (1983). *Women in the global factory* (INC Pamphlet no. 2). New York: Institute for New Communications.

Galtung, J. (1971). A structural theory of imperialism. *Journal of Peace Research, 2*, 89-117.

Glasberg, D. S., & Ward, K. (1985, April). *Third World development and foreign debt dependency.* Paper presented at the meetings of the Midwest Sociological Society, St. Louis.

Glasberg, D. S., & Ward, K. (1986, April). *Types of foreign debt dependency and inequality in the world-system.* Paper presented at the meetings of the Southern Sociological Society, New Orleans.

Gordon, L. (1977). *Woman's body, woman's right.* New York: Schocken.

Green, S. (1983). Silicon Valley's women workers: A theoretical analysis of sex-segregation in the electronics industry labor market. In J. Nash & M. Fernández Kelly (Eds.), *Women, men and the international division of labor* (pp. 273-331). Albany: SUNY Press.

Griffin, K. (1979). Underdevelopment in history. In C. Wilber (Ed.), *The political economy of underdevelopment* (pp. 77-90). New York: Random House.

Grossman, R. (1979-1980). Women's place in the integrated circuit. *Southeast Asia Chronicle 66—Pacific Research, 9,* 2-17.

Hartmann, H. (1976). Capitalism, patriarchy, and job segregation by sex. In M. Blaxall & B. Reagan (Eds.), *Women in the workplace* (pp. 137-170). Chicago: University of Chicago Press.

Hossfeld, K. (1986, August). *Their logic against them: Contradictions in sex, race, and class in the Silicon Valley.* Paper presented at the meetings of the American Sociological Association, New York.

Hull, V. (1977). Fertility, women's work, and economic class: A case study from Southeast Asia. In S. Kupinsky, (Ed.), *The fertility of working women* (pp. 35-80). New York: Praeger.

Huntington, S. (1975). Issues in women's role in economic development. *Journal of Marriage and the Family, 37*(4), 1001-1013.

Inkeles, A., & Smith, D. (1975). *Becoming modern.* Cambridge, MA: Harvard University Press.

International Center for Research on Women (ICRW). (1980a). *Keeping women out: A structural analysis of women's employment in developing countries.* Washington, DC: Agency for International Development.

International Center for Research on Women. (1980b). *The productivity of women in developing countries: Measurement issues and recommendations* (AID/otr/C-1801). Washington, DC: Agency for International Development.

International Labor Office (ILO). (1977). *Labor force estimates and projections, 1950-2000.* Geneva: Author.

Jackson, P. (1983). The safety catch. In W. Chapkis & C. Enloe (Eds.), *Of common cloth* (pp. 70-74). Amsterdam: Transnational Institute.

Jahan, R. (1979). Public policies, women and development: Reflections on a few structural problems. In R. Jahan & H. Papanek (Eds.), *Women and development* (pp. 55-70). Dacca: Bangladesh Institute of Law and International Affairs.

Jahan, R., & Papanek, H. (1979). *Women and development in Southeast Asia.* Dacca: University Press.

Jelin, E. (1977). Migration and labor force participation of Latin American women: The domestic servants in the cities. *Signs, 3*(1), 129-141.

Jelin, E. (1980). The Bahiana in the labor force in Salvador, Brazil. In J. Nash & H. Safa (Eds.), *Sex and class in Latin America* (pp. 129-146). New York: Bergin.

Joseph, G. (1980). Caribbean women: The impact of race, sex, and class. In B. Lindsey (Ed.), *Comparative perspectives of Third World women* (pp. 143-161). New York: Praeger.

Jules-Rosette, B. (1982). *Women's work in the informal sector: A Zambian case study* (Working Papers on Women in International Development no. 3). East Lansing: Michigan State University, Office of Women in International Development.

Kentor, J. (1981). Structural determinants of peripheral urbanization. *American Sociological Review, 46*, 201-211.

Koo, H., & Smith, P. (1983). Migration, the urban informal sector, and earnings in the Philippines. *Sociological Quarterly, 24*(2), 219-232.

Leghorn, L., & Parker, K. (1981). *Women's worth: Sexual economics and the world of women.* Boston: Routledge & Kegan Paul.

Lim, L. (1978). *Workers in multinational corporations: The case of the electronics industry in Malaysia and Singapore* (Michigan Occasional Papers in Women's Studies no. 9). Ann Arbor: University of Michigan.

Lim, L. (1983a). Capitalism, imperialism, and patriarchy. In J. Nash & M. Fernández Kelly (Eds.), *Women, men and the international division of labor* (pp. 70-92). Albany: SUNY Press.

Lim, L. (1983b). Are multinationals the problem? A debate. *Multinational Monitor, 4*(8), 12-16.

Lim, L. (1985). *Women workers in multinational enterprises in developing countries.* Geneva: International Labor Office.

Marshall, S. (1985). Development, dependence, and gender inequality in the Third World. *International Studies Quarterly, 29*(2), 217-240.

Mason, K. O. (1984). *The status of women, fertility and mortality: A review of the relationships* (Research Report 84-58). Ann Arbor: University of Michigan, Population Studies Center.

Mass, B. (1976). *Population target.* Brampton, Ontario: Chartus.

Mazumdar, V. (1979). Women, development and public policy. In R. Jahan & H. Papanek (Eds.), *Women and development* (pp. 39-54). Dacca: Bangladesh Institute of Law and International Affairs.

Mies, M. (1986). *Patriarchy and capital accumulation on a world scale.* London: Zed.

Milkman, R. (1976). Women's work and the economic crisis. *Review of Radical Political Economics, 8*(1), 73-97.

Mintz, S. (1971). Men, women and trade. *Comparative Studies in Society and History, 13*, 247-269.

Mueller, L. (1977). Women and men, power and powerlessness in Lesotho. *Signs, 3*, 154-166.

Muller, R. (1979). The multinational corporation and the underdevelopment of the Third World. In C. Wilber (Ed.), *The political economy of development and underdevelopment* (record ed., pp. 151-178). New York: Random House.

Nash, J. (1983). The impact of the changing international division of labor on different sectors of the labor force. In J. Nash & M. Fernández Kelly (Eds.), *Women, men, and the international division of labor* (pp. 3-38). Albany: SUNY Press.

Nash, J., & Fernández Kelly, M. (1983). *Women, men and the international division of labor.* Albany: SUNY Press.

Neumann, L. (1979-1980). Hospitality girls in the Philippines. *Southeast Asia Chronicle 66—Pacific Research, 9*, 18-23.

Newland, K. (1977). *Women and population growth: Choice beyond childbearing* (Worldwatch Paper no. 16). New York: Worldwatch Institute.

Newland, K. (1980). *Women, men, and the division of labor* (Worldwatch Paper no. 37). Washington, DC: Worldwatch Institute.

North American Congress on Latin America. (1977). *Electronics: The global industry* (Report 9, no. 4). New York: Author.

Ong, A. (1987). *Spirits of resistance and capitalist discipline.* Albany: SUNY Press.

Papanek, H. (1979). Development planning for women: The implications of women's work. In R. Jahan & H. Papanek (Eds.), *Women and development* (pp. 170-201). Dacca: Bangladesh Institute of Law and International Affairs.

Pena, D. (1985, March). *The division of labor in electronics: A comparative analysis of France, Mexico, and the U.S.* Paper presented at the meetings of the International Studies Association, Washington, DC.

Portes, A. (1976). On the sociology of national development: Theories and issues. *American Journal of Sociology, 32,* 55-85.

Portes, A. (1985). The informal sector and the world-economy: Notes on the structure of subsidized labor. In M. Timberlake (Ed.), *Urbanization and the world-system* (pp. 53-62). New York: Academic Press.

Portes, A., & Sassen-Koob, S. (1987). Making it underground: Comparative material on the informal sector in western market economics. *American Journal of Sociology, 93*(1), 30-61.

Portes, A., & Walton, J. (1981). *Labor, class, and the international system.* New York: Academic Press.

Pyle, J. (1986, August). *Export led development and the underdevelopment of women: The impact of discriminatory development policy in the Republic of Ireland.* Paper presented at the meetings of the American Sociological Association, New York.

Robert, A. (1983). The effects of the international division of labor on female workers in the textile and clothing industries. *Development and Change, 14,* 19-37.

Robertson, C. (1976). Women and socioeconomic change in Accra, Ghana. In N. Hafkin & E. Bay (Eds.), *Women in Africa* (pp. 111-134). Stanford, CA: Stanford University Press.

Rosaldo, M. (1980). The use and abuse of anthropology: Reflections on feminism and cross-cultural understanding. *Signs, 5,* 389-417.

Rubinson, R. (1976). The world-economy and distribution of income. *American Sociological Review, 41,* 638-659.

Safa, H. (1981). Runaway shops and female employment: The search for cheap labor. *Signs, 7*(2), 418-433.

Saffiotti, H. (1978). *Women in class society.* New York: Monthly Review.

Sanday, P. (1974). Female status in the public domain. In M. Rosaldo & L. Lamphere (Eds.), *Women, culture, and society* (pp. 189-206). Stanford, CA: Stanford University Press.

Sanday, P. (1981). *Female power and male dominance.* Cambridge: Cambridge University Press.

Sanger, D. (1985, June 16). Pushing America out of chips. *New York Times,* p. 18.

Sassen-Koob, S. (1983). Labor migration and the new industrial division of labor. In J. Nash & M. Fernández Kelly (Eds.), *Women, men, and the international division of labor* (pp. 175-204). Albany: SUNY Press.

Sassen-Koob, S. (1984). Notes on the incorporation of Third World women into wage-labor through immigration and off-shore production. *International Migration Review, 18*(4), 1144-1167.

Sassen-Koob, S. (1985). Capital mobility and labor migration: Their expression in core cities. In M. Timberlake (Ed.), *Urbanization in the world-economy* (pp. 231-265). New York: Academic Press.

Schmidt, W. (1985, June 23). Textiles defends its last bastion. *New York Times*, p. F-4.

Schmink, M. (1977). Dependent development and the division of labor by sex: Venezuela. *Latin American Perspectives, 4*(1-2), 153-179.

Scott, G., & Carr, M. (1985). *The impact of technology choice on rural women in Bangladesh* (World Bank Staff Working Papers no. 731). Washington, DC: World Bank.

Seager, J., & Olson, A. (1986). *Women in the world: An international atlas.* New York: Touchstone.

Seidman, A. (1981). Women and the development of underdevelopment: The African experience. In R. Dauber & M. Lain (Eds.), *Women and technological change in developing countries* (NAAS Selected Symposium no. 53, pp. 109-126). Boulder, CO: Westview.

Sen, G. (1982). Women workers and the green revolution. In L. Buneria (Ed.), *Women in development.* New York: Praeger.

Serrin, P. (1984, December 29). Textile law orders a U.S. label. *New York Times*, pp. 1, 5.

Siegel, L. (1979-1980). Orchestrating dependency. *Southeast Asia Chronicle 66—Pacific Research, 9*, 24-27.

Silvard, R. (1985). *Women . . . a world survey.* Washington, DC: World Priorities.

Simms, R., & Dumor, E. (1976-1977). Women in the urban economy of Ghana: Associational activity and the enclave economy. *African Urban Notes, 2*(3), 43-64.

Smith, J. (1984). Non wage labor and subsistence. In J. Smith, I. Wallerstein, & H. Evers (Eds.), *Households and the world-economy* (pp. 64-89). Beverly Hills, CA: Sage.

Snow, R. (1983). The new international division of labor and the U.S. labor force: The case of the electronics industry. In J. Nash & M. Fernández Kelly (Eds.), *Women, men, and the international division of labor* (pp. 39-69). Albany: SUNY Press.

Sokoloff, N. (1980). *Between money and love.* New York: Praeger.

Stallard, K., Ehrenreich, B., & Sklar, H. (1983). *Poverty and the American dream: Women and children first* (IPC Pamphlet no. 1). New York: Institute for New Communication.

Standing, G. (1978). *Labor force participation and development.* Geneva: ILO.

Standing, G. (1983). Women's work activity and fertility. In R. Bulatao & R. Lee (Eds.), *Determinants of fertility in developing countries* (Vol. 1, pp. 517-546). New York: Academic Press.

Sudarkasa, N. (1977). Women and migration in contemporary West Africa. *Signs, 3*(1), 178-189.

Tiano, S. (1984). *Maquiladoras, women's work, and unemployment in Northern Mexico* (Women in International Development Working Paper no. 43). East Lansing: Michigan State University, Office of Women in Development.

Tiano, S. (1987). Gender, work, and world capitalism. In B. Hess & M. Ferree (Eds.), *Analyzing gender.* Beverly Hills, CA: Sage.

Timberlake, M. (1985). *Urbanization and the world-economy.* New York: Academic Press.

Timberlake, M., & Kentor, J. (1983). Economic dependence, overurbanization, and economic growth: A study of less developed countries. *Sociological Quarterly, 24*(4), 489-508.

Tinker, I. (1976). The adverse impact of development on women. In I. Tinker & M. B. Bramsen (Eds.), *Women and world development* (pp. 22-34). Washington, DC: Overseas Development Council.

Todaro, M. (1985). *Economic development in the Third World.* New York: Longman.

United Nations. (1980, July 14-30). *Review and evaluation of progress achieved in the implementation of the World Plan of Action: Employment.* Paper prepared for the World Conference of the United Nations Decade for Women, Copenhagen, Denmark (A/Conf.94/8).

Von werlhof, C. (1984). The proletarian is dead: Long live the housewives? In J. Smith, I. Wallerstein, & H. Evers (Eds.), *Households and the world-economy* (pp. 131-147). Beverly Hills, CA: Sage.

Wallerstein, I. (1974). *The modern world system.* New York: Academic Press.

Ward, K. (1984). *Women in the world-system: Its impact on status and fertility.* New York: Praeger.

Ward, K. (1985a). The social consequences of the world-economic system: The economic status of women and fertility. *Review, 8*(4).

Ward, K. (1985b). Women and urbanization in the world-system. In M. Timberlake (Ed.), *Urbanization in the world-economy* (pp. 305-324). New York: Academic Press.

Ward, K. (1987). The impoverishment of U.S. women and the decline of U.S. hegemony. In T. Boswell & A. Bergesen (Eds.), *America's changing role in the world system* (pp. 275-90). New York: Praeger.

Ward, K., & Glasberg, D. S. (1986, August). *Foreign debt dependency and the economic status of women.* Paper presented at the meetings of the Society for the Study of Social Problems, New York.

Ward, K., & Pampel, F. (1985, September). Structural determinants of female labor force participation in developed nations, 1955-1975. *Social Science Quarterly, 66,* 654-667.

Wellesley Editorial Committee. (1977). Women and international development. *Signs, 3*(1).

Winter, C. (1985, June 16). A gloom settles on Silicon Valley. *Chicago Tribune,* sec. 7, pp. 1, 7.

Wolf, D. (1986, August). *Linking women's labor with the global economy: Factory daughters and their families in rural Java.* Paper presented at the meetings of the American Sociological Association, New York.

Wood, R. (1985). The aid regime and international debt. *Development and Change, 16*(2), 179-212.

Young, G. (1984). Women, development and human rights: Issues in integrated transnational production. *Journal of Applied Behavioral Science, 4,* 383-401.

Youssef, N. (1974). *Women and work in developing societies.* Berkeley: University of California Press.

Youssef, N. (1979). *Women's employment and fertility: Demographic transition or economic needs of mothers?* Washington, DC: International Center for Research on Women.

Youssef, N., & Hartley, S. (1979). Demographic indicators of the status of women in various societies. In J. Lipman-Blumen & J. Bernard (Eds.), *Sex roles and social policy* (pp. 83-112). Beverly Hills, CA: Sage.

Youssef, N., & Helter, C. (1983). Establishing the economic condition of women-headed households in the Third World. In M. Buvinic, M. Lycette, and W. McGreevy (Eds.), *Women and poverty in the Third World* (pp. 216-243). Baltimore, MD: Johns Hopkins University Press.

2

Economic Restructuring in the United States

HISPANIC WOMEN IN THE GARMENT AND ELECTRONICS INDUSTRIES

MARÍA PATRICIA FERNÁNDEZ KELLY
ANNA M. GARCÍA

This chapter concerns the employment of Hispanic women in the production of electronics and clothing in Southern California. In particular, it focuses on the way they are affected by their industry's response to the internationalization of capital investments and the influx of foreign goods. Among the changes experienced by the electronics and garment industries are increased use of subcontractors and an increase in women operating their own businesses. These changes suggest two possibilities—further erosion of the working class or consolidation of a new class of Hispanic women entrepreneurs.

Most writings on comparative international development have traditionally focused attention on Third World countries. Lately, however, there has been a paradigmatic shift in the social sciences characterized by a new emphasis on global economic and political processes as part of an integrated system of production.

The world-systems approach illustrated this change of direction, providing, since the mid-1970s, a framework that recognizes that less developed countries

AUTHORS' NOTE: This chapter is based on preliminary data obtained as part of *A Collaborative Study of Hispanic Women in Garment and Electronics Industries*, sponsored by the Ford and Tinker Foundations between 1984 and 1988. Special thanks are due to Ms. Patricia Biggers, Dr. Bill Díaz, and Mr. Henry Ramos.

are historically and structurally linked to advanced industrial nations (Waller-stein, 1974). The same thrust was echoed by students of the New International Division of Labor, who have described processes leading to the massive relocation of manufacturing operations from advanced industrial countries to politically stable low-wage areas of the world (Evans, 1985; Frobel, Heinrichs, & Kreye, 1979; Henderson, 1986; Portes & Walton, 1981).

Students of the New International Division of Labor have emphasized, in particular, the interconnection between changes at the "core" and those affecting the "periphery" and "semiperiphery." It is partly for that reason that some who began by studying export processing zones in Asia or on the U.S.-Mexico Border in the late 1970s are now exploring complementary or parallel changes in the United States and other developed nations. Advanced industrial countries are thus becoming an area of legitimate concern for students of international development (Castells, 1985).

Among the questions being asked by researchers are the following: How has the U.S. economy responded to the broad transformations caused by the internationalization of capital investments and the onslaught of cheaply made foreign goods? Are the industries affected by capital flight in the United States destined to disappear, or have they devised new strategies for survival?

This chapter provides a partial response to these questions by focusing on the employment of Hispanic women in electronics and garment production, two of the sectors that have been at the forefront of internationalization since the early 1960s. Southern California represents the largest concentration of electronics operations and the second largest center for garment production in the United States. It is, therefore, an ideal location for studying the adjustments experienced by both industries in the last two decades.[1]

Both garment and electronics production cover a broad span of alternatives in manufacturing, marketing, domestic and international competition, and the development and use of technology. Their profiles, in fact, seem antithetical to one another. Apparel manufacture retains many characteristics of early industrialization. It has been portrayed as a declining industry, subject to fashion and seasonal fluctuations and restricted by technological obsolescence. Electronics, on the other hand, is an industry on the ascent, distinguished by advanced technology and, according to some, the natural foundation of a new "information-based" economy.

Although the public image of electronics is diametrically opposed to that of garment manufacturing, the two industries share a number of features: Both sectors offer among the lowest wages to industrial workers in the United States, both rely heavily on subcontracting, and both are characterized by the predominance of small operations hiring fewer than twenty workers. More important, both industries depend heavily on the employment of women for assembly. All these traits can be understood as part of a process of economic restructuring aimed at lowering production costs and maintaining a competitive edge in the domestic and international markets.

The central argument in this chapter is that restructuring in the U.S. garment and electronics industries has entailed at least three aspects: (a) a movement toward subcontracting and decentralization of the manufacturing process; (b) an expansion of the so-called informal sector, including small shops outside government regulation as well as industrial homework; and (c) the tapping of a labor force that contains increasing numbers of women, immigrants, and ethnic minorities. As a context for the recent changes experienced by garment and electronics production, the following section briefly discusses some of the factors that have contributed to economic restructuring.

INTERNATIONALIZATION, MANUFACTURE, AND THE SERVICE ECONOMY

The movement of assembly work to export processing zones in less developed countries cannot be seen in isolation from the major shift from manufacturing to services in the United States. In the last twenty years, there has been a gradual drop in blue-collar employment and a rapid expansion in the number and range of services offered in this country. This phenomenon has affected not only light and competitive branches, such as textiles and garment manufacture, but also highly capitalized industries, such as steel and automobiles. Moreover, experts anticipate the continued decline in blue-collar manufacturing even if output rises as a result of automation. By the year 2005, less than 7% of the labor force will be involved in manufacturing, compared to 18% today. By contrast, services ranging from banking and finance to sales and janitorial work will form the largest portion of the economy (Rumberger, 1984; Rumberger & Levin, 1984; Silvestri, Lukasiewicz, & Einstein, 1983; U.S. Department of Labor, 1986).

Several causes explain the movement toward services. In part, the reduction of employment in manufacture has been due to higher educational levels and expectations on the part of young workers entering the labor force for the first time. A major recession in the mid-1970s and early 1980s displaced large numbers of people from heavy industry. Foreign competition, mainly from Japan, contributed to reduce employment in certain sectors. Finally, one of the key factors linked to the expansion of services was the transfer of industrial activities to less developed countries (Lawrence, 1984; Nash & Fernández Kelly, 1983).

Capital flight was followed during the 1970s by plant closings and drops in union membership throughout the United States (Bluestone & Harrison, 1982). In a striking counterpoint, the reduction of investment in industry was complemented by increasing labor migration mainly from Asia and Latin America. Immigrants, many of them undocumented, sought jobs in cities located at the heart of the world-system of production, and often in the very places that had been most seriously affected by the decline of industry. These phenomena have all contributed to reshape our image of the United States as an internally diversified region where changing patterns in domestic and foreign investment are causing geographical shifts in production, accentuating class differences, and creating new demands for an immigrant labor force (Sassen-Koob, 1984).

In many Third World countries, *internationalization* meant an "opening to the exterior," that is, an emphasis on export-led industrialization, the growth of export processing zones and worldwide competition to provide the cheapest labor to foreign investors. *Internationalization* has had a different meaning in the United States. Here, the term spawned new spatial images. As multinational corporations moved manufacturing operations to Asia, Latin America, and the Caribbean, the "Frostbelt" became a label for areas where industry had once thrived. The "Sunbelt" became a catchphrase for sites where high-tech was blooming. "Sunset industries" (like garment) were set in opposition to "sunrise industries" (like electronics), and many anticipated that the decaying Northeast would soon be superseded by the youthful South.

Only a few years after they were first proposed, these dichotomies are being replaced by a more complex understanding of economic restructuring as an uneven phenomenon affecting old as well as new industries. Perhaps the most important single development in this respect is the growth and diversification of electronics production. This industry has partaken of the causes and consequences of internationalization. On the one hand, advanced technology has made possible the relocation of manufacturing to distant geographical areas while maintaining administrative control in the United States (Fernández Kelly, 1985). On the other hand, domestic electronics firms have had to develop strategies to survive in a fiercely competitive market. Some of these strategies are discussed in the next section.

ADVANCED TECHNOLOGY AND
WOMEN'S WORK

Studies of the electronics industry have mostly focused on the achievements of computer technology. Greater importance may lie, however, in its embodiment of new tendencies in the relationship between employers and workers. The exportation of jobs to less developed countries, low rates of unionization, and the combination of automation in advanced industrial centers with labor-intensive operations abroad are all features of electronics manufacture (Castells, 1985; Glassmeier, Hall, & Markusen, 1985; O'Connor, 1983).

Electronics firms have been at the forefront of economic and labor management trends for more than twenty years, having demonstrated a tendency toward internationalization from the beginning. For example, in 1962 (three years after the integrated circuit was perfected), Fairchild, one of the oldest electronics manufacturers, opened the first "offshore" semiconductor assembly plant in Hong Kong. In 1966, the same corporation began operations in South Korea. General Instruments moved microelectronics assembly to

Taiwan in 1964. And only a year later, when the Mexican government intervened to provide incentives for the expansion of the Border Industrialization Program, Transistron, Motorola, and others followed a similar path. The following decade saw the incorporation of Singapore, Malaysia, and the Philippines into offshore manufacturing. Lately, the Caribbean and even some remote areas in South America have made gains as attractive locations for electronics producers (Cohen, 1986; Gall, 1982; Sanderson, 1985; Siegel, 1984).

In spite of its international thrust, electronics firms have provided growing rates of domestic employment over the last two decades. For example, from 1967 to 1980, electronics component employment in the United States grew at 2.4% a year. Between 1980 and 1983, there was an additional 2.3% increase (Scott, 1985). At present, electronics production represents the fastest growing industrial sector in the United States and it provides employment to more than one million people nationwide (Farley & Glickman, 1985).

Several factors help to explain the resilience of electronics firms in this country. First, standardized production of integrated circuits requiring low levels of quality control and abundant inputs of manual labor has been mostly relocated to Asia and Latin America. Highly advanced products requiring large investments in automation and research and development, however, are mostly assembled domestically. These products are often manufactured according to specification and, therefore, depend on the proximity to specialized markets.

Second, the same products often require the assembly of basic components, many of which are manufactured by subcontracted firms taking advantage of specialized niches in the domestic market. The highly advanced nature of electronics production has given rise to a few giant corporations employing large numbers of skilled and semiskilled personnel. The majority of electronics operations in the United States, however, are small. This feature is exemplified by data on the number of firms and size of their work forces in four types of electronics production in Southern California. Of a total 1155 firms manufacturing electronic computing equipment (SIC No. 3573), radio and TV communications equipment (SIC No. 3662), semiconductors and related devices (SIC No. 3674), and electronics components not elsewhere classified (SIC No. 3679), 564—that is, 48.8%—hired between 1 and 19 workers in 1982 (U.S. Department of Commerce, 1982).

Empirical research further shows that these small firms provide an opportunity for entrepreneurship and employment on the part of refugees, immigrants, and ethnic minorities. At least 30% of small electronics firms in Southern California are owned or managed by South East Asian refugees and Hispanics. The same ethnic groups predominate among their workers (U.S. Department of Commerce, 1982).

Third, the small size of firms and their affinity for minority and immigrant workers is also associated with a tendency toward informalization.[2] In this respect, electronics reflects yet another widespread characteristic of contemporary industrial activity: the reliance on subcontracting as part of a strategy to diversify risks and lower production costs. Subcontracting creates links between advanced sectors and producers of simple components. Workers, differentiated by ethnicity, gender, and class, are found in the various strata bound by the subcontracting chain.

Subcontracted operations capable of adapting to fluctuations in demand often fall outside the margins of legality. Small electronics firms are cited for violations of wage and hour regulations as frequently as garment factories. Employees are often paid in cash for overtime, and at the regular rates instead of the time-and-a-half wages required by law.

In addition, when activity peaks, employees in small electronics firms are allowed to take batches of components to their own homes, where they are processed at piece rates some times as low as 7 cents per unit. Home assembly is aided by the participation of family members. In Kearny Mesa, an area in San Diego County characterized by a large concentration of electronics companies, 75% of employers make regular or intermittent use of home workers.[3] The magnitude of this phenomenon is difficult to assess given its highly elusive nature. Observers in Los Angeles, Orange, and San Diego Counties, however, characterize home assembly as a common phenomenon at the lower end of the industrial hierarchy, that is, where recent or undocumented immigrants and refugees are most likely to be found.

Fourth, domestically, the electronics industry has combined the employment of highly skilled personnel with the hiring of large numbers of unskilled and semiskilled female workers, many of whom increasingly belong to ethnic minorities. The importance of this factor is stressed below.

Throughout the world, electronics firms have been characterized by the predominance of women among direct production workers. More than three million women are currently employed, directly or indirectly, in electronics manufacturing in less developed countries. Approximately a million work in similar types of production in the United States.

Electronics firms in this country originally hired local, White women who left their jobs after relatively short periods of employment, either to get married or to give attention to their families. More recently, the number of minority workers has increased. Asian and Hispanic women workers in electronics plants in California and New York are but two examples of this trend. Over 100,000 Hispanic women are employed in electronics production in Southern California alone.[4]

Historically, Southern California (i.e., Los Angeles, Orange, and San Diego Counties) has been an agricultural center reliant on the hiring of immigrants first from Asia and later from Mexico. More recently, manufacturing, defense, and aerospace have accounted for a significant proportion of that area's economy. Well-being has characterized Southern California for most of the twentieth century. The recession of the late 1970s and early 1980s brought about sharp decreases in industrial production, however. It is estimated that between 16,000 and 30,000 jobs were directly lost to plant closings in Los Angeles in 1980. The space created by these losses was filled, to a large extent, by new openings in high-tech industries.

As a result, Southern California has gradually superseded Santa Clara County—the so-called Silicon Valley—as a center for the production of high-tech goods. In 1968, there were only 30 electronics firms in Los Angeles, 12 in Orange, and 20 in San Diego; by 1975, these areas had 120, 40, and 80 firms, respectively; toward 1982, the numbers had risen to 579 in Los Angeles, 386 in Orange County, and 190 in San Diego (U.S. Department of Commerce, 1982). At present, Los Angeles contains the largest number of electronics companies in the nation while Orange County represents the fastest growing center in that type of production.

What are the factors that have determined the rapid expansion of electronics production in Southern California? Firsthand interviews with a sample of 52 electronics producers indicate that, other than the proximity to markets and research and development centers, employers are seeking benefits derived from the presence of large, affordable labor pools, comparatively low wage and unionization rates, and access to cheap land and good transportation (Castells, 1985).

In response to these requirements, local governments throughout the United States are preparing incentive packages stressing the advantages of their own areas and courting investments in high-tech. Such packages are similar in letter and spirit to "holiday programs" offered by less developed countries trying to attract foreign capital for export manufacturing. Thus the same factors that explain the decentralization of manufacturing on a world scale also clarify the reorganization of electronics production at the regional level.

Southern California boasts a comparative advantage vis-à-vis other locations in the United States. Advertisements and public affairs literature mention a good climate, the proximity to Mexico, and the availability of large numbers of trained and trainable workers in that area as positive features from the vantage point of the investor. Many of those workers are immigrants or U.S.-born citizens of Mexican ancestry. The vast majority are women.

The growing presence of Hispanic women in the lower and middle echelons of electronics firms is largely due to recent changes in the composition of local labor markets and in the number of employment alternatives faced by different types of workers. As old industrial sectors declined, workers faced new openings in industries such as electronics. The majority of jobs in that sector, however, require little or no skill. Direct production work in electronics receives the second lowest wages paid to industrial workers in this country. Jobs of that kind are not attractive for many members of the traditional labor force, particularly U.S.-born White men. Thus the recomposition of the industrial base is leading toward an increasing demand for ethnic and immigrant workers, and women in particular.

The growing significance of Hispanics in general, and of Hispanic women in particular, for contemporary industry is demonstrated by aggregate data. A comparison of the 1970 and 1980 census of population shows that Hispanics are the only ethnic group in the United States that has maintained or improved its representation in blue-collar employment. Hispanics in Los Angeles, Orange, and San Diego Counties represent only 20.5% of the total labor force in the area. Yet, they have an average labor force participation rate of 68.6% with almost half employed in the manufacturing sector. These are rates far above than those found among other ethnic groups living in the United States (Fernández Kelly & García, 1986).

Southern California, where the majority of Hispanic women are of Mexican descent, provides a good example of the labor force participation rate of minority women. Almost 53% of all Hispanic women in Los Angeles County are gainfully employed. The equivalent figures for Orange and San Diego Counties are 58.5% and 49.2%, respectively. Census data also show that approximately 35% of all women involved in direct production *nationwide* are Hispanic. These findings dispel a persistent but erroneous impression that Hispanic women's participation in the labor force is not significant. Ethnographic research further suggests that Hispanic women's involvement in wage employment has been underestimated given biases in conventional aggregate compilations. Many recent immigrants and female heads of household work informally, doing piecework at home or being hired temporarily by small underground operations.

In addition, aggregate and ethnographic data point to the importance of Hispanic women's employment in the Southern California electronics industry. For example, the presence of minorities in the large occupational category "operators, fabricators, and laborers" is striking. Fully 67% of the work force in that category in Southern California belong to minority groups. Of those, 51% are Hispanic women. In the category of "machine operators, assemblers and inspectors," minority women constitute 70% of workers. Hispanic women form 76% of that number. Finally, under "metal and plastic machine operators" (a category of special relevance to the electronics industry), ethnic minorities form 71% of the work force and Hispanic women constitute almost 80% of that figure (U.S. Department of Commerce, 1982).

The wide representation of Hispanic women in the electronics industry is noteworthy for several reasons. First, although it may seem paradoxical, electronics—the bringer of advanced technology—is predominantly an employer of unskilled and semiskilled workers, many of whom are minority women. To a large extent, employment policies in electronics manufacturing mirror national trends. U.S. Department of Labor forecasts show that the largest number of jobs over the next decade will be created in low-paying occupations in services and in the direct production of nondurable and durable goods. Electronics manufacture alone will have required fifty times more janitors than engineers by the end of the century. More than 70% of all workers in the same industry will have been involved in direct production and assembly, while only a small percentage of the labor force in electronics will be formed by high-skilled technicians, engineers, computer designers, programmers, or software developers. Most direct production workers will be women, while specialized occupations will tend to be filled by professional men. Thus electronics will remain an instance of stratification on the basis of skill and sex.

Second, capital flight and industrial relocation to the Third World have created new conditions for production in certain areas of the United States characterized by the presence of immigrants and ethnic minorities. One of the most telling aspects of electronics manufacturing in Southern California is that it often combines the employment of immigrants domestically with the relocation of certain types of assembly work to areas of the world from which those immigrants tend to come. In both cases, women are targeted as a preferred labor force. This circuit does not necessarily involve a causal relationship. Nevertheless, it does illustrate a strategy by means of which employers seek to reduce the economic and political costs of production both in advanced and less developed countries.

Third, the fact that the electronics industry is largely an employer of women underscores the importance of gender as a factor implicated in the restructuring of production (Scott, 1985). In this respect, electronics reflects national trends characterized by the unprecedented incorporation of married and unmarried females into the labor force.

Elsewhere, I have discussed the historical moments in which women have joined the labor force in large numbers (Fernández Kelly, 1983). Although women have always been wage earners, there are three periods over the last two and a half centuries when they have flooded the labor market. The first period coincided with the advent of industrial capitalism, a time of flux characterized by limited availability of capital for investment, changing technology, and emerging consumer markets. The second period paralleled World War II, when the involvement of men in armed confrontation made it necessary for women to replace them in factories and offices.

We are currently observing a third moment in which women are massively represented in the labor force. Again, this is a time of structural transformations. The internationalization of capital investments, the application of revolutionary technologies, and changes in the balance of power between employers and workers have deeply altered the conditions for profitable production and made women more attractive as prospective employees.

The reasons behind the widespread hiring of women in electronics firms throughout the world have been studied since the mid-1970s. Some industrial promoters, government officials, and researchers agree that the jobs offered by that industry require keen eyesight, manual dexterity, and a preference for minute handiwork. These characteristics are commonly believed to be possessed by women. A focus on them alone does not, however, account for the low wages associated with women's employment, or for the wage differentials that have historically characterized men and women's jobs. Women are hired primarily because they can be easily replaced, paid low wages, and kept at bay with respect to wage demands and unionization drives. This is especially true for minority and immigrant women.

One of the conclusions that can be drawn from the preceding analysis is that, in its hiring practices, wage levels, and reliance on various modes of subcontracting, the electronics industry bears striking similarities to the garment industry. These similarities cannot be considered as a coincidence. Rather, they are outcomes of similar constraints and alternatives faced by employers trying to retain a competitive edge in the domestic and international markets.

HISPANIC WOMEN, INFORMALIZATION, AND GARMENT PRODUCTION

The garment industry has been described in journalistic and scholarly writings as a sector on the decline as a result of the transfer of production mainly to Asia, the U.S.-Mexico Border, and the Caribbean. Empirical research, however, shows that this is a misleading portrayal. Garment production in general, and particularly in Los Angeles County, has expanded over time thanks in large part to the existence of mechanisms that perpetuate the use of informal labor linking established industrial operations with unlicensed subcontracted shops and homework. Nationwide, the garment industry includes approximately 24,000 firms employing about 2,000,000 people, with a $12 billion annual direct payroll. In addition, this sector indirectly employs 200,000 farmers involved in cotton and wool processing. Thus the apparel industry is larger than the automotive, steel, and electronics industries combined, and, despite the blows suffered during the last two decades, it continues displaying notable resilience in the United States (International Ladies Garment Worker's Union, 1985).

Most garments sold in this country are manufactured domestically, with Los Angeles County being second only to New York in apparel production. Approximately 46,219 women are employed as "textile, apparel, and furnishings machines operators" in that area. Almost 91% of these are minorities with 72% being Hispanic. Equivalent data for New York and Miami (the other areas with the fastest growing Hispanic populations) indicate similar trends in employment (U.S. Department of Commerce, 1982).

The history of the garment industry in Southern California is closely related to transformations experienced by apparel production in New York. The latter part of the nineteenth century witnessed the preeminence of New York as a garment producer and the emergence of California as a center of manufacture of ready-made wear for mass consumption. In the 1920s, the Los Angeles clothing industry expanded, stimulated in part by the arrival of runaway shops evading unionization drives in New York. From the very beginning, Mexican women were employed in nearly all positions of the industry. Accounts from the time describe the work force in the Los Angeles clothing industry as formed mainly by Mexican females, three-quarters of whom were between the ages of 16 and 23, two-thirds of whom were born in the United States, and nine-tenths of whom were unmarried (Taylor, 1980).

The Great Depression sent the Los Angeles garment industry into a period of turmoil, but the rise of the movie industry in the 1930s established new guidelines for fashion and fresh opportunities for production. Los Angeles began to specialize in inexpensive women's sportswear (Perlmutter, 1944). By 1944, the number of garment manufacturers in Los Angeles had grown to 900 with an workforce of 28,000 people, 75% of whom were Mexican women. The value of the product was said to be in excess of 110 million dollars. By 1975, there had been a dramatic increase of plants to an estimated 2269 with a work force of 66,000 people (Maram & Long, 1981).

During the late 1970s and 1980s, alarm over the growing employment of undocumented Mexican women, violations of the Labor Code and Tax Law, and the expansion of homework also grew. Garment contractors in Los Angeles County generated approximately 3.5 billion dollars in sales in 1983. It is estimated that between 30% and 50% of that value may have originated in home production and unregulated shops.

The impression that restructuring rather than decline has characterized the recent history of the garment industry in Southern California is confirmed by data on the number of employees hired by various types of firms over time. There was a noticeable increase in the total number of workers in the Los Angeles apparel industry, from 51,719 in 1965 to 83,424 in 1982 (U.S. Department of Commerce, 1982). The number of firms expanded and shrunk at different points during the same period.

The apparent contradiction between a declining number of companies specializing in certain types of apparel and a growing number of workers in the industry as a whole is explained by the proliferation in the number of small firms since the mid-1970s. Of 2717 registered apparel and textile manufacturers in Los Angeles County in early 1984, 1695, or 62%, employed between 1 and 19 workers; the majority of firms within that group employed between 1 and 4 people. By contrast, there has been a notable reduction in the number of plants hiring between 100 and 499 workers. Operations with larger work forces have virtually disappeared.

These findings suggest that it is the lower stratum of garment production, characterized by the existence of small licensed or unlicensed garment shops, that is expanding. These are establishments where production is relatively unstable, where a large number of undocumented immigrant workers are found, and where wage and labor code infractions are frequent.

In other words, the expansion of informal operations within garment manufacture explains the resilience of the industry over the last decade. Interviews with government officials in agencies such as the Employment Development Department of Industrial Relations, and the Wage and Hour Division of the U.S. Department of Labor further substantiate the impression that homework and other types of unregulated assembly in the garment industry have increased in the last five years.

The growth in the number of small garment operations must be seen as a symptom of deeper transformations affecting production. First, there has been a fragmentation within the apparel industry characterized by the movement of manufacturers away from direct assembly. This has entailed a reduction in the number of vertically integrated firms and an increase in decentralization of the labor process. There are fewer than 400 manufacturers in Los Angeles County at present. Large and well-known firms, which originally assembled their own products, are now mainly involved in the purchase of basic materials, design, cutting, and marketing. Sewing is invariably subcontracted out.

Second, many manufacturers combine domestic and international subcontracting, thus gaining access to different segments of the market. For example, the same firm may subcontract its "long-lead-time" standardized production to firms located in Asian export processing zones, while at the same time using the services of small domestic companies to penetrate opportunity markets demanding novelty products.

From the point of view of manufacturers, subcontracting offers the advantage of diversifying risks while at the same time allowing control over the nature and volume of output. In addition, subcontracting reduces the costs of production by diffusing the need to maintain stable labor forces. Finally, the same process mitigates the consolidation of workers' organizations, particularly unions, thus representing a potential political advantage to employers (Beneria & Roldan, 1987).

Third, the growth of subcontracting has accentuated the competitive features of the garment industry by allowing the entry of a growing number of firms, many of which are short-lived and many of which operate outside government regulation. The fragmentation of garment production has created the need for quick adaptation, speed in production, and flexibility on the part of subcontractors. This, in turn, has led to renewed violations of state and federal regulations.

Many small firms cannot weather the fluctuations of the market by operating legally, nor can they bear the costs emanating from state control. Thus they tend to evade tax and licensing expenses. They are also likely to hire workers (a large number of whom are undocumented immigrants) at peak seasons and to dismiss them perfunctorily when contracts end or when demand for a particular product wanes. Positions in these shops offer few benefits and they are the lowest paying among all industrial jobs in the United States. An example of this type of operation is home assembly. As stated earlier, homework accounts for a large portion of garment production in Southern California.

Fourth, the expansion of subcontracting has also opened new opportunities for small businesses and created new categories of buyers and intermediaries. Start-up costs in the garment industry have always been comparatively low. Thus investment in this sector has historically attracted ethnic and immigrant entrepreneurs. About 40% of small garment manufacturers in Southern Califorina are Hispanic. Most of them are U.S.-born citizens with about one-third of them being foreign-born. Ethnographic research further shows that many of these small-business persons are women.

The reorganization of garment manufacture and the growing presence of immigrant workers in Southern California has given rise to "brokers" whose function is to match garment contracts with pools of workers and contractors offering increasingly cheaper labor. Although no systematic research has been conducted on this subject, some ethnographic data are available. Brokers tend to be individuals with experience in the industry. Some are former contractors acquainted with the habits and preferences of manufacturers. Perhaps more significantly, they also tend to be members of ethnic minorities. Their bilingualism as well as their practical experience allow them to serve as a link between manufacturers and Hispanic or Indo-Chinese workers.

Brokers generally work on a commission basis. Their services may be sought by manufacturers with irregular orders for special or occasional market needs. Most often, brokers are a resource for small ethnic contractors with few employees, little entrepreneurial experience, and no established connection with formal sector producers or retailers. Small monolingual contractors use brokers as a channel to deal with an environment where language is a barrier.

Working through a broker represents a potential cost to independent contractors in the form of a commission payment out of their gains. This heightens their level of vulnerability. But there are also distinct advantages. To the newly arrived and inexperienced contractor, the broker provides invaluable skills for gaining access to orders and securing the highest pay for output.

The growing importance of brokers is consistent with the history of garment production, which has been, traditionally, a provider of entry-level jobs for immigrants. In California, Mexican women formed the preferred labor force from the inception of the industry. This feature has been maintained to the present. The number of undocumented workers seems, however, to have increased over time. According to production managers, most of the labor in the industry is newly arrived. A study of 499 workers in the Los Angeles garment industry showed that 81% of them were undocumented and 83% of them were born in Mexico (Heer & Falasco, 1981). Other studies have reached similar conclusions (Alclay, 1984; Morales, 1983). Interviews with workers engaged in industrial homework also show that many of them are undocumented and recently arrived immigrants mostly from Mexico.

The presence of immigrants in the garment industry is neither a new phenomenon nor one that can be attributed to recent economic restructuring. On the other hand, economic restructuring has accentuated the demand for immigrant workers, while at the same time mitigating the consolidation of vertically integrated firms capable of providing stable work to U.S.-born citizens.

Finally, industrial restructuring has had a peculiar impact upon Hispanic women's chances of becoming small independent subcontractors. As a result of direct interviewing with employers and women owning garment operations, two mechanisms have been identified. First, the trend toward decentralization of the labor process and the attempt to lower production costs have led many employers to encourage women workers to open their own firms. Employers often lease out idle machinery to these women while at the same time providing them with part of the orders they obtain from larger manufacturers. A case in point is the second largest contractor in San Diego County, a firm regularly hiring 80 people. The owner and manager of that company has sponsored the entrepreneurial activities of several former employees who now manage garment operations in leased commercial units located near the main firm. Each one of these minuscule enterprises hires between two and nine women, the vast majority of whom are undocumented Mexican immigrants. Work is irregular, production quotas vary significantly, and women are paid on a piece rate basis.

These operations are probably the most vulnerable in the entire subcontracting chain. Indeed, they can hardly be considered independent operations insofar as the women who manage them and their workers are directly dependent upon the mother firm. On the other hand, from the point of view of the main investors, the sponsoring of spin-off operations has distinct advantages; by transforming employees into independent subcontractors, they can discharge the costs associated with the hiring and payment of benefits to workers, which would otherwise be their responsibility.

A second mechanism leading women to become entrepreneurs emanates from the contingencies they face and the characteristics of the family units to which they belong. For example, in conducting research in Southern California, we have found instances where women with experience as operatives in the garment industry literally had to become managers or owners of small operations in order to maintain the living standards of their families. In one case, an older woman had used a sizable disability payment received by her husband to make the initial investment in five used sewing machines and in the hiring of seven workers. The small income margin between being an employer or continuing as a wage worker, as well as some autonomy in the allocation of time, were enough incentive to enter the hazardous field of business. In another instance, two young undocumented immigrants from Mexico had been provided with the necessary equipment by a former employer wishing to retire from business. Because these two women were single mothers living together, they had been able to pool savings and start a small enterprise in Los Angeles.

Finally, initial research indicates that the rationale behind Hispanic women's decisions to become entrepreneurs is not very different from the one that leads them to become involved in home assembly. In both cases, women aim at reconciling home-care responsibilities with financial need (Boris, 1985). The contradictions emanating from their involvement in nonremunerated and wage labor, however, often places them at a disadvantage in terms of competitiveness and leverage vis-à-vis large contractors.

Firsthand interviews with women who are small-scale businesspersons indicate that they live perilously on the edge of bankruptcy: their profit margins are negligible, their orders widely irregular, and their ability to master administrative charges almost nonexistent. Because of this, they are an easy target for periodic inspections, citations, and penalties assessed by state officials. Nonetheless, the measure of autonomy provided by entrepreneurial activity is fully appreciated by these women. It may be one of the unanticipated consequences of industrial restructuring that spaces are being created for the incorporation of women's potential ability as small-business persons.

CONCLUSIONS

A comparison of garment and electronics production in Southern California demonstrates that restructuring has not been confined to traditional manufacturing sectors. Instead, it has entailed a series of adjustments on the part of old as well as new industries. The internationalization of the economy was largely prompted by the attempts of companies to retain a competitive advantage in the world market. On one hand, competitiveness meant tapping pools of cheap labor in less developed countries. On the other hand, internationalization altered the conditions for production and investment in advanced industrial nations. One of the consequences of this two-pronged development has been the growing demand for immigrant and female labor in certain sectors of the U.S. economy.

In spite of their antithetical public images, garment and electronics production share several commonalities. Both are highly competitive, both are characterized by increasing fragmentation and informalization, and both depend heavily on the use of unskilled and semiskilled female labor. Our research shows that Hispanic women, many of them undocumented immigrants, are playing a decisive role in this development.

The reorganization of industry is raising questions and creating opportunities. It is possible that the expanding incorporation of Hispanics (especially recent immigrants, refugees, and undocumented workers) into garment and electronics production may reflect deteriorating conditions for labor as a whole. At the same time, the growth of subcontracting and the tendency toward informalization may be opening new paths for entrepreneurship on the part of Hispanic women and immigrants, and refugees in general. The tension between these two possibilities—further erosion of the working class or consolidation of a new class of competitive entrepreneurs—is one of the features marking the path of future international development.

NOTES

1. Under the term *Southern California* are included three counties: Los Angeles, Orange, and San Diego comprising 9121 square miles, that is, 5.7% of the total area of the state. Although proportionally small, 48% of the state's population lives in this southern portion.
2. The so-called informal sector comprises a spectrum of economic exchanges

between employers and workers falling entirely or partly outside of government regulation. The informal sector includes licensed companies that violate labor and tax legislation, unlicensed shops, and homework (see Portes, Castells, & Benton, in press).

3. Homework in electronics is legal in the state of California. Companies as well as workers participating in home assembly are, however, required to register with the Labor Commissioner. Only a small number of employers and workers fulfill this minimal proviso.

4. This figure is an estimate resulting from in-depth examination of census and statistical sources, as well as direct interviewing of public officials and employers.

REFERENCES

Alclay, R. (1984). Hispanic women in the United States: Family and work relations. *Migration Today, 12*(3), 51-63.

Beneria, L., & Roldan, M. (1987). *The crossroads of class and gender.* Chicago: University of Chicago Press.

Bluestone, B., & Harrison, B. (1982). *The deindustrialization of America.* New York: Basic Books.

Boris, E. (1985). Regulating industrial homework: The triumph of sacred motherhood. *Journal of American History, 71*(4), 745-763.

Castells, M. (1985). *New technologies, world development, and structural transformation: The trends and the debate,* Report Prepared for the Committee for a Just World Peace, Abbaye de Royaumont Ile-de-France.

Cohen, R. (1986, October 17). Tierra del Fuego: Microchips and sheep. *The Wall Street Journal,* p. 32.

Evans, P. (1985). Transnational linkages and the economic role of the state: An analysis of developing and industrialized nations in the post-World War II period. In P. Evans, D. Rueschemeyer, & T. Sckocpol (Eds.), *Bringing the state back in.* New York: Cambridge University Press.

Farley, J., & Glickman, N. (1985). *R and D as an economic development strategy: The Microelectronics and Computer Technology Corporation comes to Austin Texas.* Austin: University of Texas. Lyndon Johnson School of Public Affairs.

Fernández Kelly, M. P. (1983). *For we are sold. I and my people: Women and industry in Mexico's frontier.* Albany: State University of New York Press.

Fernández Kelly, M. P. (1985). Contemporary production and the new international division of labor. In S. Sanderson (Ed.), *The Americas in the new international division of labor.* New York: Holmes and Meier.

Fernández Kelly, M. P., & García, A. M. (1986). The making of an underground economy: Hispanic women, home work, and the advanced capitalist state. *Urban Anthropology, 14*(1-3), 59-90.

Frobel, F., Heinrichs, J., & Kreye, O. (1979). *The new international division of labour.* New York: Cambridge University Press.

Gall, N. (1982, February 15). Close the door, they come in the window. *Forbes,* pp. 80-82.

Glassmeier, A., Hall, P., & Markusen, A. R. (1985). *Recent evidence on high-technology industries' spatial tendencies: A preliminary investigation* (Working paper no. 417). Berkeley: University of California, Institute of Urban and Regional Development.

Heer, D., & Falasco, D. (1981). *The socioeconomic status of recent mothers of Mexican origin in Los Angeles County: A comparison of undocumented migrants, legal migrants, and native citizens.* Paper presented at the meeting of the International Union for the Scientific Study of Population, Manila, The Philippines.

Henderson, J. (1986). The new international division of labor and American semi-conductor production in South-East Asia. In D. Watt, C. Dixon, & D. Drakakis-Smith (Eds.), *Multinational companies in the Third World.* London: Croom Helm.

International Ladies Garment Workers' Union, Research Department. (1985). *Conditions in the women's garment industry.* New York: Author.

Lawrence, R. Z. (1984). *Can America compete?* Washington, DC: Brookings Institution.

Maram, S., & Long, S. (1981). *The labor market impact of Hispanic undocumented workers: A case study of the garment industry in L.A. County.* Fullerton: California State University.

Morales, R. (1983). Transitional labor: undocumented laborers in Los Angeles automobile industry. *International Migration Review, 17,* 510-596.

Nash, J., & Fernández Kelly, M. P. (1983). *Women, men and the new international division of labor.* Albany: State University of New York Press.

O'Connor, D. (1983, May 12-15). *Changing patterns of international production in the semiconductor industry: The role of transnational corporation.* Paper prepared for the Conference on Microelectronics in Transition, University of California at Santa Cruz.

Perlmutter, M. (1944). *The rag bizness.* Los Angeles: Author.

Portes, A., & Castells, M. (in press). World underneath. In A. Portes, M. Castells, & L. Benton (Eds.), *The informal economy: Comparative studies in advanced and Third World societies.* Baltimore, MD: Johns Hopkins University Press.

Portes, A., Castells, M., & Benton, L. (Eds.). (in press). *The informal economy: Comparative studies in advanced and Third World societies.* Baltimore, MD: Johns Hopkins University Press.

Portes, A., & Walton, J. (1981). *Labor, class and the international system.* New York: Academic Press.

Rumberger, R. W. (1984). High technology and job loss. *Technology in Society, 6,* 263-284.

Rumberger, R. W., & Levin, H. M. (1984). *Forecasting the impact of new technologies on the future job market,* Research Report. Stanford, CA: Stanford University, School of Education.

Sanderson, S. (Ed.). (1985). *The American in the new international division of labor.* New York: Holmes and Meier.

Sassen-Koob, S. (1984). The new labor demand in global cities. *In Urban Affairs Annual Reviews. Vol. 26: Cities in transformation* (pp. 139-171). Beverly Hills, CA: Sage.

Scott, A. J. (1985). *High technology industry and territorial development: The rise of the Orange County Complex, 1955-84,* Research Report. Los Angeles: University of California at Los Angeles, Department of Geography.

Siegel, L. (1984). *Delicate bonds: The semiconductor industry.* Mountain View, CA: Pacific Studies Center.

Silvestri, G. T., Lukasiewicz, J. M., & Einstein, M. A. (1983, November). Occupational employment projections through 1995. *Monthly Labor Review,* pp. 37-49.

Taylor, P. S. (1980). Mexican women in Los Angeles industry in 1928. *Aztlan, International Journal of Chicano Studies Research, 11*(1), 99-129.

U.S. Department of Commerce, Bureau of the Census. (1982). *County business patterns.* Washington, DC: Government Printing Office.

U.S. Department of Labor, Bureau of Labor Statistics. (1986). *Statistical abstract of the United States.* Washington, DC: Government Printing Office.

Wallerstein, I. (1974). *The modern world system.* New York: Academic Press.

3

The Mobilization of Women in the Bolivian Debt Crisis

JUNE NASH

The debt crisis in Bolivia, as in many countries of Latin America, is bringing about economic stagnation and impoverishment for increasing sectors of the population. Government welfare programs are curtailed as the International Monetary Fund imposes stringent conditions for payment of the debt. More women than ever before are forced to seek a livelihood in the "informal" economy, engaging in petty trade, casual labor in agriculture, and scavenging. Household strategies for survival, deploying members in the work force both within and outside of the country, call upon resources women have always cultivated in kinship and neighborhood settings. As the crisis deepens, the class struggle has moved from the sites of production to the household and community, and the right to survive becomes a revolutionary issue. Women's primary responsibility for the survival of family members puts them in the vanguard of political mobilization around these claims to live.

In the current debt crisis in Latin America, conditions set by international financial circles for repayment of the debt are transforming the economies of the hemisphere. The "orthodox strategies" used by the International Monetary fund (IMF), including limitation of imports and capital investment, have had a negative effect on debt payment because of reduced economic activity within the

AUTHOR'S NOTE: Fieldwork was carried out with money provided by the Professional Staff Congress of the City University of New York in the summers of 1985 and 1986. I am grateful for the research assistance of Rodrigo Muñoz, who accompanied me in my travels to Cochabamba and Santa Cruz in 1985. Rosario León and Cecelia Salazar joined me when we interviewed participants in the March for Bread and Peace, and Cecelia accompanied me on my trip to the mining communities in 1986. I benefited from their questioning and reflections in the interviewing and interpretation.

debtor countries and a reduction of the market for foreign manufacturers (Devlin, 1985). These strategies have led to a net outflow of capital from developing countries to industrial centers since 1980, resulting in reductions in consumption and stagnation in production.

The fragile democracies in Argentina, Bolivia, Brazil, and Peru that bear the debt burden imposed by earlier military dictatorships are crippled in their ability to respond to the pressing needs of their citizens. Social welfare budgets directed toward health, education, and housing are minimized as servicing on the debt becomes more onerous. Because the prime target of these programs are women and children, they are forced into ever increasing impoverishment. The struggle to survive in the mushrooming neighborhoods of the cities of Peru (Andreas, 1986), Chile (Lewis & Petras, 1986), and other countries of the Third World is radicalizing the political life of urban poor women, and rural women have found a distinct voice within the agricultural confederations (Dandler & Madeiros, 1985).

In the emerging economic structure of debt-ridden countries, there is greater participation of women in the growing service sector and "informal" economy than ever before. By *informal economy,* I mean work outside of the organized institutions of government or private capitalism, in which income is derived from self-initiated activities such as street vending, garbage recycling, prostitution, and begging. These activities yield very low returns and none of the benefits workers have won in the formal economy (Arizpe, 1977). In rural areas, women tend to retreat into household subsistence production, where diversification of activities by various members of a family enable them to survive the crisis in the growing uncertainties of economic life (Dandler & Madeiros, 1985). In their role as housewives, they are especially alert to the threat to life in the declining economy. This role is doubly threatened as male wage earners have lost their jobs and oftentimes drifted from home in search of work elsewhere. The governments of the indebted countries, under pressure from the International Monetary Fund, have reduced expenditures on health, welfare, and education budgets, as noted above, and have closed or turned over to private enterprise the nationalized industries that maintained legal standards of wages and benefits. In this process of denationalization and deindustrialization, the class struggle has shifted its locus from the workplace to the home and community as demands for the right to life have replaced claims for higher wages. Women are often in the vanguard of the movements that make these demands.

ECONOMIC RESTRUCTURING IN BOLIVIA

Although landlocked in the heart of the southern hemisphere, Bolivia has always relied on world markets for the sale of its natural resources. The precipitous decline in the prices of commodities on the world market, in particular tin and oil, which were Bolivia's major exports, has shaken the foundations of the economy. Added to this is the debt crisis brought about by inflated buying during the military regimes of Colonel Hugo Banzer from 1971 to 1978 and a series of military dictators until the return to democracy in 1982 when President Siles Zuazo took power. Banzer incurred $US2,234,458,000 of debt in the 1970s when U.S. banks were eager to loan the glut of petroleum dollars from OPEC countries. His successors (with brief intermissions of democratically elected presidents Guevara and Gueiler), Generals Pereda, Padilla, Natusch, García Meza, and Torrelio, borrowed another billion and a half in the five years until 1982, when Siles Zuazo was seated in the presidency he had won in 1978. With sharply declining production in the mines due to the accumulated failure to renew technology and explore for future veins in the period of the military, Siles Zuazo was forced to borrow another half billion from international banks.

The resulting debt of almost $5 billion may seem insignificant in comparison with that of Brazil and Mexico, where it surpasses $100 billion, but it requires 60% of Bolivia's dwindling exports to service the interest and amortization annually. In a country where the average annual income is $288, the debt, if distributed per capita, amounts to $552 (Strengers, 1985). Bolivia was the first Latin American nation to fail to pay the servicing of the debt in 1981. The renegotiation of the debt during General García Meza's term of office, from July 1980 to August 1981, set disastrous conditions in the interest rates and terms for repayment. The publicly announced failure to meet the debt service in 1984 carried with it the loss of international credit and the complete collapse of Bolivian currency. The official rate of exchange during President Siles Zuazo's term of office, from October 1982 to July 1985, rose to 67,000 bolivianos to one U.S. dollar, but the unofficial or "parallel" rate was 350,000 bolivianos to a dollar just before the elections of August 1985 (Strengers, 1985). No sector of the population (except those involved in the drug trade that has become a $4-billion industry) could endure the rampant inflation that exceeded 100% per month.

Following the election of President Paz Estenssoro in July 1985, the national currency was allowed to "float" on the exchange market, reaching 1,900,000 bolivianos per U.S. dollar. Prices remain at all-time highs while wages have declined relative to the dollar. The New Economic Policy that Paz Estenssoro introduced shortly after his election incorporated the neoliberal philosophy of the IMF adviser from Harvard, Jeffrey Sachs. This called for withdrawal of the government from nationalized enterprises, closing of the major mines, and taxing all citizens, including subsistence farmers. The 1986 budget reveals these priorities more than any other instrument. It allocated 36.5% of expenditures to the foreign debt, 22.3% for "defense" (which in Bolivia is uniquely a defense against popular uprisings), 11% to education, 1.9% to health, and 28.3% for "other items" (Centro de Documentación e Información [CEDOIN], 1986, p. 1).

As the currency fell in the international market, prices rose dramatically. The impact of these dramatic fluctuations in the exchange rate and cost of living has affected all classes. Professionals, bureaucrats, teachers, and small entrepreneurs in the flagging manufacturing sector (H. Buechler, 1986; J.-M. Buechler, 1986) have been forced to cut basic consumption to the minimum in order to survive. Although the debt crisis cut across class strata, its impact on different sectors of the economy and on different regions of the country has affected women in very different ways. The "dollarization" of the economy—converting prices to the dollar exchange as a response to variations in the exchange rate—occurred most rapidly in the major market centers of La Paz, Santa Cruz, and Cochabamba. Women are the major force in the urban markets, both as sellers and buyers. As sellers, they fared better than fixed-income workers or professionals, and, as buyers, they organized boycotts of speculators. In the mining communities, housewives stood at the center of the storm in the raging inflationary spiral. As long as the mining centers received subsidized food in the commissaries, they were insulated from the most adverse affects of the cost-of-living increase. But by March 1985, there was very little food supplied to the mines and housewives protested in a major mobilization in La Paz. Mining was the sector most adversely affected by Paz Estenssoro's New Economic Policies, which called for closure of the major mines in 1986. Subsistence peasants of the Cochabamba Valley were less adversely affected than wage workers, but the control exerted by Siles Zuazo's government over prices of commodities that they sold in the market resulted in protests expressed in road blockades in Santa Cruz and Cochabamba. Women joined men in these actions and in addition promoted self-help groups that channeled contributions from overseas.

I shall compare the impact of the crisis in three areas, the mining centers of Oruro and Siglo XX-Catavi, the agricultural and trucking center of Cocha-bamba, and the agroindustrial area of Santa Cruz in the periods June and July 1985 and August 1986 when I did research on the subject. In the absence of national hegemonic control exercised by any of the political parties, each region experienced the crisis in ways that were expressed in terms of regional ideologies (Laserna, 1985, pp. 128-129). As the crisis moved from a pervasive threat to an acute state of emergency in the 12-month period from June 1985 to July 1986, there was an expansion of protest from enclave mining sectors to the civic committees of Oruro and Potosí, and to the universities throughout the country. This process of generalizing protest that had its origins in particular regional economies was systematically suppressed by the Bolivian armed forces. The presence of U.S. troops stationed in the Beni from July 14, 1986, for the supposed purpose of controlling the drug traffic, added to the apprehension of leaders in the university, unions, and civic committees who were mounting a campaign to counter government policies to meet the debt payments.

In the course of the year 1985-1986, the focus of my research shifted from one of looking at women's strategies for coping with the crisis to their participation in protest movements as the economy moved from one of general inflationary crisis to one of acute emergency in particular sectors after the New Economic Policies went into effect. The presence of women in the political struggles that developed, along with the sharpening of the crisis, has changed the nature of class struggle from one based on conflict in the workplace to one focused on the right to life in the context of the family and community.

ECONOMIC STRATEGIES FOR SURVIVAL

The Highland Mining Centers

The highland mining centers have been developed as the main export economy in Bolivia since the colonial period. The state of Oruro, which held silver mines opened by the Inca prior to the conquest, became the banking and university center for the tin mines at the end of the nineteenth century and continued to yield important revenues throughout the 1970s. Potosí, with its "Cerro Rico," or "rich hill," with its many mines, produced enough silver, people say, to build a bridge from the New World to the Spanish capital city of Madrid. Despite its decline in the period of industrialization, it continues to be the scene of small extractive enterprises up to the present.

The metaphor implied in a bridge is significant, given that the mining sector provided over 90% of the balance of payments up until the 1970s. The mining economy fell into decline during the 1980s when the price of tin declined and the costs of production rose. The nationalized Bolivian Mining Company (COMIBOL) sold its metals at the official rate of 67,000 bolivianos to the U.S. dollar but bought machinery and supplies at the unofficial rate of 300-500 bolivianos to one U.S. dollar. This discrepancy, combined with the low productivity of the mines after years of military rule when capital investments were made in geological exploration for new veins and technology, meant that the mines were exhausted by the year 1982 when Hernán Siles Zuazo came to power (Ugarteche, 1985).

Because the mines, like all national enterprises, suffered from the official exchange rate, the Bolivian Workers' Center (COB), which unites all unions in the country in a single organization, proposed the explicit use of the "parallel" (underground) exchange rate in their purchases as well as sales, and that they buy supplies directly in bulk to avoid losses on the exchange rate given in the national bank. They called for postponement of the debt service and payment of the service charges at the import sector rate.

By 1985, the mines were losing thousands of dollars each month. Recognizing the threat this posed to the survival of the nationalized mines, the Federation of Mine Workers' Unions of Bolivia (FSTMB) called for government investments in state enterprises to improve the productivity of the workers by upgrading the machinery, searching for new veins, and concentrating the 90-million tons of slag pile where the level of metal was about 0.26—equal to that taken from the interior mine shafts.

The turning point from worker action at the site of production to workers' and housewives' actions in the public arena came in the period from March to

May 1985 when miners converged on La Paz to urge the government to bring supplies and tools to the mining centers. Their demands had little effect on the falling government of Siles Zuazo, however, because they could not be backed by economic force. Indeed, a workers' strike would have saved the company money, because it was operating the mines at a cost of $US14 million a month and producing only $US8 million at the official rate of return. Although the mining company might thereby have saved money, there would also have been *no* production and no income to miners.

When I visited the major nationalized mining centers in June 1985, I was particularly interested in interviewing the leaders of the Housewives' Associations who had played such an important part in the march on La Paz that had taken place in March. These associations had been organized in most of the major mines in the 1960s when wives of union members who were imprisoned by President René Barrientos mobilized political support to gain their husbands' freedom. They gained strength and importance throughout the 1960s and 1970s in their struggles against political repression by the military regimes. During the height of repression in the military regime of Hugo Banzer, who had seized power in a military coup in 1971, members of the Housewives' Association entered into a hunger strike that brought his downfall in 1978.

I spoke with Domitila Barrios de Chungara, a leading figure in the hunger strike initiated by the Housewives' Association and author of *Let Me Speak,* about her participation in the march to La Paz.

She told me that she had entered the presidential palace with the women who confronted President Siles with their demands for food in the mines. She expressed dissatisfaction with the results of that movement, and concluded that it was no longer the time for strikes and protest marches.

When I asked the president of the Housewives' Association of the San José Mine in Oruro what she thought of the march on La Paz, she replied:

> It's clear that we didn't gain anything. The government only promised to help, but has not fulfilled their obligation. We still don't have any meat, we don't have bread, we don't have sugar, and we don't have rice. There are homes that have ten children and these homes suffer more than most.

After the La Paz march, the women developed lower-key, direct contact of delegations from each mine that traveled to La Paz to tell government officials about the shortages of food in the mining centers. In addition to political activities, the Housewives' Association promoted survival techniques that included pooling money on payday to buy supplies in bulk. Households in the mining centers were eating almost no meat, relying on potatoes and noodles with vegetables as the mainstay of meals. Because wages were often not paid on time, it was extremely difficult to procure basic food supplies on the open market when they were no longer available in the mine company store. As their needs increased because of the termination of public programs such as school lunches, many women traveled to Cochabamba to work in the harvest, returning with corn, vegetables, and oil rather than receiving pay.

Throughout 1985, there was a sharp attrition in employment in the mines, with more than 8000 miners laid off. Many of these men have gone to the lowlands in the southeastern department of Santa Cruz where land was promised to colonizers. Sometimes they left behind their wives and children. Others have joined the thousands of unemployed in Cochabamba, and countless other discouraged workers have found jobs in the cocaine production centers of Beni, Chapari, and the Yungas.

As yet, women in the mining communities have not yet adopted an independent political position. Despite the increasing number of desertions as men seek work elsewhere, and the growing significance of their own strategies for gaining a living for themselves and their children, women continue to define themselves as housewives and make their appeals to government in those terms. External agencies have brought in garment work to enable the women to earn money on their own, but such economic independence was not an expressed demand. The awareness that women without men must live on very meager resources makes them fearful of striking out on their own, and their demands continue to be phrased in terms of homemakers.

When I returned to the mining centers a year after Paz Estenssoro was installed in office, production in the mines had come to a standstill. The miners had attempted to demonstrate the possibility of increasing productivity in April and May of 1986, but the lack of materials and technology doomed any such effort. The Federation of Mine Workers Unions (FSTMB) declared an indefinite strike until the administration would provide the needed supplies, and demanded a response from the government on its emergency plan. This strike was an attempt to forestall the government decree calling for the closing of marginal mines, transfers to cooperatives of others, and sales of more profitable mines to private companies.

The resistance of the mining communities to the threat of closing the mines reached a peak in the 21st National Congress of Miners on May 12 and 13, 1986. For the first time, the National Committee of Housewives sent an official delegation of 50 women to the Congress and the delegates adopted a resolution that gave them the right to voice and vote in the meetings. *Socavón* (1986), the official publication of the Center for the Promotion of the Mines, summed up the significance of the women's presence:

> This act [providing credentials to the women] verifies that even women of the mining community are discriminated against, despite their experience in the work and their decisive participation in critical periods for the working class. We speak of discrimination in the sense that the women of the mines, in suffering daily the reverses of fortune in the system, are being exploited indirectly through the wages of their husbands that do not cover the household expenses, an experience that permits them to mature more quickly and to hold a critical outlook on their

problems, making possible the search for alternative solutions compatible with their experience.

The recommendations of the Congress to close some of the nationalized mines and turn others into cooperatives were submitted to the national representatives in the parliament and President Paz Estenssoro. When the government failed to respond to the petitions of the FSTMB to save the nationalized mines, miners organized a March for Life and Peace that began on July 19 and was brought to an end by the army on July 28. Their actions in that historic march, supported by civic committees of the departments of Oruro and Potosí, teachers, farmers, and factory workers, are described below.

Cochabamba Valley

Throughout the colonial and independence period when the mines were the important centers for export production, Cochabamba served as a peripheral area supplying food and labor reserves (Laserna, 1982, pp. 1-15). Following the Revolution of 1952, the abolition of the *latifundia* (large landholding) and control by the tin oligarchy, Cochabamba became the key interchange in the new orbit between La Paz and Santa Cruz, where petroleum and gas production along with commercialized agriculture and cattle raising promoted new directions in the cash economy. Development in the area after the Revolution of 1952 tied small plot farming to a cash economy without providing the basis for mobility in the wider economy (Laserna, 1982). Price controls on basic foods during the Siles Zuazo government meant that small farmers have become progressively impoverished with the introduction of commercialized cultivation and transportation services.

The polarization of income became acute after the Banzer coup when prices for semicommercial and commercial crops such as sugar and cotton rose while those for subsistence crops such as rice and wheat were controlled at levels that actually decreased as inflation advanced. In the growing opposition to government policies, peasants took action by constructing road blockades in 1973. These were so effective that Banzer sent out the armed forces with tanks and machine guns, an action that resulted in the massacre of hundreds of peasants (Justice and Peace Commission, 1974).

Regional protests in Cochabamba peaked again in 1978 when workers and students joined a civic strike to demand higher wages to meet the inflation in the cost of living. The rebellion widened in 1980 as broad sectors of the population rejected the rule of General García Meza. The rejection of military rule became nationwide in 1982 as a general strike, already undertaken in Cochabamba, Santa Cruz, and Oruro, was decreed for all workers by the Bolivian Workers' Center (COB).

In the growing crisis of the 1980s, members of households in Cochabamba expanded the scope of strategies that they had traditionally used. These included migration to other departments or outside the country, particularly Argentina and Brazil; diversification of crops and productive activities undertaken by various members of the family; and intensification of petty vending. As Dandler and Madeiros (1985) have shown, these strategies are dependent on the retention of strong family ties, which are the primary responsibility of women. The resources that women employ in cultivating these ties include, according to Dandler and Madeiros (1985, p. 10), not only land, capital, and technology, but also time, information, social networks, identity, and historical memory to detect opportunities in situations of limited economy. Women and the families they bear are the ties that keep migrants to other regions of the country or to Argentina and Brazil returning to their home bases. The remittances that they receive enable them to capitalize their ventures in petty vending and to make improvements on homes and commercial establishments. Women's activities, as Dandler and Madeiros summarize from scores of interviews, vary in their life cycle in accord with domestic responsibilities. In the high valleys of Cochabamba, girls engage in pastoral activities, helping in the kitchen and with younger children, weeding, and knitting. When they marry, they often become engaged in a trade, working with their husbands until children are born. This restricts their geographic mobility but they often knit and embroider items for sale. Those who migrate to Argentina with their husbands engage in agricultural work in harvest time or in "informal work" selling food, clothing, or even starting boardinghouses for compatriots.

Few data are available for Cochabamba on the incidence of female-headed households—an increasing phenomenon worldwide (Buvinic, Youssef, & Von Elm, 1978)—and undoubtedly a serious problem in Bolivia with its rising out-migration. Most of the respondents in the studies carried out by the Center for the Study of the Economic and Social Situation (CERES) treated the migration of men as a temporary phenomenon, and indeed there seemed to be a high ratio of returned migrants. One incentive was the favorable balance of exchange between Bolivian and Argentinean currency so that men do better earning money in Argentina and returning to Bolivia to spend it. Even when the nuclear family is disrupted as a residential unit, extended families continue to operate as a resource base where money can be pooled and redistributed (Dandler & Madeiros, 1985).

The "careful organization of multiple, small earnings in the context of the family" is the chief mechanism of survival in the face of the lack of a state welfare program (Dandler & Madeiros, 1985, p. 39). Flexibility in the face of violent fluctuations in the economy is the crux of the strategy of women who supervise these household economies. In June 1985, I spoke about how the crisis affected the life of her family with Doña Felicia, a housewife who had been engaged in market vending with her mother as a young girl and sporadically during her marriage to a clerk in a research organization. She stated:

Prices have been going up for the past three years. Now in the market no one deals with 20 or 50 boliviano bills; everything is in 100s. Potatoes have gone up to 800 for an arroba. A kilo of tomatoes is 400. I can't even tell my husband how much I will need for the month since it varies so much. We are eating less each week. I didn't bring home any sugar, rice or noodles. Everything is in short supply. So with the situation like that, in the month of October of last year I began to start an egg business. I bought 200 eggs that cost 400 bolivianos and I sold them for 800. That helped me meet my own expenses.

Doña Felicia had eight children: one is chronically ill, two are in grade school, three are in college, and the rest are self-supporting. She has cut down food rations in order to make ends meet. At lunchtime, Doña Felicia does not serve a second course as she was accustomed. There are no desserts except for birthday cakes. Yet, she is among the more fortunate because her husband has a steady job and regularly turns over money for household expenses.

Women with children under 5 years of age are able to receive basic supplies of milk, flour, and noodles from the "Mothers' Clubs" that get their supplies through donations to the churches from abroad. The women pay the cost of delivering the goods to their locales. These groups vary in the impact they have on women's mobilization. In some cases, as in the one I witnessed in Cochabamba, they promote a sense of dependency on the donor, cultivating conformity to a given status structure. In other cases, as in Santa Cruz, which I describe below, the Mothers' Clubs promote self-help projects that may even enhance the power and autonomy of women. The following excerpt from my field notes illustrates the first kind of response:

In June 1985, I attended a meeting of a Mothers' Club in the outskirts of Cochabamba. A Belgian priest addressed the group of 50 or more women on the topic of marriage, baptism and the family. In the course of his talk he asked rhetorically, "Who are the three people one needs to ensure a family?" When no one answered, he responded, "The Father, the Son and the Holy Ghost." He went on to ask, "Why do we call on these three?" "Christ sacrificed his life for us," one woman ventured. The priest agreed but added that there is a "deeper" reason. "These three called us to a new life more perfect than before. The three are a family. And what is the relation between the father and the son?" A woman responded, "The father conceived the son." The priest corrected her, saying that the relation was through the Holy Ghost, the relation of love between the Father and Son was personified in the Holy Ghost. He then asked the group, "What exists between father and mother?" and hastily answered before anyone could intervene, "Love." He proceeded without pausing for audience participation:

"This is the image of God in us. Is it just to have free love? It is unjust. We are not owners of our children. God is the only owner. Parents should reflect on the future of their children."

A young woman broke in at that point to say, "But they can't because they are preoccupied trying to get the basic necessities. All of us Bolivians are preoccupied with our stomachs." The priest said, "I don't deny this, but let us look at the problem in greater depth. We aren't living by bread alone . . . You may be living a desperate life and want to escape, but you should not give in to egoism. The church will help you go from desperation to hope." The young woman broke in to say, "The church teaches our children the catechism, but it should teach them something more . . . " but her voice was drowned out as the women moved to the storehouse where the food was kept and gathered up their shares to take home to their families.

When I asked women in the Mothers' Clubs who was at fault for the crisis, they agreed that it was because of their own self-centeredness. "We are not putting the country before ourselves." And when I asked them "Who is taking advantage of the crisis?" they answered almost in unison, "We all are. We are not putting our country before ourselves."

The group of women who attended the meeting of the Mothers' Club included wives of retired miners, employees of the municipality and small establishments, as well as women engaged in petty trade. Their consciousness does not come directly from their life situation but rather is filtered through the institutional channels that are mediating the crisis and permitting survival for those who conform to an imposed ideology. Although some of the younger women questioned the priest's message, which stressed conformity to the Christian ideals of family life, the group did not develop an independent line of thinking. This ideal stressing the male trinity as the central focus of family is in striking contrast to the reality women face. Often abandoned by men as the economic crisis heightens, women are left to cope with the multiple stresses of hunger, starving children, and a bleak outlook for the future. Yet the response cultivated by the church encourages the meekness and self-blame revealed in their responses to the questions I raised. This lack of class consciousness, fostered by some segments of the church, contrasts with the political awareness of the women in the mining communities who blame the crisis on the military leaders of the 1970s and early 1980s who left the country with the debt burden.

The outlook and strategies of the women living in the cities contrast with those of women in the countryside. Carmen Madeiros, a research investigator with the Center for the Study of Economic and Social Reality (CERES), has interviewed over 100 families of Ucurena. She found that women are constantly traveling, selling goods, shoring up the bonds between relatives who become a valuable resource in the crisis, and engaging in harvest and other agricultural work. They do not have time to attend Mothers' Club meetings, nor do they share the ideology of dependence encouraged by the church.

Southeastern Agroindustrial Area of Santa Cruz

In contrast to the small landholder agricultural areas of Cochabamba, the agroindustrial area of the southeast in the department of Santa Cruz grew enormously in population and gross agricultural production in the 1970s. This growth was a result both of increased revenues from the oil fields that were taken over from Gulf Corporation and nationalized in 1969 and of investments by the government and U.S. aid that assisted the development of large privately owned plantations raising sugar and cotton. The wealth of the cocaine traffic was even more evident in Santa Cruz in June 1985 than in Cochabamba, where "Dish" antennas and Mercedes Benzes indicate the homes of the traffickers. In Santa Cruz, whole neighborhoods of luxurious homes, many of them radiating out from the Holiday Inn, are patrolled by private police forces bearing machine guns. There is no mystery as to who is in the drug traffic; the illegal wealth is flaunted and admired.

This wealth coexists with miserable impoverishment of agricultural workers who are cut off from the domestic networks that make life possible in Cochabamba. Frontier communities extend far out into the formerly forested area as colonizers are dispossessed of the lands they clear when they cannot pay their debts or when unscrupulous government agents negate their claims. With each takeover, the colonists penetrate farther into the hinterland. The large commercial farms are worked by itinerant farm workers, including women and children who are bused in from the declining mining centers of Potosí and Oruro, or by colonizers who are dispossessed of their lands.

My arrival in Santa Cruz coincided with the meeting of the Confederation of Farmers' Unions, which was formed by these colonizers and farm laborers, in the office of the Ministry of Campesino affairs. The unions had carried out a blockade of the highways a week before, where their demands for government assistance in credit, medical, and subsistence needs were publicized. Most of the delegates who spoke felt that the blockade had failed to mobilize any resources to help the small farmers. I spoke with Lydia Flores, secretary of the Women's Affairs Committee of the Confederación Sindical de Trabajadores Campesinos Unidos, about conditions of the migrants. She told me that the farmers who produce rice and sell it for 4 or 5 million bolivianos a hundredweight do not cover their cost of production. "It is difficult to live," she told me, "because of the escalating cost of living." In 1980, she could buy a hundredweight of sugar, a tin of lard, and 20 kilos of noodles with the sale of one hundredweight of rice that she and her husband raised, but in 1985, with the same proceeds, she could not even buy a tin of lard. Health conditions are miserable and clinics are at great distances. Most of the sickness results from amoebas because there is no potable water in the frontier districts and most of the children have diarrhea. Nurses in the team that visits the frontier districts said that the children's hair is turning a reddish blond because of malnutrition and that there is a great deal of conjunctivitis. Little international medical aid reaches these lands, although government health teams have given injections against contagious diseases.

The daily wage for fieldworkers is 300–350,000 bolivianos a day, about 50 cents. Even skilled masons make less than a dollar. Although some of the workers who cultivate cotton and sugarcane are organized in unions, the children who are trucked in from Potosí often do not even have their parents to defend them, and they work just for their daily food. The government workers in charge of labor (CEJIS) are aware of the situation, but are unable to enforce the law because of lack of personnel. A report by CEJIS field-worker Hortensia

Sanchez Caballero, in May 1985, noted the following conditions in various plantations and frontier colonies:

Guapilo: Children less than 14 years work the same number of hours as adults but do not receive the same wages. Observed two children, a girl of 8 and a boy of 5 who were not on the employment lists of the company but worked to help maintain their families. They received tea with bread, soup of corn gruel for lunch and supper. Two communal dormitories that lack bathrooms, electricity and beds are the only habitation, and there is only one water faucet.

CORGEPAT: This is a military zone with cattle and agriculture where 800 women and children, 80 percent of whom are from Potosí, work. They have good housing with electric light, water, a hospital and school up to the fifth grade.

Pozo 5: 40 adults with 34 children of both sexes between the ages of 5 and 14 work in the harvest. They are fed a breakfast of tea and toasted corn. Lunch consists of corn kernels toasted and the same is given for supper. Most of the workers suffer diarrhea, vomiting, sores and eye infection. There are no schools.

Pozo 6: 18 children under 14 years of age work and receive a breakfast of coffee and bread, lunch with rice and noodles and supper the same. Most suffer malnutrition, sores and eye infection, live in communal housing without beds. Two faucets provided.

Zona M: Workers from Uyuni in Potosí include 4 of 6 children and adults. Breakfast is tea with bread, lunch rice and potatoes with meat once a week. Fathers receive their wages. A school is provided for 32 students up to fifth grade. The students work during harvest along with their parents. Children age 1-5 work on Saturdays and Sundays.

Cooperative July 5, Pozo 9: 35 minors were contracted by landowner without their parents. They have suffered from intoxication by insecticides, infected bites, diarrhea, stomachaches and malnutrition. Breakfast consists of tea with bread, rice and noodle soup.

The CEJIS office estimates that there are 70,000 workers who have migrated to the Department of Santa Cruz from highland areas, particularly the mining centers. They were promised facilities and land, but neither of these has been forthcoming. Inflation has wiped out any savings and the colonists lack transportation to take their crops to harvest. Because of these conditions, the farmers turn to coca production because they do not receive anything for other crops. This further distorts the economy, causing scarcities in food crops.

The state of Santa Cruz had more help from international agencies than the other departments I visited, although this did not always reach the settlements far from the highways. The Mothers' Clubs, of which there are 102 in the department, promote a variety of self-help projects in addition to distributing food. I visited the town of Montero, about 100 miles from the capital city, where there was a store run by the Mothers' Club. Because of the high rate of inflation, the women who organized the store lost its operating capital in May and June of

1985. While the prices of all the products the women buy have increased, the products that they raise have not increased at the same rate. In addition to the store, the Mothers' Club runs an institute for teaching dressmaking and beauty care as well as a bakery. Shortages in supplies of flour and other necessities constantly frustrate the women, who have very limited access to transportation. During Siles Zuazo's presidency, the price control on these basic supplies meant that flour, noodles, rice, and sugar were in short supply everywhere. Agronomists were working through the clubs to introduce kitchen gardens to help supplement food supplies.

The discourse in the meeting of the Mothers' Club that I attended in Montero differed considerably from that in the meeting run by the priest in Cochabamba. The president of the club dealt directly with the economic problems confronted by the group as they dealt with the daily crises in the store, the bakery, and the training classes. When I asked the same questions I had posed to the women in Cochabamba, the women expressed feelings that the crisis was the fault of poor government and that the continual strikes by the Bolivian Workers Central (COB) reduced the possibilities for recuperation. They had little hope for the elections. Like the women in campesino organizations, they have turned from political parties to seeking solutions in local action groups to improve water supplies and medical attention and, most of all, to secure food for their families.

THE STRUGGLE FOR SURVIVAL AND
THE MARCH FOR LIFE AND BREAD

In these three strategic regions, the highland mining area, the Cochabamba valleys, and the lowlands of Santa Cruz, we can see the collapse of the productive base of the country. This collapse has transformed the political mobilization from one based on the class struggle, formulated in terms of the relations in production, to one based on the struggle for life and bread, involving broad sectors of the population. In this changing struggle, the role of women in the reproduction of society has become a critical basis for their entry into political action against IMF-imposed regulations. The importance of women has been officially recognized by the Federation of Mine Workers' Unions of Bolivia (FSTMB), where the Housewives' Associations have achieved membership in the National Committee with the right to vote. The teachers' unions, in which women are a majority, are playing a more militant role than workers in many other organized industries. Women in agriculture have organized a national committee distinct from that of male agricultural workers in the Confederación Sindical Única de Trabajadores Campesinos de Bolivia (CSUTCB).

The struggles of organized labor are joined by broadly based civic committees in the departments of Potosí and Oruro that are most threatened by Paz Estenssoro's New Economic Policy. In July 1986, these committees united in a Pact for Survival in which union, civic, professional, and university organizations participated. The most important contingent was made up of teachers, mostly women, who recognized the impact of the decrees on the educational system and the entire municipal structure. On July 4, 1986, there were massive meetings in each department in which the thousands of participants declared a state of emergency and called upon the government to reply to their demands to keep the mines open. When the government failed to respond in the time stated, the Civic Committees of both departments declared a general strike that included miners in all of the mines in these departments. The policies of the government have succeeded in uniting the unemployed and dispossessed more than any other political action since the overthrow of the military in 1982. These policies threaten the basic social welfare not only of thousands of workers and peasants but also the entire population of merchants, schoolteachers, and service workers in the departments of Oruro and Potosí. The Housewives' Association that sent a delegation to the 21st National Conference of the FSTMB mounted a strong campaign against the destruction of the mining centers that had served as the backbone of the export economy. Peasants have, ever since the presidency of Lidia Gueiler (November 1979 to July 17, 1980), resisted the recommendations of the IMF, which included increases in prices for transportation, raw materials, and gas, at the same time that prices for the peasants' products were frozen. Their current struggle against the Tax Law is a continuation of their attempts to save the smallholder economy from destruction by government levies on their products. The high unemployment rates that are officially recognized as 20%, along with increasing costs of living, make the question of survival a central issue in the present struggle.

The decline in the mining economy combined with the influx of workers in drug traffic provoked the crisis that led to the invitation of U.S. troops into Bolivia in 1986. They arrived on July 14 at the time of intense mobilization of people against the conditions required by the International Monetary Fund to pay off the debt. The rising opposition to the decrees, expressed in strikes and blockades throughout the country, set the stage for the introduction of U.S. troops. Many Bolivians interpret the increase in repressive forces, both from the United States as well as internally, as a response to the rising popular reaction against IMF-imposed conditions for paying back the debt. The freezing of salaries in nationalized enterprises, the removal of price controls and subsidies for food for the poor, the restriction in social services are all measures that the IMF has imposed in other debt-ridden countries to control inflation by cutting back the demand for goods by the people (Devlin, 1985; Grounds, 1984). In Bolivia's case, the measures have been extended to a restructuring of the economy around private enterprises, which rules out the gains they felt were the achievements of the 1952 revolution.

The opposition to the New Economic Policy reached a climax shortly after the arrival of U.S. troops. The FSTMB organized a March for Life and Bread that started out from the mining center of Oruro on August 22 and planned to arrive in La Paz on August 29. The Housewives' Association, civic committees, teachers' union, farmers' unions, and factory workers enthusiastically supported the march that included groups from all the major centers affected by the decree, particularly those in the departments of Potosí and Oruro that were threatened by a total shutdown.

These forces joined together with civic committees in the departments of Oruro and Potosí—which represented a broad coalition of merchants, religious leaders, and government employees—in the March for Life and Bread of August 22-29, 1986. On Tuesday, August 26, the marchers arrived at the halfway point of Patacamaya, where they were met by tanks and troops. After some discussion, the organizers of the march convinced the government to withdraw the troops, and they proceeded to Calamarca, about 70 kilometers short of their goal.

In the massive mobilization of over 7000 people, the people arrived without incident in the town of Calamarca, 40 miles short of La Paz—the goal in their march to bring the plight of the mining communities to President Paz Estenssoro and his ministry. There they were met by delegations of peasants who helped in the preparation and distribution of food. All day Wednesday, marchers arrived in the sun-baked farming village, carrying their union banners, bedrolls, water flasks, and coca leaves. Some women even carried babies. Reporters compared the waves of weary travelers to the biblical exodus from Egypt, and the streams of dust-laden travelers evoked images of the great pilgrimages in human history. There was a kind of faith and conviction in the justice of their cause that seemed to inspire the group. There was no show of violence or rowdiness even as the cold evening winds chilled the long lines of marchers standing in line for food. The church was filled with hundreds who sought shelter, and the overflow settled in the walled yards of the peasants. The prevailing spirit was one of cooperative camaraderie, as Red Cross workers and volunteers from religious centers massaged the leg muscles and treated the blisters of the marchers.

Despite the observable peaceful intent and tenor of the marchers, Paz Estenssoro declared a state of siege and sent in four regiments to surround the marchers early on Thursday morning, August 28. While fighter planes and helicopters buzzed the masses of marchers detained in the town, armored tanks and troops prevented Red Cross vehicles, press representatives, and even parliamentary representatives from entering the town.

I joined some women from the mining center of Oruro to bring food behind the lines of soldiers spread out a few yards apart from the highway to the plaza of Calamarca. When I arrived behind the lines, I walked down to the highway, where I saw a score of women from Siglo XX sitting on the highway at the edge of a Bolivian flag that they had spread between them and rows of soldiers standing with their rifles pointed at them. Behind them were students, singing songs of protest, and around them were grouped thousands of the marchers.

"The paramilitary forces pushed us out of the church early in the morning," a woman from Oruro told us, and we slept on the road. The snow began to fall at three or two in the morning. We had a bonfire in the center and we sang insults to the government. The cold was fierce. The people of the town were prevented from giving us shelter, and the military forces ordered them not to sell us any bread.

The army intended to evacuate the marchers by forcing them into army trucks. The women resisted. "We do not know if you are going to take us away and kill us," they said. The marchers waited on the road all that day, contained by soldiers with their machine guns held in readiness. Some wanted to challenge the detention and continue the march. "We have walked 170 kilometers only to be kept from our goal," one woman shouted at the soldiers, and another cried, "There is nothing to eat in the mines. We have had no rations of meat or sugar or flour and our children are hungry!" But union leaders did their best to contain the crowd. "We don't want to have people killed," Filemón Escobar, leader of the Siglo XX miners' union, shouted as women cried out their frustration to the soldiers.

The marchers waited on the road until 35 buses of the National Transport Company were sent to take the people back to their districts. On the following day, workers in Siglo XX declared a hunger strike. Dozens set up pickets in the mine and in social clubs in the district. The strike spread to the San José mine in Oruro and to Huanuni, Colquecharca, and Potosí. Housewives joined the miners on the fifth day, with the national leadership coming to La Paz, where they took up quarters in the offices of the Newspaper *Presencia,* in the Federation of Journalists, and in the theater of the university.

The state of siege order remained in effect throughout the weeks that followed. The government rounded up rectors of the Universities of Potosí and Cochabamba. Over 200 leaders of unions, student groups, and civic groups as well as intellectuals who had criticized the government's New Economic Policy were arrested and some sent to the jail for political prisoners called "Puerto Rico." Yet as the repression increased, the Episcopal Conference of the Catholic church succeeded in initiating a dialogue between the leaders of the Federation of Mine Workers Unions of Bolivia (FSTMB) and the government. The number of hunger strikers increased during the two weeks of the dialogue. It was not, as some claimed, instigated by the leaders of the FSTMB; it was a rank and file movement initiated by the miners and their families, joined by university students and others who felt that they were setting the agenda for the larger dialogue between the government and the people. They demanded that the mines be preserved as state enterprises and that the process of nationalization be extended to include some private mines. They called for freedom for those who were detained, and, finally, they called for removal of the U.S. troops from Bolivia. One woman in the hunger strike told us, "We are defending the national sovereignty against Yanky imperialism. The National Revolutionary Movement (MNR) and the National Democratic Action (ADN) [parties of the right in power] are servants of Yanky imperialism and have accepted U.S. armed forces in order to repress the people."

The dialogue between mine federation leaders and the government came to an end on September 13. The agreement signed by both parties included provisions to keep the mines open and retain them as state property, with closing permitted after a careful study by professional geologists and economists. It approved the release of university, civic, and union leaders who had been detained, and it promised freedom of action for civic and union groups.

The women and men who had undertaken the hunger strike continued their action throughout the following week to ensure government compliance with the agreement. They questioned the democratic base of a government that used massive repression against a peaceful movement. Members of the Federation of Mine Workers Unions remained divided over issues of supplies to the mine centers and the amount of leave pay allotted to workers who were dismissed in the week following the signing of the agreement. But the government faces a clear mandate to respond to the united appeal of thousands of Bolivians who reject the New Economic Policy promoted by the International Monetary Fund or to renounce its claims to being a democracy.

U.S. troops remained quartered in the Beni throughout October 1986, despite the opposition of leaders in political parties and unions who question whether they have done anything more than divert the routes used to traffic cocaine. The U.S. government considered the possibility of extending similar troop operations to Peru, Colombia, and Ecuador, citing the fall in the price of coca as a sign of the success of the operation. But on October 10, 3000 Bolivians intervened when the troops attempted to arrest two men accused of being drug traffickers. On October 19, the Minister of the Interior announced that the 170 U.S. soldiers would be withdrawn in November, leaving the helicopters that they had brought with them for the antidrug campaign (*New York Times,* October 19, 1986). This promise was fulfilled, but in the interim that the U.S. soldiers remained in the country, the government succeeded in dispersing the miners from the major centers and in diffusing the attack on the New Economic Policies that had been demanded by the IMF.

Despite the apparent failure of the mobilization to reverse policies in the government of Paz Estenssoro, we can see the force of unified action against tremendous odds. This potential force will not be forgotten as the crisis widens. The mining centers succeeded in generalizing their crisis to include small plot agricultural workers of the highlands. Civic committees of the departments of Potosí and Oruro have made at least a temporary alliance of diverse classes that may become the basis for a more lasting hegemony of groups that find their interests threatened by antinationalist moves. The protest against the government's new economic policies has found many allies in Cochabamba, where squatter communities of migrants from the lowlands have gone in search of work. Whether the agroindustrial interests of Santa Cruz will succeed in incorporating the many migrants in those zones in reaffirming the power of right wing political parties, which now dominate the parliament, will depend in part on the success of the export-oriented agriculture and its ability to absorb workers. Because this does not appear to be envisioned in their present policies, there may be a resurgence of peasant federations that might join with those of the altiplano to unify this divided nation. The government's action in admitting 5000 Chinese immigrants to agricultural lands in the lowlands may promote the same antagonisms that Banzer's government engendered in the 1970s when they opened up the colonizing areas to South African immigrants.

In all of these struggles, women have promoted survival strategies where they could; and where there was little chance of success in customary economic solutions, they have turned to political mobilization. The threat to life promotes the mobilization of women as autonomous political figures (Nash, 1979). The economic decline of the mining sector weakened the position of organized labor in making its claims on the basis of yielding surplus value in production. The acceptance of women in the Housewives' Association of the mining center as fully accredited voting delegates in the June 1986 Congress of the Federation of Bolivian Mine Workers Unions is both a sign of the weakening of labor's position and a turn from claims based on the role of labor in production to claims based on the needs of the household to survive. This shift in the mining sector is finding an echo in the Federation of Campesinos as women's groups call for an autonomous position that would clarify the needs of the domestic economy in the restructuring of agriculture. Their input could be decisive in shaping of Bolivia's economy in the future.

REFERENCES

Andreas, C. (1986). The barriada as locus of revolutionary organization in dependent capitalistic societies: The case of Peru. *Resources for Feminist Research* [Special Issue on Feminism and State Processes], *15*(1), 25-27.

Arizpe, L. (1977). Women in the informal labor sector: The case of Mexico City. *Signs, 3*(1), 25-37.

Buechler, H. (1986, October). *Dealing with the economic depression in Bolivia: Male strategies in small firms.* Paper delivered at the meetings of the Latin American Studies Association, Boston.

Buechler, J.-M. (1986, October). *Dealing with the economic depression in Bolivia: Female strategies among small scale urban producers and market venders.* Paper delivered at the meetings of the Latin American Studies Association, Boston.

Buvinic, M., Youssef, N., & Von Elm, B. (1978). *Women-headed households: The ignored factor in development planning.* Washington, DC: International Center for Research on Women.

Center for the Promotion of the Mines. (1986, July). *Socavón, 33.*

Centro de Documentación e Información (CEDOIN). (1986). *Boletin.* La Paz: Author.

Dandler, J., & Madeiros, C. (1985, December). *La migración temporal de Cochabamba, Bolivia a la Argentina: Trayectorias e impacto en el lugar de origen* (mimeo). La Paz: CERES.

Devlin, R. T. (1985, December). External debt and crisis: The decline of the orthodox procedures. *CEPAL Review, 27*, 35-52 (Comité Económica para América Latina).

Grounds, R. L. (1984, August). Orthodox adjustment programmes in Latin America. *CEPAL Review, 23,* 41-79.

Justice and Peace Commission. (1974, January). *The massacre of the valley* (mimeo). Bolivia: Catholic Church.

Laserna, R. (1982). *Constitución y desarrollo regional de Cochabamba.* La Paz: CERES.

Laserna, R. (1985). La protesta territorial. In R. Laserna (compiler), *Democracia y conflicto social.* La Paz: CERES.

Lewis, F. I., & Petras, J. (1986, Fall). Chile's poor in the struggle for democracy. *Latin American Perspectives,* pp. 5-25.

Nash, J. (1979). Resistance as protest: Women in the struggle of Bolivian tin mining communities. In R. Rohrlich-Leavitt (Ed.), *Women cross-culturally, change and challenge* (pp. 261-274). The Hague: Mouton.

Strengers, J. (1985). *La pesada carga de la deuda.* La Paz: CEDOIN.

Ugarteche, O. (1985). La situación Latinoamericana. *La Deuda* [La Paz: FLACSO].

4

The Interaction of Women's Work and Family Roles in the U.S.S.R.

GAIL WARSHOFSKY LAPIDUS

The Soviet effort to devise policies that would simultaneously guarantee women equal treatment as workers and citizens and special treatment as mothers has had distinctive consequences for women's work and family roles. Despite rising educational attainments, and their visibility in a number of scientific and professional occupations, Soviet women tend to be concentrated in economic sectors and occupations that rank low in status and pay, and they are underrepresented in managerial positions. A sexual division of labor persists within the family as well, reflecting traditional assumptions about what constitutes men's and women's work. Soviet discussion of the problems created by women's "double burden" has become notably more frank in recent years as ritual self-congratulation has been superseded by growing alarm about rising divorce rates, declining birth rates, and growing evidence of serious strain. Current policy debates reveal sharply varying diagnoses and recommendations, while Gorbachev's economic and social reforms portend far-reaching but as yet contradictory changes in women's work and family roles. To this day, Soviet policy remains premised on the assumption that women's equality depends on a shift of functions from the private to the public sector rather than on a redefinition of male as well as female roles.

In the industrial societies of Europe and the United States, as in the developing countries of the Third World, the relationship between changes in women's

AUTHOR'S NOTE: This chapter was completed while I was a Fellow at the Center for Advanced Study in the Behavioral Sciences, with financial support from the National Science Foundation #BNS 84-11738. I should like to express my appreciation to Jennifer Sheck and Russ Faeges for their research assistance, and to Harriet Presser for helpful insights and suggestions.

economic roles and changes in the structure and functions of the family has attracted growing attention from social scientists and policymakers alike. The scope and patterns of female employment, it is increasingly recognized, critically influence key features of economic and social behavior and, most important, fertility.

For policy analysts concerned with Third World issues, these linkages present an opportunity rather than a problem: They hold out the prospect that development strategies that enhance the educational and employment opportunities of women will not only increase national income but also may contribute significantly to population control. In Europe and the United States, by contrast, these linkages are a source of concern. Rising levels of female labor force participation have been accompanied by rising divorce rates and declining birthrates, provoking widespread anxiety that the family itself is threatened by current trends. A whole array of economic and social programs are undergoing reevaluation with a view to their impact on family stability and family size, and long-standing debates over what constitutes "equal protection" of workers who are also women have been reignited.

Because of its special relevance to all these concerns, the Soviet experience deserves the close attention of social scientists and policy analysts alike. Extensive reliance on female labor has been a central feature of Soviet economic development for several decades, with important consequences for virtually every aspect of economic and social life. Today, the Soviet Union claims the highest female labor force participation rates of any industrial society with over 85% of women engaged in full-time work or study, and women constituting 51% of all workers and employees. At the same time, rising divorce rates and sharply declining birthrates have made the single-child family the norm in the urban European part of the country, while large families remain widespread in the Moslem regions of Soviet Central Asia. Indeed, important regional and ethnic variations linked to sociocultural as well as economic differences make the Soviet Union a fascinating universe for comparative study.

But the Soviet experience is important above all because the effort to develop policies that simultaneously guarantee women equal treatment as citizens and workers and special treatment as mothers has had some distinctive consequences for women's work and family roles. The promise of the new Communist Party Program of 1986 that "favorable conditions will be created that will enable women to combine motherhood with active participation in work and social activities" (*Programme*, 1986) is a clear admission that this goal has not yet been attained.

Until the late 1960s, Soviet writings interpreted high rates of female employment as unambiguous evidence that socialism and sexual equality went hand in hand, and that Soviet policy had created optimal conditions for the harmonious combination of women's work and family roles. In recent years, however, ritual self-congratulation has given way to serious self-criticism. A growing array of studies by Soviet scholars, as well as numerous Soviet novels and films, document at length the conflicting demands of women's dual roles, the constraints they place on occupational mobility, and their harmful effects on the health of women workers and the well-being of their families (Dogle, 1977; Gruzdeva & Chertikhina, 1983; Iuk, 1975; Kharchev, 1977; Kotliar & Turchaninova, 1975; Mikhailiuk, 1970; Novikova, 1985; Sakharova, 1973; Shishkan, 1976; "Trud i Byt Zhenshchin," 1978). A succession of scholarly conferences, trade union meetings, and Communist Party gatherings devoted to problems of female labor and *byt* (everyday life) have yielded an abundance of often conflicting diagnoses, recommendations, and goals (Buckley, 1986; Kharchev & Golod, 1971; "Povyshat' Politicheskuiu Proizvodstvennuiu," 1975; Solov'ev, Lazauskas, & Iankova, 1970; SSA, 1972).

These discussions and initiatives reveal a growing Soviet recognition that economic objectives pursued without regard to their social consequences not only risk failure but also threaten to exacerbate what are already perceived to be acute social problems. Consequently, significant changes in the training and utilization of female labor depend on, and are likely to elicit further changes in, a broad array of social institutions, especially the family. Family and population policies will in turn directly affect the future size and quality of the Soviet labor force.

In this chapter, I will first sketch a profile of the Soviet female labor force and its place in the national economy. I will then examine the interaction of female work and family roles and the major sources of strain between them. A concluding section will explore the variety of Soviet responses to the dilemma raised by this interdependence and their possible implications for broader economic and social policies, particularly in the context of Mikhail Gorbachev's commitment to significant economic reform. By treating the work and family roles of Soviet women as not merely the outcome of personal characteristics and preferences but as behavior that is shaped by a specific structural context, this study will also point to the distinctive way in which the Soviet pattern of development has joined family and economic systems, and it will illuminate several of its most salient, and problematic, consequences.

THE HISTORICAL LEGACY

The role of women in the Soviet labor force has been shaped by a distinctive set of assumptions and historical developments that influence Soviet policy to this day. Central to the Soviet approach—as it was to Marxist and Leninist theory—was the conviction that women's entry into social production held the key to the creation of a genuinely socialist society. Economic participation was associated with political mobilization, and industry with progress. The factory would forge new Soviet men and women—politically conscious, technically skilled builders of a new society. The family, by contrast, was initially seen as the very antithesis of the factory, the embodiment of tradition and backwardness; as Bukharin put it, the "most conservative stronghold of the old regime" (Geiger, 1968, p. 52).

To free women from dependence and isolation, and to redirect their energies and loyalties from private to public domains, it was crucial, in the view of the revolutionary Bolsheviks, to deprive the family of its economic base and replace its most important educational and social functions with publicly provided services. The nationalization of industry and the collectivization of agriculture would divest the family of its economic power; the expansion of public education and institutional child care would diminish its influence over the socialization of children; and the creation of public laundries and dining rooms would complete the shift of family functions to the wider society and free women for participation in the labor force. The economic independence of women would deal the final blow to the traditional family structure. No longer dependent on marriage for economic support, women would enter both work and family roles on an equal basis with men.

But the political and economic mobilization of women envisioned in revolutionary ideology was not intended to supplant childbearing. Rather, maternity itself was transformed into a social function. It was the very contribution of maternity to the needs of the state that justified special measures to safeguard it. Early Soviet policies therefore recognized the potential contribution of women to both production and reproduction, and attempted to provide conditions for the simultaneous performance of both. In short, the Soviet approach sought women's equality through a shift of functions from the private domain to the public rather than, as in contemporary feminist strategy, through a redefinition of male and female roles.

Stalinist priorities, however, precluded any major shift of family functions to the larger society. Radical visions of communal organization premised on the "withering away of the family" came under attack in the Stalin era. At the same time, the family's importance for social stability, economic performance, and population growth received increasing official recognition. Growing reliance on the family for the performance of critical social functions was accompanied by a new emphasis on women's domestic and maternal responsibilities. Simultaneously, Stalin's industrialization strategy, with its extreme emphasis on heavy industry, limited the development of consumer industries and services, compelling the household to provide itself with a wide range of goods and services that are normally shifted outside it in the course of economic development. In the U.S.S.R., the underdevelopment of social services meant that rising female employment outside the household would supplement rather than replace female labor within it.

Soviet norms and institutions thus ultimately rested upon the premise that women, but not men, had dual roles. On the one hand, female employment was encouraged by measures that accorded women equal rights with men, expanded their educational opportunities and professional training, and shifted some of the additional costs of female labor from the individual enterprise to the larger society. At the same time, the growth of female industrial employment was exceptionally dependent on special arrangements to accommodate the continuing heavy burden of family responsibilities. The effort to make female occupational roles permeable to family needs created especially sharp differences in the conditions of male and female labor. The result was a distinctive pattern of linkages between the family and the occupational system that had fundamentally different consequences for women and men.

FEMALE LABOR AND THE
SOVIET ECONOMY

Although Soviet policy rested from the start on an ideological commitment to the full participation of women in social production, it was the inauguration of rapid industrialization under the First Five-Year Plan in 1928 that transformed a politically desired objective into a pressing economic need. Rapid economic expansion created a rising demand for industrial labor at the same time that falling real income and a growing deficit of males increased the supply of female labor. Between 1932 and 1940, women formed the overwhelming majority of new recruits into industry; by 1940, the number of women workers and employees had risen from 3 million to 13 million, almost 40% of the total industrial work force. Increases in the proportion of women in many traditionally male branches of industry were striking: In coal mining and iron and steel production, for example, where women had constituted under 10% of the labor force in 1929, 25% of the workers in 1938 were women.

The demand for female labor was given added impetus by World War II, when a new influx of women workers replaced the millions of mobilized men. The cumulative casualties of war and civil war, of collectivization, purges, and deportations, and, ultimately, of World War II had created a severe deficit of males. In 1946, there were only 59 men for every 100 women in the 35 to 59 age group. This demographic imbalance affected the supply of female labor, as well as the demand for it, by obliging large numbers of women to become self-supporting. Political deportations and wartime losses transformed wives and widows into heads of households; in addition, a large proportion of Soviet women were deprived of any opportunity to marry because of the scarcity of men. Female-headed households made up almost 30% of the total in 1959, leading a distinguished economist to observe that "women could not but work, because their earnings are the basic source of income for the family." To this day, regional variations in the proportion of economically active women are correlated with marital status.

The gradual return to demographic normality in the postwar period, combined with the steady improvement of living standards, might have been expected to diminish the pressures for high female employment. Yet between 1960 and the early 1970s, an additional 25 million women were added to the Soviet labor force, raising their numbers to above 51% of the total. Today, over 87% of working-age women are now either employed or studying full-time; their average length of employment rose from 28.7 to 33.5 years between 1960 and 1970; and the average number of nonworking years dropped from 12.3 to 3.6 (Kotliar & Turchaninova, 1975, pp. 106-107). The only major untapped reserves

TABLE 4.1
Average Annual Number and Percentage of
Female Workers and Employees, 1922-1985

Year	Total of Workers and Employees (in thousands)	Number of Female Workers and Employees (in thousands)	Women as Percentage of Total
1922	6,200	1,560	25
1926	9,900	2,265	23
1928	11,400	2,795	24
1940	33,900	13,190	39
1945	28,600	15,920	56
1950	40,400	19,180	47
1955	50,300	23,040	46
1960	62,000	29,250	47
1965	76,900	37,680	49
1970	90,200	45,800	51
1976	104,235	53,632	51
1980	112,480	57,700	51
1985	116,829	59,669	51

SOURCE: TsSU SSSR (1972b, pp. 345, 348, 1975b, pp. 28-29, 1977, p. 470, 1979, pp. 178-179, 1980, pp. 387-388, 391, 1981, p. 160, 1985a, p. 409), "Zhenshchiny v SSSR" (1980, p. 70), "Zhenshchiny v SSSR" (1986, p .53).
NOTE: Women constituted 55% of the total population in 1959 and 63.4% of the age cohort 35 and over; by 1985, the figure had dropped to 53%.

of female labor in the U.S.S.R. today are found in the Central Asian and Transcaucasian republics, where female participation rates outside agriculture—especially among the local nationalities—remain extremely low (Ubaidullaeva, 1987).

The continuing climb in female participation rates in recent years is partly the result of explicit official policies. In the face of acute labor shortages caused by the slowdown in population growth and the exhaustion of rural manpower reserves, the Soviet leadership launched an intensive effort in the early 1960s to draw housewives into the workplace. The rapid growth of the service sector, and white-collar employment generally, facilitated the influx of older and relatively less skilled women. At the same time, a major expansion of child-care facilities made it easier for young mothers to accept employment, and several increases in the minimum wage and in pension benefits sharply raised the cost, in forgone income, of remaining unemployed.

High female participation rates also reflect continuing economic pressures. Soviet wage scales and pensions are not designed to support a family of dependents on the income of a single breadwinner. The average monthly wage, for example, is less than two-thirds of what is required to support a family of four at even the officially recognized level of "material well-being." Opinion surveys of women factory workers clearly demonstrate that economic need is the major determinant of female employment, and that family income and female labor force participation are inversely related (Kharchev & Golod, 1971, pp. 38-69; Osipov & Shchepan'skii, 1969, pp. 444, 456). As a team of Soviet labor economists put it:

> The supply of female labor is more elastic [than that of males]. It depends to a greater degree on the extent to which a family's requirements are satisfied by the earnings of the head of the family [the male] and by income from public consumption funds. The lower the level at which these requirements are being satisfied, the more the family needs earnings from its women. (Guseinov & Korchagin, 1971, p. 49)

The fact that participation rates have continued to rise despite palpable economic improvements during the past 15 years, however, suggests that other forces are also at work. "Economic need" is itself relative; as rising aspirations outrun rising incomes, a second income may still appear essential. Moreover, rising wages increase the opportunity cost of not being employed, encouraging women to prefer employment to either larger families or more leisure. This factor becomes all the more significant as educational attainments rise, because, in the Soviet Union as elsewhere, education and professionalism tend to strengthen labor force attachment.

Soviet ideology reinforces economic pressures by emphasizing the intrinsic value of work, as well as its contribution to economic independence, social status, and personal satisfaction. The role of "mere housewife" has been sharply devalued in Soviet society. As Soviet surveys indicate, relatively few women would withdraw from the labor force even if it became economically feasible (Iankova, 1975, p. 43; Mikhailiuk, 1970, p. 24; Pimenova, 1966, pp. 36-39). It is therefore unlikely that improved living standards will precipitate a substantial decline in female participation rates in the years ahead. But there is widespread interest among women in the possibility of part-time work, which has been virtually absent until quite recently. Were the opportunities for part-time work to expand significantly, the intensity of female labor force participation could diminish somewhat.

The large scale of female participation in Soviet economic life, however, has not obliterated many features that, in the U.S.S.R. as elsewhere, distinguish male and female employment. Indeed, the sharpest line of differentiation among Soviet workers today is that of sex. In the occupational structure as in the family, sex remains a significant basis for the allocation of social roles, with the result that male and female workers differ in the distribution of income, skill, status, power, and even time.

PATTERNS OF FEMALE EMPLOYMENT

Despite the massive scope of female participation in the Soviet labor force, here as in the West, women tend to predominate in economic sectors and occupations that rank low in status and pay, and they are underrepresented in the more prestigious professions and in managerial positions. In industry, as in the economy as a whole, women are heavily concentrated in a relatively small number of areas, and are significantly underrepresented in others. Although half of all industrial workers are women, three industrial branches—machine building and metalworking, textiles, and the food industry—account for 70% of all female industrial employment. Women constitute over 80% of food and textile workers and over 90% of garment workers, but less than 30% of the workers in coal, lumber, electric power, and mineral extraction.

Moreover, in industrial employment as in the professions, women are concentrated at lower levels of the occupational pyramid. Although Soviet data are scarce, they clearly indicate that, even as women begin to enter the middle and upper ranks of industry, they continue to predominate in low-level, unmechanized, and unskilled jobs. Thus, in a typical industrial city studied in a Soviet survey, approximately 4% of the women workers were highly skilled; 30% were of average skill; and 66% were low-skilled, compared to 31%, 50%, and 19%, respectively, for men (Sonin, 1973, pp. 362-363). Within individual enterprises, a similar pattern prevails. In a group of machine-building enterprises studied by another Soviet research team, almost 95% of the women workers, but only 5% of the men, occupied the three lowest skill classification. No women at all were found in the highest classification (Kotliar & Turchaninova, 1975, pp. 67-68). Although it is often assumed that technological progress will bring greater equality, increasing mechanization not infrequently widens the gap between men and women workers. The massive influx of older and less-educated women into industry in the 1960s, for example, resulted in an increase in their share of unskilled, manual jobs. Newly mechanized and automated work went primarily to males.

Women are better represented among technical specialists than among skilled workers in industry, and they occupy a particularly prominent place in teaching and medicine, although even here the proportion of women declines at higher levels of the pyramid. Women are still largely absent from positions of managerial authority. To be sure, the proportion of women among enterprise directors, for example, rose from a mere 1% in 1956 to 9% in 1975, and to 11% in 1985, but females have emphatically not moved into management to the extent that their training, experience, and proportion of the relevant age cohort would warrant.

Women workers manifest lower levels of sociopolitical participation than their male counterparts, although such activities may actually consume a greater share of their free time than is the case for males. Moreover, at every level of education and occupational attainment, women workers are far less likely than men to become Communist Party members. They constitute only 28% of total Party membership, and are virtually absent from the Soviet political elite. The proportion of women in the Central Committee of the Communist Party has never exceeded 5% since 1918, and only one woman has ever been a member of the Politburo ("KPSS v tsifrakh," 1986, p. 24; Lapidus, 1978, pp. 216-217).

The limited occupational mobility of women in industry is compounded by their lower enrollment rate in programs to raise professional qualifications. Only one-third of the women workers in a Soviet study expressed a desire to upgrade their skills, compared with over one-half the men, and they had less confidence that their efforts would be suitably rewarded (Kotliar & Turchaninova, 1975, pp. 76-84). According to the findings of other studies, young women workers raise their qualifications at the same rate as their male counterparts when their situations are identical; but from ages 21 to 25, when family responsibilities fall increasingly on their shoulders, their participation diminishes (Bliakhman, Zdravomyslov, & Shkaratan, 1965, p. 66; Gruzdeva & Chertikhina, 1975, p. 97). Family responsibilities also limit women's occupational mobility. Soviet studies of labor turnover in Novosibirsk indicate that women leave their jobs half as often as men because of dissatisfaction with the job content or pay, and that 59% of women who change jobs take a step down in occupational status (Antosenkov & Kupriianova, 1977, pp. 48-50, 77; Kotliar et al., 1982, p. 100; Reznik, 1982, p. 111). Extensive Soviet reliance on combining full-time work with study is particularly disadvantageous to women with families; the enrollment of women in evening programs virtually ceases with the birth of a child. The low level of professional and sociopolitical involvement of women workers both reflects their economic position and reinforces it; here, as elsewhere, limited aspirations are a function of limited opportunities.

THE EARNINGS GAP

The uneven distribution of women across economic sectors and occupations, combined with their underrepresentation in positions of high skill and responsibility, results in a considerable gap between male and female earnings. Although the absence of national wage data by sex makes it necessary to rely on more fragmentary figures based on local surveys or on émigré samples, the cumulative evidence points to full-time female earnings that are to 65% to 70% of males' (Lapidus, 1982, pp. xxi-xxvii; Ofer & Vinokur, 1981). This 30% to 35% gap is narrower than the 40% gulf in the United States and several West European countries, but wider than the 27% spread prevailing in Scandinavia.

The wage disparity is all the more surprising in view of official assertions that women are guaranteed equal pay for equal work and in light of the fact that the educational attainment of much of the female industrial labor force actually exceeds that of males, that female labor force participation is more continuous in the U.S.S.R. than in the West, and that virtually all employed women work full-time.

The explanation is to be found in certain features of Soviet economic organization and policy, and not only in the distinctive characteristics of the female labor force. First, economic sectors and industrial branches with high wage levels and greater wage differentials—such as heavy industry and construction—are precisely those in which women are underrepresented; those

TABLE 4.2

Distribution of Women Workers and Employees, and
Average Monthly Earnings, by Economic Sector

Economic Sector	Number of Women Workers and Employees	Women as Percentage of Labor Force	Average Monthly Earnings (rubles)
Construction	3,002,000	28	236.6
Transport	2,211,000	24	220.3
Industry (production personnel)	1,662,000	49	210.6
Science and scientific services	2,344,160	52	202.4
Nationwide	59,669,000	51	190.01
Agriculture (state sector)			182.1
Credit and state insurance	588,240	86	180.9
Apparatus of government and economic administration	1,780,860	67	166.2
Communications			159.5
Education	7,267,500	75	150.0
Trade, public catering, materials and equipment, supply and sales	7,565,040	76	149.2
Housing and municipal economy, everyday services	2,440,350	51	146.6
Arts	229,000	50	145.3
Public health, physical culture, social welfare	5,471,040	82	132.8
Culture	1,017,500	74	117.3

SOURCE: Figures on female labor and on earnings from TsSU SSSR (1985b, p. 51, 1986, pp. 391, 394, 397-398); percentages are for 1983. Current figures for industry, construction, and transport are unavailable; those used here are from TsSU SSSR (1976, pp. 542-543, 546-547).

that have a high concentration of female employees—light industry and the services—are also those in which lower wage levels and narrower differentials prevail. In construction, where women constituted 28% of the labor force in 1985, monthly earnings averaged 236.6 rubles; in public health and physical culture, where females make up 84% of the work force, they averaged 132.8 rubles.

Also contributing to the earnings gap is the fact that blue-collar occupations are more highly rewarded than most white-collar ones, even when white-collar employees have higher levels of educational attainment. For example, in 1985, the average wage of industrial workers was 211.7 rubles a month, and of white-collar personnel in industry, 164.6 (TsSU SSSR, 1986, p. 397). A detailed portrait of the social structure of a group of Leningrad machine-building enterprises revealed that the occupational categories with the highest proportion of women were at the bottom of the scale in income, but in the middle range in educational level; unskilled manual workers had lower educational levels but received higher incomes (Shkaratan, 1967, p. 36). Thus the large-scale movement of women into white-collar and professional occupations in the U.S.S.R., including teaching and medicine, has been associated with a profound decline in their average status and pay relative to skilled blue-collar employment. Moreover, work considered especially difficult or dangerous is particularly lucrative, but often forbidden to women.

Soviet sources often attribute the earnings gap to differences in the qualifications and productivity of male and female workers, but the evidence suggests that this explanation is not sufficient. Although Soviet law requires that equal work receive equal pay, there is in practice no mechanism to ensure that women are placed in positions commensurate with their training and skills. Women are thus frequently overqualified for the jobs they hold. A study of industrial enterprises in Taganrog came to the startling conclusion that 40% of all female workers with higher or secondary specialized education occupied low-skill industrial positions, compared to 6% of comparable males; only 10% of these highly educated women, compared to 46% of their male counterparts, occupied high-skill positions. Most striking of all was the fact that the distribution of the male labor force *as a whole*, without respect to education, was more favorable than the distribution of this highly educated female contingent (Gruzdeva, 1975, p. 94; Zdravomyslov, Rozhin, & Iadov, 1967). A recent study of young workers found a similar pattern. Because women confront a narrower range of choices in the job market, because they attach more weight to a job's compatibility with domestic responsibilities than to its content, and because the jobs most readily available to women are those where lower wages prevail, lower earnings are not exclusively a result of lower qualifications or productivity. Women workers are frequently more qualified, as well as more reliable and productive, than their male counterparts.

Finally, the possibility of direct wage discrimination cannot be completely ruled out. A Western analysis of unpublished Soviet wage data concluded that only one-fourth of an average male-female wage differential of 40 rubles per month could be attributed to the combined effects of sex differences in distribution across education, age, economic sector, and levels of skills or responsibility (Swafford, 1978, pp. 661-665).

What is clear, then, is that equality of economic opportunity for women has not followed automatically from higher levels of educational attainment and labor force participation. In the U.S.S.R. as in the U.S., the process of earnings attainment is sharply different for men and women. Men derive greater benefits from educational and occupational attainments, even when women's work experience and levels of current labor force participation are comparable.

It is often argued—in the Soviet Union as in the West—that these patterns reflect not discrimination but fundamental differences in the occupational preferences and valuations of men and women. Soviet studies have made it abundantly clear that, from early childhood through adolescence and on into adulthood, boys and girls diverge in their educational and occupational choices. Fewer adult women express an interest in a career as opposed to a job, and, in choosing a job, women attach more weight to convenience than to content. Yet these individual choices are made within a socially structured context of opportunities and costs.

Three features of the Soviet system deserve to be singled out for their role in shaping women's preferences and choices. First, despite the fact that Soviet women have entered many scientific and technical fields, sexual stereotyping of occupations has not been eliminated; in fact, it has been explicitly sustained by official attitudes and policies. Measures that restrict the hiring of women for jobs considered unsuitable, or "harmful to the female organism," that limit their employment in heavy or dangerous work, and that encourage their entry into suitably "female" occupations serve to channel and not merely to protect female labor. Although the rationale for particular classifications is now being questioned, the distinction in principle between "men's work" and "women's work"—based on biological and psychological stereotypes—remains unchallenged. Soviet labor economists routinely write of the need to create working conditions that correspond to the "anatomical-physiological peculiarities of the female organism and likewise to the moral-ethical temperament of women." They assume that "the psycho-physiological make-up of women permits them to carry out certain kinds of work more successfully than men, such as work demanding assiduity, attention, accuracy and precision" (Kotliar & Shlemin, 1974, p. 111; Manevich, 1971, p. 168). It is consistent with these assumptions, therefore, that each of the 1100 occupations for which training is offered at Soviet technical-vocational institutions is explicitly designated for males, for females, or for both sexes, and that only 714 of the total are accessible to women.

Second, female occupational choices are profoundly influenced by the continuing identification of authority with men.[1] As many Soviet sources testify, women who pursue demanding careers encounter subtle but widespread prejudices, which impede their professional mobility and limit their accession to positions of responsibility. According to a recent Soviet study, women are widely, though erroneously, believed to have less initiative and creativity than men, and to be less suited for managerial positions (Pavlova, 1971). Even among highly educated scientific workers, men *and* women have a strong preference for males in supervisory roles (Shubkin & Kochetov, 1968). After a comprehensive discussion of the recruitment and training of industrial executives in the pages of a leading intellectual journal, *Literaturnaia gazeta*, it took a letter from an irate female reader to point out that "for some reason it seems taken for granted that an executive is a man" (*Literaturnaia gazeta*, 1976, p. 10).

This problem has not gone unrecognized in political circles. Complaints that insufficient attention is paid to recruiting women for responsible positions occur with monotonous regularity in official pronouncements. At one meeting of a provincial Communist Party committee, the underrepresentation of women in positions of authority was explicitly attributed to the presence of "a certain psychological barrier": "On the one hand, a number of leaders fear to entrust women with responsible positions, and on the other, women themselves demonstrate timidity, doubting their strength and refusing under various pretexts, a transfer to leadership positions" ("Povyshat' politicheskuiu proizvod-stvennuiu," 1975, p. 44).

Dubious about the utility of further exhortation, and impatient with the slow pace of change, one labor specialist proposed a more radical solution: the adoption of sexual quotas, with the number of women in managerial positions to be proportional to the number of women working under their jurisdiction (Tolkunova, 1967, p. 103). Most recently, Gorbachev himself called for the promotion of more women to positions of authority, and named a veteran trade union official, Biryukova, to the Party Secretariat. But the overall proportion of women in key political positions has not changed significantly since his accession to power.

A third social determinant of the pattern of female employment is the official treatment of household and family responsibilities as primarily and properly the domain of women. Persistent cultural norms are reinforced by a body of legislation that adjusts the terms of female, but not male, employment to family needs. At the same time, shortages of consumer goods and everyday services make household responsibilities especially onerous. Thus the fundamental assumption of Soviet economic and family policy—that women, and women only, have dual roles—effectively assigns women a distinctive position in both the occupational and the family systems, and has important consequences for their behavior in both domains.

FEMALE WORKERS AND
THE FAMILY

Just as family roles affect the scope and pattern of female employment, so women's work affects many aspects of family life, including patterns of marriage and divorce, fertility, and the family division of labor. Marxist-Leninist ideology assumed from the start that women's participation in social production would have a beneficial effect on their status and authority within the family. Soviet scholars share the view of Western sociologists that education, occupational status, income, and social participation are resources that directly influence family authority; and they contend that, by reducing disparities in these areas between men and women, socialism has guaranteed the independence of women in marriage, enhanced their power within the family, and produced a more egalitarian pattern of family life.

Current patterns of marriage and divorce in the U.S.S.R. offer some support for this view. A combination of early marriage, a relatively universal marriage rate, a large male-female age difference at the time of marriage, and a low rate of divorce is characteristic of many traditional agricultural societies; the pattern indicates women's limited status and opportunities outside the family by comparison with the value attached to reproductive potential within it. This pattern still predominates in the largely agricultural and Moslem regions of Soviet Central Asia. By contrast, access to education, to employment, and to independent income, typical of the more developed, European regions of the U.S.S.R., tends to enhance a woman's freedom to enter or leave marriage by reducing the relative value of the resources gained through marriage. Thus the proportion of married women is considerably higher in Uzbekistan than in the Russian Republic. Over 90% of all females between the ages of 25 and 39 in Uzbekistan are married, compared to 83% of the same group in Russia (TsSU SSSR, 1972a, pp. 263-268). Second, the mean age of marriage is lower in the Central Asian republic; a large number of women marry at extremely early ages. In 1970, 47 of every 1000 16- and 17-year-old girls in Uzbekistan were married, compared with 20 of their Russian counterparts; for 18- and 19-year-olds, the corresponding figures were 343 and 159, respectively (TsSU SSSR, 1972a, pp. 263-268). Finally, the age disparity between spouses was considerably smaller in the Russian Republic. Of all marriages registered in 1973, 64% of the grooms and 73% of the brides were 24 and under in the R.S.F.S.R.; in Uzbekistan, this was true of 61% of the grooms and 81% of the brides (TsSU SSSR, 1975a, pp. 172-173).

The greater disparity in educational and occupational resources of males and females in Central Asia is associated with higher rates of marriage, with earlier marriage, and with a higher level of family stability as well. Divorce rates are only one-third as high in Central Asia as in the Russian Republic; 1.1 divorces were registered per thousand population in Uzbekistan in 1973, compared to 3.2 in the R.S.F.S.R. (Chuiko, 1975, p. 134; TsSU, 1972a, pp. 263-68; TsSU SSSR, 1975a, pp. 150-165). The higher divorce rates in the Russian Republic are also associated with a growing tendency for women to initiate divorce actions (IOI, 1984, p. 47).

Nevertheless, a considerable disparity in economic resources and prospects between males and females persists in even the most developed regions of the U.S.S.R., and may be increasing with the rising number of female-headed households (Chuiko, 1975, p. 145; Kharchev, 1964, p. 212). As one distinguished Soviet family sociologist concluded, "The material position and social prestige of the husband has not lost its significance at the present time. Its role has only weakened" (Chuiko, 1975, p. 142).

A second way in which female employment affects family structure is through its influence on childbearing. An inverse relationship between female employment and fertility was first established in the 1930s; the distinguished

TABLE 4.3

Distribution of Births in Relation to Occupational Position
of Mother, Moscow Region, 1965 (as percentage of
total number of births in each group)

Mother's Occupational Position	Proportion of Families with Given Number of Children						Average Births per Woman
	1	2	3	4	5	Total	
Unskilled and low-skilled workers	43.3	44.9	9.3	1.7	0.8	100	1.7
Skilled and highly skilled workers	60.8	35.3	3.0	–	0.9	100	1.4
Service sector	66.6	27.4	4.8	0.6	0.6	100	1.4
Technicians and comparable categories	78.2	20.7	1.1	–	–	100	1.2
Engineers and comparable categories	73.6	25.8	0.6	–	–	100	1.3

SOURCE: Sysenko (1974, pp. 37, 40).

economist S. G. Strumilin found that, in the Soviet Union, housewives bore twice as many children as working women (Strumilin, 1964, p. 140). More recent studies show that, although the gap has narrowed, nonworking women have 20%-25% more children than do their working counterparts; and the latter have 2.5 times as many abortions (Musatov, 1967, p. 321; Nemchenko, 1973, pp. 35-36; Shlindman & Zvidrin'sh, 1973, p. 74). This difference helps to account for the inverse correlation of urbanization with birthrates. By the early 1970s, the one-child family was the norm in the urban regions of the U.S.S.R., except among the Moslem population, where large families are still widespread.

Lower urban birthrates are partly the result of structural factors that reduce fertility potential: lower marriage rates, later marriage age, and a high divorce rate. They are also the result of decisions to restrict childbearing. Urban women both desire and expect fewer children than rural women, and women in large cities expect to bear fewer children than their counterparts in small cities; the figures reach an alarming low of 1.69 in Moscow and 1.55 in Leningrad (Belova, 1975, pp. 109, 129; Borisov, 1976, pp. 72-77; Sysenko, 1974, pp. 36-40).

Birthrates also vary with educational attainment, occupational status, and professional skill. White-collar mothers have far fewer children than workers, and workers have fewer than collective farmers. Among workers, family size is

TABLE 4.4

Ideal and Expected Number of Children in the Opinion of
Women by Educational Level and per Capita Family Income

Group According to per Capita Family Income		According to the views of women with the following educational levels:			
	Average	Higher and Incomplete Higher	General and Specialized Secondary	Incomplete Secondary	Primary and Lower
Average ideal number of children:					
I (lowest)	4.10	3.98	3.88	3.96	4.29
II	3.01	3.22	2.96	2.97	3.07
III	2.71	2.74	2.63	2.72	2.83
IV	2.58	2.56	2.53	2.63	2.68
V (highest)	2.57	2.51	2.54	2.64	2.77
average for all 5 groups	2.88	2.67	2.72	2.90	3.25
Average expected number of children:					
I	4.23	3.91	3.59	4.00	4.65
II	2.65	2.78	2.50	2.60	2.87
III	2.15	2.09	2.03	2.20	2.39
IV	1.92	1.84	1.84	2.01	2.17
V	1.87	1.71	1.85	2.03	2.15
average for all 5 groups	2.41	1.99	2.12	2.47	3.10

SOURCE: Belova (1975, p. 146).

inversely related to skill level. The highest proportion of third, fourth, and fifth children is found among unskilled workers and those with low qualifications; relatively few large families are found among workers with high qualifications or with engineering and technical skills.

These variations in birthrates reflect differences in reproductive norms: The more demanding and rewarding a woman's occupation, the less value she attaches to children and the greater the cost of having more than one. A recent survey of newlyweds found that fewer worker-brides desired either no children or one child than did their white-collar counterparts; and almost twice as many women workers as women engineers and technicians wished to have three or more children. In the absence of countervailing measures, therefore, further increases in the proportion of women in white-collar or highly skilled jobs, along with further urbanization, are likely to result in still further declines in the rate of population growth.

In seeking to reverse these trends, Soviet scholars and planners have noted with interest that most women have fewer children than they appear to desire. This gap has led some to conclude that specific obstacles—limited financial resources, poor housing, and crowded preschool facilities—are responsible for low urban birthrates, and that measures to alleviate these problems would have a positive effect on fertility. But Soviet investigations of the relationship between income and fertility have yielded contradictory results; subjective perceptions of family needs play a crucial mediating role. Moreover, the effects of education on reproductive motivations and behavior are difficult to entangle from those of income. Although it would appear that birthrates are inversely correlated with the female educational level, some evidence suggests that a slight upturn in both desired and actual family size may occur at very high levels of education and income.

Consequently, the efforts of the last ten years to strengthen the family and reverse the declining birthrate have had disappointing results, a leading Soviet family sociologist recently confessed. Today, the largest number of children are born to women with only primary education and only a third as many to those with higher education. According to the latest data, 3433 children are born to every 1000 women lacking even primary education and 2718 to those with primary education, compared to 1167 for those with secondary education and 1279 to those with higher education (Kharchev, 1986, p. 32).

The tendency for increased female education, employment, and level of professional qualification to be associated with lower rates of marriage, later marriage, high rates of divorce, and declining family size, and for stable family patterns and high birthrates to be found among the least "liberated" Soviet women, have provoked an understandable concern. Not only do these trends challenge the heretofore unquestioned assumption that socialist societies enjoy a steady increase in population; they also raise the prospect that the goals may be fundamentally incompatible with each other. As the prominent Soviet sociologist, the late A. G. Kharchev, noted ruefully:

> Although growing prosperity since the end of World War II has strengthened the family, the positive influence is not as direct as had been expected. Life shows that improved conditions and equal rights for both sexes do not automatically strengthen the institution of marriage (Kharchev, 1972, p. 58.).

A broad array of Soviet writings have argued that women's entry into the work force has resulted in greater female authority within the family, greater male participation in housework, and a more egalitarian pattern of family decision making. Yet this pattern is not fully corroborated by a voluminous body of Soviet time-budget investigations. Although men and women devote roughly equal time to paid employment and physiological needs, working women devote on average 28 hours per week to housework compared to about 12 hours per week for men; men enjoy 50% more leisure time than women.

Within the family, a sharply defined sexual division of labor persists. A first

TABLE 4.5
A Comparison of Time Budgets of Male and Female Workers

Time-Budget Categories	Percentage of Week Devoted to Given Activity		Ratio of Time Spent by Females in Given Category to that of Males
	Males	Females	
Working time			
low	28	27	
high	32	31	
average	30	29	.96
Physiological needs			
low	38	37	
high	42	40	
average	41	39	.95
Housework			
low	5	11	
high	10	22	
average	8	19	2.37
Leisure time			
low	16	9	
high	25	17	
average	21	13	.62

SOURCE: Gordon and Klopov (1972), Patrushev (1966), Petrosian (1965), Prudenskii (1961), Artemov et al. (1967), Geidane et al. (1976), Pishchulin (1976).
NOTE: The table was compiled by standardizing the data presented in the cited
studies into percentages of time in a seven-day week. In the Soviet usage, "working
time" includes both actual work and time connected with work, as in travel; "physiological needs" include eating, sleeping, and self-care; "housework" includes shopping, food preparation, care of the household and possessions, and direct physical
care of young children; "leisure time" includes hobbies, public activities, activities
with children, study, and various forms of amusement and rest.

category of activities, such as gardening and repairs, is predominantly male; a
second, including shopping and cleaning house, is predominantly female but
shared to some degree by males; a third group of activities, including cooking
and laundry, is performed almost exclusively by women. In short, nearly 75% of
domestic duties fall to women; the remainder are shared with husbands and
other family members (Iankova, 1970a, p. 43; Slesarev & Iankova, 1969, pp.
430-431).

Although Soviet studies do not systematically explore the impact of different
variables on time usage, several conclusions may be drawn (Lapidus, 1979, pp.
256-258). First, male-female differences in the allocation of time are apparent,

TABLE 4.6

Male-Female Differences in Time Use
by Occupational Group, Leningrad 1966

	Time Expenditure as Percentage of 24-Hour Day							
Occupational Category	*Working Time*		*Physiological Needs*		*Housework*		*Leisure*	
	M	F	M	F	M	F	M	F
Unskilled workers	35.8	35.7	35.9	34.0	10.3	20.2	18.0	10.1
Workers of average skill	37.3	36.6	33.9	34.6	9.1	17.5	19.7	11.3
Skilled manual workers	36.5	37.0	33.6	33.9	9.9	15.2	20.0	13.9
Skilled workers on machinery	37.4	35.7	35.2	34.9	7.8	15.2	19.6	14.2
Personnel in highly skilled mental work	40.3	37.5	34.9	33.8	8.6	15.2	16.2	12.5
Managerial personnel	42.5	39.2	34.4	33.2	7.1	14.7	16.0	12.9

SOURCE: Trufanov (1973, p. 106).

even among single students living in dormitories. Second, this basic male-female differential increases with marriage: The share of housework performed by husbands does not offset the additional time spent by wives. Third, there is a positive relationship between female employment outside the home and male help within. Fourth, the male-female differential is sharply increased with the birth of a first child. Finally, educational level seems to have an important effect on the allocation of time to domestic chores, but not necessarily on the participation of males in them. A study of time use among workers with higher or specialized secondary education found that, although the total amount of time devoted to housework was lower, the male-female differential was actually larger than that found in worker families of lower educational qualifications (Gruzdeva, 1975, p. 9). Even high female educational attainments fail to obliterate sharp sex-role differences; the five most prevalent daily activities of women with specialized education differ far more from those of comparable males than from the activities of women with only four grades of schooling.

The effects of socioeconomic or occupational status are even more difficult to tease out of the Soviet data. As with education, the evidence suggests that the male-female division of labor does not necessarily become more equal at higher levels of the social hierarchy. At every level of the occupational ladder, the total working time of employed women exceeds that of males. Contrary to the assertions of several Soviet scholars, the reduction in women's housework and an increase in leisure time is not so much a result of greater male help as it is of the availability of household appliances and services that higher income brings.

The time devoted to housework by males varies with the demands of their work roles and with their job and educational levels. Blue-collar males actually devote more time to housework than their white-collar counterparts. The latter—particularly those engaged in demanding careers—devote more time to work, study, and social participation, and less time to household chores, than any other category.

Unfortunately, no data are available that would enable us to analyze the effects of relative male and female income on the family division of labor. Several Western studies have suggested that family members allocate time according to their comparative advantage in the production of market and domestic goods and services, and that comparative advantage is in turn determined by a combination of relative wage rates and efficiency in home production. If this hypothesis is correct, we might expect to find that, in families where the income of the wife is substantially higher than that of the husband, he would participate comparatively more in domestic production than in families where the wife's income is lower. Were such a trend indeed emerging in the U.S.S.R., however, it would probably receive prominent mention in Soviet writings.

In light of these patterns, it is unrealistic to assume that further economic development will bring a dramatic decline in women's household responsibilities or a sharp increase in leisure time. The available Soviet data appear to support instead an American study that concluded that gains wrought by labor-saving technology in the past few decades have not been translated into substantial increases in women's spare time (Vanek, 1974). As a distinguished Soviet sociologist has argued, women do not simply shed their former duties as development occurs; they acquire new ones. Higher standards of housekeeping and child rearing have created new responsibilities, and the breakup of extended families means that tasks once shared between two generations of women now fall exclusively on one (Iankova, 1970a, 1970b).

Nor will future reductions in female working time automatically yield the increase in leisure many Soviet writers anticipate. The shift from a six-day to a five-day workweek in 1967 yielded a comparatively greater increase in male leisure than in female, as did a recent experiment with shortening the workday of women factory workers (Gordon & Rimashevskaia, 1972, pp. 24, 62-79; Porokhniuk & Shepeleva, 1975, p. 102-108). An experiment in Kostroma found that a one-hour reduction of women's working time yielded half an hour of free time, with the other half-hour devoted to household chores (Pimenova, 1974, p. 131). In both cases, men took advantage of the opportunity to reduce their share of household chores, but women devoted more of the additional time to child care and domestic responsibilities than to study, social participation, or leisure pursuits.

The combination of full-time employment and heavy domestic chores is responsible for the limited amount of time available to women workers for raising their professional qualifications, mastering more complex jobs, or assuming responsible administrative posts. Women's educational efforts virtually cease with the birth of a child, but family responsibilities have little effect on the ability of male workers to continue their studies. As two Soviet authors explicitly recognize, men combine employment with study by limiting the time they devote to family chores, at the expense of other members of the household, who, in effect, subsidize these educational pursuits.

> From everything that we know about the structure of urban life, we can assert that [free time] is obtained by increasing the housework of working and non-working women—mothers, wives, and other relatives. This is the "contribution" that they make to their children's and husbands' further education. And much evidence . . . shows that this is no "loan" repaid with interest, but a "free grant." Consequently, a cause that is on the whole progressive is "paid for" not just by society and not just by those of its members who obtain the fruits of a higher education. Combination of work and study has become so widespread in the U.S.S.R. partly because it has been supported by the other part of society—people who often do not participate in study at all and even suffer a certain loss on education's account. (Gordon & Klopov, 1972, pp. 200-201)

By freeing males from the performance of routine household and child-care chores, which would otherwise divert time and energy from educational, professional, and political pursuits, women workers in effect advance the occupational mobility of males at the cost of their own.

THE INTERDEPENDENCE OF WORK AND FAMILY ROLES

This profile of the female labor force has pointed to the ways in which women's work and family roles interact, and to the effects of this interaction in producing a sharp differentiation between the activities of male and female workers. For men and women alike, work and family roles are inversely related and tend to compete with each other for time and energy. In the case of women, however, it is family roles that are assigned primacy and that define the nature and rhythms of female employment. The consequences are frankly acknowledged by a Soviet analyst:

> Women do indeed choose easier jobs, with convenient hours, close to home and with pleasant co-workers and managers, but not because they lack initiative. They choose these jobs because their combination of social roles is difficult. (Pavlova, 1971)

Soviet women's family responsibilities intrude into the workplace—and are accommodated by it—to a degree unusual in contemporary industrial societies. Provisions for pregnancy leaves, for leave to care for sick children, for nursing infants during work hours, and for exemptions of pregnant women and mothers from heavy work, overtime, or travel are predicated on the view that child rearing and other "exclusively female" family responsibilities take a certain priority that work arrangements must accommodate. The illness of family members is responsible for high rates of female, not male, absenteeism. Women are explicitly encouraged to view work from the perspective of their roles as wives and mothers.

This limited insulation of female work roles from family roles results in characteristic patterns of female behavior. As two Soviet specialists observed, "Many female workers stated that when at work they cannot put the house and children out of their mind. The women value jobs requiring simple automatic responses that can be performed adequately despite these mental distractions" (Kharchev & Golod, 1971, pp. 63-64). Women workers are less demanding than their male counterparts, as is generally true of workers whose mobility is blocked and whose work satisfaction depends less on the content of their jobs than on working conditions. Under these circumstances, it is understandable that married women are seriously underrepresented in enterprise activities requiring additional commitments of time and energy, as well as in volunteer movements and in public affairs generally.

The opposite is the case for males. An extensive network of evening and correspondence courses attended overwhelmingly by males, the numerous assignments requiring travel away from home, and the proliferation of Party meetings and sociopolitical obligations in which males predominate are all predicated on the assumption that they constitute legitimate claims on male time and energy even at the expense of family responsibilities. The fact, as Kharchev put it, that "while men often think about production work at home, women frequently think about domestic concerns at work" (Kharchev, 1972, pp. 60-61) reflects a fundamental difference in the structure of male and female work and family roles. The boundaries between occupational and family systems are permeable—but in opposite directions for men and women.

Male and female roles, like work and family roles, are also interdependent and mutually reinforcing (Pleck, 1977, pp. 417-427). Women are integrated into the labor force in segregated and subordinate roles. Horizontal occupational differentiation and vertical stratification by sex effectively shield male roles from competition by women and limit the situations in which females exercise authority over males. Norms that classify occupations as especially suitable for women, or that give women authority primarily when it is exercised over other women, create a dual labor market that helps insulate male jobs from the effects of rising female employment, and that preserves male predominance in positions of responsibility and leadership. This pattern is as characteristic of the political arena as it is of the economy.

A parallel pattern is found within the family itself. Norms that sustain a sexual division of labor by defining housework and child care as preeminently "women's work" also serve to insulate the male role from pressures for increased participation in domestic work as women take on paid employment. The effect is to create a domestic counterpart to the dual labor market; one part of the labor supply does not take on certain types of work even when there is a surplus of them, while the other part is overburdened and leaves needed work undone. At best, men help with housework and child care; no fundamental redefinition of male roles is involved.

The sexual division of labor both on the job and at home, combined with the differential permeability of the work-family boundary for males and females, have cushioned the strains created by changing female roles. The effects have not been altogether benign. As the massive participation of women in full-time paid employment erodes the traditional rationale for a sexual division of labor within the family, it has increased the level of conflict between men and women over the division of domestic tasks.

These domestic tensions have received eloquent expression in contemporary Soviet fiction. Natalia Baranskaia's evocation of a "week like any other" in the harried life of a young Soviet scientific worker captures the findings of innumerable time-budget studies in one dramatic image of the family evening: The husband pores over his newspapers and professional journals, while the wife, her scientific research forgotten, is swallowed up by laundry, mending, child care, and the family supper (Baranskaia, 1969).

Domestic conflict has also received growing attention from Soviet journalists and social scientists (Shlapentokh, 1984, pp. 202-211). "Many families now have been turned into real fields of battle," observed one Soviet journalist (Riurikov, 1983, p. 3). "The family has become fragile and vulnerable," writes a demographer (Zvindrin'sh, 1983, p. 68). Yet a third comments:

> The present transitional period implies that there is no consensus among couples on the nature of family life, about the roles of husband and wife, about their respective duties in housework, about the upbringing of children, and on many other questions. The modern, urban, educated woman is not inclined to be resigned to her low position in the family, since the Soviet woman legally is equal to the man in production and social life. (Perevedentsev, 1982, p. 30)

These rising resentments, Soviet analysts argue, are contributing to alcoholism and high divorce rates and are a potential source of disenchantment with the institution of the family itself.

A second source of strain is the extreme tension between female work and family roles as currently defined. Working women everywhere devote less time to domestic labor than do housewives, and, in this respect, Soviet women are no exception. But the pressure in the Soviet Union to reduce family commitments has implications for larger political priorities; it entails the deliberate limitation of family size. Taking a benign view of this trend, one Soviet writer noted:

> The current decline in the birth rate has certain negative consequences—e.g., it will contribute to the manpower shortage—but it also has some positive aspects. It can be viewed, in part, as a spontaneous response by women to their excessive work load and lack of equality with men—a response that consists of eliminating the single factor over which they have the greatest control. The falling birthrate is an important—in fact indispensable—lever that women can use in their effort to achieve full equality with men. (Riurikov, 1977, p. 119)

From the point of view of many in the Soviet leadership, however, low birthrates in regions with high female labor force participation, and the predominance of one-child families in urban areas, are the most dramatic and the most extreme, undesirable, and threatening manifestations of female resistance to the combined pressures of work and family. By impinging on a wide range of economic, political, and military concerns, they have compelled fundamental reconsideration of the whole spectrum of policies involving female work and family roles.

POLICY DILEMMAS AND OPTIONS

The irreplaceable contribution of women to both production and reproduction presents the Soviet leadership with a classic policy dilemma. Soviet development has induced two mutually contradictory processes. By opening a new range of educational and professional options for women, it has encouraged them to acquire new skills, values, orientations, and aspirations that compete with their traditional domestic roles. At the same time, the high value attached to the family, the critical social roles assigned to it, and the large investments of time and energy needed to sustain it seriously constrain women's occupational commitments and achievements.

The resulting "contradictions," in the language of Soviet analysts, between the occupational and family roles of working women have an extremely high economic, demographic, and social cost. They adversely affect women's health and welfare, as well as their opportunities for professional and personal development; they "engender tensions and conflicts in internal family relations, lead to a weakening of control over the conduct of children and a deterioration of their upbringing, and, finally, [they are] one of the basic causes of the declining birthrate" (Kharchev, 1970, p. 19; Shishkan, 1976, p. 38).

These tensions may be increased rather than diminished by current economic, demographic, and technological trends. Undeniably, the growing availability of consumer goods and services will lighten some of the heaviest burdens; rising wages have made it increasingly possible for worker families to share in the "consumption revolution" of the past two decades. Other structural changes may prove less favorable to women's professional mobility. To the extent that extraordinary circumstances in the past—a severe deficit of males coinciding with a fundamental transformation of the economic and social structure—created unprecedented opportunities and pressures for female occupational mobility, the return to demographic normality for younger age cohorts, in the context of a relative saturation of elite positions, is likely to slow both the impetus and the real opportunities for the advancement of women in the educational and occupational structure and to increase the competition for valued positions.

The scientific-technological revolution and the shift from manufacturing to services may also adversely affect the structure of female employment. Without major changes in the system of vocational training and placement, women are likely to face growing problems of entry into highly skilled technical employment and to be absorbed in growing numbers into routine white-collar and service occupations, particularly if part-time employment opportunities are expanded. The major economic reforms now being introduced would further accelerate this process. Such jobs may be more compatible with family responsibilities but less commensurate with women's training, ability, and aspirations.

Thus it is with a heightened sense of urgency that the Soviet leadership has begun to confront the complex issues surrounding female labor and its social requisites and consequences. Enlisting the aid of social scientists as well as several newly created legislative and administrative bodies, it has launched a serious and sustained quest for a strategy that will encourage a more effective use of scarce labor resources without further compromising family stability, and that will also reverse the declining birthrate in the developed regions of the U.S.S.R.

A first group of proposed measures is aimed at redistributing female labor resources by removing women from employment in unsafe and unhealthy conditions; transferring them from low-skilled, nonmechanized, and heavy labor to more skilled and suitable jobs, and achieving a demographically more balanced regional labor market by providing a better mix of "men's" and "women's" work. A number of critics have also urged that upgrading the skills of women workers be given higher priority and increased incentives, and that, following the example of the G.D.R., vocational programs be adapted to the schedules and responsibilities of working mothers (Kostakov, 1976, pp. 101-160; Kotliar & Shlemin, 1974, pp. 110-119; Sergeeva, 1976, pp. 37-46).

A second group of proposals would improve the working conditions of the female labor force. Despite the elaborate provisions of protective labor legislation, complaints abound that existing regulations are inadequate and their requirements widely violated. The employment of women in hazardous and unhealthy conditions that are "harmful to the female organism" remains a problem of considerable magnitude. Moreover, although a number of critics have called for a thorough revision of the list of occupations forbidden to women, they have also noted that hazardous conditions are widespread even in industries—such as textiles—that are considered especially suited to women. Some experts have urged that existing protective legislation be tightened and that an effort be made to reduce night work, overtime, and inconvenient work shifts for women.

Some analysts have even advocated reducing the "intensity" of female labor by introducing differentiated work norms. Insisting that women's contributions to the domestic economy and to childbearing constitute socially useful labor not paid for by society, these writers have urged that women be assigned reduced work norms, and even a shortened working day, without loss of pay (Iankova, 1975, pp. 44-46; Iuk, 1975, p. 122; Sakharova, 1973). By refusing to exclude women's domestic responsibilities from the definition of "work," and by arguing that working mothers have a right to be compensated for the double shift they perform, the advocates of such measures are not only insisting that socially useful labor be properly rewarded, they are also putting the blame for current shortcomings on the shoulders of policymakers. Needless to say, such proposals have not been widely endorsed.

A third group of recommendations would increase the supply of consumer and everyday services to reduce the strain of women's dual roles. The economic and social costs of inadequate services and child-care facilities have received particular attention in recent years. A growing number of studies argue that investments in refrigerators, public laundries, or rapid transit would generate savings of time that would more than compensate for initial investments. Calls for the more rapid expansion of preschool facilities are coupled with reminders that the lack of such facilities contributes to underemployment of women, high rates of turnover, and lowered productivity. Moreover, the slow pace of progress in "revolutionizing everyday life" has encouraged a number of writers to press for greater reliance on private and cooperative arrangements. They call for parent nurseries in housing developments, economic unions of families to share the burdens of shopping and repairs, and even the creation of bureaus to provide nannies and governesses for child care.

Taken together, these three groups of recommendations amount to an agenda for slow but incremental reform to reduce the conflict between female work and family roles, but not to eradicate the distinction between "men's" and "women's" work. They rest on the assumption that a combination of technological progress and socioeconomic reform sponsored by a benevolent Party leadership will serve as a sufficient solvent of sexual inequality and will obviate the need for more far-reaching changes in the structure of family or work. It is conceivable that the present balance of the two can be maintained indefinitely, but many Soviet experts believe that the problem will, in fact, require a more controversial set of choices.

One option with vocal advocates is an all-out effort to elevate the social status and material rewards associated with reproduction, even if this results in a decline in female labor-force participation. Alarmed by the current birthrate, a number of prominent Soviet scholars have urged that a comprehensive population policy receive highest priority "regardless of any considerations that may be advanced from an economic, ecological, sociological, or any other point of view" (Urlanis, 1974, p. 283). They call for measures to enhance fertility potential, to alter social values in favor of larger families, to increase the economic incentives for larger families, and to modify the pension system to reward child rearing as well as production.

The central and most controversial aspect of this pronatalist position is its desire to transform maternity into professional, paid, social labor. Financial subsidies, tailored not to the direct costs of children but to the opportunity cost of female labor, would be offered to induce new mothers to withdraw from the labor force for periods of up to three years; a sliding scale of benefits tied to wage levels would ensure a more equal distribution of births among different social strata. The costs of such a program, its advocates argue, would be offset by its long-term contribution to the labor supply and by the more immediate savings generated by a cutback in public nurseries. Viewing high maternal employment as a temporarily necessary evil, they argue that, at the present stage of its economic development, Soviet society can afford, and would greatly benefit from, a shift toward family upbringing of young children.

Measures such as these could widen the options of many women, but they have potentially far-reaching economic and social costs. To have the desired demographic effect, they would entail relatively long interruptions in female labor force participation, which could result in a deterioration or obsolescence of skills and could pose substantial problems of retraining and reentry. Moreover, the lower return on investments in women's education might adversely affect their educational opportunities and increase the reluctance of employers to hire or train them for skilled and responsible positions. By assigning primacy to female family and reproductive functions while reducing the scope and centrality of female employment, by increasing the permeability of female work roles to family responsibilities, and by forestalling a more equal division of family responsibilities, this entire approach, in the view of its critics, represents an unacceptable step backward. It would re-create a division of labor based on sex.

A radically different set of policy options derives from the premise that the more effective use of female labor, not stimulation of fertility, is the overriding priority. Arguing that work is of critical importance to women's social status and personal development as well as to the economy, and that economic progress and national power depend on the *quality* of the labor force rather than on its size, proponents urge the further expansion of women's economic role in terms of greater equality with men—along with a reduction in the household burdens that inhibit it.

"Women have no need of 'light work,' but of qualified work, commensurate with their professional preparation and training, their education, and their talents," insisted one commentator (Berezovskaia, 1975, p. 12). Not "protection" but assignment to positions of responsibility should receive priority. Recognizing that women's "double burden" reduces their ability to raise their skill levels, to master more complex jobs, and to undertake more responsible duties, this approach calls for a more equal sharing of family responsibilities. As one prominent sociologist put it:

> The entry of women into the sphere of social production presupposes the return of men to the family. If women had remained within the family, in order to produce the same quantity of material wealth it would have been necessary for men to work almost twice as much. From this point of view it is possible to say that women liberated men from half of their heavy work. Why, then, should some men not wish, in their turn, to take upon themselves half of "light" women's work? (Iurkevich, 1970, p. 192)

But even the most outspoken of Soviet feminists emphasize the biological and psychological differences between men and women, and attach high value to women's family and maternal roles. Unlike some of their Western counterparts, they do not embrace the notion of transcending gender in the allocation of social roles.

Emphasizing that new attitudes are a precondition for new patterns of behavior, and refusing to treat them as a purely private and personal matter, a number of writers call for a more systematic intervention by state, Party, and public organizations to inculcate egalitarian values. The postrevolutionary Women's Department *(Zhenotdel)* is recalled and held up as a model by one labor economist, who explicitly regrets its premature abolition:

> The resolution of this problem can occur only as a result of a complex of political, economic, and organizational measures. . . . Unfortunately, the whole system of institutions created in the process of socialist construction for the resolution of the complex problem of women's work and everyday life . . . was liquidated before it had completely fulfilled its special tasks. (Sonin, 1973, pp. 378-379)

The more immediate problems faced by working mothers with young children would be alleviated by an expansion of part-time work rather than by extended maternity leaves (Martirosian, 1976, pp. 54-61; Novitskii & Babkina, 1973, pp. 133-140; Shishkan, 1971, pp. 42-47). By making it possible for more women to enter the labor force, and by enabling mothers to maintain some continuity of employment without sacrificing the time available for child rearing and family chores, part-time employment would meet the needs of many women workers without incurring the extremely high costs of the more radical pronatalist program.

Clearly, the introduction of part-time work on a large scale would raise a host of unresolved problems (Moses, 1983). It is far more feasible in routine white-collar and service occupations than in highly skilled technical positions or supervisory jobs. In industry, it would require the creation of special sectors and assembly lines that would segregate part-time workers from the full-time labor force. In all likelihood, it would increase the concentration of women in low-skilled and poorly remunerated jobs. In addition, if recent experiments with shortened workdays are any indication, it is also likely to forestall a more equal division of household responsibilities. Recent small-scale experiments with flextime are, therefore, especially promising precisely because of its potential for avoiding an intensification of the sexual division of labor.

NEW POLICY INITIATIVES

Even if the Soviet leadership has been relatively slow in coming to an awareness of the economic and demographic issues reviewed here, these issues have gradually come to occupy an important place on the political agenda. Under Leonid Brezhnev, a number of specific measures "to improve the conditions of labor and everyday life of working women" were included in the

10th Five-Year Plan outlined at the 25th Party Congress in March 1976, as well as in the new Soviet Constitution of 1977. The State Committee on Labor and Wages was reorganized with a broader mandate and renamed the State Committee on Labor and Social Questions; and, in October 1976, new standing commissions were created in both chambers of the Supreme Soviet and in the soviets of all republics to address the special problems of women workers and mothers. In an address to the Trade Union Congress, Brezhnev (1977) explicitly recognized the problem and committed himself to further initiatives: "We men ... have thus far done far from all we could to ease the dual burden that [women] bear both at home and in production."

In effect, the measures introduced under Brezhnev sought to strike a balance between a labor-extensive strategy and a labor-intensive one. On the one hand, they encouraged high female participation rates by raising minimum wages, expanding the child-care network, modifying the pension system, and exploring the possibilities for expansion of part-time work. At the same time, concern over declining birthrates was evident in the family allowance program introduced in 1974, which extended maternity leave benefits to *kolkhoz* (collective farm) women, liberalized sick leave for parents of young children, and expanded partially paid maternity leave to a full year. In this as in other areas, however, the Brezhnev leadership failed to act with the vigor and decisiveness necessary to address the problem adequately.

The accession of Mikhail Gorbachev to the Soviet leadership, and his efforts to promote a far-reaching reform of the Soviet system, may have a more significant impact on women's roles. Although the overall thrust of his efforts remains unclear, he has already given women's issues high visibility. Indeed, his initial campaign against alcoholism (a major "women's issue" in the Soviet context), the prominent role and unprecedented visibility of his wife, Raisa, and his energetic advocacy of the promotion of more women in political life have apparently won considerable support among women. The larger implications of several of his key initiatives for women's roles, however, remain contradictory.

In the economic realm, Gorbachev's effort to promote more rapid economic growth and increased technological innovation by stimulating greater competition within the workplace, the release of surplus workers, and increased wage differentiation, could conceivably operate to the disadvantage of women workers. Coupled with his call for the expansion of the service sector, including individual and cooperative enterprises, it may well foreshadow a long-term shift in female labor force participation from industrial to service employment, as well as expansion of part-time work (Kostakov, 1986).

Moreover, although Gorbachev's initiatives may promote more active participation of women in political life, they may also reinforce the tendency to focus this participation on "women's issues." Gorbachev's speech to the 27th Party Congress in February 1986 broke new ground in calling for the creation of a national women's organization that would link a network of local women's councils to the Soviet Women's Committee and "exert an important influence on the resolution of a broad range of social questions in the life of our society"

(Gorbachev, 1986, p. 1). In January 1987, a National Conference of Women was convened, and the Party's Central Committee laid before it an array of tasks ranging from the protection of maternity to the defense of peace ("All-Union Conference of Women," 1987, pp. 1, 3). The effort gave high visibility and media attention to the issue of women's roles, but the focus of this new organization's activities remains to be defined. Similarly, Gorbachev's appointment of Alexandra Biryukova to the party's powerful Secretariat was the first such high-level appointment in 25 years, but her portfolio is social affairs.

Finally, a new attention to social and family policy, accompanied by a desire to strengthen the position of the family, is also unclear in its thrust and consequences. Acknowledging the economic and social costs of so many broken homes, Gorbachev has promised to provide more part-time jobs for women who want to spend more time with their families, to increase child allowances for poorer families, to expand preschool care for children whose mothers work, and to extend partly paid maternity leave to 18 months. A major reform of the pension system is also in preparation. These efforts could enhance the welfare of poorer families, and particularly of female-headed households which account for a high proportion of those in poverty. But Gorbachev's broader economic and social policies could have far-reaching consequences for women's roles in Soviet economic life, and these changes will not be necessarily benign.

At the present stage of Soviet economic and social development, the interdependence of work and family roles poses a qualitatively new range of problems for Soviet policymakers. The Soviet experience clearly demonstrates the degree to which women's movement into industrial employment can be accelerated and channeled through the deliberate use of public policy. The most critical problems of the years ahead, however, for the U.S.S.R. as well as for the West, will no longer center on removing the formal obstacles to women's entry into a world of work designed for men, but on adapting both occupational and family patterns, as well as traditional male and female roles, to a new array of social and human needs.

NOTE

1. A parallel identification of genuine creativity with men is widespread in scientific work and scholarship more generally. As two prominent male scholars argued recently, "The increase in the number of women with scholarly degrees accounts for the decrease in the number of those who really develop science. . . . The 'rebellious' spirit, the predisposition to search for new, non-traditional methods in science are more typical among men than women. This has been established by psychologists and experts in the science of science. Therefore, the broad feminization of science contributes to the slackening in the development of new branches of science, even if women make their contribution in the accumulation of facts" (Sokolov & Reimers, 1983, p. 77).

REFERENCES

All-Union Conference of Women. (1987, February 1). *Pravda*.

Andriushkiavichene, I. (1970). Zhenskii trud i problema svobodnogo vremeni. In N. Solov'ev, Iv. Lazauskas, & Z. A. Iankova (Eds.), *Problemy byta, braka i sem'i* (pp. 78-86). Vil'nius: Mintis.

Antosenkov, E. G., & Kupriianova, Z. V. (1977). *Tendentsii v tekuchesti rabochikh kadrov.* Novosibirsk: Nauka.

Artemov, V. A., Bolgov, V. I., & Vol'skaia, O. V. et al. (1967). *Statistika biudzhetov vremeni trudiashchikhsia.* Moscow: Statistika.

Baranskaia, N. (1969). Nedelia kak nedelia. *Novyi mir, 11*, 22-55.

Belova, V. A. (1975). *Chislo detei v sem'e.* Moscow: Statistika.

Berezovskaia, S. (1975, June 25). Prestizh—zabota nasha obshchaia. *Literaturnaia gazeta, 12.*

Berliner, J. S. (1987). *Soviet female labor force participation: A regional cross-section analysis* (Monograph 177). Cambridge: Harvard Russian Research Center.

Bliakhman, L. S., Zdravomyslov, A. G., & Shkaratan, O. I. (1965). *Dvizhenie rabochei sily na promyshlennykh predpriiatiiakh.* Moscow: Ekonomika.

Borisov, V. A. (1976). *Perspektivy rozhdaemosti.* Moscow: Statistika.

Brezhnev, L. I. (1977, March 22). Rech' tovarishcha Brezhneva, L. I. *Pravda,* pp. 1-3.

Buckley, M. (Ed.). (1986). *Soviet social scientists talking: An official debate about women.* London: Macmillan.

Chuiko, L. V. (1975). *Braki i razvody.* Moscow: Statistika.

Dirzhinskaite, R. (1975). Sovetskaia zhenshchina—aktivnyi stroitel' kommunizma. *Partiinaia zhizn', 20,* 23-28.

Dogle, N. V. (1977). *Usloviia zhizni i zdorov'e tekstil'shchits.* Moscow: Meditsina.

Geiger, K. (1968). *The family in Soviet Russia.* Cambridge, MA: Harvard University Press.

Geidane, I. M., Gosha, Z. Z., Zvindrin'sh, I. V. et al. (1976). *Balans vremeni naseleniia Latviiskoi SSR.* Riga: Zinatne.

Gorbachev, M. S. (1986, February 26). Politicheskii doklad Tsentral'nogo Komiteta KPSS XXVII s'ezdu Kommunisticheskoi partii Sovetskogo Soiuza. *Pravda.*

Gordon, L. A., & Klopov, E. V. (1972). *Chelovek posle raboty.* Moscow: Nauka.

Gordon, L. A., & Rimashevskaia, N. M. (1972). *Piatidnevnaia rabochaia nedelia i svobodnoe vremia trudiashchikhsia.* Moscow: Mysl'.

Gruzdeva, E. B. (1975). Osobennosti obraza zhizni "intelligentnykh rabochikh." *Rabochii klass i sovremennyi mir, 2,* 91-99.

Gruzdeva, E. B., & Chertikhina, E. S. (1975). Zhenshchiny v obshchestvennom proizvodstve razvitogo sotsializma. *Rabochii klass i sovremennyi mir, 6,* 133-147.

Gruzdeva, E. B., & Chertikhina, E. S. (1983). *Trud i byt sovetskikh zhenshchin.* Moscow: Politizdat.

Guseinov, G., & Korchagin, V. (1971). Voprosy trudovykh resursov. *Voprosy ekonomiki, 2,* 45-51.

Iankova, Z. A. (1970a). O bytovykh roliakh rabotaiushchei zhenshchiny. In N. Solov'ev, I. Lazauskas, & Z. A. Iankova (Eds.), *Problemy byta, braka i sem'i* (pp. 42-49). Vil'nius: Mintis.

Iankova, Z. A. (1970b). O semeino-bytovykh roliakh rabotaiushchei zhenshchiny. *Sotsial'nye issledovaniia, 4,* 76-87.

Iankova, Z. A. (1975). Razvitie lichnosti zhenshchiny v sovetskom obshchestve. *Sotsiologicheskie issledovaniia, 4,* 42-51.

Institut obshchestvennoe issledovanie. (1984). *Sotsial'nye posledstviia razvoda.* Moscow: Sovetskaia sotsiologicheskaia assotsiatsiia.

Iuk, Z. M. (1975). *Trud zhenshchiny i sem'ia.* Minsk: Belarus'.

Iurkevich, N. G. (1970). *Sovetskaia sem'ia; funktsii i usloviia stabil'nosti.* Minsk: Belorusskii gosudarstvennii universitet.

Kharchev, A. G. (1964). *Brak i sem'ia v SSSR.* Moscow: Mysl'.

Kharchev, A. G. (1970). Byt i sem'ia. In N. Solov'ev, I. Lazauskas, & Z. A. Iankova (Eds.), *Problemy byta, braka i sem'i* (pp. 9-22). Vil'nius: Mintis.

Kharchev, A. G. (1972). *Zhurnalist, 11.*

Kharchev, A. G. (Ed.). (1977). *Izmenenie polozheniia zhenschchiny i sem'ia.* Moscow: Nauka.

Kharchev, A. G. (1986). Issledovaniia sem'i: Na poroge novogo etapa. *Sotsiologicheskie issledovanie, 3,* 22-33.

Kharchev, A. G., & Golod, S. I. (1969). Proizvodstvennaia rabota zhenshchin i sem'ia. In G. V. Osipov & I. Shchepan'skii (Eds.), *Sotsial'nye problemy truda i proizvodstva* (pp. 416-438). Moscow: Mysl'.

Kharchev, A. G., & Golod, S. I. (1971). *Professional'naia rabota zhenshchin i sem'ia.* Leningrad: Nauka.

Kostakov, V. G. (1976). *Trudovye resursy piatiletki.* Moscow: Politizdat.

Kostakov, V. G. (1986). Chelovek i progress. *Sovietskaia kultura,* February 1, p. 3.

Kotliar, A. E. (1973). Voprosy izucheniia struktury zaniatosti po poly v territorial'nom razreze. In A. Z. Maikov (Ed.), *Problemy ratsional'nogo ispol'zovaniia trudovykh resursov* (pp. 400-453). Moscow: Ekonomika.

Kotliar, A. E. et al. (1982). *Dvizhenie rabochii sily v krupnom gorode.* Moscow: Finansy i statistika.

Kotliar, A. E., & Shlemin, A. (1974). Problemy ratsional'noi zaniatosti zhenshchin. *Sotsialisticheskii trud, 7,* 110-119.

Kotliar, A. E., & Turchaninova, S. I. (1975). *Zaniatost' zhenshchin v proizvodstve.* Moscow: Statistika.

KPSS v tsifrakh. (1986). *Partiinaia zhizn', 14,* 19-32.

Lapidus, G. W. (1978). *Women in Soviet society.* Berkeley: University of California.

Lapidus, G. W. (Ed.). (1979). The female industrial labor force: Dilemmas, reassessments, options. In A. Kahan & B. Ruble, *Industrial labor in the USSR.* New York: Pergamon.

Lapidus, G. W. (Ed.). (1982). *Women, work and family in the USSR.* Armonk: M. E. Sharpe.

Literaturnaia gazeta. (1976, 15 September). [Letter to the editor].

Manevich, E. L. (Ed.). (1971). *Osnovnye problemy ratsional'nogo ispol'zovaniia trudovykh resursov v SSSR.* Moscow: Nauka.

Martirosian, E. R. (1976). Pravovoe regulirovanie nepolnogo rabochego vremeni. *Sovetskoe gosudarstvo i pravo, 10,* 54-61.

Mikhailiuk, V. B. (1970). *Ispol'zovanie zhenskogo truda v narodnom khoziaistve.* Moscow: Ekonomika.

Moses, J. (1983). *The politics of women and work in the Soviet Union and the United States.* Berkeley, CA: Institute of International Studies.

Musatov, I. M. (1967). *Sotsial'nye problemy trudovykh resursov v SSSR.* Moscow: Mysl'.

Nemchenko, V. (1973). Mezhotraslevoe dvizhenie trudovykh resursov. In D. E. Valentei et al. (Eds.), *Narodonaselenie.* Moscow: Statistika.

Novikova, E. E. (1985). *Zhenshchina v razvitom sotsialisticheskom obshchestve.* Moscow: Mysl'.

Novitskii, A., & Babkina, M. (1973). Nepolnoe rabochee vremia i zaniatost' naseleniia. *Voprosy ekonomiki, 7,* 133-140.

Ofer, G., & Vinokur, A. (1981). Earnings differentials by sex in the Soviet Union: A first look. In S. Rosefielde (Ed.), *Economic welfare and the economics of Soviet socialism* (pp. 127-162). Cambridge: Cambridge University Press.

Osipov, G. V., & Shchepan'skii, I. (Eds.). (1969). *Sotsial'nye problemy truda i proizvodstva* (pp. 416-438). Moscow: Mysl'.

Patrushev, V. D. (1966). *Vremia kak ekonomicheskaia kategoriia.* Moscow: Mysl'.

Pavlova, M. (1971, September 22). Kar'era Ireny. *Liternaturnaia gazeta, 13.*

Perevedentsev, V. I. (1982). *270 millionov.* Moscow: Finansy i Statistika.

Petrosian, G. S. (1965). *Vnerabochee vremia trudiashchikhsia v SSSR.* Moscow: Ekonomika.

Pimenova, A. L. (1966). Sem'ia i perspektivy razvitiia obshchestvennogo truda zhenshchin pri sotsializme. *Nauchnye doklady vysshei shkoly: Filosofskie nauki, 3,* 35-45.

Pimenova, V. N. (1974). *Svobodnoe vremia v sotsialisticheskom obshchestve.* Moscow: Nauka.

Pishchulin, N. P. (1976). *Proizvodstvennyi kollektiv, chelovek i svobodnoe vremia.* Moscow: Profizdat.

Pleck, J. H. (1977). The work-family role system. *Social Problems, 4,* 417-427.

Porokhniuk, E. V., & Shepeleva, M. S. (1975). O sovmeshchenii proizvodstvennykh i semeinykh funktsii zhenshchin-rabotnits. *Sotsiologicheskie issledovaniia, 4,* 102-108.

Povyshat' politicheskuiu proizvodstvennuiu aktivnost' zhenshchin: s plenuma ivanskogo obkoma KPSS. (1975). *Partiinaia shizn', 16,* 39-45.

Programme of the Communist Party of the Soviet Union. (1986). Moscow: Novosti.

Prudenskii, G. A. (Ed.). (1961). *Vnerabochee vremia trudiaschikhsia.* Novosibirsk: Sibirskoe otdelenie AN SSSR.

Reznik, S. D. (1982). *Trudovye resursy v stroitel'stve.* Moscow: Stroiizdat.

Riurikov, I. B. (1977). Ieti i obshchestvo. *Voprosy filosofii, 4,* 111-121.

Riurikov, I. B. (1983, July 9). Mestorozhdenia schast'ia. *Pravda,* p. 3.

Rzhanitsyna, L. (1979). Aktual'nye problemy zhenskogo truda v SSSR. *Sotsialisticheskii trud, 3,* 58-67.

Sakharova, N. A. (1973). *Optimal'nye vozmozhnosti ispol'zovaniia zhenskogo truda v sfere obshchestvennogo proizvodstva.* Kiev: Vishcha shkola.

Sergeeva, G. P. (1976). O professional'noi strukture rabotaiushchikh zhenshchin. *Planovoe khoziaistvo, 11,* 37-46.

Shishkan, N. M. (1971). Nepolnyi rabochii den' dlia zhenshchin v usloviiakh sotsializma. *Nauchnye doklady vysshei shkoly: Ekonomicheskie nauki, 8,* 42-47.

Shishkan, N. M. (1976). *Trud zhenschchin v usloviiakh razvitogo sotsializma.* Kishinev: Shtiinsta.

Shkaratan, O. I. (1967). Sotsial'naia struktura sovetskogo rabochego klassa. *Voprosy filosofii, 1,* 28-39.

Shlapentokh, V. (1984). *Love, marriage and friendship in the Soviet Union.* New York: Praeger.

Shlindman, S., & Zvidrin'sh, P. (1973). *Izuchenie rozhdaremosti.* Moscow: Statistika.

Shubkin, V. N., & Kochetov, G. M. (1968). Rukovoditel', kollega, podchinennyi. *Sotsial'nye issledovaniia, 2,* 143-155.

Slesarev, G. A., & Iankova, Z. A. (1969). Zhenshchina na promyshlennom predpriiatii i v sem'e. In G. V. Osipov & I. Shchepan'skii (Eds.), *Sotsial'nye problemy truda i proizvodstva* (pp. 439-456). Moscow: Mysl'.

Sokolov, B., & Reimers, I. (1983). Effektivnye formi upravleniia nauka. *EKO, 9,* 72-87.

Solov'ev, N., Lazauskas, I., & Iankova, Z. A. (Eds.). (1970). *Problemy byta, braka i sem'i.* Vil'nius: Mintis.

Sovetskaia sotsiologicheskaia assotsiatsiia (SSA). (1972). *Dinamika izmeneniia polozheniia zhenshchiny i sem'ia* (3 vols.). Moscow: Institut konkretnykh sotsial'nykh issledovanii AN SSSR.

Sonin, M. I. (1973). Aktual'nye sotsial'no-ekonomicheskie problemy zaniatosti zhenshchin. In A. Z. Maikov, (Ed.), *Problemy ratsional'nogo ispol'zovaniia trudovykh resurov* (pp. 352-379). Moscow: Ekonomika.

Strumilin, S. G. (1964). *Izbrannye proizvedeniia. Vol. 3: Problemy ekonomiki: truda.* Moscow: Nauka.

Swafford, M. (1978). Sex differences in Soviet earnings. *American Sociological Review, 5*, 657-673.

Sysenko, V. (1974). Differentsiatsiia rozhdaemosti v krupnom gorode. In D. I. Valentei et al. (Eds.), *Demograficheskii analiz rozhdaemosti.* Moscow: Statistika.

Tatarinova, N. I. (1971). Zhenskii trud. In E. L. Manevich (Ed.), *Osnovnye problemy ratsional'nogo ispol'zovaniia trudovykh resursov v SSSR* (pp. 161-194). Moscow: Nauka.

Tolkunova, V. N. (1967). *Pravo zhenshchchin na trud i ego garantii.* Moscow: Iuridicheskaia Literatura.

Trud i byt zhenshchin. (1978). *EKO, 3.*

Trufanov, I. P. (1973). *Problemy byta gorodskogo naseleniia SSSR.* Leningrad: Leningradskii gosudarstvennyi universitet.

Tsentral'noe statisticheskoe upravlenie pri Sovete Ministrov SSSR (TsSU SSSR). (1972a). *Itogi vsesoiuznoi perepisi naseleniia 1970 goda* (Vol. 2). Moscow: Statistika.

Tsentral'noe statisticheskoe upravlenie pri Sovete Ministrov SSSR (TsSU SSSR). (1972b). *Narodnoe khoziaistvo SSSR: 1922-1972.* Moscow: Statistika.

Tsentral'noe statisticheskoe upravlenie pri Sovete Ministrov SSSR (TsSU SSSR). (1975a). *Naselenie SSSR 1973.* Moscow: Statistika.

Tsentral'noe statisticheskoe upravlenie pri Sovete Ministrov SSSR (TsSU SSSR). (1975b). *Zhenshchiny v SSSR.* Moscow: Statistika.

Tsentral'noe statisticheskoe upravlenie pri Sovete Ministrov SSSR (TsSU SSSR). (1976). *Narodnoe khoziaistvo SSSR v 1975 g.* Moscow: Statistika.

Tsentral'noe statisticheskoe upravlenie pri Sovete Ministrov SSSR (TsSU SSSR). (1977). *Narodnoe khoziaistvo SSSR 60 let.* Moscow: Statistika.

Tsentral'noe statisticheskoe upravlenie pri Sovete Ministrov SSSR (TsSU SSSR). (1979). *SSSR v tsifrakh v 1978 godu: kratkii statisticheskii sbornik.* Moscow: Statistika.

Tsentral'noe statisticheskoe upravlenie pri Sovete Ministrov SSSR (TsSU SSSR). (1980). *Narodnoe khoziaistvo SSSR v 1979 godu.* Moscow: Statistika.

Tsentral'noe statisticheskoe upravlenie pri Sovete Ministrov SSSR (TsSU SSSR). (1981). *SSSR v tsifrakh v 1980 godu: kratkii statisticheskii sbornik.* Moscow: Finansy i statistika.

Tsentral'noe statisticheskoe upravlenie pri Sovete Ministrov SSSR (TsSU SSSR). (1985a). *Narodnoe khoziaistvo SSSR v 1984 g.* Moscow: Finansy i statistika.

Tsentral'noe statisticheskoe upravlenie pri Sovete Ministrov SSSR (TsSU SSSR). (1985b). *Zhenshchiny i deti v SSSR.* Moscow: Finansy i statistika.

Tsentral'noe statisticheskoe upravlenie pri Sovete Ministrov SSSR (TsSU SSSR). (1986). *Narodnoe khoziaistvo SSSR v 1985g.* Moscow: Finansy i statistika.

Ubaidullaeva, R. (1987). *Selskaia zhizn.* March 24, p. 2.

Urlanis, B. (1974). *Problemy dinamiki naseleniia SSSR.* Moscow: Nauka.

Vanek, J. (1974). Time spent in housework. *Scientific American, 5*, 116-120.

Volkov, A. (1983). Rozhdaemost i "defitsit zhenikhov." In E. Vasileva (Ed.), *Rozhdae-most': izvestnoe i neizvestnoe* (pp. 13-17). Moscow: Finansy i statistika.

Zdravomyslov, A. G., Rozhin, V. P., & Iadov, V. A. (Eds.). (1967). *Chelovek i ego rabota*. Moscow: Mysl'.

Zhenshchiny v SSSR. (1980). *Vestnik statistiki, 1*, 69-79.

Zhenshchiny v SSSR. (1986). *Vestnik statistiki, 1*, 51-67.

Zvindrin'sh, P. P. (1983). Stabil'nost' brakov i rozhdaemost'. In E. Vasileva (Ed.), *Rozhdaemost': Izvestnoe i neizvestnoe* (pp. 61-69). Moscow: Finansy i statistika.

5

The Effect of Sex Composition of the Workplace on Friendship, Romance, and Sex at Work

ELINA HAAVIO-MANNILA
KAISA KAUPPINEN-TOROPAINEN
IRJA KANDOLIN

The fact that men and women work together in the formal work organization provides an environment for the emergence of informal cross-sex interactions, friendships and romance, and sexual harrasment. In Helsinki in 1984-1985, 234 interviews with 102 men and 132 women in male-dominated, female-dominated, and mixed occupational groups were conducted. The mutual activity of men and women such as talking together and helping each other was assumed to affect cross-sex friendship, workplace romances, and sexual harassment. Mutual activities of men and women proved to be sufficient for cross-sex friendship. Workplace romances, however, were mainly associated with individual factors. Sexual harassment occurred as a result of an eroticized atmosphere at work.

INFORMAL INTERACTION AND SENTIMENTS
OF LIKING BETWEEN THE SEXES
IN THE WORK SETTING

Organizational research maintains a distinction between *instrumental ties*, or those arising in the course of carrying out appointed work roles, and *informal social relations* that enhance and impede the attainment of formal organizational goals (Lincoln & Miller, 1979). Thus organizations provide a potential environment for romantic relationships, even though this is not prescribed by bureaucratic rules. An organization provides routine interaction over time and allows people to discover attractive aspects of others (Quinn, 1977).

Informal interaction between men and women at work includes social chatting, reciprocal help, and exchange of confidences (Anderson, 1984). Informal interaction may even develop into a workplace romance. According to Homans (1951), in work organizations, formal work activity is accompanied by informal interaction and feelings of liking. This type of interaction is usually reciprocal. There are also asymmetrical or nonreciprocal interactions between men and women, for example, sexual harassment, which in public discussions and research literature has been looked upon in four ways: as a consequence of sexism in society; as reflecting unequal, exploitative power relationships at work; as a personal matter that occasionally gets out of hand; or as aberrant and nonprofessional behavior (Gutek, 1985).

Informal social interactions, friendships, and romances between men and women are sometimes viewed as disturbances in the organization (Collins, 1983) or the family. The threat to the family was expressed clearly in the responses of two-thirds of the Finnish male manual workers, interviewed in 1967, who agreed with the statement: "For peace in the family, it is important that men's and women's jobs are kept separate" (Haavio-Mannila & Stolte-Heiskanen, 1969, p. 56). Thus marital status is a factor affecting friendship and attraction between men and women at work, though a married person may also be perceived as a less threatening potential friend than a single person.

Most studies dealing with workplace romances make no distinction between romantic feelings of love and sexual relationships. Indeed, there are almost incestlike taboos against sexual relationships between coworkers in many workplaces (Zetterberg, 1966). The most universal restriction of friendship has been to limit it to persons of the same sex. There are relatively few references in anthropology to socially approved close friendships between men and women that have no significant courtship of sexual implication (Bell, 1984).

The fact that informal interaction is restricted within one-sex groups can be explained partially by homosocial tendencies. Lipman-Blumen (1976) defined *homosociality* as seeking enjoyment and/or preference for the company of the same sex. At work, men's homosociality means that women do not receive the valuable information, resources, or support that often come with inclusion in men's networks. Cross-sex interaction gives more status to women than to men, as the Swedish sociologist Gerd Lindgren (1983) has pointed out. Accordingly, women are more eager to seek the company of men than vice versa. Women's preferences are heterosocial.

According to an early Finnish study (Haavio-Mannila, 1968), men showed more homosocial tendencies than women. Men preferred male company, but women preferred the company of both men and women at work, when such company concerned discussion about politics and professional matters. The difference between the sexes has diminished since then, but even in 1981, there were more homosocial preferences among men than among women (Haavio-Mannila et al., 1984).

In the Nordic countries, friendship networks are homogeneous in their gender composition, though less so in Denmark than in Finland, Norway, and Sweden (Jaakkola & Karisto, 1976). Only young people tend to have more heterogeneous friendship networks. Even though married couples often meet other married couples, and those who work come into contact with people of the opposite sex while they are on the job, social norms do not favor the establishment or maintenance of close friendships with people of the opposite sex. In the United States, friendship between married women and men is mostly found among the college-educated middle class. Many of these friendships start at work, where white-collar employees and professionals are more likely than their working-class counterparts to have colleagues of the opposite sex (Rubin, 1985).

FACTORS INFLUENCING INTERACTIONS, FRIENDSHIPS, AND ROMANCES BETWEEN MEN AND WOMEN: DEFINITIONS

Our aim is to examine different types of cross-sex interactions, including friendships, romances, and sexual harassment. The idea is to locate potential factors that contribute to the various types of informal cross-sex interaction.

Sex Composition of the Workplace

The sex composition of the workplace determines the extent and type of informal interaction and attraction between women and men at work. Gutek (1985) examined sociosexual interaction in work settings in terms of *sex-role spillover*, which means the carryover into the workplace of gender-based expectations for behavior. Sex-role spillover has different consequences for women in female-dominated, in male-dominated, or in integrated workplaces. When the sex ratios were unequal, a wide range of social-sexual behavior (e.g., sexual touching, sexual harassment) occurred. Sex-integrated work showed less sex-role spillover and fewer problems with sociosexual interaction at work.

Gruber and Bjorn (1982) expected that a low representation of women in a work area would lead to harassment, but that was not the case among blue-collar auto workers. Women whose proportional representation was less than the plant average were not harassed to the same extent as women in more numerically proportionate areas. According to their analysis, a very small proportion of women were not perceived as a threat; women became threatening only when more of them entered a work area.

In this article, *sex-segregation of work* was determined by two criteria: (a) daily contacts at work with people of the same sex: physical sex-segregation; and (b) sharing the same work tasks with people of the same sex: functional sex-segregation (Kauppinen-Toropainen et al., 1984, 1988). The subjects were divided into three groups according to the sex-segregation of work:

(1) Work was classified as segregated if it was done mostly or only by members of one's own sex, and daily contacts were only or mostly with one's own sex.

(2) Work was classified as complementary if men and women performed different sorts of work but had daily contacts with each other.

(3) Work and the worker were classified as token if a person performed roughly the same sort of work as members of the opposite sex, but very few of the workers were of one's own sex (see also Kanter, 1977).

Quality of Work

An important aspect of the quality of work is *autonomy*. In this article, *autonomy of work* was measured on a scale that included such indicators as the work is not repetitive, one uses knowledge and skills derived from earlier education, one makes decisions about one's own work, one contributes to decisions, and one has a challenging job. Autonomy also includes freedom to move in the work environment and to make contacts with coworkers. Accordingly, it would seem easier for people with more autonomous jobs to cross the traditional gender barrier in informal work contacts. Haavio-Mannila (1982) found that, among women, workplace romances were connected with a high-status and autonomous job. In a study of 281 men and 296 women working in urban areas in Finland, about 40% of women with autonomous, challenging, and well-paying jobs had had workplace romances, compared with only about 25% of women with less autonomous and lower-status jobs. Among men, the tendency was in the opposite direction, though the difference between autonomous and less autonomous jobs was not significant.

Disharmonious Atmosphere

A connection has also been found between the social atmosphere of the workplace and workplace romances. Among urban, employed Finns, workplace romances were found most often in workplaces where the social atmosphere was disharmonious. Of those with a disharmonious atmosphere, 42% had had workplace romances, compared with 20% with a harmonious atmosphere: Workplace romances were more likely to occur when the relations between workmates were distant and formal (37%) than when they were close and less formal (25%) (Haavio-Mannila, 1982). According to Haavio-Mannila, romances between men and women may function as "safety valves," where a close dyadic relationship becomes a compensatory mechanism by means of which one can cope with the strains and conflicts at work. In this article, we studied the *social atmosphere* by analyzing the occurrence of intrigues, cliques, envy, and social isolation with regard to coworkers, and discrimination and favoritism shown by supervisors.

Erotic Atmosphere

Eroticizing of work-related cross-sex interactions and friendship creates an erotically loaded atmosphere in the workplace. According to Liljeström (1981),

Attitude toward Flirting	Eroticized Atmosphere at Work	
	Low	High
Negative	1. Erotically neutral atmosphere	3. Overerotic atmosphere
Positive	2. Undererotic atmosphere	4. Erotically excited atmosphere

Figure 5.1   Erotic Atmosphere at Work

noticing sexual stimulation everywhere is part of *erotic war.* Its opposite is *erotic peace,* which means that sexual stimulation is restrained to certain zones and relations at work. In the case of erotic war, norms are unclear and ambivalent, whereas in peace, they are straightforward and clear. In erotic war, romance becomes a sport and the sporting aspect attains intrinsic value as a source of satisfaction. In the erotically peaceful situation, workplace romances give joy and stimulation, or they are a step in the search for a genuine relationship. Security during erotic war lies in control and scoring, and during erotic peace, in trust and dependence.

In this study, *eroticized atmosphere at work* was measured by two criteria: (a) friendship between men and women is unwarrantedly eroticized; and (b) friendly touching is misunderstood as a sexual signal. The correlation between the two variables was .57 for women and .30 for men.

In addition, two criteria measured the subject's own *attitude toward flirting at work:* (a) enjoyment of light flirting; and (b) being flattered if someone pays sexual attention. The correlation between the two variables was .38 for women and .50 for men.

The two dimensions of eroticized atmosphere and the subject's own attitude toward flirting did not correlate with each other. The correlation between them for both men and women was .05. A cross-tabulation of these two dimensions gave the following typology of *erotic atmosphere* (shown in Figure 5.1).

An erotically neutral atmosphere means that there is a low eroticized atmosphere at the workplace, and workers are negative about flirting (cell 1 of Figure 5.1). The erotically excited atmosphere includes a highly eroticized atmosphere, where workers enjoy expressions of sexuality (cell 4). Thus the erotic atmosphere includes both the perceived outside atmosphere and the subjective attitudes toward sexually colored behavior at work.

Other individual factors influencing interaction with the opposite sex were the person's *self-rated sex appeal* and *sociability.* In this article, *sociability* was measured on a scale that included such indicators as likes to be with other people, likes company, open-minded, easygoing, and talkative.

RESEARCH SCHEMA

The framework for this study is Homans's theory (1951): Mutual activity of men and women in the workplace leads to informal cross-sex interactions, friendship and romance, and sexual harassment. We assume that the friendships, romances, and other erotic or sexual behavior are facilitated or hampered by other structural and individual factors, discussed above.

Within this research schema, the following questions were posed:

(1) Will an erotically excited atmosphere inhibit interaction, friendship, and romance between men and women and encourage sexual harassment?

(2) Will a disharmonious atmosphere at work lead to more workplace romances than a harmonious atmosphere?

(3) Are high-autonomy jobs connected with more cross-sex interaction, friendship, and romance than low-autonomy jobs?

(4) Will such individual factors as self-rated sex appeal and sociability be related to cross-sex interactions, friendships, and romance at work? Do those who rate their sex appeal and sociability as being high have more cross-sex friends and workplace romances than those who rate their sex appeal and sociability as being low? Will a positive attitude toward flirting and a high self-rated sex appeal be connected with sexual harassment?

RESEARCH DATA

The research data were obtained through personal interviews conducted in 1984-1985 in Helsinki as part of a larger study on women and men in men's and women's jobs. The interviewees were selected with the assistance of trade unions and employers. The results presented in this chapter are based on the answers of male and female engineers, nursery school teachers, and factory workers, and female secretaries.

About 60 people were interviewed in each occupational group—half men and half women. The number of women interviewed was 132, the number of men 102. The structured interview included 200 questions. The topics covered the social structure and culture of the workplace, working conditions, the quality of the work, job satisfaction, interaction, and social support at work, and several personality factors such as self-esteem and sex-role orientation. The interviews were conducted at the workplace during paid working hours.

ASSOCIATIONS AMONG DIFFERENT
TYPES OF CROSS-SEX
INTERACTIONS AND LIKING

Table 5.1 presents the correlations among sexually neutral interaction (chatting and receiving help with personal problems), cross-sex liking (friendship

TABLE 5.1

Correlations Among Indicators of Cross-Sex Interactions,
Cross-Sex Liking, and Sexual Harassment Among
Men and Women at Work

	Chatting		Help		Friendship		Workplace Romances	
	Men	Women	Men	Women	Men	Women	Men	Women
Cross-sex interaction								
daily chatting	–	–						
receiving help with personal problems	.17	.33***	–	–				
Cross-sex liking								
friendship	.29**	.48***	.36**	.38**	–	–		
workplace romances	.24*	.16	.31**	.05	.29**	.19*	–	–
Sexual harassment								
sexually harassed in last 24 months	.20*	.15	.17	.08	.29**	.14	.31**	.09

*p < .05; **p < .01; ***p < .001.

and workplace romances), and sexual harassment between men and women in the workplace.

Sexually neutral interaction was strongly related to cross-sex liking among men and women. The more sexually neutral activity—chatting and helping—between men and women, the more men and women established friendships with each other. Also, workplace romances were, among men, associated with chatting and receiving help with personal matters from women. Generally, for men, friendship, workplace romances, and sexual harassment correlated with each other (on the average, .30). Sexual harassment among women was not correlated with either sexually neutral factors or with indicators of liking. Also, the correlation between friendship and workplace romances was quite low among women (.19). The fact that, among men but not among women, sexual harassment correlated with sexually neutral interaction and with cross-sex liking suggests that sexual harassment has a different meaning to men and women.

SEX COMPOSITION AT WORK AND CROSS-SEX INTERACTIONS, CROSS-SEX LIKING, AND SEXUAL HARASSMENT

The influence of the type and degree of sex-segregation in the workplace on informal cross-sex interactions, cross-sex liking, and sexual harassment is shown in Table 5.2. Two-thirds of the sex-segregated men were industrial workers and one-third were engineers. Three-fourths of the complementary male group were engineers, the others were industrial workers. All token men were nursery school teachers. Among women, almost half (48%) of the sex-segregated group consisted of nursery school teachers, almost one-fourth (23%) were secretaries, and the rest were industrial workers. Half of the women's complementary group were secretaries, 36% were industrial workers, and 14% nursery school teachers. All token women were engineers.

Women's segregated and complementary groups were occupationally more heterogeneous than men's because both included secretaries, which were not part of our male sample.

Table 5.2 shows that daily chatting with members of the opposite sex was related to the sex structure of the workplace; both men and women in complementary and token groups reported more daily chatting with each other than men and women in sex-segregated work. Also, receiving help with personal problems from a workmate of the opposite sex was associated with sex structure in the same way.

A total of 79% of token women and 59% of token men had cross-sex friends in the workplace. Only 23% of women and 19% of men in sex-segregated jobs had cross-sex friends. For men, daily contact with women was enough to establish a cross-sex friendship; there were no statistically significant differences in this matter between men either in complementary or in token groups. For women, the situation was different; token women had male friends more often than women in complementary work.

What affected cross-sex friendship also affected workplace romances. Men in token (34%) and in complementary groups (45%) had more workplace romances than men in sex-segregated work (15%). The availability of women seemed to be enough for men to become attracted to a female workmate. For women, the situation was different; more token women (58%) than women either in complementary (29%) or in sex-segregated (36%) work reported workplace romances. For women, it was apparently necessary to share the same tasks in order to become emotionally involved. For both men and women, about one-half of the workplace romances resulted in sexual relationships.

Altogether, 20% of men had been sexually harassed during the past 24 months, whereas 31% of women had been objects of sexual harassment. The difference in rates of harassment between men and women was not statistically significant. Token women reported more sexual harassment than did the other women, and the difference between token women and women in sex-segregated work was statistically significant at the .05 level. For men, sexual harassment was not related to sex-segregation. Most incidences of sexual harassment were quite mild. The most common form, sexual teasing and joking, was reported by 37% of token women, compared with 29% of women in complementary jobs and 14% of women in sex-segregated work.

TABLE 5.2

Relationship of Type of Sex Composition of Workplace to Cross-Sex Interactions, Cross-Sex Liking, and Sexual Harassment (in percentages)

	Men					Women				
	Sex-Segregated	Complementary	Tokens	Total	$P <$	Sex-Segregated	Complementary	Tokens	Total	$P <$
Cross-sex interactions: has daily chats with workmates of the opposite sex	54	86	100	78	.001	29	78	97	67	.001
has received help with personal problems from workmates of opposite sex	13	22	37	23	.05	14	23	33	23	n.s.
Cross-sex liking: has cross-sex friends at work	19	65	59	45	n.s.	23	36	79	42	.001
has had workplace romance during service with present employer	15	45	34	24	.05	36	29	58	35	.05
Sexual harassment: has been sexually harassed at work during 24 months[a]	15	26	22	20	n.s.	19	33	45	31	.05
(N)	(41)	(29)	(32)	(102)		(44)	(55)	(33)	(132)	

a. During the past 24 months has at work experienced incidents of sexual harassment, for example, actual or attempted rape or sexual assault; unwanted pressure for sexual favors; deliberate touching; leaning over; cornering or pinching; sexually suggestive looks or gestures; letters; phone calls; materials of sexual nature; or sexual teasing, jokes, or questions (Tangri et al., 1982).

132   SEX COMPOSITION OF THE WORKPLACE

THE COMBINED INFLUENCE OF THE
STRUCTURAL AND INDIVIDUAL FACTORS ON
CROSS-SEX FRIENDSHIP, WORKPLACE
ROMANCES, AND SEXUAL HARASSMENT

Table 5.3 shows results of three different regression analyses made separately for men and women. The two forms of cross-sex liking—friendship and workplace romances—as well as sexual harassment were the dependent variables. Structural factors (mutual activity, autonomy at work, intrigues at work, and eroticized atmosphere in the workplace) and individual factors (positive attitude toward flirting, self-rated sex appeal, sociability, age, and marital status) were independent variables. The regression analyses allow us to examine the explanatory power of each variable when the other variables of the model are simultaneously held constant.

Cross-sex friendship was explained by mutual activity. Among men, it was associated with daily cross-sex contacts, and among women, with the mutual activity of men and women at work. *Workplace romances,* as reported by men, were related to other factors: high autonomy at work and disharmonious atmosphere at work. Also, individual factors such as self-rated sociability and a positive attitude toward flirting were related to workplace romances for men. Young single men were more often involved in romantic relationships at work than were older and married men. For women, workplace romances were explained only by individual factors: a positive attitude toward flirting, a high self-rated sex appeal, and sociability. No structural factors were related to workplace romances among women. A disharmonious atmosphere at work (intrigues at work) was slightly associated with workplace romances.

Sexual harassment was mainly affected by two structural features: mutual activity of men and women and an eroticized atmosphere at work. Single women were harassed more often than married women. Other individual factors, such as a positive attitude toward flirting or a high self-rated sex appeal, were not related to sexual harassment. In summary, there are different mechanisms to explain cross-sex friendship, on the one hand, and workplace romances, on the other. Romances were more dependent on individual factors than friendships, which were more clearly dependent on structural factors. Sexual harassment was connected with an eroticized atmosphere at work.

EROTIC ATMOSPHERE AT WORK

When the men and women in the study were classified according to the typology of erotic atmosphere shown in Figure 5.1, it was found that more men than women worked in an erotically excited atmosphere. The portion of women was higher in an erotically neutral atmosphere:

TABLE 5.3

Regression Model Explaining Men's and Women's Cross-Sex Liking–Friendships and Workplace Romances–and Sexual Harassment at Work (standardized regression coefficients)

Explaining Variable	Friendship		Workplace Romances		Sexual Harassment	
	Men	Women	Men	Women	Men	Women
Joint activity in the formal work organization[a]	.33**	.46***	.13	.15	.20*	.16*
High autonomy at work[b]	.10	−.03	.29**	.05	−.12	−.04
Disharmonious atmosphere in the workplace[c]	.13	.08	.27**	.15	−.01	.09
Eroticized atmosphere in the workplace[d]	.07	.04	−.06	−.04	.22**	.16*
Positive toward flirting[e]	−.07	.12	.19*	.21**	.10	.02
Young age	−.07	−.04	.24*	.13	.07	.04
Single	.01	.01	.19*	.05	.00	.16*
High self-rated sex appeal	.12	.05	.10	.17*	−.05	.10
Is sociable[f]	.02	.03	.19*	.21**	.10	.00
Proportion of variance explained	19%	26%	25%	18%	19%	12%

a. Except for men in explaining friendships, the scale includes both sharing the same work tasks and having daily contacts at work with the other sex. The variable is the same as the independent variable in Table 5.2. Men's friendships are explained by daily contacts with women.
b. Scale based on five indicators: makes decisions about one's own work, the work is not repetitive, uses knowledge and skills derived from earlier education or experience, contributes to decisions, and has a challenging job. Reliability (Cronbach's alpha) is .79 for women and .77 for men.
c. Scale based on seven indicators: cliques, envy, exclusion, scapegoating, not sharing job-related information, discrimination, and favoritism. Reliability (Cronbach's alpha) is .75 for women and .67 for men.
d. Scale based on two indicators: even without cause, friendship between men and women is often or sometimes thought to signify a romantic or sexual relationship (in the workplace); and a friendly touch is often misunderstood (in the workplace). Correlation coefficients were .57 for women and .30 for men.
e. Scale based on two indicators: enjoys light flirting at work, and feels flattered if somebody pays sexual attention to him or her. Correlation coefficients were .38 for women and .50 for men.
f. Scale based on five indicators: likes to be with other people, likes company, open-minded, easygoing, talkative. Reliability (Cronbach's alpha) is .82 for women and .80 for men.
*p < .05; **p < .01; ***p < .001.

TABLE 5.4

Cross-Sex Friendship, Workplace Romances, and Sexual Harassment
Explored According to the Erotic Atmosphere at Work

	Erotically Neutral		Undererotic		Overerotic		Erotically Excited	
	Men %	Women %	Men %	Women %	Men %	Women %	Men %	Women %
Has had cross-sex friends at work	44 (18)	30 (27)	59 (22)	54 (28)	31 (16)	38 (34)	51 (33)	45 (39)
Has had a workplace romance during service with present employer	12	15	32	43	6	29	33	50
Object of sexual harassment at work during past 24 months	13	27	9	29	19	28	34	35

NOTE: Numbers within parentheses in the first row indicate number of respondents.

		Women	Men
1.	Erotically neutral atmosphere	27	18
2.	Undererotic atmosphere	20	25
3.	Overerotic atmosphere	31	18
4.	Erotically excited atmosphere	22	38
		100	99
		(102)	(132)

Sex-segregation and an erotic atmosphere did not overlap with each other.
The correlation between sex-segregation and eroticized atmosphere was .01 for
women and −.16 for men. A positive attitude toward flirting did not correlate
with sex-segregation (r = −.02 for women and −.04 for men). Table 5.4 shows how
friendship, workplace romances, and sexual harassment vary according to the
erotic atmosphere at work.

Cross-sex friendships were not related to the erotic atmosphere at work;
however, *workplace romances* were. Only 6% of men in overerotic workplaces
reported having a workplace romance compared with 33% of men in erotically
excited workplaces. Among women, an erotically neutral workplace also
generated few workplace romances; only 15% had workplace romances
compared with 43% of women in undererotic and 51% of women in erotically
excited workplaces.

Sexual harassment was not related to the erotic atmosphere among women.
Although the differences were not statistically significant, women reported more

incidences of harassment in an erotically excited workplace (35%) than other workplaces. Men in undererotic workplaces reported less sexual harassment (9%) than men in erotically excited workplaces, where 34% reported incidences of harassment.

SUMMARY AND DISCUSSION

Women and men are segregated from each other occupationally, at the job level and at the workplace level. In this study, we analyzed the consequences of sex-segregation on non-work-related interactions between men and women at work. Different mechanisms affected different kinds of cross-sex interaction and cross-sex liking. The mutual activity of men and women was related to cross-sex friendship. Workplace romances were more dependent on individual factors, whereas sexual harassment as an example of an asymmetrical interaction was associated with the eroticized mutual activity of men and women.

The questions posed in this study were partly supported by our results. Men with more *autonomous jobs* had workplace romances more often than men with less autonomous jobs. Autonomy was not related with the other indicators of cross-sex interaction. *Social atmosphere in the workplace* among men, but not among women, was related to workplace romances. Men in disharmonious workplaces reported romantic relationships more often than men in more harmonious workplaces. Apparently, for men but not for women, workplace romances operate as a "safety valve," an interpretation suggested by Haavio-Mannila (1982). Social atmosphere in the workplace was not related with other cross-sex interaction variables. An *eroticized atmosphere* was related to sexual harassment among men and women. Within an eroticized atmosphere, men and women reported more incidences of sexual harassment than men and women within a less eroticized atmosphere. An eroticized atmosphere was not related to sentiments of liking.

Self-rated sociability was related to workplace romances among men and women. Those with high self-rated sociability reported romantic relationships at work more often than those with low self-rated sociability. Also, a *positive attitude toward flirting at work* was related to workplace romances among both sexes. Those men and women whose attitude was positive toward flirting reported workplace romances more often than those whose attitude was less favorable.

It was noteworthy that a positive attitude toward flirting and self-rated sex appeal were *not* related to sexual harassment. Harassment was mainly dependent on an eroticized atmosphere in the workplace (e.g., where interaction between men and women was unwarrantedly eroticized).

For both men and women, becoming an object of sexual harassment was related to the sex structure of the workplace and to its eroticized atmosphere. Working together with the opposite sex in workplaces where friendship between men and women was eroticized created an atmosphere favorable to sexual harassment. In all, 31% of women and 20% of men reported incidences of sexual harassment during the past 24 months.

These figures were strikingly similar with our recent results, dealing with 957 women and 887 men representing 12 occupations with different sex ratios. According to that study, 34% of women and 26% of men reported incidences of sexual harassment. The gender difference in our results was smaller than that of most British or American studies (Dziech & Weiner, 1984; Gutek, 1985). Consistent with American and British studies was the finding that token women were more sensitive to sexual harassment than women working either in complementary or in sex-segregated work (Gutek, 1985). Token women were in a double-bind situation; they reported a great deal of sexual harassment, on the one hand, and a great deal of workplace romances, on the other. In each job category, single women were sexually harassed more often than married women. One implication of our results is that if eroticizing tendencies in working life are suppressed, some sexual harassment can be prevented (see also Gutek, 1985, chap. 9).

REFERENCES

Anderson, L. (1984). *Aging and loneliness.* Stockholm: University of Stockholm, Department of Sociology.

Bell, R. R. (1984, October). *Sexuality and cross gender friendships.* Paper presented at the National Council on Family Relations Annual Meetings, San Francisco.

Collins, E.G.C. (1983, September-October). Managers and lovers. *Harvard Business Review.*

Dziech, B. W., & Weiner, L. (1984). *The lecherous professor: Sexual harassment on campus.* Boston: Beacon.

Gruber, J. E., & Bjorn, L. (1982). Blue-collar blues: The sexual harassment of women autoworkers. *Work and Occupations, 9*(3), 271-298.

Gutek, B. A. (1985). *Sex and the workplace.* San Francisco: Jossey-Bass.

Haavio-Mannila, E. (1968). *Suomalainen nainen ja mies* [The Finnish woman and man]. Porvoo: WSOY.

Haavio-Mannila, E. (1982). Työn laatu ja työpaikkarakkaudet [Quality of work and workplace romances]. *Sosiologia, 19*(4), 225-236.

Haavio-Mannila, E., Jallinoja, R., & Strandell, H. (1984). *Perhe, työ ja tunteet* [Family, work and emotions]. Juva: WSOY.

Haavio-Mannila, E., & Stolte-Heiskanen, V. (1969). Työ ja ihmissuhteet Valkeakosken tehtailla [Work and human relations in the factories of Valkeakoski]. *Kaikuja Hämeestä, 7* (Hämeenlinna: Arvi A. Karisto).

Homans, G. C. (1951). *The human group.* New York: Routledge & Kegan Paul.

Jaakkola, M., & Karisto, A. (1976). *Friendship networks in the Scandinavian countries* (Research Reports 11). Helsinki: University of Helsinki, Research Group for Comparative Sociology.

Kanter, R. M. (1977). Some effects of proportions of group life: Skewed sex ratios and responses to token women. *American Journal of Sociology, 82*, 965-990.

Kauppinen-Toropainen, K., Haavio-Mannila, E. & Kandolin, I. (1984). Women at work in Finland. In M. J. Davidson & C. L. Cooper (Eds.), *Working women: An international survey*. Chichester: John Wiley.

Kauppinen-Toropainen, K., Kandolin, I., & Haavio-Mannila, E. (1988). Sex segregation and quality of women's work. *Journal of Occupational Behavior, 9*, 15-27.

Liljeström, R. (1981). Könsroller och sexualitet [Gender roles and sexuality]. In *Prosition*. Stockholm: Liber Forlag.

Lincoln, J. R., & Miller, J. (1979, June). Work and friendship ties in organizations. *Administrative Science Quarterly, 24*, 181-199.

Lindgren, G. (1983). Konssegregeringen i arbetslivet och "kvinnlig" heterosocialitet [Gender segregation in work life and "female" heterosociability]. In *Sociologi i brytningstid*. Umeå: Umeå Universitet, Sociologiska institutionen.

Lipman-Blumen, J. (1976). Toward a homosocial theory of sex roles: An explanation of the sex segregation of social institutions. *Signs, 1*(3, Part 2), 15-31.

Quinn, R. E. (1977). Coping with cupid: The formation, impact, and management of romantic relationships in organizations. *Administrative Science Quarterly, 22*, 3-45.

Rubin, L. B. (1985). *Just friends: The role of friendship in our lives*. New York: Harper & Row.

Tangri, S., Burt, M. R., & Johnson, L. B. (1982). Sexual harassment at work: Three explanatory models. *Journal of Social Issues, 38*(4), 33-54.

Zetterberg, H. (1966). Den hemliga rangordningen [The secret rank order]. *Sociologisk forskning*, no. 3.

6

Stress in Dual-Earner Families

SUZAN N.C. LEWIS
CARY L. COOPER

This chapter provides a review of research on dual-earner couples, within an occupational stress framework. Evidence concerning sources of stress for dual-earner spouses is first discussed followed by consideration of the impact of these stressors on well-being. In addition, a brief discussion of the situation vis-à-vis dual-earners in the United Kingdom is included. Finally, the implications of the literature, and the situation facing British couples, are considered in terms of sex-role ideology, and some suggestions for future research and practice are presented.

Heightened concern for the quality of working life, together with mounting evidence of a relationship between stress and illness (Holmes & Masuda, 1974; Kasl, 1978) have generated an accumulating literature on sources and manifestations of occupational stress (Cooper & Smith, 1985; French, Caplan, & Harrison, 1982). There has been much criticism, however, of the relative neglect of factors beyond the work environment, and particular recognition recently of the interdependence of work and family in relation to well-being (Burke & Bradshaw, 1981; Glowinkowski & Cooper, 1985; Kasl, 1978). It has been argued that the home-work interface is especially significant for employed parents (Lewis & Cooper, 1983).

Parallel research initiatives on work and family have been stimulated by demographic and social trends. The increasing rate of employment of married women with children, a group who have traditionally fulfilled the role of full-time homemaker, has produced a growing research interest in two-earner families. The early research was designed primarily to chart social changes in the evolution of the family (Fogarty, Rapoport, & Rapoport, 1971; Rapoport & Rapoport, 1969) and this perspective is reflected in the ever expanding literature on dual-earner couples and marital satisfaction (Burke & Weir, 1976; Chassin, Zeiss, Cooper, & Reaven, 1985; House, 1986; Yogev & Brett, 1985b). Thus, just as early occupational stress research within organizational psychology tended to neglect the impact of extraorganizational influences, family psychologists and sociologists studying dual-earners have been concerned with family dynamics to a greater extent than occupational experiences (Gutek, Nakamura, & Nieva, 1980). Currently, however, interest in work-family interrelationships is producing a shift in emphasis and convergence of these two lines of research, reflected in concern about the impact of both occupational and family experiences, and their interface, on the well-being of employed spouses (Nieva, 1985; Sekaran, 1983, 1985; Voydanoff & Kelly, 1984).

The term *stress*, although by no means new, has increasingly become an integral part of everyday vocabulary. As numerous authors have noted, however, there is much diversity in the definitions of *stress* used in research (Glowinkowski & Cooper, 1985; Jick & Burke, 1982; Monat & Lazarus, 1985). The earliest models of stress were physiological, the most influential being that of Selye (1956), who defined *stress* as a nonspecific response of the body to any demand. More recent models of stress have emphasized the impact of psychological variables, and especially the interaction between the person and the environment, in the perception of and reaction to stress (French, Caplan, & Harrison, 1982; Lazarus, 1966). Thus it is not the situation that is inherently stressful, but it may be appraised as such by the individual. Characteristics of both individuals and situations are therefore implicated, with signs of stress indicating an individual's inability to cope with perceived environmental demands. Definitional confusion has arisen because of the use of the word *stress* to denote a stimulus, or property of the environment, and a response, or state of the individual, which may be inferred from recurring signs and symptoms. The view of stress as an individual response to demands that are appraised as stressful, appears to be the most useful in considering the impact of work and family pressures on two-earner couples. The term *stressor* will be used to denote sources of stress in the following discussion.

Reviews of research into occupational stress have identified a number of pressures in the work environment, including role strain, overload, underutilization of skills, inequity, and lack of control (Cooper & Marshall, 1976; French, Caplan, & Harrison, 1982). In addition, certain personality and attitudinal variables, such as Type A (i.e., hurried, pressured) behavior and work commitment, have consistently been shown to moderate the impact of potentially stressful situations (Caplan & Jones, 1975; Davidson & Cooper, 1983; Sekaran, 1983, 1985). All these pressures and individual variables may be involved to some extent in work-family management problems facing dual-earner couples, and may be manifested in symptoms of stress (see Figure 6.1). It is our contention that most sources of stress from the home-work interface arise out of the social context, particularly as a consequence of gender role attitudes, which are internalized, and also reflected externally in organizational and state policies.

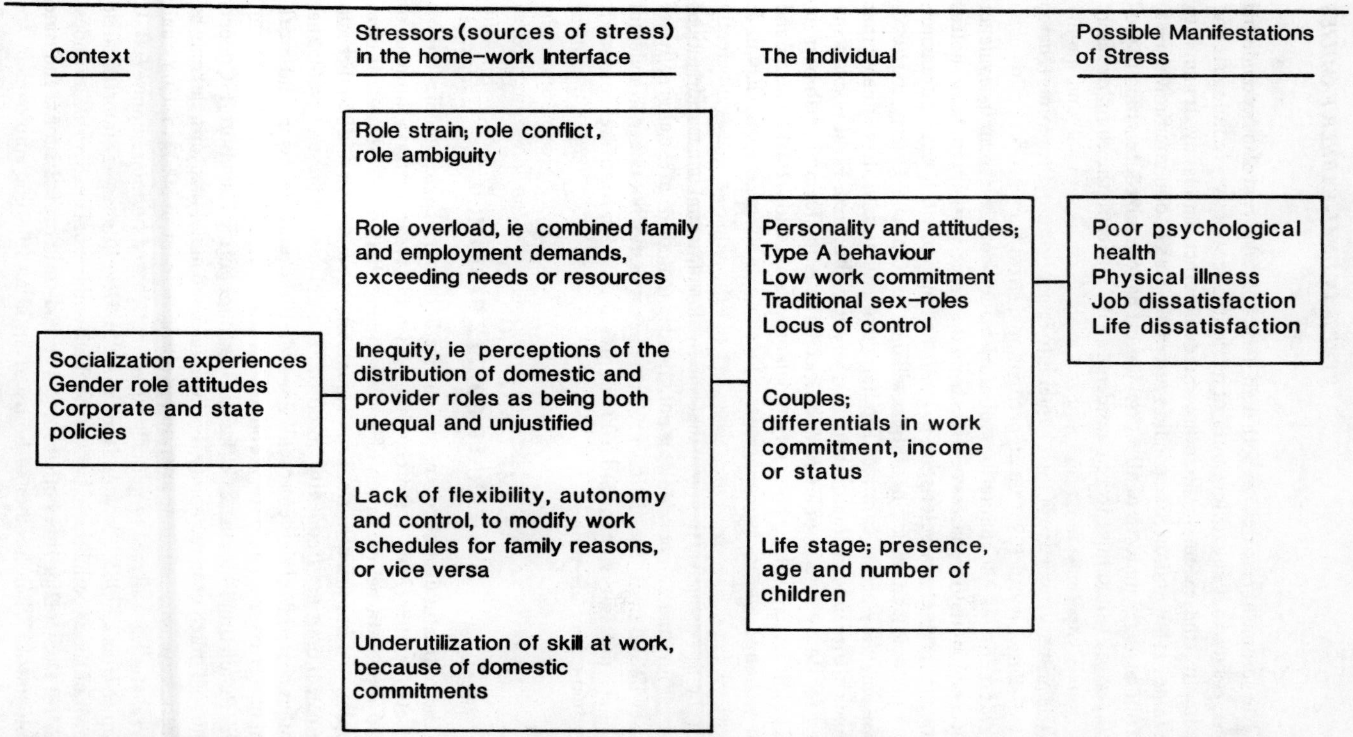

Context	Stressors (sources of stress) in the home–work Interface	The Individual	Possible Manifestations of Stress
Socialization experiences Gender role attitudes Corporate and state policies	Role strain; role conflict, role ambiguity Role overload, ie combined family and employment demands, exceeding needs or resources Inequity, ie perceptions of the distribution of domestic and provider roles as being both unequal and unjustified Lack of flexibility, autonomy and control, to modify work schedules for family reasons, or vice versa Underutilization of skill at work, because of domestic commitments	Personality and attitudes; Type A behaviour Low work commitment Traditional sex-roles Locus of control Couples; differentials in work commitment, income or status Life stage: presence, age and number of children	Poor psychological health Physical illness Job dissatisfaction Life dissatisfaction

Figure 6.1. A Model of Stress in Dual-Earner Couples

141

The volume of research on both dual-earner couples, and also occupational stress, is such that any review must, of necessity, be selective. In the interest of parsimony, the extensive literature on dual-earner family dynamics (e.g., Hoffman, 1986) and on job-specific sources of stress (Cooper & Smith, 1985) will not be our main focus of attention. It must be recognized, however, that all these factors would have to be considered to do justice to the complexities of individuals' experiences.

The primary objective of this chapter is to review some of the recent research on two-earner couples, within an occupational stress framework. Following a consideration of the limitations of dual-earner couple research, evidence concerning potential sources of stress from the home-work interface, as well as certain individual characteristics, as illustrated in Figure 6.1, will be discussed. Some possible manifestations of stress will then be examined. Clearly, sources of stress may vary across cultures. The particular situation vis-à-vis dual-earner parents in the United Kingdom will therefore be highlighted. Finally, sources of stress for dual-earner couples, and the specific situation facing British couples, will be interpreted in terms of sex-role ideology. Implications for attitudinal and policy change, and stress management, together with related research, will be suggested.

It should be stated at this point that a discussion of sources and manifestations of stress for dual-earner couples is not intended to imply that the alternative of housewife and single-breadwinner roles are less stressful, but rather to highlight issues as a necessary step toward reducing pressures and maximizing the rewards of a dual-earner life-style.

SOME LIMITATIONS OF
TWO-EARNER COUPLE RESEARCH

There are a number of conceptual and methodological issues and limitations in the two-earner family research, which will be discussed briefly at this stage to avoid repetition below. Much of the literature is biased toward middle-class couples, and important variations in employment conditions and number and age of children are frequently obscured. The original interest in two-earner families centered on the "emergent" life-style of the middle-class, professional, dual-career couple (Fogarty, Rapoport, & Rapoport, 1971; Huser & Grant, 1978; Pendleton, Paloma, & Garland, 1982; Rapoport & Rapoport, 1969), and is thus of limited generalizability. The dynamics of couples with jobs, rather than careers, have received some attention (Keith & Schafer, 1980; Lein, 1979), and several studies analyzed large-scale survey data based on more representative samples (Pleck, 1985; Pleck & Staines, 1985). Nevertheless, more needs to be known of the experiences of two-earner blue-collar workers.

Most studies state that both members of dual-earner couples are in full-time employment. When number of hours constituting full-time employment are specified, however, these vary from a minimum of 20 hours a week (Pleck &

Staines, 1985) to 35 hours (Chassin, Zeiss, Cooper, & Reaven, 1985; House, 1986). Other research includes couples in which one partner, usually the wife, may be employed part-time (Pleck & Staines, 1985). Differences among dual-earners in relation to hours of employment are further obscured by the failure of much research to consider variables such as flexibility or convenience of work schedules.

The original definition of *two-earner couples* referred to the combining of two jobs with the raising of children (Rapoport & Rapoport, 1969). Nevertheless, not all research specifies whether or not there are children in the family (Huser & Grant, 1978; Pendleton, Paloma, & Garland, 1982). Other studies group together parents of children up to the age of 18 (Bryson, Bryson, & Johnson, 1978; Holohan & Gilbert, 1979; Sekaran, 1983, 1985, 1986). The impact of the specific pressures affecting parents of one or more children of different ages is thus frequently obscured.

Much of the research on dual-earner couples is "women-centered." Often, different techniques of assessment are used with female and male subjects (Berk, 1985) or extraneous variables controlled more strictly for wives than husbands (Weingarten, 1978). Certain questions, especially those relating to domestic work, are frequently asked only in relation to wives (Pleck, 1985; Robinson, 1977). The perception of problems of balancing home and work as women's issues perpetuates the belief that domestic and family work are primarily their responsibilities (see also Lapidus, this volume; Roby & Uttal, this volume). Women's roles cannot and do not change in isolation, and a full understanding of dual-earner dynamics requires the examination of the experiences of both wives and husbands, and the mutual impact of adapting to developing roles. Implicit assumptions about appropriate gender roles are also reflected in research questions addressed. Thus the impact of wives' employment on husbands' mental health has been investigated (Fendrich, 1984; Rosenfield, 1980) while the impact of husbands' unemployment on families is of greater concern (Fagin & Little, 1984).

Finally, it should be noted that recent research on dual-earner couples has been predominantly American. Cross-cultural research would be valuable in highlighting the impact of different social contexts. A comparison of professional couples in the East and West suggests that many of the issues are similar in spite of differences in prevailing ideologies (Lapidus, Chapter 4, this volume; Rueschemeyer, 1981) but this may not generalize to nonprofessionals. In the United Kingdom, recognition of converging roles of men and women has been reflected in research interest in employed mothers (Apter, 1985; Moss & Fonda, 1980; Sharpe, 1984) and in the fatherhood role (Beail, 1985; Beail & McGuire, 1982), but research into dual-earner couples is fairly sparse (Lewis, 1986; Rapoport & Rapoport, 1969, 1971). The weight of dual-earner couple research to be discussed in the following sections is therefore American. Its applicability to other settings, such as the United Kingdom, remains an empirical question.

SOURCES OF STRESS

Role Conflict and Ambiguity

Role strain, in terms of role conflict and role ambiguity at work, have consistently been identified as significant stressors associated with a range of negative physical and psychological outcomes (Davidson & Cooper, 1983; French, Caplan, & Harrison, 1982). *Role conflict* refers to the appraisal of conflicting demands within one role, or between different roles, while *role ambiguity* denotes uncertainty about the expectations associated with a particular role. Potential for role strain exists for dual-earners because women's employment roles, and men's paternal and homemaking roles, may interfere with the demands of their traditional activities, causing time-based conflict, and also conflict with societal expectations, producing role ambiguity or identity dilemmas. Contemporary women are also exposed to divergent cultural directives, due to early socialization extolling the exclusivity of the maternal role, and current egalitarian thinking that encourages the seeking of fulfillment beyond motherhood through employment (Hock, Gnezde, & McBride, 1984; Johnson & Johnson, 1980).

There is abundant evidence of work-family role conflict and identity dilemmas for mothers from a range of occupational groups in the United States (Gilbert, Holohan, & Manning, 1981; Hock, Gnezde, & McBride, 1984; Kamerman, 1980) and in the United Kingdom (Moss & Fonda, 1980; Pollert, 1981; Sharpe, 1984). Feelings of guilt and efforts to overcompensate by spending more time with children and hence exacerbating role overload are frequently reported consequences (Hoffman, 1979). There is evidence too of role conflict for men (Barling, 1986; Greenhaus & Kopelman, 1981), although most research fails to focus specifically on men with employed wives. Greenhaus and Kopelman (1981) reported no differences between male managers with employed and nonemployed wives in amount of work-family conflict, but those married to managerial or professional women, who may exert more pressure for egalitarian relationships, reported more role conflict than other men. Thus the dual-earner life-style with both spouses in demanding occupations creates substantial conflict for husbands, while women report conflict, irrespective of their type of occupation.

Research focusing on couples rather than employed on women or men independently indicates that role conflict is much greater for dual-earner parents than nonparents (Pleck, Staines, & Lang, 1978) and work-parenting conflict is greater for mothers than fathers (Holohan & Gilbert, 1979; Johnson & Johnson, 1980; Keith & Schafer, 1980; Lewis, 1986; Sekaran, 1983, 1985). Chassin, Zeiss, Cooper, and Reaven (1985) required mothers and fathers of preschool-aged children to describe the roles of working woman, working man, husband, wife, mother, and father. The results indicated that the characteristics of the working woman role were perceived as quite distinct from the other two roles, while the three male roles were rated as more similar to each other. There were also significant differences between wives and husbands in their perceptions of the spouse and parent roles, implying the potential for intrarole conflict due to lack of agreement by occupants of complementary roles. The authors argue that men appear to be more tied to traditional role values concerning the role of the wife, which creates difficulty for women in simultaneously fulfilling the roles of worker, wife, and mother in their husbands', but not in their own, eyes.

The potential for role strain associated with parenthood may begin prior to the birth of a first child. The belief in the primacy of the maternal role, which remains pervasive among employed women expecting their first child (Hock, Gnezde, & McBride, 1984), and the widely held expectation that childbirth marks the end of a woman's career, if only temporarily, impose considerable pressure. Not surprisingly, employed pregnant women frequently feel ambivalent about future employment plans (Behrman, 1980; Daniel, 1980; Hock, Gnezde, & McBride, 1984). Nevertheless, Lewis (1986) found no evidence that this conflict was manifested in symptoms of stress for couples expecting their first child, and intending to maintain a dual-earner life-style.

Consequences of Role Strain for
Dual-Earner Parents

For dual-earner parents, role strain is associated with poor mental health and diminished job and life satisfaction (Keith & Schafer, 1980; Lewis, 1986; Sekaran, 1983, 1985), which is consistent with evidence on occupational stress. The process by which role pressures affect parents' well-being, however, appears to differ for employed mothers and fathers. Sekaran (1985) examined paths to mental health in a sample of 166 dual-career couples with children up to the age of 18. Multiple role stresses were associated with job and life dissatisfaction of women and men, but exerted a direct negative effect on the mental health of wives only. Sekaran interprets her results as indicating that women continue to be overburdened with domestic and family responsibilities, the stress of which may directly impair mental health.

Summary: Role Strain

Traditional expectations concerning gender roles create the potential for role ambiguity and conflict for dual-earner parents, and may be a source of considerable stress. Attitudes toward the maternal role are such that employed mothers experience the greatest role strain and consequently may be particularly vulnerable to psychological ill health.

OVERLOAD

A second consequence of multiple roles is the potential for overload. This implies the appraisal of overall workload as exceeding needs or resources, and has been identified as an important source of occupational stress (French,

Caplan, & Harrison, 1982). Overload dilemmas are consistently reported by dual-earners, and tend to be disproportionately experienced by wives (Bryson, Bryson, & Johnson, 1978; Gilbert, Holohan, & Manning, 1981; Rapoport & Rapoport, 1976). Yogev (1982), however, in a study of married professional women, found no significant correlation between objective overload in terms of number of hours worked at home and in employment, and subjective overload. Thus, consistent with psychological models of stress (Lazarus, 1966), workload will only become a source of stress if it is cognitively appraised as "too much." Nevertheless, it remains possible that there is a threshold beyond which a specific objective overload may have negative consequences. This is likely to be determined not only by employment load, but also the extent to which domestic roles are shared by spouses.

Domestic Overload

As women increasingly share the breadwinner role, a rational response would be increased sharing in the domestic sphere also, but this has been slower to occur. Employed women still perform the majority of domestic work, although recent evidence suggests that the extent of this inequality may be decreasing (Nyquist, Slivken, Spence, & Helmreich, 1985; Pleck, 1985). Some of the most dramatic evidence of women's overload associated with "dual roles" comes from studies of British women factory workers (Pollert, 1981; Shimmin, 1984). Some of the women interviewed by Pollert (1981) claimed at first that their husbands shared domestic work but, on closer questioning, it emerged that "sharing" meant limited delegation. Women took total domestic responsibility and also performed most of the daily drudgery. The distinction between performing and taking responsibility for tasks has been noted elsewhere (Berk, 1985; Oakley, 1974). Rapoport and Rapoport (1976, 1978) described the sense of responsibility for domestic work as one of the key bottlenecks to sex-role change. Beliefs about responsibilities may explain why women tend to experience multiple roles simultaneously while men experience them sequentially (Hall, 1972). Research noting this distinction between task performance and responsibility indicates that two-earner husbands are increasing their domestic contributions, especially in terms of child-care involvement, but that the distribution of responsibility still tends to be along fairly traditional lines, irrespective of socioeconomic status or sex-role attitudes (Berk, 1985; Nyquist, Slivken, Spence, & Helmreich, 1985; Pleck, 1985). Responsibility may, of course, be a source of satisfaction, but too much responsibility, especially responsibility for people, can be a source of stress (French, Caplan, & Harrison, 1982; Wardwell, Hyman, & Bahnson, 1964).

Consequences of Domestic Overload

Household overload appears to be associated with depression for employed wives (Pearlin, 1975), and involvement in household work linked with depression for dual-worker husbands (Keith & Schafer, 1980). In relation to child care, however, there is substantial evidence that increased paternal involvement improves psychological health for parents of both sexes (Clarke, 1983; Kessler & McCrae, 1982; Lee, 1983; Pleck, 1985). The impact of domestic work on job satisfaction has received less attention but it has been suggested that both partners may feel that their productivity and occupational achievement is constrained by home responsibilities (Holmstrom, 1972; Hunt & Hunt, 1982). Lewis (1986), however, found that greater domestic responsibility was associated with job dissatisfaction for a sample of British two-earner mothers, and not for their partners. This may be due to negative spillover from home to work, or may be a consequence of restricted occupational choice for women with major domestic responsibilities (O'Neil, 1985).

Employment Overload:
Sources and Consequences

Pleck (1977) proposed that if and when ideological support for the traditional division of labor in the home breaks down, then the objective demands of the male paid work role will emerge as a primary constraint on men's family work. The "male model of the work role" that has evolved in Western society calls for continuous paid work from education to retirement, and the subordination of all other roles. This model fails to meet the needs of men and women in egalitarian two-earner families with children. Insofar as traditional gender role expectations govern involvement in family and work, however, it is possible that husbands may experience greater overload than wives from their employment role. The strain on families associated with long working hours of highly successful men with nonemployed wives has frequently been described (Kanter, 1977; Seidenberg, 1973). The potential strains are obviously greater when both partners are employed, particularly in what Handy (1978) has termed "greedy occupations," that is, occupations such as management, which require a great deal of time and commitment from employees. Such problems are, however, not limited to men, nor to high-status occupations. Long working hours are associated with pressure and symptoms of stress in a range of two-earner couples (Keith & Schafer, 1980; Pleck & Staines, 1985; Pleck, Staines, & Lang, 1978). In a survey of single- and dual-earners, Pleck, Staines, and Lang (1978) found that excessive, demanding, inflexible schedules were a major cause of work-family interference leading to impaired health and to reduced job and life satisfaction. Reanalyzing the data for men and women in dual-earner couples, who reported their own and their spouses' employment experiences, Pleck and Staines (1985) concluded that men worked at their jobs for longer, more inconvenient, and more stressful hours than wives. This result may be, however, confounded by the nature of the sample. While the criterion of full-time employment for respondents was at least 20 hours a week, no such restrictions were placed on respondents' partners. Thus the sample effectively included part-time employees, who are more likely to be women.

The Combined Family Workday

Recent research based on national survey data has extended the analysis of the effects of work schedules of two-earner spouses by examining crossover effects of each partner's schedule on the other's family life (Pleck & Staines, 1983, 1985) and by using as the unit of analysis couples' combined work in family and employment or the "family workday" (Kingston & Nock, 1985; Nock & Kingston, 1984). Pleck and Staines (1985) failed to confirm the hypothesis that husbands' work schedules would have a greater impact on partners' family lives than those of wives, who would continue to perform "dual roles" irrespective of job commitments. The authors noted, however, that the results may be biased by selective factors, as wives whose work schedules are so demanding as to interfere with family life may reduce, or cease, their employment commitment. Congruent with this argument, Kingston and Nock (1985) found that any necessary adjustments to the combined family workday were made by wives. Chassin, Zeiss, Cooper, and Reaven (1985) reported that reduction of paid workload by wives, after a one-year follow-up period, was predicted not by their own self-role incongruence, but by their husbands' perception of them as failing to fulfill the maternal role. Thus many wives may be pressured into decreasing workload in order to reduce overall family stress.

Summary: Overload

Overload denotes multiple demands exceeding resources. The evidence suggests that employed women are more likely than men to experience overload from domestic work and responsibility and that this may be a source of stress. Overload emanating mainly from the employment role may be experienced by both sexes, although there is some indication that expectations surrounding the male role may create more job-related stress for dual-earner husbands. Couples tend to cope with their combined work and family loads by increasing their commitments in line with traditional expectations, such that if adjustments are necessary, women are more likely to reduce their paid workload and increase their domestic involvement.

UNDERUTILIZATION OF SKILLS

Insofar as stress is a consequence of lack of fit between the needs of an individual and the demands of the situation (French, Caplan, & Harrison, 1982), job "underload," or underutilization of skills, is a potential stressor when the need for challenge exceeds that offered in the work situation. Pressure of this nature is usually associated with boring, repetitive, understimulating work (Cox, 1985) or with underpromotion (Langrish, 1981). Reduction of job involvement during the period of maximum parental responsibility may create risk of job underload. The potential for underload stress in dual-earner parents has received little attention due to the more prevalent and pressing problems of overload associated with managing multiple roles. Lewis (1986), however, described cases of women who returned from maternity leave to be reinstated in less demanding jobs than those they occupied previously, and who consequently were bored and frustrated at work. It cannot be assumed that lack of challenge at work will be compensated for by additional domestic demands. A reduction in workload demands may be necessary for some employed parents, in order to avoid overload, but may be a source of stress to others. Previous research has indicated that women in dual-earner couples may avoid the stress experienced by wives and mothers without an employment role (Crosby, 1984; Ferree, 1976). Nevertheless, the mere fact of having a job does not guarantee full utilization of skills and abilities, particularly as women tend to be overrepresented in low level, unchallenging, undemanding jobs.

INEQUITY

The stressfulness of any workload or role is partly determined by processes of social comparison. Workers who believe that they are unfairly or inequitably treated in relation to others are less satisfied, regardless of objective workload (Pritchard, Dunnette, & Jorgenson, 1972). This applies whether individuals feel over- or underbenefited, although the latter situation is usually more distressing. Rapoport and Rapoport (1976) proposed that role satisfaction within dual-career couples would also depend upon equitable sharing. *Inequity* refers to the appraisal of fairness in a relationship, through comparison of one's own efforts and rewards with those of a relevant other, and it is to be distinguished from the less subjective concept of equality. In the family context, judgments about what is equitable will be influenced not only by actual time spent in homemaking and employment by each spouse, but also by perceptions of gender-related responsibilities and the value of each partner's contribution in each domain. Research in this area tends to be woman-centered, and emphasizes perceptions of equity in domestic work to a greater extent than equity in the provider role.

Pleck (1985) reported that the only significant predictor of employed women's desire for greater husband participation in domestic work or child care was husbands' present level of involvement. Wives' own objective load, or sex-role attitudes, were not significant predictors. Thus dissatisfaction is related to social comparison rather than actual load. Predictors of husbands' attitudes were not investigated. Nevertheless, not all women perceive their situation as inequitable even if disproportionately overloaded, and therefore domestic load is not an inevitable pressure. The majority of women, or couples, report fairly high levels of satisfaction with their roles, and with their partners' contributions (Berk, 1985; Pleck, 1985; Robinson, 1977; Schafer & Keith, 1980). This may be attributable to stereotyped attitudes toward responsibilities, and the widespread tendency to regard men's domestic contributions as "help." Indeed, many early studies asked only wives about their satisfaction with domestic roles, and inquired whether they desired more "help" from their husbands (Robinson, 1977). Any ambivalence women might have felt in relation to sex roles would be reinforced by the assumption underlying this question. LaRossa and LaRossa (1981), using an exchange theory framework, propose that greater husband domestic contributions would not be desired if perceived as assistance rather than shared responsibility, as this implies that favors would be expected in return.

Consequences of Inequity

Equity theory predicts that perception of overbenefit, as well as underbenefit, will be distressing. There is evidence that perceptions of inequity in domestic, provider, and companionship roles are a source of depression for husbands and wives, whether the inequity is in their favor or their partner's (Schafer & Keith, 1980), thus confirming the significance of social comparison in determining the stressfulness of workloads. Equity also predicts marital satisfaction for dual-earner wives, but not their husbands, who are more satisfied if they perceive themselves as doing less than their share (Yogev & Brett, 1985b). The positive impact of greater paternal child-care involvement on parents' well-being, discussed earlier, may be interpreted in terms of creating a more equitable situation. No parallel effect has been noted in relation to the sharing of domestic work, however. One reason for men's reluctance to become more involved in nonmarket work may be that, because they tend, on average, to contribute more to the family income, they perceive their lower level of domestic work as equitable. Many women may accept greater domestic responsibility and reduced work commitment for the same reasons but, in doing so, decrease opportunities for narrowing income differentials and therefore perpetuate the situation. Clearly, issues of equality at work and at home are inseparable and interrelated in their effect on family and work stress.

Summary: Inequity

Inequity exists when individuals believe they are performing more, or, theoretically, less than their fair share of work in comparison with another. There is some evidence that wives' dissatisfaction with their domestic and child-care load is more contingent upon their husbands' contributions then their own loads, and hence on appraisal of inequity. Stereotyped views of responsibility as well as the gender gap in income level, however, may prevent inequalities from being perceived as inequitable. Little is known about husbands' perceptions of equity due to the largely woman-centered approach to this research question.

AUTONOMY/CONTROL

Considerable experimental evidence suggests that, if individuals believe that they have control over stressful events, they are less likely to be adversely affected (Cornelius & Averill, 1980). Conversely, lack of control or autonomy is associated with stress. For two-earner couples, the potential stressfulness of long working hours or inconvenient schedules may be modified if these are undertaken voluntarily, or if some control can be exercised over hours worked, thus reducing feelings of helplessness. Lack of control over overtime, but not overtime itself, is an important predictor of work-family interference (Pleck, Staines, & Lang, 1978). The moderating effects of autonomy on potentially stressful schedules appears to differ, however, for husbands and wives. Discretionary time spent on job-related activities beyond normal work hours increases job satisfaction for dual-career husbands, but is associated with decreased job satisfaction for wives (Sekaran, 1983, 1985). Similarly, Kingston and Nock (1985) reported that longer working hours were associated with higher family satisfaction for two-earner husbands, but not wives. It appears that, yet again, the greater domestic and child-care responsibilities of women prevent them from benefiting from extra work involvement, even if voluntarily undertaken.

Flexible Work

Control over normal, rather than extra, work hours may be increased by flextime systems. Theoretically at least, such systems should enable spouses to arrange their schedules to be compatible with family needs. Flexible work schedules in the face of inflexible nonwork schedules, such as schools or nurseries, however, may fail to increase perceived control, and hence have no advantage in terms of increased well-being (Krausz & Freibach, 1983). Even if flexibility does increase the perception of autonomy, the impact appears to be moderated by sex-role attitudes. In families with traditional perceptions of gender-related responsibilities, flextime enables women to fit in more tasks rather than encouraging a redistribution of roles (Bohen & Viveros-Long, 1981) and hence does little to reduce family management stress for those with the greatest need. For men who have "radical" or egalitarian attitudes toward parental responsibilities, however (but not for other men), flextime facilitates greater involvement in child care and reduces stress associated with the parental role (Lee, 1983).

Informal Restrictions on Autonomy

The perception of control over work schedules is restricted not only by organizational policies but also informal norms and attitudes of people at work. It has been argued that men are not expected to allow family to interfere with work (Pleck, 1977) and that those who do so are perceived as less desirable or less committed employees (Lamb, Russell, & Sagi, 1983). Stereotyped views concerning men's work and family roles may exacerbate stress by restricting feelings of autonomy at work and, consequently, perpetuating inequity at home. The prevalence of such prejudices and consequences for occupational health, together with the effectiveness of strategies for reducing stereotypes, are areas requiring further investigation.

Summary: Autonomy and Control

The stress associated with long or inconvenient hours of work may be reduced for dual-earners if they perceive themselves as having autonomy to modify schedules for family reasons. Informal norms, based on stereotyped views of men and women's work and family roles, as well as formal organizational policies, may restrict perceptions of control. Flextime is one potential means of increasing individual autonomy, but tends to be ineffective in reducing work-family management stress from inequitable burdens except for employees with non-sex-typed attitudes.

Finally, whether or not individuals perceive themselves as helpless, or able to exercise autonomy in relation to work schedules, may depend upon individual as well as situational factors. Locus of control, or generalized beliefs concerning whether or not control is possible in life (Lefcourt, 1966), may be relevant in this respect, and should be examined as a possible mediator of dual-earner work-family stress in future research.

PERSONALITY AND ATTITUDINAL
DIFFERENCES AND STRESS

An emphasis on aspects of the environment or demands associated with multiple roles may fail to take sufficient account of personal meanings of situations. Sources of pressure in managing work and family evoke different reactions in different people. The possible moderating influences of locus of control and need for challenge have already been mentioned. Other personality and attitudinal factors that may influence the way in which dual-earners appraise and cope with stress include Type A coronary-prone behavior, work orientation, and sex-role attitudes.

Type A Behavior

Type A behavior has been widely investigated in occupational stress research, although rarely in dual-earner contexts. The Type A behavior pattern is characterized by extreme competitiveness of speech, tension of facial muscles, and feelings of being continually under pressure of time and responsibility. It was originally described by cardiologists Freidman and Rosenman (Friedman & Rosenman, 1974; Rosenman, Friedman, & Strauss, 1964) and has been the individual difference variable most investigated in stress research because of the accumulating evidence that it plays a causal role in illness, particularly coronary heart disease (Rosenman, Brand, Jenkins, Friedman, & Wurm, 1975). Type A behavior was originally thought to be more prevalent in men than women (Friedman & Rosenman, 1974) but studies controlling for occupational status report no gender differences in this behavioral pattern (Waldron, 1978b). Employed women tend to have higher Type A scores than housewives (Waldron, 1978a), due to either self-selection or the impact of a time-pressured life-style. Friedman and Rosenman (1974) maintained that an environmental challenge must always serve as a fuse for Type A behavior, but Type A individuals appear to perceive challenge in more situations than other (Type B) individuals (Burnham, Pennebaker, & Glass, 1975). They also tend to select themselves into more demanding situations (Burke & Desca, 1982). The direction of causality in relation to Type A behavior is therefore unclear.

There is considerable evidence that Type A behavior is associated with stress at work (Caplan & Jones, 1975; Davidson & Cooper, 1983). Type A individuals tend to work long hours, often under constant deadline pressure (Friedman & Rosenman, 1974; Howard, Cunningham, & Rechnitzer, 1977) and to be more dissatisfied with their workload (Brief, Rude, & Rabinowitz, 1983; Waldron, 1978a). The extra workload of Type A individuals, and the tendency to become so involved in work that other aspects of life are relatively neglected (Jenkins, 1971), auger badly for family life. Even in single-earner families, Type A men report greater work-family interference and lower marital satisfaction than their Type B counterparts (Burke, Weir, & DuWors, 1980), and wives of Type A men report poorer mental health and lower marital satisfaction than wives of Type B husbands (Burke, Weir, & DuWors, 1979). The majority of research on Type A behavior and families has failed to specify employment status of wives. In a study of dual-earners, however, Lewis (1986) found that Type A behavior was associated with poor mental health for both spouses, while life satisfaction was higher for Type A men, and job and life satisfaction higher for Type B women. This may be because Type A behavior is more normatively acceptable male behavior. The question of whether Type A behavior is a consequence or a source of pressure for dual-earners—and the dynamics whereby it exacerbates stress or affects coping mechanisms—is an area requiring further research.

Commitment to Work

Orientation to work, defined in terms of career commitment or salience, and job involvement, are variables that have received much research attention in the dual-earner family literature. It is usually assumed that a high level of commitment to or involvement in either work or family precludes high investment in the other area, but this is not necessarily the case (Yogev & Brett, 1985a). Indeed, high commitment to both work and family is particularly characteristic of professional, dual-career couples (Gilbert, Holohan, & Manning, 1981; Rueschemeyer, 1981). Contrary to traditional expectations, there are no gender differences in career salience among dual-earner couples (Sekaran, 1982, 1983, 1985), but there is evidence of husbands' greater job involvement and discretionary time spent on job-related activities (Sekaran, 1985). Thus husbands and wives appear to differ in their behavior, probably due to nonmarket responsibilities, but not in their attitudes toward work.

There is some controversy over whether high or low work commitment is more stressful for dual-earners, and whether this differs for wives and husbands. Insofar as energy expands to enable individuals to meet the expectations of roles to which they are highly committed (Marks, 1977), high commitment to the employment role should reduce the stress of multiple demands. On the other hand, high levels of commitment to two or more highly salient roles is likely to exacerbate role conflict. Evidence from studies of employed mothers support the latter view, particularly in relation to middle-class or professional women (Gilbert, Holohan, & Manning, 1981; Pearlin, 1975). Research focusing on dual-earner couples consistently shows, however, that high commitment to work is associated with improved mental health and satisfaction for both husbands and wives (Holohan & Gilbert, 1979; Lewis, 1986; Sekaran, 1983, 1985). These findings are not necessarily incompatible, as positive commitment to work may enable mothers to cope with subsequent role conflict. Evidence that the protective effect of high levels of work commitment is greater for husbands than wives (Bailyn, 1970; Lewis, 1986) is congruent with this argument.

Given that the traditional pattern of family relationships has endorsed husbands' high commitment to and involvement in the breadwinner role, and wives' subordination of work to family commitment, it appears particularly inappropriate to examine the impact of work orientation at the individual level only. Dual-earner couples frequently diverge from this normative pattern, and similarity rather than complementarity of work and family orientations is becoming more prevalent (Yogev & Brett, 1985a). This may be due not only to women's increased work commitment but also to the reduction of work involvement by husbands of employed wives (Gould & Werbel, 1983). Changes in family patterns of work commitment and involvement have raised questions concerning the impact of each spouse's work orientation on their partners. There is evidence that this impact may differ for women and men. In a sample of married women students, similarity of career salience, irrespective of whether it was high or low, was associated with low work-family conflict (Beutell & Greenhaus, 1982). The situation in which wives have higher work commitment than husbands, however, may be very stressful for men (Lewis, 1986), particularly if wives achieve higher occupational status (Hiller & Philliber, 1982) or earn higher or equivalent salaries (Fendrich, 1984). Wives who achieve higher occupational status than their husbands may reduce marital tension by changing to a lower-status job (Hiller & Philliber, 1982). Many employed wives may thus reduce their commitment to work, as a consequence of marital dynamics, and in doing so be deprived of an important source of protection against stress.

Sex-Role Attitudes

The potential for stress associated with nontraditional patterns of work orientation implies that sex-role attitudes may be the key individual attitudinal variable, moderating stress for dual-earners. A dual-earner marriage does not necessarily result from, nor lead to, androgynous attitudes (House, 1986) and, therefore, a range of sex-role attitudes are represented among two-earner couples. Better fit between sex-role attitude and marital style can be predicted, however, for sex-typed single-earners than dual-earners. Evidence that this lack of fit is a source of stress is largely restricted to impact on marital satisfaction (Hiller & Philliber, 1982; House, 1986), although profeminist attitudes and awareness of social influence have been reported to reduce role conflict for professional couples (Holohan & Gilbert, 1979). It should be noted, however, that nontraditional sex-role attitudes are not always reflected in behavior, particularly in the domestic sphere (Araji, 1977). The relationship between sex-role attitudes and division of household labor and responsibility has consistently been shown to be slight, at best (Beckman & Hauser, 1979; Bird, Bird, & Scruggs, 1984; Pleck, 1985). Merely professing non-sex-typed attitudes, therefore, does not necessarily guarantee an equitable relationship and may equally fail to reduce other sex-role-based sources of stress.

NUMBER AND AGE OF CHILDREN

As indicated previously, two-earner parents experience more stress than nonparents, and the pressures are especially salient for parents of preschool children (Holohan & Gilbert, 1979; Lewis, 1986; Pleck, Staines, & Lang, 1978). The strains may increase with the number of children (Keith & Schafer, 1980) especially for wives (Bryson, Bryson, & Johnson, 1978). Sekaran (1985) found a positive relationship between number of children and mental health for wives, however, which she speculated may be due to emotional and practical support given to mothers by older children. Presence, age, and number of children are frequently neglected in research on dual-earner couples. A clearer understanding of the needs of dual-earners at different stages requires that these factors be included as key independent variables in future research.

SOME MANIFESTATIONS OF STRESS

There is a growing body of evidence to suggest that occupational stress is a causal factor in physical diseases (Margolis, Kroes, & Quinn, 1974) and is also associated with poor mental health (French, Caplan, & Harrison, 1982) and decreased job and life satisfaction (Davidson & Cooper, 1983). Some consequences of occupational and nonwork stressors for two-earner couples have been discussed above. It would be misleading, however, to give the impression that the two-earner life-style is inevitably and inherently stressful. It is undeniably demanding, and couples frequently complain of costs such as persistent fatigue and lack of time for leisure activities; however, evidence indicates that costs tend to be balanced by considerable benefits including increased personal fulfillment of wives and extra income (Crosby, 1984; House, 1986; Pendleton, Paloma, & Garland, 1982).

Although women in dual-earner couples may experience as many as, or more demands than, their partners, any negative impact of this life-style on psychological well-being may be greater for husbands. The evidence concerning wives' employment and husbands' psychological distress is not entirely consistent. Burke and Weir (1976) reported poorer psychological and physical health among a sample of accountants and engineers with employed wives than among single-earners. Booth (1977, 1979), using a more representative sample, however, found no significant effect of wives' employment on husbands' well-being, with a trend toward better health in two-earner men. Subsequently, several studies indicated that husbands with employed wives were in poorer mental health than single breadwinners (Kessler & McCrae, 1982; Roberts & O'Keefe, 1981; Rosenfield, 1980) although employment had a positive impact on wives' mental health (Kessler & McCrae, 1982). In an attempt to resolve inconsistencies, Fendrich (1984) applied meta analysis techniques to combine results of a further replication and previous findings and concluded that, although the overall correlation between wives' employment and husbands' psychological distress was positive, it was nonsignificant. It has been suggested that the inconsistency in these results may be due to neglect of moderating variables (Fendrich, 1984). Presence and age of children may be relevant factors. Lewis (1986) found that fathers of young children reported significantly more psychosomatic symptoms than childless men in dual-earner couples. Dual-earner men also report lower levels of happiness when there are children in the home (Benin & Nienstedt, 1985). Because paternal involvement in child care may improve well-being, as discussed earlier, it is possible that additional pressures are experienced at this stage due to the organizational expectations that family should not interfere with work, thus limiting opportunities for involvement in child care.

Research indicates that normative sex differences in psychological health continue to exist in dual-earner couples (Sekaran, 1986), but that the differences are smaller than in single-earner couples (Kessler & McCrae, 1981). The tendency for women in society generally to report poorer mental health has been attributed to their traditional roles (Gove, 1972; Gove & Tudor, 1973). Also, stress is more likely to be manifested in psychological distress by women and in physical illness by men (Jick & Mitz, 1985).

Therefore, any increase in psychological distress manifested by husbands of employed wives may be the consequence of a convergence of roles. The corollary to this might be an increase in stress-related physical illnesses, such as coronary heart disease, in employed women, as they increasingly experience the job-related pressures previously associated with male breadwinners. Generally, employed women, like their male counterparts, tend to enjoy better physical health than the unemployed with their limited roles (Verbrugge, 1983, 1984), but certain categories of employed women may be vulnerable to stress-related illness. The Framingham Heart Study identified combinations of factors, including motherhood, clerical work, and blue-collar husband, as increasing women's risk of heart disease (Haynes, Eaker, & Feinlab, 1983; Haynes, Feinlab, & Kannel, 1980). The women in this study, however, were working prior to 1960, when women's employment was discouraged; they received little support at home or at work; and clerical work was devalued and unrewarding. Evidence that contemporary American clerical women tend to be healthier than other occupational groups suggests that changes in social attitudes and conditions may have important consequences for health (Verbrugge, 1984). The combination of stressors that pose a risk to the physical health of employed women and their partners nevertheless requires clarification. Research on dual-earner couples has predominantly examined psychological manifestations of stress, but possible implications for physical health should not be overlooked.

DUAL-EARNER FAMILIES IN THE UNITED KINGDOM

If two-earner couples are defined very broadly as those in which both partners are economically active, the life-style is becoming increasingly prevalent among U.K. families without children or with children aged five or older (i.e., school age). The situation in which both partners are in full-time employment and raise children, however, remains a minority choice. Only 6.2% of married mothers with preschool-aged children and 36% of mothers whose youngest child is aged 16 or over are employed full-time outside the home (Joshi, 1984). Full-time employment of both parents of preschool-aged children in intact families thus remains exceptional and may even be perceived as "deviant." In contrast, 51.8% of married mothers of preschool children were employed in the United States in 1984, of whom 58.9% were full-time (Hoffman, 1986). In a recent U.K. national survey, 60% of the women believed that mothers of young children should not be employed, and 25% believed that they should only take a job in cases of financial necessity (Martin & Roberts, 1984). In a similar survey in the 1960s (Hunt, 1968), 93% of women believed that mothers should stay at home, or should work outside the home only if economically essential. There has, therefore, been some shift in attitudes, but it is very slight. A high proportion of employed and unemployed men also believe that mothers of young children should not be employed outside the home (Bell, McKee, & Priestly, 1983). Employed mothers of young children, therefore, are subjected to tremendous normative pressure, and their partners too are likely to be affected by societal attitudes.

Women's discontinuous working patterns remain one significant cause of their low incomes relative to men's (Joshi, 1984, but see also Gwartney-Gibbs, this volume). Equal opportunity legislation in the 1970s aims to protect women against dismissal on the grounds of pregnancy, and to provide them with rights and facilities to combine continuous careers with childbearing. Subject to certain conditions, women have the opportunity to take maternity leave, with the right to reinstatement up to 29 weeks after childbirth. In practice, however, the rights are so narrowly defined that many women do not qualify (Breugel, 1983; Daniel, 1980). Further erosions of maternity-related rights have been proposed recently in the interests of "building businesses, not barriers" (U.K. Government, 1986). Furthermore, the demand for child-care facilities far exceeds supply (Lockwood & Knowles, 1984), which, together with the prevailing assumption that children are ultimately mothers' responsibility, has meant that the majority of women have been unable to take up their reinstatement rights (Daniel, 1980). Of those who do take maternity leave, most women's experiences are favorable, but some report pressures associated with stereotyped attitudes of employers, demotion, accumulation of work during their absence, or even, in spite of the law, dismissal (Daniel, 1980; Lewis, 1986).

Stereotyped attitudes concerning parental responsibilities are also reflected in policies toward paternity or parental leave. The EEC published a European draft directive on parental leave and leave for family reasons in 1983. If adopted, this directive, which is based on the assumption that men and women are equally responsible for children, would require all member states to provide parental leave rights for either parent of a child under 2, and paid leave for pressing family reasons, such as illness of a spouse or child. The British government has persistently voted against this directive, arguing that such legislation is inappropriate and should be left to voluntary negotiations. Some form of parental and family leave is already provided by most other European countries. Paternity leave of various forms exists to some extent in the United Kingdom too, but there is no legal requirement for its provision, and many men still suffer penalties ranging from employer hostility to job loss if they take time off work around the time of the birth (Bell, McKee, & Priestly, 1983). The lack of paid leave in the case of a child's illness, which is again based on the view that mothers are, or should be, at home, is a source of considerable pressure for two-earner parents (Lewis, 1986). Recognition by a minority of organizations that they will lose valued skills, training, and experience unless they take measures to help employees accommodate domestic commitments has led to various initiatives to remove or minimize career breaks (Truman, 1986). These include part-time and flexible working, job sharing, home working, counseling, and also reentry and retainer schemes that enable career breaks to be taken without loss of seniority. Such schemes, although potentially useful, are relatively rare and tend to be aimed exclusively at women. Therefore, the spirit of the European initiative is far from influential at this stage.

The minority status of two-earner families with young children, together with state policies in relation to child-care provision and family leave, reflect the continuing belief that children are the responsibility of mothers, while the breadwinner role is the prime responsibility of fathers. These views suggest the potential for stress for those who elect to follow a "nontraditional" pattern. As both employment patterns and attitudes concerning maternal employment have changed much less in the United Kingdom than in the United States, there is obviously a need for more research based on contemporary British samples. The little evidence available suggests that most couples cope well with these pressures, but examination of case studies indicates considerable stress for certain two-earner families in an unresponsive society (Lewis, 1986).

CONCLUSIONS AND IMPLICATIONS FOR FUTURE RESEARCH AND PRACTICE

Sex Role and Ideology

Ostensibly, research on dual-earner couples and stress appears to have proceeded atheoretically (Gutek, Larwood, & Stromberg, 1986). Nevertheless, commentators have noted that most research is based, at least implicitly, in role theory (Kingston & Nock, 1985). The stress of the two-earner life-style is a consequence of roles competing for scarce time and, even more fundamentally, the uncertainty associated with roles in transition. Two-earner couples are "nontraditional" in that the breadwinner and domestic roles are combined at least to some extent for both partners, as opposed to a gender-based role division. At the same time, dual-earners are the product of their socialization, so that traditional gender role expectations, even if unarticulated, or overtly rejected, underlie pressures such as guilt and conflict in employed mothers, and the discomfort experienced by men if their major provider role is threatened by wives' high work commitment, occupational status, or income. Policies such as those in the United Kingdom, described above, which are based on stereotyped views of maternal responsibility, not only present obstacles to be overcome by dual-earner parents, but also reinforce role-related conflicts. Much of the stress associated with the two-earner life-style is not inevitable, but rather the consequence of normative pressures, traditional sex roles, or problems encountered by couples attempting to enact more egalitarian sex roles. Dual-career families are no new phenomenon, and researchers have been describing "roles in transition" for nearly two decades (Rapoport & Rapoport, 1969). A crucial question now is to consider "if" and "how" it might be possible to accelerate the transitional process by direct attempts at attitude and policy change.

Implications for Attitude and Policy Change

Corporate and state policies both reflect and influence current ideology, often helping to perpetuate norms that lag behind social reality (Rapoport & Rapoport, 1971; Walsh & Kelleher, 1987). Thus changes in policies to facilitate equal commitment to work and family by both partners who elect to adopt a dual-earner life-style may be instrumental in changing attitudes that underlie much work-family pressure.

An important step in mitigating the pressure on two-earner spouses is to promote an understanding of their dilemmas among management, where single-earner men and single or child-free women are often overrepresented (Davidson & Cooper, 1983). Management training programs might include sessions in which issues concerning dual-earner couples and related stereotypes are examined. The traditional view that women, especially mothers, are not highly committed to their jobs may become self-fulfilling, as a determinant of important organizational commitment for women, as for men, is satisfaction with promotional opportunities (Bhagat & Chassie, 1981), and assumptions about maternal responsibilities may influence promotional decisions (Rosen & Jerdee, 1974). Equally, the stereotyped view that fathers who allow family involvement to encroach upon their work are undesirable employees (Lamb, Russel, & Sagi, 1983) should be questioned.

Institutional policies such as flextime, part-time work, and job sharing, which might facilitate the combining of multiple roles for dual-earners, often fail to reduce stress for the people at whom they are aimed, because of traditional gender role attitudes (Bohen & Viveros-Long, 1981; Lee, 1983). Part-time work, for instance, is an option most frequently considered by mothers, and undertaken in addition to traditional domestic responsibilities (O'Neil, 1985), thus increasing overload and reducing promotional opportunities. Alternative work strategies could be actively encouraged for men as well as women during the stage of early parenting by the safeguarding of promotional opportunities and seniority. This may help to equalize the family-work load among spouses, and also enhance the psychological health of fathers in dual-earner families by enabling them to make a greater contribution to child care (Lee, 1983; Pleck, 1985).

The provision of good child-care facilities and parental leave including paid leave for either parent to care for a sick child are all essential measures in any attempt to change attitudes and behavior in relation to family responsibilities. The recognition that parenting is a shared venture in intact couples requires that attention be given to exploring solutions to work-family management problems for both men and women. It is imperative, however, that any policy changes should be monitored and evaluated, as employers are likely to require persuasive documentation of both individual and organizational benefit before offering policies that would support dual-earner families (Crouter, 1984).

Stress Management

Given that societal attitudes are slow to change, a crucial intermediate goal must be the identification of effective coping strategies and the design of stress management programs. Research examining strategies that enable dual-earners to resist social pressures and effectively manage multiple roles is useful but tends to look only at women (Gilbert, Holohan, & Manning, 1981; Harrison & Minor, 1978). Cognitive strategies, however, such as the recognition of societal influence, have been identified as effective means of reducing role conflict (Gilbert & Holohan, 1982) and represent teachable skills. A second line of research with implications for stress management concerns the identification of individual difference variables moderating the effects of stressors. If it is not possible to alter situations, it may be practical to reduce stress by programs for modifying Type A behavior, maximizing work commitment, or increasing internality of locus of control. Another personality variable that has been shown to moderate the effects of stress is that of personality "hardiness" (Kobasa, 1982; Kobasa & Puccetti, 1983). The "hardy" personality comprises three dimensions: commitment, control, and challenge; all of which have been discussed earlier, as relevant to the experience of stress in dual-earners. Hardiness has been shown to moderate the negative effects of interrole conflict for men (Barling, 1986) and may buffer the effects of other work-family stressors for dual-earner women and men. As it may be possible to enhance hardiness through direct training and counseling (Maddi & Kobasa, 1984), the possible moderating effect of this variable for dual-earners merits investigation.

Future Generations

The validity of research on two-earner couples is time-bound, being inextricably linked with social change. Many of the pressures facing the earliest generations of dual-earners stem from their own experiences as children in traditional single-breadwinner homes. A question for future research concerns the impact on younger generations of dual-earner couples, of being raised by employed parents struggling with the conflicts and pressures of an emergent life-style.

CONCLUSION

The evidence reviewed indicates that the potential for stress in dual-earners is largely the product of internalized and institutionalized social expectations. The institutionalization of traditional sex-role expectations is further illustrated by family policies and social attitudes in the United Kingdom. Nevertheless, most dual-earners cope well and derive positive satisfaction from their life-style, although the experiences of husbands and wives differ, and stress is also moderated by certain personality and attitudinal variables. It may be practical to design programs to enable dual-earners to avoid and manage stress. A major task for the future, however, is to consider strategies for accelerating change in societal attitudes and practice, hence possibly preventing many of the sources of stress for dual-earners.

REFERENCES

Apter, T. (1985). *Why women don't have wives: Professional success and motherhood.* London: Macmillan.

Araji, S. K. (1977). Husbands' and wives' attitude-behavior congruence on family roles. *Journal of Marriage and the Family, 39*, 309-320.

Bailyn, L. (1970). Career and family orientations of husbands and wives in relation to marital happiness. *Human Relations, 23*, 97-113.

Barling, J. (1986). Interrole conflict and marital functioning amongst employed fathers. *Journal of Occupational Behaviour, 7*(1), 1-9.

Beail, N. (1985). Fathers and infant caretaking. *Journal of Reproductive Infant Psychology, 3*, 53-64.

Beail, N., & McGuire, J. (Eds). (1982). *Fathers psychological perspectives.* London: Junction Books.

Beckman, L. J., & Hauser, B. B. (1979). The more you have, the more you do: Sex role attitudes and household behavior. *Psychology of Women Quarterly, 4*, 160-174.

Behrman, D. L. (1980). *Family and/or career: Plans of first time mothers.* Ann Arbor: University of Michigan Research Press.

Bell, C. McKee, L., & Priestly, K. (1983). *Fathers, childbirth and work.* Manchester: Equal Opportunities Commission.

Benin, M. H., & Nienstedt, B. C. (1985). Happiness in single and dual earner families: The effects of marital happiness, job satisfaction, and life cycle. *Journal of Marriage and the Family, 47*, 975-984.

Berk, S. F. (1985). *The gender factory.* New York: Plenum.

Beutell, N. J., & Greenhaus, J. H. (1982). Interrole conflict among married women: The influence of husband and wife characteristics on conflict and coping behavior. *Journal of Vocational Behavior, 21*, 99-110.

Bhagat, R. S., & Chassie, M. B. (1981). Determinants of organizational commitment in working women. *Journal of Occupational Behaviour, 2*, 17-30.

Bird, G. W., Bird, G. A., & Scruggs, M. (1984). Determinants of family task sharing: A study of husbands and wives. *Journal of Marriage and the Family, 46*, 345-355.

Bohen, B. H., & Viveros-Long, A. (1981). *Balancing jobs and family life: Do flexible work schedules help?* Philadelphia: Temple University Press.

Booth, A. (1977). Wife's employment and husband's stress: A replication and a refutation. *Journal of Marriage and the Family, 39*, 645-650.

Booth, A. (1979). Does wives' employment cause stress for husbands? *Family Coordinator, 4*, 445-449.

Brief, A. P., Rude, D. E., & Rabinowitz, S. (1983). The impact of Type A behaviour pattern on subjective workload and depression. *Journal of Occupational Behaviour, 4*, 157-164.

Breugel, I. (1983). Women's employment, legislation and the labour market. In J. Lewis (Ed.), *Women's welfare, women's rights.* London: Croom Helm.

Bryson, R., Bryson, J. B., & Johnson, M. F. (1978). Family size, satisfaction and productivity in two-earner couples. *Psychology of Women Quarterly, 3*(1), 67-77.

Burke, R. J., & Bradshaw, P. I. (1981). Occupational and life stress and the family. *Small Group Behaviour, 12*(3), 329-375.

Burke, R. J., & Desca, E. (1982). Career success and personal failure experiences and the Type A behaviour pattern. *Journal of Occupational Behaviour, 3*, 161-170.

Burke, R. J., & Weir, T. (1976). Relationship of wives' employment status to husband, wife and pair satisfaction and performance. *Journal of Marriage and the Family, 30,* 279-287.

Burke, R. J., Weir, T., & DuWors, R. E. (1979). Type A behaviour of administrators and wife's reports of marital satisfaction and well-being. *Journal of Applied Psychology, 64,* 57-65.

Burke, R. J., Weir, T., & DuWors, R. E. (1980). Work demands on administrators and spouse well-being. *Human Relations, 33*(4), 253-278.

Burnham, M. A. Pennebaker, J. W., & Glass, D. C. (1975). Time consciousness, achievement striving and the Type A coronary prone behavior pattern. *Journal of Abnormal Psychology, 84*(1), 76-79.

Caplan, R. D., & Jones, K. W. (1975). Effects of workload, role ambiguity and personality Type A on anxiety, depression and heart rate. *Journal of Applied Psychology, 60,* 713-719.

Chassin, L., Zeiss, A., Cooper, K., & Reaven, J. (1985). Role perceptions, self-role congruence and marital satisfaction in dual worker couples with pre-school children. *Social Psychology Quarterly, 48*(4), 301-311.

Chesney, M. A., & Rosenman, R. H. (1983). Specificity in stress models: Examples drawn from Type A behaviour. In C. L. Cooper (Ed.), *Stress research: Issues for the eighties.* London: John Wiley.

Clarke, A. W. (1983). The relationship between family participation and health. *Journal of Occupational Behaviour, 4,* 237-239.

Cooper, C. L., & Marshall, J. (1976). Occupational sources of stress: A review of the literature relating to coronary heart disease, and mental ill health. *Journal of Occupational Psychology, 49,* 11-28.

Cooper, C. L., & Smith, M. J. (Eds.). (1985). Job stress and blue collar work. New York: John Wiley.

Cornelius, R. R., & Averill, J. R. (1980). The influence of various types of control on psychophysiological stress reactions. *Journal of Research in Personality, 14,* 503-517.

Cox, T. (1985). Repetitive work: Occupational stress & health. In C. L. Cooper & M. J. Smith (Eds.), *Job stress and blue collar work* (pp. 83-113). New York: John Wiley.

Crosby, F. (1984). Job satisfaction and domestic life. In M. D. Lee & R. Kanuago (Eds.), *Management of work and personal life.* New York: Praeger.

Crouter, A. C. (1984). Spillover from family to work: The neglected side of the work-family interface. *Human Relations, 37*(6), 425-447.

Daniel, W. W. (1980). *Maternity rights: The experience of women.* London: Policy Studies Unit.

Davidson, M. J., & Cooper, C. L. (1983). *Stress and the woman manager.* Oxford: Martin Robertson.

Fagin, L., & Little, M. (1984). *The forsaken families.* Harmondsworth, England: Penguin.

Fendrich, M. (1984). Wives' employment & husbands' distress: A meta-analysis and a replication. *Journal of Marriage and the Family, 46,* 871-879.

Ferree, M. H. (1976). Working class jobs: Housework and paid work as sources of satisfaction. *Social Problems, 23,* 431-441.

French, J.R.P., Caplan, R. D., & Harrison, R. V. (1982). *The mechanisms of job stress and strain.* New York: John Wiley.

Fogarty, M. P., Rapoport, R., & Rapoport, R. N. (1971). *Sex, career and family.* Beverly Hills, CA: Sage.

Friedman, M., & Rosenman, R. H. (1974). *Type A behavior and your heart*. New York: Knopf.

Gilbert, L. A., & Holohan, C. K. (1982). Conflicts between student/professional, parental and self development roles: A comparison of high & low effective copers. *Human Relations, 35*, 635-648.

Gilbert, L. A., Holohan, C. K., & Manning, L. (1981). Coping with conflict between professional and maternal roles. *Family Relations, 30* , 419-426.

Glowinkowski, S. P., & Cooper, C. L. (1985). Current issues in organizational stress research. *Bulletin of the British Psychological Society, 38*, 212-216.

Gould, S., & Werbel, J. D. (1983). Work involvement: A comparison of dual wage earner and single wage earner families. *Journal of Applied Psychology, 2*, 313-319.

Gove, W. R. (1972). The relationship between sex roles, marital status and mental illness. *Social Forces, 51*, 34-44.

Gove, W. R., & Tudor, J. (1973). Adult sex roles and mental illness. *American Journal of Sociology, 78*, 812-835.

Greenhaus, J. H., & Kopelman, R. E. (1981). Conflict between work and non-work roles: Implications for the career planning process. *Human Resource Planning, 4*, 1-10.

Gutek, B. A., Larwood, L., & Stromberg, A. H. (1986). Women at work. In C. L. Cooper & T. Robertson (Eds.), *International review of industrial and organizational psychology* (pp. 217-234). London: John Wiley.

Gutek, B. A., Nakumura, C. Y., & Nieva, V. F. (1980). The interdependence of work and family roles. *Journal of Occupational Behaviour, 2*(1), 1-17.

Hall, D. T. (1972). A model of coping with role conflict. The role behavior of college educated women. *Administrative Science Quarterly, 1*(7), 471-486.

Handy, C. (1978). Going against the grain: Working couples and greedy occupations. In R. Rapoport & R. N. Rapoport (Eds.), *Working couples*. New York: Harper & Row.

Harrison, A. O., & Minor, J. H. (1978). Interrole conflict, coping strategies and satisfaction among black working wives. *Journal of Marriage and the Family, 40*, 799-805.

Haynes, S. G., Eaker, E. D., & Feinlab, M. (1983). The effect of employment, family and job stress on coronary heart disease patterns in women. In E. B. Gold (Ed.), *The changing risk of disease in women: An epidemiological approach*. Lexington, MA: D. C. Heath.

Haynes, S. G., Feinlab, M., & Kannel, W. B. (1980). The relationship of psychosocial factors to coronary heart disease in the Framingham Study. *American Journal of Epidemiology, 111*, 37-58.

Hiller, D. V., & Philliber, W. W. (1982). Predicting marital and career success among dual career couples. *Journal of Marriage and the Family, 44*, 53-62.

Hock, E., Gnezde, M. T., & McBride, S. W. (1984). Mothers of infants: Attitudes towards employment and motherhood following birth of the first child. *Journal of Marriage and the Family, 46*, pp. 425-431.

Hoffman, L. W. (1979). Maternal employment: 1979. *American Psychologist, 34*(10), 859-865.

Hoffman, L. W. (1986). Work, family and the child. In M. S. Pollock & R. O. Perloff (Eds.), *Psychology and work: Master lectures*. Washington, DC: American Psychological Association.

Holmes, T. H., & Masuda, M. (1974). Life change & illness susceptibility. In B. S. Dohrenwend & B. P. Dohrenwend (Eds.), *Stressful life events: Their nature and effects* (pp. 45-72). New York: John Wiley.

Holmstrom, L. L. (1972). *The two-career family*. Cambridge, MA: Schenkman.

Holohan, C. K., & Gilbert, L. A. (1979). Conflict between major life roles: Women and men in dual career couples. *Human Relations, 32*(6), 451-467.

House, E. A. (1986). Sex role orientation and mental satisfaction in dual and one provider couples. *Sex Roles, 14*, 245-259.

Howard, J. H., Cunningham, D. A., & Rechnitzer, P. A. (1977). Work patterns associated with Type A behaviour: A managerial population. *Human Relations, 30*(9), 825-836.

Hunt, A. (1968). *A survey of women's employment*. London: Her Majesty's Stationery Office.

Hunt, J. G., & Hunt, L. L. (1982). Dual-career families: Vanguard of the future, or residue of the past? In J. Aldous (Ed.), *Two paychecks: Life in dual earner families*. Beverly Hills, CA: Sage.

Huser, W. R., & Grant, C. W. (1978). A study of husbands and wives from dual career and traditional career families. *Psychology of Women Quarterly, 3*(1), 78-87.

Jenkins, C. D. (1971). Psychological and social precursors of coronary disease. *New England Journal of Medicine, 284*(5), 244-255.

Jick, T. D., & Burke, R. J. (1982). Occupational stress, recent findings and new directions. *Journal of Occupational Behaviour, 3*, 1-3.

Jick, T. D., & Mitz, C. F. (1985). Sex differences in work stress. *Academy of Management Review, 10*(3), 408-420.

Johnson, C. L., & Johnson, F. A. (1980). Parenthood, marriage and careers: Situational constraints and role strain. In Repitone Rockwell (Eds.), *Dual career couples*. London: Sage.

Joshi, H. (1984). *Women's participation in paid work: Further analysis of the women in employment survey*, Paper no. 45. London: Department of Employment.

Kamerman, S. B. (1980). *Parenting in an unresponsive society*. New York: Free Press.

Kanter, R. M. (1977). *Work and family in the United States*. New York: Russel Sage.

Kasl, S. V. (1978). Epidemiological contributions to the study of work stress. In C. L. Cooper & R. Payne (Eds.), *Stress at work* (pp. 3-51). New York: Wiley.

Keith, P. M., & Schafer, R. B. (1980). Role strain and depression in two job families. *Family Relations, 29*, 483-488.

Kessler, R. C., & McCrae, J. A. (1981). Trends in the relationship between sex and psychological distress: 1957-1976. *American Sociological Review, 46*, 443-452.

Kessler, R. C., & McCrae, J. A. (1982). The effect of wives' employment on the mental health of married men and women. *American Sociological Review, 47*, 216-227.

Kingston, P. W., & Nock, S. L. (1985). Consequences of the family work day. *Journal of Marriage and the Family, 47*, 621-629.

Kobasa, S. (1982). The hardy personality: Towards on social psychology of stress & health. In G. S. Sanders & J. Suls (Eds.), *Social psychology of stress and illness*. Hillsdale, NJ: Lawrence Erlbaum.

Kobasa, S., & Puccetti, M. (1983). Personality and social resources in stress resistance. *Journal of Personality & Social Psychology, 45*, 839-850.

Krausz, M., & Freibach, N. (1983). Effects of flexible working time for employed women upon satisfaction, strains and absenteeism. *Journal of Occupational Psychology, 56*, 155-159.

Lamb, M. E., Russell, G., & Sagi, A. (1983). *Fatherhood and family policy*. Hillsdale, NJ: Lawrence Erlbaum.

Langrish, S. (1981). Why don't women progress to management jobs? *Business Graduates, 11*, 12-13.

LaRossa, R., & LaRossa, M. M. (1981). *Transition to parenthood: How infants change families*. Beverly Hills, CA: Sage.

Lazarus, R. S. (1966). *Psychological stress and the coping process*. New York: McGraw Hill.

Lee, R. A. (1983). Flexi-time and conjugal roles. *Journal of Occupational Behaviour, 4*, 297-315.

Lefcourt, H. M. (1966). *Locus of control*. Hillsdale, NJ: Lawrence Erlbaum.

Lein, L. (1979). Male participation in home life: Impact of social support and breadwinner responsibility on the allocation of tasks. *Family Coordinator, 26*, 489-495.

Lewis, S. N. (1986). *Occupational stress and two-earner couples: A lifestage approach*. Unpublished doctoral dissertation, University of Manchester, Institute of Science & Technology.

Lewis, S. N., & Cooper, C. L. (1983). The stress of combining occupational and parental roles: A review of the literature. *Bulletin of the British Psychological Society, 36*, 341-345.

Lockwood, B., & Knowles, W. (1984). Women at work in Great Britain. In M. J. Davidson & C. L. Cooper (Eds.), *Working women: An international survey*. Chichester: John Wiley.

Maddi, S. R., & Kobasa, S. C. (1984). *The hardy executive: Health under stress*. Illinois: Dow-Jones Irwin.

Maret, E., & Feinlab, B. (1984). The distribution of household labor among women in dual earner families. *Journal of Marriage and the Family, 46*, 357-364.

Margolis, B., Kroes, W., & Quinn, R. (1974). Job stress: An unlisted occupational hazard. *Journal of Occupational Medicine, 1*, 659-661.

Marks, S. (1977). Multiple roles and role strain: Some notes on human energy, time and commitment. *American Sociological Review, 42*, 921-938.

Martin, J., & Roberts, C. (1984). Women and employment: A lifetime perspective. London: Office of Population Consensus and Surveys, Her Majesty's Stationery Office.

Monat, A., & Lazarus, R. S. (Eds.). (1985). *Stress and coping*. New York: Columbia University Press.

Moss, P., & Fonda, N. (1980). *Work and family*. London: Temple Smith.

Nieva, V. (1985). Work and family linkages. In L. Larwood, A. H. Stromberg, & B. A. Gutek (Eds.), *Women and work: An annual review* (Vol. 1). Beverly Hills, CA: Sage.

Nock, S. L., & Kingston, P. W. (1984). The family work day. *Journal of Marriage and the Family, 46*, 333-343.

Nyquist, L., Slivken, K., Spence, J. T., & Helmreich, R. L. (1985). Household responsibilities in middle class couples: The contribution of demographic and personality variables. *Sex Roles, 12*(1/2), 15-34.

Oakley, A. (1974). *Housewife*. London: Allen Lane.

O'Neil, J. (1985). Role differentiation and the gender gap in wage rates. In L. Larwood, A. H. Stromberg, & B. A. Gutek (Eds.), *Women and work: An annual review* (Vol. 1). Beverly Hills, CA: Sage.

Paloma, M. M., & Garland, T. (1971). The married professional women: A study in the tolerance of domestication. *Journal of Marriage and the Family, 33*, 531-540.

Pearlin, L. I. (1975). Sex roles and depression. In N. Dalen & H. Ginsberg (Eds.), *Life span developmental psychology*. New York: Academic Press.

Pendleton, B. F., Paloma, M. M., & Garland, T. N. (1982). An approach to quantifying the needs of dual career families. *Human Relations, 35*(1), 69-82.

Pleck, J .H. (1977). The work-family role system. *Social Problems, 24*, 417-427.

Pleck, J. H. (1981). *The male sex role.* Cambridge: M.I.T. Press.

Pleck, J. H. (1985). *Working wives/working husbands.* Beverly Hills, CA: Sage.

Pleck, J. H., & Staines, G. L. (1983). Work schedules and work family conflict in two-earner couples. In J. Aldous (Ed.), *Two paychecks: Life in dual earner families.* Beverly Hills, CA: Sage.

Pleck, J. H., & Staines, G. L. (1985). Work schedules and family life in two-earner couples. *Journal of Family Issues, 6*(1), 68-82.

Pleck, J. H., Staines, G. L., & Lang, L. (1978). *Work and family life: First reports on work-family interference and workers' formal child care arrangements, from the 1977 Quality of Employment Survey* (Working Paper no. 11). Cambridge, MA: Wellesley College, Center for Research on Women.

Pollert, A. (1981). *Girls, wives, factory lives.* London: Macmillan.

Pritchard, R. D., Dunnette, M. D., & Jorgenson, D. O. (1972). Effects on perceptions of equity and inequity on worker performance and satisfaction. *Journal of Applied Psychology, 56*, 75-94.

Rapoport, R., & Rapoport, R. N. (1969). The dual-earner family: A variant pattern and social change. *Human Relations, 22*, 3-30.

Rapoport, R., & Rapoport, R. N. (1971). *Dual career families.* London: Penguin.

Rapoport, R., & Rapoport, R. N. (1976). *Dual career families re-examined.* New York: Harper & Row.

Rapoport, R. N., & Rapoport, R. (1978). Dual career families: Progress and prospects. *Marriage and Family Review, 1*(5), 1-12.

Roberts, R., & O'Keefe, S. (1981). Sex differences in depression. *Journal of Health and Social Behaviour, 21*, 33-42.

Robinson, J. P. (1977). *How Americans use time: A socio-psychological analysis.* New York: Praeger.

Rosen, B., & Jerdee, T. H. (1974). Influence of sex-role stereotypes on personnel decisions. *Journal of Applied Psychology, 59*(1), 9-14.

Rosenfield, S. (1980). Sex differences in depression: Do women always have higher rates? *Journal of Health & Social Behaviour, 21*, 33-42.

Rosenman, R. H., Brand, R. J., Jenkins, C. D., Friedman, M., & Wurm, M. (1975). Coronary heart disease in the Western Collaborative Group Study: Final follow-up experiences of eight years. *Journal of American Medical Association, 233*, 872-887.

Rosenman, R. H., & Chesney, M. A. (1980). The relationship of Type A behaviour to coronary heart disease. *Activistas Nervosa Superior, 22*(1), 1-45.

Rosenman, R. H., Friedman, M., & Strauss, R. (1964). A predictive study of CHD. *Journal of American Medical Association, 189*, 15-22.

Rueschemeyer, M. (1981). *Professional work and marriage: An East-West comparison.* London: Macmillan.

Schafer, R. B., & Keith, P. M. (1980). Equity and depression among married couples. *Social Psychology Quarterly, 43*(4), 430-435.

Seidenberg, R. (1973). *Corporate wives: Corporate casualties.* New York: AMACOM.

Sekaran, U. (1982). An investigation of the career salience of men and women in dual career families. *Journal of Vocational Behaviour, 20*(1), 11-119.

Sekaran, U. (1983). Factors influencing the quality of life in dual career families. *Journal of Occupational Psychology, 56*(2), 129-138.

Sekaran, U. (1985). The path to mental health: An exploratory study of husbands and wives in dual career families. *Journal of Occupational Psychology, 58*(2), 129-138.

Sekaran, U. (1986). Significant differences in quality of life factors and their correlates: A function of differences in career orientation, or gender? *Sex Roles, 4*, 261-279.

Selye, H. (1956). The stress concept: Past, present and future. In C. L. Cooper (Ed.), *Stress research: Issues for the eighties*. New York: John Wiley.

Sharpe, S. (1984). *Double identity: The lives of working mothers*. Harmondsworth: Penguin.

Shimmin, S. (1984). Pressures on factory women; between the devil and the deep blue sea. *Ergonomics, 27*(3), 511-519.

Staines, G. L., & Pleck, J. H. (1984). Non-standard work schedules, and family life. *Journal of Applied Psychology, 69*(3), 513-523.

Truman, C. (1986). *A positive approach to the career break* (A report to the Manpower Services Commission). Manchester: University of Manchester, Institute of Science and Technology.

U.K. Government. (1986). *Building businesses not barriers* (U.K. Government White Paper). London: Her Majesty's Stationery Office.

Verbrugge, L. H. (1983). Multiple roles and physical health of women and men. *Journal of Health and Social Behaviour, 24*, 16-30.

Verbrugge, L. H. (1984). Physical health of clerical workers in the U.S., Framingham and Detroit. *Women & Health, 9*(1), 17-41.

Voydanoff, P., & Kelly, R. F. (1984). Determinants of work-related family problems among employed parents. *Journal of Marriage and the Family, 46*, 881-892.

Waldron, I. (1978a). The coronary prone behavior pattern, blood pressure, employment and socio-economic status in women. *Journal of Psychosomatic Research, 22*, 79-87.

Waldron, I. (1978b). Type A behavior pattern and coronary heart disease in men and women. *Social Science and Medicine, 128*, 167-170.

Walsh, D. C., & Kelleher, S. E. (1987). The "corporate perspective" on the health of women at work. In A. H. Stromberg, L. Larwood, & B. A. Gutek (Eds.), *Women and work: An annual review* (Vol. 2, pp. 117-142). Newbury Park, CA: Sage.

Wardwell, W. I., Hyman, M. M., & Bahnson, C. B. (1964). Stress and coronary disease in three field studies. *Journal of Chronic Diseases, 17*, 73-84.

Weingarten, K. (1978). The employment pattern of professional couples and their distribution of involvement in their family. *Psychology of Women Quarterly, 3*(1), 43-52.

Yogev, S. (1982a). Are professional women overworked? Objective versus subjective perception of role loads. *Journal of Occupational Psychology, 55*(3), 165-170.

Yogev, S., & Brett, J. (1985a). Patterns of work and family involvement among single and dual earner couples. *Journal of Applied Psychology, 70*(4), 754-768.

Yogev, S., & Brett, J. (1985b). Perceptions of the division of household and childcare and marital satisfaction. *Journal of Marriage and the Family, 47*, 609-618.

7

Women's Work Experience and the "Rusty Skills" Hypothesis

A RECONCEPTUALIZATION AND REEVALUATION OF THE EVIDENCE

PATRICIA A. GWARTNEY-GIBBS

This research contrasts two ways of examining lifetime work experience in relation to earnings: as *characteristics* (intensity, duration with employers, mobility between employers, and intermittency) and as *length* (months employed or not). Distinguishing between the characteristics and the length of work experience disentangles two previously confused concepts in human capital theory: time spent out of labor force and intermittency (multiple labor force entries or exits). Highly detailed work histories from a purposive sample of three groups of married women show the expected patterns of work interruption associated with childbearing, but challenge the notion that employment discontinuity is penalized in later earnings. Rather, the results support the hypothesis that, net of time spent out the labor force, intermittency is a rational strategy for maintaining work skills. The conclusions assess the implications of this research for human capital theory, discrimination theory, and public policy.

The wage gap between the sexes remains one of the most persistent research puzzles in economics and sociology. Repeated efforts to explain it have

AUTHOR'S NOTE: This research benefited from the comments of the reviewers and editors of this volume, and, in the past, M. Corcoran, R. Farley, P. Siegel, and L. Waite. Thanks go to Linda Kelm and Ron Larsen for word-processing assistance. The material in this project was prepared in part under Grant No. DD-26-80-025 from the Social Science Research Council. Researchers undertaking such projects under Council sponsorship are encouraged to express freely their professional judgment. Therefore, the points of view of opinions stated in this document do not necessarily represent the official position or policy of the Social Science Research Council.

produced inconsistent results and succeeded in accounting for only a portion of the male-female earnings differential. Women's work experience has been a promising factor in that explanation, because researchers and policymakers often argue that the quantity and quality of their experience is substantially different from men's.

Intermittency in employment—that is, the idea that women go in and out of the labor force in response to marriage and childbearing—has been a major explanation of the wage gap, particularly in human capital theory. In their now-classic study, Mincer and Polachek (1974) characterized *intermittency* as the "discontinuity of work experience" due to "several entries into and exits from the labor force after leaving school." They attributed intermittency in employment to women's traditional household and child-caring responsibilities in families' divisions of home and market labor. During time spent out of the labor force work, skills become "rusty" or "atrophy," thereby lowering the value of women's human capital and subsequent earning.[1] Even though numerous researchers have documented that structural characteristics of employment (such as occupational segregation, industrial sector, and firms' characteristics) can detrimentally influence women's earnings independently of their individual characteristics (e.g., Roos, 1981; Taylor, Gwartney-Gibbs, & Farley, 1986), this notion of intermittency in women's work histories remains a pervasive and intuitively appealing explanation of the wage gap between the sexes, even in the structuralist literature.

Recently, Treiman (1985) and others (Hartmann, Roos, & Treiman, 1985; O'Neill, 1985) have called for a reexamination of women's lifetime work experience and its relationship to earnings in order to help understand sex differentials in employment. Despite a long tradition of sociological research on work histories (e.g., Broom & Smith, 1963; Davidson & Anderson, 1937; Form & Miller, 1949; Gusfield, 1961; Reiss, 1961; Wilensky, 1961) and numerous related studies on job and occupational mobility, detailed work histories of women remain relatively unexamined (for exceptions, see Mulvey, 1963; Palmer, 1954), due in part to a lack of adequate data (see Treiman, 1985). The research reported here uses a sociological approach to study women's work histories and focuses on economists' concerns about intermittency and its relationship to earnings.

Below, I argue that the concept of intermittency in human capital research has been both inadequately modeled and inadequately measured. To substantiate these claims, I first review the theory and findings regarding women's work intermittency and earnings in key previous studies, with critical attention to these studies' measurement of intermittency as the *length* of nonwork. I then present a new method of modeling work histories, which captures the *characteristics* of work experience, including an exact measure of intermittency. I illustrate this new model by examining the lifetime work histories of a purposive sample of three groups of married women: employed childless, employed mothers, and nonemployed mothers. The results of the new model reveal distinct patterns of work experience for the groups and support most hypotheses regarding the relationship between work experience and earnings. The results fail, however, to support the "rusty skills" hypothesis. Instead, they provide evidence for the alternative hypothesis that intermittency is a rational strategy for keeping work skills from depreciating during long spells out of the labor force, and should therefore be rewarded. I conclude by assessing the theoretical and public policy implications of these findings.

KEY PRIOR RESEARCH ON
INTERMITTENCY IN WOMEN'S WORK

Mincer and Polachek's (1974) theoretical work puts a great deal of emphasis on the extent to which intermittency in women's work lowers their wages. They, and subsequent researchers (e.g., Corcoran, 1978; Corcoran & Duncan, 1979), hypothesize that intermittency in past work experience has the following consequences: (a) less human capital investment (i.e., general and firm-specific training) occurs overall for those with discontinuous labor force participation; (b) the timing of human capital investments, especially specific training, is concentrated later in life; (c) human capital, especially general training, depreciates in value during spells of nonemployment; that is, work skills "get rusty" or "atrophy" in periods of nonuse.

For the first two hypotheses, well-established empirical support exists. Women with children, who are the most likely to have discontinuous work experience, accumulate less work experience overall than women without children (Mincer & Polachek, 1974). In addition, they tend to concentrate this human capital investment in the years after children have reached school age, whereas women without children tend to invest more heavily early in adulthood. Thus discontinuities in work experience associated with childbearing do indeed appear to affect the timing and overall accumulation of employment-related human capital investments over the lifetime.

Empirical tests of the depreciation, or rusty skills, hypothesis, however, have produced mixed results. Mincer and Polachek interpreted negative regression coefficients on the length of spells of nonemployment as the depreciation of work skills. But in a replication of their work, after correcting for coding errors in the National Longitudinal Survey (NLS) work history data, Sandell and Shapiro (1978) found that the size of those coefficients dropped by a factor of three and became insignificant. In replications using data from the Panel Study of Income Dynamics (PSID),[2] Corcoran (1978) and Corcoran and Duncan (1979) found negative coefficients on "home time" for women aged 30 to 45, like Mincer and Polachek, but these results disappeared when the same model was applied to women aged 18 to 64. Mincer and Ofek (1982) showed that women are penalized for intermittency upon reentry to the labor force, but these penalties soon evaporate with continued work; they interpret this as the "restoration" of human capital.[3]

The inconsistency of empirical support regarding the depreciation hypothesis may be due to inadequate data, or inadequate conceptualizations of intermittency and lifetime work experience, or both. For example, even though the notion of intermittency was crucial to Mincer and Polachek's theoretical framework, they did not measure intermittency directly, that is, as the number of employment interruptions. Rather, the length of nonemployment between predetermined lifetime events (school, marriage, and the birth of the first child) was used as a proxy for intermittency. The length of time spent unemployed or out of the labor force is clearly not synonymous with the number of spells of nonemployment. Moreover, *length of work* in the NLS retrospective work history data used by Mincer and Polachek was defined as the number of years a woman worked six months or more. If women's jobs are intermittent and of short duration, as the authors suggest, then jobs that lasted less than six months were not counted as employment, and therefore the length of nonemployment is likely to have been overestimated. (The length of nonemployment may have been underestimated, however, for those who worked less than a year but more than six months. The net effect of these countervailing biases is unknown.)

Corcoran (1978) and Corcoran and Duncan (1979) improved upon Mincer and Polachek by adding a direct, but crude, measure of intermittency—a dummy variable indicating that an individual experienced two or more interruptions of a year or longer in the work life. They also included measures of the length of employment and nonemployment that were not bounded by predetermined lifetime events. These different measures revealed that the continuity of work experience and the frequency of labor force withdrawals did not significantly affect later earnings of women in the PSID.

RECONCEPTUALIZING INTERMITTENCY AND WORK EXPERIENCE

The brief review above shows that, even though human capital theorists' ideas about intermittency and earnings seem reasonable, empirical results on the rusty skills hypothesis have been unstable and sensitive to how intermittency has been measured. Particularly confusing has been a tendency not to distinguish between (a) the length of nonemployment and (b) multiple labor force entries (or exits) when operationalizing intermittency.

Disentangling the concept of intermittency from the concept of months out of the labor force raises theoretical questions: If employment skills erode only, or primarily, as a function of time, then researchers need to be concerned only with some count of time spent out of the labor force (and, presumably, time out of school or training, because these are investments in human capital, like work experience). But such measures do not capture intermittency *per se*. Intermittency involves entries into, or withdrawals from, the labor force, and implicitly raises notions of the timing of nonemployment in individuals' work histories. Multiple labor force exits may be a crude indicator of rusty skills, but more likely they signal unreliability to future employers, depending on the number of previous exits and the length of previous employment spells. On the other hand, multiple labor force entries may signal a taste for employment, particularly among homemakers whose "first jobs" are their households. During long spells out of the labor force, periodic reentries may be desirable, from social learning theory, to keep skills honed. (By definition, the sum of labor force entries for employed persons is one greater than the sum of exits.)

Substantively, the distinction between intermittency and time spent out of the labor force means that someone who has accumulated 100 months of nonemployment in several discrete spells may receive different penalties for rusty skills than someone else who has accumulated 100 months of nonemployment all at once, even though they both may have accumulated 200 months of employment experience at different points in their lives. Defined in this way, intermittency is a *characteristic* of lifetime work experience that should have a net effect on later earnings over and above the effects of the *length* of nonemployment. While the length of nonemployment provides information about the *quantity* of an individual's stock of human capital, intermittency provides information about the *quality* of that human capital.

Whether the net effect of intermittency will be negative or positive, however, is open to interpretation. The rational actor may have work history patterns that exhibit both long nonemployment and many short spells of work, as a strategy for maintaining work skills (general training). Under such circumstances, the length of nonemployment may bear a net negative relationship to later earnings, but intermittency should have a net positive effect. On the other hand, many short spells of work may indicate to employers that the new hire is at risk to dropping out again and is therefore not a good candidate for on-the-job training. This may result in a net negative relationship with earnings for both intermittency and the length of nonemployment, at least in the short term.

Distinguishing intermittency from unemployment in this manner helps to clarify aspects of both human capital theory and, regarding employers' behavior, discrimination theory. Still, these notions of work experience capture only part of the richness of individuals' work histories that may have consequences for later earnings. Within one spell of employment, for example, individuals may change employers, work for long or short durations with employers, and work part- or full-time. These variations in work experience are likely to influence future employers' hiring and wage-setting decisions, as well as their willingness to invest in workers' training. Below, I develop hypotheses for three additional characteristics of lifetime work experience that may also add to the understanding of the effects of work experience on earnings, namely: mobility between employers, the duration of work with employers, and the intensity of past work.

Mobility between employers. The concept of intermittency, that is, multiple spells of employment, may be distinguished from mobility, that is, multiple employers within a spell of work. Intermittency measures the number of discrete spells of nonemployment (or employment), but workers may have several employers within one continuous spell of work.

Mobility between employers can occur in several forms in an individual's work life, each with different consequences for later earnings (see Felmlee, 1982). First, multiple employers within a spell of work may be viewed as strategic job changing. Workers may change employers to move up occupational ladders and to take advantage of new opportunities, such as higher earnings, greater prestige, and more opportunity for promotion. Strategic job changing may augment an individual's human capital and result in higher earnings later on.

On the other hand, mobility between employers may be viewed as job instability. Frequent employer changes within a spell of work may be due to dissatisfaction with earnings, hours, job tasks, or opportunities, or to being fired or laid off. This kind of mobility is unlikely to augment workers' general or specific training, and may result in being labeled unreliable by potential employers.

Duration. The duration of time spent with an employer indicates the degree of seniority and tenure within a firm, as well as the amount of firm-specific training received. Workers who have had long attachments to prior employers are likely to be viewed by prospective employers as more reliable and as better risks for on-the-job training than workers with short attachments.

Intensity. The intensity of past work experience also influences later earnings. Corcoran (1978) and Corcoran and Duncan (1979) found that the proportion of years spent working full-time significantly increased later earnings. Although their measure does not account for varying levels of part-time employment over the work life, it suggests that people who are employed part-time may not accrue as much (or the same kind of) firm-specific training as full-time workers do. Part-time employment may signal that women workers in particular are constrained by location and family responsibilities.

Precisely how part-time work experience affects later earnings encompasses several possibilities. Part-time work may be worth proportionally less; that is, 200 months worked half-time may be worth half as much to later earnings as 200 months worked full-time. Alternatively, part-time work may be worth little or nothing at all to later earnings if subsequent employers discount it or if employers do not invest in training part-time workers.

The earnings effects of these four characteristics of work experience— intermittency, mobility, duration, and intensity—are expected to be contingent upon the other characteristics. Ten years of part-time employment with several employers broken by several spells of nonemployment, for example, may be worth less than ten years of continuous part-time employment with one employer. These characteristics of lifetime work experience represent aspects of the quality of individual's work histories that may inform both the hiring and the wage-determination decisions of prospective and current employers, independent of the quantity (or length) of past employment or lack of employment.

This reconceptualization of work experience in terms of characteristics rather than length has the added advantage of being easily modeled. Equation 1 expresses the characteristics of work experience parsimoniously:

$$W_i = H_i * D_i * E_i * S_i = \frac{W_i}{m_i} * \frac{m_i}{e_i} * \frac{e_i}{S_i} * S_i \qquad [1]$$

where, for the i-th woman: W_i = total hours worked in the lifetime; H_i = Intensity: average hours of work per month of work; D_i = Duration: average months of work per employer; E_i = Mobility: average number of employers per spell of work; S_i = Intermittency: total number of spells of work; m_i = total number of months of work; e_i = total number of employers.

The measures of intensity, duration and mobility are quotients derived from the number of hours, months, employers, and spells worked in the lifetime. Total lifetime work experience, W_i, is defined as the product of the four components given above.

The work history data required to implement this new model of work experience must be highly detailed, including information on hours and months worked for each employer over the work life, as well as information on periods of nonwork. The PSID and NLS of Mature Women contain some detailed data on women's work at selected points in the life course, but not at points in between and without sufficient detail for the model proposed above. Hill's (1977) and Maret's (1983) analyses of women's work histories from the PSID and NLS, respectively, use models of work experience similar to the one presented here, but reflect the limitations of these data sets (see also Angle, 1980). Detailed continuous-event or retrospective work histories on a large, national sample of women are not available in the United States, although they are available in some other countries (see Treiman, 1985). For these reasons, and for hypothesis testing, I test the new model of work experience presented above using highly detailed retrospective work histories from a somewhat unusual data source.

METHODS

Data and Sample

The data used in this investigation have exact measures of the timing of women's labor force entries and exits, as well as hours and months worked, and employers for every job held in the lifetime. The data were gathered in the fall 1978 "Study of Family Life" by the Survey Research Center at the University of Michigan. Interviews conducted with 299 married couples in the Detroit metropolitan area included detailed retrospective histories of work, education, marital status, and childbearing for both husbands and wives.[4] Only data for wives are examined in this analysis. All of the women in the sample are White, aged 30 to 45 in 1978[5], married at least five years, and (if working) employed 20 or more hours per week for pay for at least the prior year.

The sample was stratified into three types of married couples: The first group comprises dual-earner couples without children (n = 68); the second, dual-earner couples with children (n = 116); and the third, single-earner couples (husband working, wife out of the labor force) with children (n = 115). The three types of couples were identified and sampled independently. A comparison of the sample to the Detroit SMSA and the nation revealed that the two groups of mothers are similar to comparable groups of women in the population (Gwartney-Gibbs, 1981). The childless women are, however, a "rare element"; results for them are presented for illustrative and comparative purposes, but can be generalized only with caution.

The three types of women represent "ideal types" in married women's degrees of labor force attachment over the work life.[6] Comparisons among them are expected to show the greatest possible variation in both length and characteristics of work experience for married women. The childless women are expected to have built their work lives around childlessness and to adhere most closely to the male model of human capital investment over the lifetime, including virtually continuous work histories. The employed mothers are expected to have discontinuous work experience, due to the demands of childbearing and child rearing. Comparison of this group to the prior group allows me to determine how children, net of marriage, effect the length and characteristics of work experience and subsequent earnings. The nonemployed mothers are expected to evidence the weakest labor force attachments.

Demographic profiles of the three groups of women indicate that the childless women are generally younger and therefore less experienced, but better educated, married later, with higher earnings and combined family incomes, and have spent a slightly smaller proportion of their work lives in female-typed occupations than the two groups of women with children (Gwartney-Gibbs, 1981). Differences between the employed and nonemployed mothers in age, education, ages at marriage and first birth, number of children, and household income are insignificant.

Measures of Work Experience

To calculate the four characteristics of lifetime work experience presented earlier, W_i (total hours of work from the end of high school to the date of the interview) was estimated as the number of hours worked per week on each job, multiplied by the number of months worked on each job, times 4.333 (assuming 4.333 weeks in each month), summed across jobs. Then, using information on total number of months worked, number of employers, and number of spells of work (delineated by entries into/exits from the labor force), W_i was broken down into the four components that characterize lifetime work experience, that is, intensity, duration, mobility, and intermittency.

Next, three mutually exclusive, but not uncorrelated, measures of the length of time spent employed and not employed were created: (a) number of months spent out of the labor force or school;[7] (b) number of months of tenure with the current employer; and (c) number of months of work experience prior to tenure with the current employer. These direct measures of the length of lifetime work experience, when summed together with time spent in education, account for the total period since respondents were approximately age 6. In the next section, these measures are examined and compared for the three types of women.

Analysis

The analysis explores characteristics of lifetime work experience as a supplement and as an alternative to measures of the lengths of employment and nonemployment, with particular attention to different patterns of work experience associated with the employment and parental statuses of the three groups of married women, and to the consequences of these different patterns for later earnings.

The analysis begins with a descriptive discussion of the length and characteristics of work experience for the three groups of married women. To test hypotheses about differences between employed childless women and employed mothers, and between employed mothers and nonemployed mothers, t-tests of differences in means are used.

To examine the earnings effects of the length and characteristics of work experience, ordinary least squares regressions are used. Three basic models are estimated: The first includes measures of the *length* of employment and nonemployment; the second includes measures of the *characteristics* of work experience; and the third includes both. The models are reestimated including a dummy variable for parental status, and then reestimated again to allow for interactive effects between parental status and the other independent variables in predicting earnings. Analyses of covariance are used to test for the equality of coefficients and intercepts between the two groups of employed women.

RESULTS

Descriptive Discussion of
Lifetime Work Experience

The childless employed women in the sample are expected to have had more intense lifetime work experience, greater duration of work per employer, and less intermittency in their work histories than employed mothers, because their work lives have not been constrained by the responsibilities of childbearing and child rearing. The results confirm these expectations (Table 7.1). The average childless woman in the sample worked 162 hours per working month (full-time), compared to just 147 hours for working mothers. Women without children averaged 47 months per employer for 5.25 employers over the lifetime. Although the employed mothers had about the same number of employers, they averaged only 28 months per employer, significantly less. Mobility between employers was also significantly higher for childless women than employed mothers: 3.3 employers per spell versus 2.1. This is not so surprising, however, considering that the average length of spells for the childless women is more than twice as long as for the employed mothers: 115 months compared to 54 months, respectively.

The hypothesized differences are also evident for intermittency and months out of the labor force. Women without children averaged two long spells of employment in the lifetime, with only 4.25 months spent, on average, between the two spells. The employed women with children averaged three spells of employment, with 77 months out of the labor force distributed between them. Childless women averaged significantly greater tenure with their current employers and hours of work in the previous year, as well as somewhat greater work experience prior to tenure. These results confirm that the presence of children is related to important differences in women's patterns of lifetime work experience.

Among the two groups of women with children, those employed are expected to have had more months of work experience than those not employed, but there is no a priori reason to expect that the intensity, duration, mobility, or intermittency of past work should be different. These two groups differ significantly, however, on nearly every measure of lifetime work experience.

The work histories of employed mothers are characterized by greater duration of months with employers, but lower intensity (hours of work) than nonemployed mothers. The latter tend to work in brief but intense bursts; that is, employed mothers averaged 147 hours per working month, compared to 156 hours per month for nonemployed mothers. But they tended to work somewhat longer with employers, averaging 28 months per employer for 5.6 employers, whereas the nonemployed mothers averaged only 22 months per employer for 4 employers.

The lengths of employment and nonemployment for the two groups of mothers are virtually opposites. Employed mothers averaged 137 months of work and 77 months of nonwork, while the others averaged 71 months of work and 131 months of nonwork. Given these patterns, the greater intermittency of employed mothers (3.1 spells of work, on average, compared to 2.2 for nonemployed mothers) may signal a commitment or taste for paid work (particularly part-time work), rather than a lack of such traits.

Overall, these descriptive results show significantly different patterns in both the quantity and the quality of lifetime work experience associated with different employment and parental statuses. Married women in the sample who are childless evince greater continuity, intensity, and duration in their work histories than women with children, as expected. Employed mothers' work histories show greater discontinuity and less intensity of work than nonemployed mothers, but

TABLE 7.1

Descriptive Statistics on Characteristics and Length of Lifetime Work Experience

Lifetime Work Experience Variables	Employment-Parental Status						t-Tests of Difference in Means	
	I. Employed, Childless		II. Employed Mothers		III. Nonemployed Mothers		Is to IIs[a]	IIs to IIIs[b]
	x	s	x	s	x	s		
Characteristics								
intensity (W_i/m_i)	162	23	147	31	156	37	3.40*	2.02*
duration (m_i/e_i)	47	38	28	18	22	21	4.62*	2.22*
mobility (e_i/S_i)	3.29	2.39	2.13	1.60	2.08	1.44	3.93*	.27
intermittency (No. of spells, S_i)	2.01	1.19	3.09	1.34	2.20	1.40	5.48*	4.95*
Components of characteristics								
hours worked (W_i)	28,031	10,471	20,080	9,774	11,569	7,688	5.19*	7.35*
months worked (m_i)	172	57	137	63	71	45	3.87*	9.14*
number of employers (e_i)	5.25	2.73	5.57	2.38	3.90	2.29	.83	5.41*
months per spell	115	71	54	43	42	38	7.34*	2.16*
Length								
months out of the labor force	4.25	8.80	77	70	131	75	8.65*	5.60*
months tenure with current employer	66	46	41	42	—	—	3.77*	—
months experience prior to current employer	106	60	96	55	—	—	1.17	—
hours of work in previous year	1,971	390	1,623	650	—	—	4.01*	—

a. Degrees of freedom: $n_I - n_{II} = 182$.
b. Degrees of freedom: $n_{II} - n_{III} = 229$.
*p < .05.

179

their length of work is greater, suggesting a taste for market work, which is not predicted by human capital theory. Thus measures of the length of employment or nonemployment alone do not fully capture intermittency and other aspects of work experience that may have consequences for earnings. Indeed, for employed mothers in this sample, high intermittency coexists with long accumulations of months of work.

Work Experience and Earnings:
The Cost of Having Children

In 1977, childless married women in the sample earned $15,235 on average, significantly more than the $8179 earned by employed mothers (t = 8.41, p < .05). (Because the nonemployed mothers had no earnings in the year prior to the survey, they are excluded from this portion of the analysis.) To what extent are the childless women's greater earnings associated with their distinctly different patterns of work experience, their parental status, or some combination of the two?

To answer these questions, first, Model 1 estimates annual earnings[8] as a function of the *length* variables (months spent out of the labor force, months of tenure in current job, and months of prior employment experience) with four control variables (hours worked, years of education, a dummy variable for a female-typed occupation, and a dummy variable indicating that a promotion was received in the current job). To examine the net impact of parenthood on earnings, Model 2 contains the same basic equation as Model 1 plus a dummy variable for parental status (1 = childless).

Next, Model 3 estimates earnings including the *characteristics* of work experience (intensity, duration, mobility, and intermittency) with the control variables, but excluding the length of work experience (prior experience and tenure), because the multiplicative terms of work experience (Equation 1) are substantively equivalent to the length of work experience. Model 4 is the same basic equation plus parental status.

Finally, Model 5 estimates earnings as a function of *both* the length and the characteristics of work experience, to determine whether either significantly adds to our understanding of the effect of work experience on earnings. Model 6 adds parental status.

Table 7.2 shows the six estimated models. For each pair of models, the addition of parental status adds significantly to the explained variance of the equation, as indicated by the F-statistics for increments in R-squared at the base of the table; that is, the regression intercept for employed mothers is significantly different from that of childless women. Substantively, the coefficients show that childlessness is associated with a net reward of roughly $3000 per year.

So, parenthood has an important net effect on earnings, over and above the effects of work experience. But does parenthood *interact* with work experience in its relationship to earnings? On the basis of the quite different work history patterns found in the descriptive results, we expect it to. To test this, interactive

TABLE 7.2
Regressions of Annual Earnings on the Characteristics and Length of Lifetime Work Experience: Pooled and Separated by Parental Status

Independent Variables	Model 1 β	Model 1 t	Model 2 β	Model 2 t	Model 3 β	Model 3 t	Model 4 β	Model 4 t	Model 5 β	Model 5 t	Model 6 β	Model 6 t
Characteristics												
intensity					34.9*	2.72	26.4*	2.08	37.2*	2.90	29.0*	2.28
duration					61.4*	3.87	51.5*	3.28	50.5*	2.58	38.1*	1.96
employer mobility					705*	2.86	622*	2.58	624*	2.22	504	1.83
intermittency					426	1.25	498	1.50	429	1.11	442	1.17
Length												
months out of labor force	−8.36	1.10	3.61	.47	−6.91	1.00	.39	.06	−4.76	.93	3.14	.42
months tenure in current job	32.4*	3.44	28.2*	3.14					18.2	1.72	18.9	1.84
months prior experience	10.6	1.52	11.5	1.73					.75	.09	3.24	.41
Parental status												
1 = childless			3,665*	4.54			2,812*	3.31			2788*	3.28
Control												
hours worked in year	3.52*	5.31	3.31*	5.27	2.94*	4.44	2.97*	4.62	2.61*	3.85	2.67*	4.04
years education	975*	5.43	933*	5.46	1,042*	5.73	982*	5.53	1,077*	5.82	1,027*	5.69
1 = current job > 75% female	−1,429*	2.02	−1,012	1.50	−1,183	1.75	−920	1.39	−1,315*	1.96	−1,023	1.54
1 = promotion in current job	2,267*	2.45	1,994*	2.27	1,657	1.88	1,556	1.81	2,041*	2.27	1,933*	2.21
intercept	−11,228*	3.08	−12,247*	3.53	−18,967*	4.28	−18,036*	4.17	−19,774*	4.41	−19,031*	4.36
adjusted R²	.476		.528		.514		.540		.519		.545	
F-statistic	24.7*		26.6*		22.5*		22.5*		18.9*		19.2*	
degrees of freedom	7,177		8,176		9,175		10,174		11,173		12,172	

NOTE: F statistics (degrees of freedom) for increment in R^2: Models 2 and 1, F = 19.3 (1,176); Models 4 and 3, F = 9.8 (1,173); Models 6 and 5, F = 9.8 (1,171); Models 6 and 2, F = 1.60 (4,171); Models 6 and 4, F = .94 (2,171).
*p < .05.

models were estimated, that is, models that allow for interactive effects between parental status and the independent variables. Using F-tests for increments in explained variance, however, none of the interactive models sufficiently improved upon Models 2, 4, and 6; that is, I could not reject the null hypothesis of no interactions. From this I infer that the slopes for childless women and mothers are essentially the same and, consequently, do not present the results of the interactive models here. Instead, I elaborate the results for Models 2, 4, and 6 below.

Contributing to doubts about the rusty skills hypothesis, Model 2 shows that time spent out of the labor force has an insignificant, although negative, relationship to later earnings when tenure on the current job and prior work experience are controlled (see Sandell & Shapiro, 1978, p. 106). While each additional month of tenure on the current job (indicating firm-specific training) is associated with an extra $28 per year in earnings, prior experience (indicating general training) is not significantly related to earnings. This suggests that prior experience may be of importance in initial job and wage decisions by employers, but it does not have a long-lasting influence on earnings.

Results for the new model of the characteristics of work experience in Model 4 confirm expectations. Regarding the intensity of work, each extra hour of work per month of work experience is worth an additional $26 per year on the current job. Each additional month spent with an employer increments annual earnings by $52. The coefficient for mobility between employers suggests that women engage in strategic job changing; an employer change during a spell of work is associated with $622 extra per year with the current employer.

The fact that neither intermittency nor months out of the labor force in Model 4 is significantly associated with current earnings again casts doubt on the rusty skills hypothesis. Indeed, the positive regression coefficient suggests that intermittency is not penalized, but rather that repeated returns to the labor force are rewarded. The possibility remains that short-term negative effects of intermittency and/or months out of the labor force are not captured in this analysis (see Mincer & Ofek, 1982), as childless women and working mothers in this sample averaged 5.5 and 3.4 years of tenure, respectively, and so any penalties they may have experienced could have been recouped.

When the characteristics and length of work experience are included in the same earnings equation (Model 6), intensity and duration remain significantly related to current earnings, but mobility and tenure drop to insignificance. Moreover, the increment in explained variance of Model 6 over Models 2 and 4 is insignificant. This indicates that characteristics of work experience do not add significantly to equations that include length alone; but neither do measures of the length of work experience add significantly to equations that include characteristics alone.

Overall, the direction and significance of the regression coefficients support hypotheses derived for characteristics of lifetime work experience more consistently than hypotheses concerning the lengths of work and nonwork. Thus the new model of lifetime work experience appears to capture better the features of work experience that have consequences for earnings. No matter what the model fashioned, however, using exact measures of intermittency and months out of the labor force, no support is found for the widely debated rusty skills, or depreciation, hypothesis. Moreover, even though certain features of work experience correspond with parenthood, as expected, parenthood does not interact significantly with work experience in its relationship to earnings.

CONCLUSIONS

This research has presented a new way of modeling lifetime work experience to examine its relationship to earnings. Four variables—the intensity of past work, duration of work with employers, mobility between employers within a spell of work, and intermittency (number of discrete spells of work)—were defined as multiplicative components of total hours of lifetime work experience. Each is an exact and theoretically meaningful component of lifetime work experience, which reveals significant differences in married women's patterns of work experience that have consequences for later earnings.

Reconceptualizing work experience in terms of the *quality* (or characteristics) instead of simply the *quantity* (or length) of past employment and nonemployment enabled me to distinguish between two previously confused concepts: intermittency and time spent out of the labor force. The theoretical consequences of this are twofold: On one hand, I argued that though work skills may "get rusty" with nonemployment, periodic labor force entries may maintain human capital by keeping skills honed. This insight is not inconsistent with human capital theory. Rather, it amplifies and extends human capital theory in a direction that can explain intermittency as rational behavior for lifelong maximization of earnings. On the other hand, this reconceptualization amplifies discrimination theory by explaining how intermittency may influence employers' hiring, job placement, and wage decisions. In particular, intermittency may signal unreliability to employers and serve as a reason for denying women adequate wages, on-the-job training, and other opportunities. The empirical results were consistent with the first argument.

Using data from a purposive sample of three groups of married women, the length and characteristics of work experience illustrated sharply different patterns of lifetime work experience. Comparing employed childless women to employed mothers, the mothers worked less intensely and continuously in the past, and for shorter durations and less intensely for their current employers, than the childless women. This confirms that the presence of children alters not only the length but the characteristics of women's lifetime patterns of work experience. Comparing employed and nonemployed mothers in the sample (who were, on average, equivalent in all other respects), the latter typically work in brief, intense bursts, while employed mothers typically worked for longer durations, part-time, and with greater intermittency. These differences between the two groups of mothers, first, confirm that the presence of children alone is not enough to explain mothers' different work history patterns, suggesting differences in preferences for paid work. Second, these findings demonstrate that relatively high levels of intermittency and long durations with employers coexist in the work history patterns of some women, contrary to the assumptions of human capital theory.

The results of the earnings regressions supported hypotheses derived for the new model of work experience more consistently and strongly than hypotheses for the lengths of employment and nonemployment typically used by human capital theorists. Despite exact measures of intermittency and nonemployment, I found no support for the rusty skills hypothesis. Rather, the data suggest that intermittency is rewarded, as alternately hypothesized. Thus brief periodic employment appears to be a good strategy for maintaining employment skills during life cycle stages when women devote their primary energies to the family.

Childless women's work experience patterns would presumably place them in a more advantageous position than employed mothers vis-à-vis employers in wage-setting decisions. Childlessness was found to have a strong net positive effect on earnings, but analyses of covariance indicated that parental status does not interact with the work experience regressors. This implies two possible explanations: Childless women in the sample may earn more than employed mothers because they have more intensity, duration, months, and hours of work, and more strategic mobility between employers, not because they have a different kind of work experience. Alternatively, if employers discriminate against parents, perhaps anticipating work interruptions, then childless women may earn more simply because they are not parents.

These empirical results, while based upon more detailed work history data than are typically available, should be regarded as tentative and in need of replication, for they are limited by the age cohort, period, and geography of the sample.[9]

For public policymaking, the theory, method, and findings presented here suggest that the most prevalent explanation of the wage gap—"rusty skills" associated with intermittent labor force participation and nonemployment—needs rethinking. Even though employment skills may depreciate during married women's typically long spells out of the labor force, this research suggests that the frequent labor force reentries among at least some women, particularly mothers, help to maintain those work skills, and, consistent with Mincer and Ofek (1982), that even "rusty" skills are quickly restored with continued employment. Thus the depreciation hypothesis apparently explains only the sex-wage gap for that proportion of the female population that has recently reentered the labor force. Beyond those narrow bounds, discrimination and structuralist explanations may offer the best explanations, and therefore the best arenas for remedies, of the sex-wage gap.

NOTES

1. *Human capital* comprises workers' skills and qualifications obtained in education, work experience, and on-the-job training (Becker, 1957; Mincer, 1974). From human capital theory, workers' investments in human capital determine their marginal productivity on the job and associated earnings. For reviews of human capital theory in relation to women's earnings, see Blau (1984), Corcoran, Duncan, and Ponza (1984), England and Farkas (1986), and Larwood, Stromberg, and Gutek (1985).

2. The Panel Study of Income Dynamics (PSID) has followed the economic behavior of 5000 families since 1968. The National Longitudinal Surveys (NLS) has gathered data on the labor market experience of four cohorts of mature and youthful men and women for varying lengths of time. The Inter-University Consortium for Political and Social Research (ICPSR), Institute for Social Research, University of Michigan, provides these data and documentation at cost to member universities.

3. Others have extended research on the depreciation hypothesis to include the relationship between occupational sex segregation, intermittency, and earnings (e.g., Corcoran, Duncan, & Ponza, 1984; England, 1982, 1984; Polachek, 1976, 1979, 1981). Due to length considerations, this chapter does not review these studies or examine intermittency's relationship to occupational segregation (see, however, Gwartney-Gibbs, 1987). These studies have the same problems in conceptualizing intermittency, in part due to limitations in the NLS and PSID data used, as discussed in the text.

4. In order to catch potential errors of recall, which are an inherent problem with all retrospective data, I compared individual's work, educational, marital, and fertility histories, and contacted respondents by telephone to correct seeming inconsistencies (e.g., when a respondent reported simultaneously going to school full-time and working full-time).

5. The age restriction parallels that of the NLS sample of mature women and was designed to help ensure that the childless group in the sample were forgone parents, not deferred mothers.

6. A crucial link in explaining sex inequality in earnings concerns the joint decisions made by married couples about how to allocate their productive and reproductive resources. Consider a hypothetical range of sexual divisions of labor within married couples in which, at one end of the continuum, wives and husbands equally concentrate their resources on market achievement; at the other end of the continuum, wives' efforts are devoted to work in the home and husband' are devoted to the market; and in between, wives' resources are divided between household and market work. The sample used here is designed to represent these three points on a hypothetical continuum of the divisions of household and market labor within married couples. The dual-earner childless couples in the sample represent the prior end of the continuum, in which the resources of both spouses are concentrated on market achievement, not on reproduction. Dual-earner couples with children represent the middle range of the continuum, in which wives' resources are divided between home and market production. The work experience of this group is particularly important to understand, because the labor force participation of this type of woman has increased more rapidly than any other group since World War II. Single-earner (husband working) couples with children represent "traditional" married couples who split their joint resources between husbands' market achievement and wives' work in the home. The distribution of the population of married couples on this hypothetical continuum is expected to be skewed toward the latter end, so only a very large

probability sample would yield enough couples representing the entire range of internal divisions of labor within the home, and such data are not available. (For more details on the sample, see Gwartney-Gibbs, 1981.)

7. Months and years in school are human capital investments, like work experience. Distinguishing time spent in school from time spent out of the labor force allows for a purer measure of periods of no human capital investment. If time spent in school was included as part of time spent out of the labor force, some years of education would be effectively double-counted in the earnings equations that follow, that is, as part of both the education variable and the time spent out of the labor force variable.

8. The skew typically observed in earnings distributions is not apparent in this purposive sample, allowing use of metric rather than logged earnings.

9. Unfortunately, the widespread use of this new method of characterizing lifetime work histories may be precluded by a lack of adequate data. Data from the PSID and NLS are not sufficiently detailed to use this model exactly, although, with interpolation between time points, estimates of certain of the components could be created (e.g., Angle, 1980; Hill, 1977). Work history data for women in Great Britain (Dex, 1984), Australia (Funder, 1986; Young, 1978), Malaysia, Austria, Hungary, and Japan (see Treiman, 1985) hold promise, but postsurvey coding and data reduction are hurdles that cannot go unmentioned. Even without exact data on each component of characteristics of lifetime work experience (hours and months of work, employers, and labor force entries and exits), the work history model used in this research is flexible. Referring back to Equation 1, for example, in the absence of information on hours of work over the lifetime, researchers could still calculate terms for duration, mobility, and intermittency. And lacking only data on employers, terms of intensity, the length of spells of work, and intermittency could be included.

REFERENCES

Angle, J. (1980). The cumulative experience method of analysis of longitudinal surveys. *Sociological Methods and Research, 8*(2), 209-231.

Becker, G. S. (1957). *The economics of discrimination.* Chicago: University of Chicago Press.

Blau, F. D. (1984). Discrimination against women: Theory and evidence. In W. A. Darity, Jr. (Ed.), *Labor economics: Modern views.* Boston: Kluwer Nijhoff.

Broom, L., & Smith, J. H. (1963). Bridging occupations. *British Journal of Sociology, 14,* 321-334.

Corcoran, M. (1978). Work experience, work interruption and wages. In G. J. Duncan & J. M. Morgan (Eds.), *5000 American families: Patterns of economic progress* (Vol. 6). Ann Arbor, MI: Institute for Social Research.

Corcoran, M., & Duncan, G. J. (1979). Work history, labor force attachment and earnings differences between the races and sexes. *Journal of Human Resources, 14*(1), 3-20.

Corcoran, M., Duncan, G. J., & Ponza, M. (1984). Work experience, job segregation, and wages. In B. F. Reskin (Ed.), *Sex segregation in the workplace: Trends, explanations, remedies.* Washington, DC: National Academy Press.

Davidson, P. E., & Anderson, D. (1937). *Occupational mobility in an American community.* Palo Alto, CA: Stanford University Press.

Dex, S. (1984). Work history analysis, women, and large scale data sets. *Sociological Review, 32*(4), 637-661.

England, P. (1982). The failure of human capital theory to explain occupational sex segregation. *Journal of Human Resources, 17*(3), 358-370.

England, P., & Farkas, G. (1986). *Households, employment and gender: A Social,* explanations of occupational sex segregation. *Social Forces, 62*(33), 726-749.

England, P., & Farkas, G. (1986). *Households, employment and gender: A social, economic, and demographic view.* New York: Aldine.

Felmlee, D. H. (1982). Women's job mobility processes within and between employers. *American Sociological Review, 47,* 142-151.

Form, W. H., & Miller, D. C. (1949). Occupational career pattern as a sociological instrument. *American Journal of Sociology, 54,* 317-329.

Funder, K. (1986). Work and the marriage partnership. Chapter 5 in P. McDonald (Ed.), *Settling up: Property and income division on divorce in Australia.* Englewood Cliffs, NJ: Prentice-Hall.

Gusfield, J. (1961). Occupational roles and forms of enterprise. *American Journal of Sociology, 66,* 571-580.

Gwartney-Gibbs, P. A. (1981). *Married women's work experience: Intermittency and sex-typed occupations.* Unpublished doctoral dissertation, University of Michigan, Department of Sociology.

Gwartney-Gibbs, P. A. (1987). *Occupational segregation and lifetime work experience: A test of the Polachek hypothesis.* Paper presented at the annual meeting of the American Sociological Association.

Hartmann, H. I., Roos, P. A., & Treiman, D. J. (1985). An agenda for basic research on comparable worth. In H. I. Hartmann (Ed.), *Comparable worth: New directions for research.* Washington, DC: National Academy Press.

Hill, D. H. (1977). *A dynamic analysis of the labor force participation of married women.* Unpublished doctoral dissertation, University of Michigan, Department of Economics.

Larwood, L., Stromberg, A. H., & Gutek, B. A. (Eds.). (1985). *Women and work: An annual review.* Vol. 1. Beverly Hills, CA: Sage.

Maret, E. (1983). *Women's career patterns: Influences on work stability.* Lanham, MD: University Press of America.

Mincer, J. (1974). *Schooling, experience, and earnings.* New York: National Bureau of Economic Research.

Mincer, J., & Ofek, H. (1982). Interrupted work careers: Depreciation and restoration of human capital. *Journal of Human Resources, 17,* 1-24.

Mincer, J., & Polachek, S. W. (1974). Family investments in human capital: Earnings of women. *Journal of Political Economy, 82,* S76-S108.

Mincer, J., & Polachek, S. W. (1978). Women's earnings examined. *Journal of Human Resources, 13,* 118-134.

Mulvey, M. C. (1963). Psychological and social factors in predictions of career patterns of women. *Genetic Psychology Monographs, 68,* 309-386.

O'Neill, J. (1985). Role differentiation and the gender gap in wages. In L. Larwood, A. H. Stromberg, & B. A. Gutek (Eds.), *Women and work: An annual review.* Beverly Hills, CA: Sage.

Palmer, G. L. (1954). *Labor mobility in six cities.* New York: Social Science Research Council.

Polachek, S. W. (1975). Discontinuous labor force participation and its effect on women's market earnings. In C. B. Lloyd (Ed.), *Sex, discrimination and the division of labor.* New York: Columbia University Press.

Polachek, S. W. (1976). Occupational segregation: An alternative hypothesis. *Journal of Contemporary Business, 5*, 1-12.

Polachek, S. W. (1979). Occupational segregation among women: Theory, evidence, and a prognosis. In C. B. Lloyd, E. S. Andrews, & C. L. Gilroy (Eds.), *Women in the labor market.* New York: Columbia University Press.

Polachek, S. W. (1981). Occupational self-selection: A human capital approach to sex differences in the occupational structure. *Review of Economics and Statistics, 58*, 60-69.

Reiss, A. J. (1961). *Occupations and social status.* New York: Free Press.

Reskin, B. F. (Ed.). (1984). *Sex segregation in the workplace: Trends, explanations, and remedies.* Washington, DC: National Academy Press.

Roos, P. A. (1981). Sex stratification in the workplace: Male-female differences in the economic returns to occupation. *Social Science Research, 10*, 195-224.

Sandell, S. H., & Shapiro, D. (1978). An exchange: The theory of human capital and the earnings of women: A reexamination of the evidence. *Journal of Human Resources, 13*, 103-117.

Taylor, P. A., Gwartney-Gibbs, P. A., & Farley, R. (1986). The changing structure of earnings inequality: 1960-1980. *Research in Social Stratification and Mobility, 5*, 105-138. [R. V. Robinson, Ed.]

Treiman, D. J. (1985). The work histories of women and men: What we know and what we need to find out. In A. S. Rossi (Ed.), *Gender and the life course.* New York: Aldine.

Wilensky, H. S. (1961). Orderly careers and social participation: The impact of work history on social integration in the middle mass. *American Sociological Review, 26*, 525-539.

Young, C. M. (1978). Work sequences of women during the family life cycle. *Journal of Marriage and the Family, 40*, 401-411.

8

Women's Relationships with Women in the Workplace

VIRGINIA E. O'LEARY

The popular and professional literature relevant to women's relationships with women in the workplace is reviewed with an eye toward explicating what little is known empirically about the topic and identifying questions that need to be addressed to understand these relationships better. Heavy reliance is placed upon the social psychological literature, much of it reporting the results of laboratory studies. Confirmation or disconfirmation of laboratory findings in the field are noted, and the results obtained in the two research settings are examined. Drawing on the work of Hall (1985), information pertinent to the perception of women in the workplace, as both bosses and subordinates, is conceived as a vertical dimension labeled "Working for Women." Horizontal relationships among women are discussed in a section headed "Working with Women." This section also includes a brief exploration of some of the current work on women's relational concerns, including female bonding. Avenues for further research are identified.

Despite substantial interest in issues relevant to women and work in the last 15 years (see Davidson & Cooper, 1984; Larwood, Stromberg, & Gutek, 1985; Nieva & Gutek, 1981), relatively little attention has been focused on women's relations with women in work settings. The literature that does exist may best be described as fugitive, in that it is widely scattered among professional (see Aries, 1976; Bartol & Martin, 1986; Dion, 1985) and popular sources (see Albin, 1984; French, 1985; Slade, 1984), and frequently relies on person observation and speculation, rather than systematic demonstration. The purpose of the current chapter is to review this fugitive literature with the end of specifying what is known about women's relationships with women in the workplace and identifying questions that need to be addressed to understand these relationships better.

In 1986, the Department of Labor reported that, for the first time in history, more than 50% of adult women were in the labor force. As women workers constitute an increasingly large proportion of the labor force in the roles of both subordinates and superiors, the need to understand how the dynamics of their relationships are affected by issues of sex and gender increases as well. For example, in Schein's (1984) view,

> When both the boss and the secretary are women, there is the potential for an unusually productive relationship as the woman boss may be less inclined to demean the role of another woman and more inclined to afford her respect and responsibility. However, the potential for an unusually unproductive relationship between women also exists if the woman boss is insecure and afraid of being identified as "one of the girls." (cited by Slade, 1984, p. 26)

The extent to which one or the other potential is actually realized in women's working relationships with others has yet to be documented, although the weight of the popular anecdotal evidence appears to favor the latter explanation (see Agins, 1986).

Because the literature relevant to women's relationships with women in the workplace in widely scattered through psychological and sociological journals, as well as the popular press, and because no single topic is covered extensively, the task of organizing the material was a difficult one. As a result, the topics covered are necessarily selective and arbitrary. The reader will quickly discern that there is a heavy reliance upon the extant social psychological literature, much of it reporting the results of laboratory studies. An attempt is made to note the confirmation or disconfirmation of laboratory findings in the field where appropriate, and the results obtained in the two research settings are explored in a section comparing them. Much of the material covered deals either explicitly or implicitly with the topic of women and power. Drawing on the work of Hall (1985), information pertinent to the perceptions of women in the workplace, as both bosses and subordinates, is conceived as a vertical work dimension labeled "Working for Women." Horizontal relationships among women are discussed in a section labeled "Working with Women." This section also includes a brief exploration of some of the current work pertinent to women's relational concerns (i.e., Chodorow, 1978; Goldberg, Clinchy, Belenky, & Tarule, 1987; Kaplan & Surrey, 1984), including female bonding. The application of this work to the general topic of women working with women is necessarily speculative, and, it is hoped, provocative. The final section, "Implications," attempts to summarize what is empirically known about women's relationships with women in the workplace and to identify avenues for future research on the topic.

WORKING FOR WOMEN

The Woman Boss

In a recently published book, *How to Work for a Woman Boss,* Bern (1987) details "over 280 coping strategies that will help you to adjust to this new phenomenon in the workplace." The book contains seven self-administered questionnaires designed to assist those whose bosses are women in identifying their management styles as "non listeners, power brokers, nonmanagement managers, or hesitant decision-makers etc." Clearly, the underlying premise is that working for a woman is problematic, a situation with which one must learn to cope. The depiction of women in positions of status and power as problematic is pervasive.

Much of the early writing relevant to high-status women in the workplace focused on their solo (Wolman & Frank, 1975) or token (Kanter, 1977; Laws, 1975) status. Nieva and Gutek (1981) suggest that the price extracted from women even peripherally included in a predominantly male work group includes a willingness to turn against other women, to ignore disparaging remarks about women, and to contribute to the derogation of other women. Such women have been labeled as "Queen Bees" (Staines, Travis, & Jayerante, 1973).

Queen Bees. Queen Bees are described by Staines and his colleagues as women who have achieved professional success and are antifeminist. They are strongly individualistic and tend to deny the existence of discrimination based on sex. Despite the fact that they often hold positions of power and could help other women, they do not offer their support. It has been widely assumed that Queen Bees are not supportive because they fear that the success of other women would challenge their own positions of power in organizations, a power maintained at the cost of other, lower-status women (Kanter, 1977).

Bardwick (1977) has offered a very different interpretation of the behavior of powerful women so frequently labeled by less powerful women as Queen Bees. In her view, personally powerful women are self-actualized (Maslow, 1962). As such, they enjoy a high degree of ego integration. They are secure in their relationships with others, lack the need to gain at others' expense, and have confidence in themselves. They do not see themselves as having or as holding on to power. Rather, they think of power in terms of increased responsibility. They therefore find it difficult to understand the animosity they engender among those women who view power as a zero-sum game, that is, if power is held by one woman in an organization, it is therefore not available to other women.

Unlike their more powerful peers, these less powerful women define *power* as the ability to be coercive, potent, and free: They do not equate power with the assumption of greater responsibility. Bardwick (1977) sees the disparity between the concept and the experience of power among the powerful and powerless as fundamental to understanding the conflict so frequently observed between the two groups; a conflict rendered almost inevitable by the differential meaning assigned to power by women who have it and those who do not.

Bardwick's alternative explanation for Queen Beeism is intriguing. It offers a rationale for powerful women's reluctance to support their weaker peers, anchored in a sensitivity to their positions as the targets of ambivalence rather than to their personal ambition. To offer assistance to someone who demands your support—while simultaneously resenting you for being in a position to provide it—is difficult, at best.

Conceptually consistent with Bardwick's speculation, there is some suggestion in the literature relevant to women mentors' relationships with their "mentees," that breakdowns in those relationships occur when mentees' demands for attention exceed their mentors' expectations for reciprocity (O'Leary, 1987a). It may be that situations involving the violation of expectations that women hold for one another's behavior result in the kind of affective intensity stereotypically attributed more often to women's same-sex relationships than to men's.

Unfortunately, there have not been any direct empirical tests of Bardwick's hypotheses regarding either the differential perceptions of power among women who have it and those who do not or the causes of women's reluctance to provide support to other women when they are in a position to so do. There is, however, some evidence to suggest that women's perception of power, grounded in their own secondary status in the sex-gender system (Lipman-Blumen, 1984), differs from that of men. Lipman-Blumen labels men's power strategies as macro-manipulation, and women's as micromanipulation. She claims these two contrasting strategies constitute the dialectic of the gender-power game.

Women and power. Through their long history as a subordinate group, women have learned how to survive in a world structured by the dominant group's definitions, rules, rewards, and punishments. "The only realistic response of many women to such overwhelming institutionally based macro-manipulation is micromanipulation, the use of interpersonal behaviors and practices to influence, if not control the balance of power" (Lipman-Blumen, 1984, p. 30).

Restricted to micromanipulation, women become well versed in interpreting the unspoken intentions, even the body language, of the powerful. "They learn to anticipate their governor's behavior, to evoke as well as to smother pleasure, anger, joy, and bafflement in their rulers, to charm, to outsmart, even to dangle the powerful over the abyss of desire and anguish" (Lipman-Blumen, 1984, p. 30). By various interpersonal strategies of micromanipulation, women have learned to sway and change, circumvent, and subvert the decisions of the powerful to which they seemingly have acquiesced.

In this view, any attempt to understand the relationships among women must necessarily involve an analysis of the power relationships among subordinates. All women exist within a larger social context that confines them, regardless of status, to subordinate positions vis-à-vis men. It is, therefore, not surprising that women who attempt to exert power by using the (direct) tactics of the superior (males) group are regarded as at least deviant, if not threatening, by both men and women. Macromanipulation by the less powerful is a violation of the "natural" order. This is consistent with Moss and Frieze's (1984) findings that, although women are familiar with both male (instrumental) and female (socioemotional) strategies for occupational success, they are also very aware of the need to match the strategy with the task in role-appropriate ways. Success in female-dominated careers, such as nursing, is probably enhanced by the use of micromanipulative strategies such as "honesty" and "grace in accepting criticism," whereas the direct assumption of "leadership" is more likely to be a prerequisite to traditional (male) managerial success. Thus women's relationships with other women may be expected to vary depending on the sex composition of the occupation itself. Within female-dominated occupations, the demonstration of women's competence and leadership abilities, strategies directed toward upward mobility, may be viewed as relatively inappropriate.

Recently, Eagly (1986) has proposed a social-role theory of sex differences, which argues that gender roles directly induce stereotypic sex differences because these roles tend to be behaviorally confirmed. The predominance of women in domestic social roles indirectly supports the stereotypes of women as communal because women's domestic roles are an important source of peoples' expectations about female characteristics. Women's predominance in low-status roles also underlies peoples' expectations about their submissiveness (Eagly & Steffen, 1984; Eagly & Wood, 1982), and women respond by behaving in a manner consistent with these expectations.

It is clear that expectations concerning appropriate conduct differ markedly for women and men in a variety of settings. Therefore, it should not be surprising that their social behavior differs in a fashion that parallels these expectations. The impact of social roles on behavior may be particularly strong in settings where role-related expectations conflict; for example, women in upper-level management risk negative evaluations if they violate expectations for the female-appropriate use of power by resorting to direct or macromanipulative strategies (Falbo, Hazen, & Linimon, 1982).

Strong support for the social-role theory of sex differences was recently obtained by Snodgrass (1985) in several studies exploring the impact of sex (male versus female) and role (superior versus subordinate) on interpersonal sensitivity. When the superior/subordinate role was crossed with sex in both a teacher-learner situation and in three separate business-related tasks, women showed no advantage over men in interpersonal sensitivity. Those in the subordinate role, however, regardless of sex, were more sensitive to the other person's feelings about them than were those in the superior role. According to Snodgrass, "women's intuition" might be more aptly labeled "subordinates' intuition." Undoubtedly, those who are less powerful have a greater need to be aware of the feelings and reactions of their superiors in order to respond to their needs and to acquire their favor.

Of particular relevance to the attempt to shed some light on women's relationships with other women in the workplace were the role-by-sex interactions that Snodgrass (1985) obtained. Not surprisingly, women were generally more sensitive than men regardless of the role to which they were assigned. Women were less sensitive toward other women, however; an effect that was most pronounced when women "teachers" were paired with women "learners," perhaps reflecting women's awareness of their lower status in the larger sex-gender system.

In the last several years, role-relevant explanations for women's differential status in the marketplace have assumed prominence over person- (as opposed to situation-) centered, and often trait-deficit, ones (Brown, 1979; Deaux, 1979;

Terborg, 1977; Smith & Grenier, 1982), at least in the professional literature (Riger & Galligan, 1980). Unfortunately, the opposite obtains in the popular press (see Freedman, 1986).

Studies, beginning with Kanter's *Men and Women of the Corporation* (1977), have argued that structural factors prevent women from performing successfully (Cann, 1984; Harlan & Weiss, 1981; Kanter, 1983; West, 1982). Both the person-centered and the structural perspectives, however, focus on women's deficits—stressing that women can adopt traditional (male) strategies either by changing themselves or by breaking down the structural barriers that prevent them from attaining their due (Stratham, 1985). Either way, women who desire power and status in the workplace are viewed as problems with which to cope. Given this view of women in the workplace, it is little wonder that no one wants a boss who is a woman.

Stereotypes of women bosses. The popular literature abounds with stereotypic portrayals of women bosses. Typically, these stereotypes are based on the interaction styles adopted by women bosses with their subordinates. For example, Jacobs (1979) describes six types of women bosses: the "motherly boss," who is warm and generous but also very demanding; the "sibling boss," who behaves much like an older sister, encouraging her subordinates' talents until they begin to grow and mature; the "dean-of-women" boss, reminiscent of the sorority house mother, encouraging everyone to pitch in; the "nit-picking" boss, who constantly nags about tiny details; the "buck-passing" boss, who adopts a we-are-all-alike posture and refuses to provide direction or to accept responsibility; and the "boss lady," who is ruthlessly successful and totally demanding. It is interesting to note the female bias inherent in the stereotypic conceptions of women bosses described by Jacobs. With the exception of the "boss lady," each of the other types possesses traits characteristically attributed more frequently to women than to men (Broverman et al., 1972).

Jacobs also acknowledges the existence of a "perfect" woman boss, described as brisk, efficient, trusting, and respectful of others. The perfect woman boss helps those who work for her to do their best and to grow professionally. Notably, in the case of the perfect boss, it is the possession of the very traits associated with stereotypic femininity, such as nurturance, that contributes to the growth of subordinates. Such bosses might appropriately be labeled "androgynous" in Sargent's (1984) terms, or "good mothers" in Bardwick's (1977). If they were men, they would likely be labeled "good mentors" (Kram, 1986).

The only source of information about the stereotypic woman boss is found in popular sources. When Virginia Schein's work on managerial stereotypes was published in the professional literature in 1973 and 1975, respectively, it was widely assumed that the stereotypic woman boss had been identified as "male," because, in Schein's terms, to think manager was to think male. In fact, Schein only asked her subjects (employers of large insurance firms) to characterize "Man," "Manager," and "Woman." When it was determined by Schein that the male profile was more like the managerial one than the female profile, the stereotypic woman boss was widely assumed to possess the requisite male characteristics to ensure success in the workplace. No empirical demonstration of the existence of a woman boss stereotype has been conducted to date.

In a recent poll by WBZ-TV's *Evening Magazine* (1986), men who worked for women were asked what they liked best and least about their bosses. Men indicated that their women bosses' least liked characteristics were moodiness and emotionality. They, however, most liked the fact that their bosses exhibited interpersonal sensitivity, that is, they got along well with others in the workplace. Comparisons are not available for employees' ratings of the best and least liked characteristics of men bosses. Perhaps even more important, the extent to which identical behavior on the part of women and men is differentially labeled and attributed to different causes is not well understood (see O'Leary & Hansen, 1983). For example, it is possible that a male boss's display of impatience in the workplace is likely to be labeled as appropriate task-oriented behavior caused by his interest in beating the competition, while the identical behavior of a woman is likely to labeled moodiness, caused by her emotionality or raging hormones. Differential causal attributions based on sex lead to differential responses (O'Leary & Hansen, 1985). Many laboratory studies that examine sex-determined attributions fail to find evidence for sex-of-subject differences (Nieva & Gutek, 1980; O'Leary & Hansen, 1985), suggesting that men and women agree about the characteristics and traits that differentiate the sexes.

Attitudes toward women bosses. Recent evidence suggests that the expressed attitudes of both men and women toward working women are increasingly positive (Kahn & Crosby, 1985). On the other hand, there has been little if any change in people's global preferences for male bosses, at least among those who do not have a woman boss (O'Leary & Ickovics, 1987). In addition, evidence for the pervasive belief that men make better leaders than women remains strong (Broverman, Vogel, Broverman, Clarkson, & Rosenkrantz, 1972; Offermann, 1986; Powell & Butterfield, 1979) although there have been no empirical demonstrations of sex differences in leadership aptitudes or managerial styles (Brown, 1979; Dobbins & Platz, 1986; Kanter, 1977). Nevertheless, managers act as if the belief in women's inferior leadership ability accurately reflects reality (see Brown, 1979; Kahn & Crosby, 1985; O'Leary, 1974).

A classic study of male attitudes toward women executives was published in the *Harvard Business Review* in 1965 (Bowman, Worthy, & Greyser, 1965). Men sampled felt women had no appreciable (negative) effect on efficiency and production; one-third of those sampled felt that women had a "bad" effect on employee morale; 51% of the male respondents felt that women were temperamentally unfit for management; 81% agreed that women would feel uncomfortable working for a woman; and almost one-fifth of the women in the sample concurred. Twenty years later, another survey of *Harvard Business Review* subscribers (Sutton & Moore, 1985) revealed that men's attitudes have changed more than women's.

In general, men indicated that they were willing to accept women as colleagues and treat them as competent equals, but more than half of the respondents did not believe that women would ever be wholly accepted in business. Twice as many women as men expressed this view. The percentage of executives who thought that women would be uncomfortable working for other women actually increased from 1965 to 1985, although few thought that men would feel uncomfortable working for a woman. Indeed, the number of men who expressed an unfavorable basic attitude toward women executives declined dramatically from 41% in 1965 to 5% in 1985. The extent to which this decline can be accounted for in terms of social desirability, rather than actual attitude change, cannot be determined.

The authors suggest that the "growing adversarial relations" between women bosses and women subordinates may be explained in one of three ways. Women bosses, eager to mold their women subordinates into competent corporate women, may place greater demands on them than do men. In return, the women subordinates may be both resentful of the pressure and disappointed at the lack of warmth and support to which they believe a woman boss entitles them. Second, women subordinates may (accurately) perceive themselves to be in direct competition with their women bosses for the scarce number of advanced corporate positions available to women. Finally, to the extent that there is a marked age discrepancy between a (young) boss and her (older) subordinate, tensions may be exacerbated.

In 1974, Rosen and Jerdee found evidence that even the best intentioned managers fall back on traditional ideas about women's proper roles, resulting in women's failure to receive the organizational support their male counterparts routinely enjoy. Several years later, a Gallup poll (1978) revealed that women prefer men bosses and would rather deal with men than women in a variety of occupations. Apparently, women are particularly likely to express prejudice against women in positions of authority.

In a sample of academic and nonacademic men and women employed at a midwestern university, Ferber, Huber, and Spitze (1979) found that highly educated women and men who are similarly educated or married to professional women are least likely to prefer male bosses to female ones. In line with research that shows that knowledge reduces stereotypic thinking, exposure to women bosses resulted in increased preferences for them. Interestingly, both women and men respondents were more likely to generalize their positive experiences with competent women to other women than their experiences with competent men to other men, perhaps because the latter represent the benchmark for such behavior (see O'Leary & Hansen, 1985).

Two interpretations have been offered to explain the preference of workers for male over female superiors. The first focuses on the oft-cited fact that women's traits are assumed to be antithetical to those requisite for a competent (male) manager (Schein, 1973, 1975). The other points to the power differentials "enjoyed" by men versus women, concluding that it is only reasonable to prefer a more powerful superior, who can obtain greater rewards for and bestow greater status on *his* subordinates (Kanter, 1983). In this regard, Gutek (1985) found that women subordinates were equally satisfied with a male or female boss, whereas men were less satisfied with a female unless their own income and job status were controlled, in which case their bias for male bosses disappeared. Both perspectives, in attempting to explain women's failings in managerial roles, focus on the negative aspects of women's assumption of those roles. The possibility that women might bring something of value that is uniquely their own to the workplace is seldom considered. Indeed, management has found it necessary to offer T-groups to assist male managers lacking in interpersonal sensitivity, and to offer assertiveness training to bolster women's ability to confront issues and people directly. Deficits are identified in both cases, but the value of extant strengths is taken for granted and apparently dismissed, particularly when those strengths are interpersonal in nature.

Secretaries' perceptions of their bosses. In 1984, the National Commission on Working Women reported that nearly one-third of all employed women worked in administrative support and clerical occupations. To date, most of the research on sex and status in the workplace has been unidirectional. It has focused on the evaluation of subordinates by superiors—with the experimenters looking for the effects of sex and status on these evaluations (Dion, 1985). There has been relatively little research investigating the perceptions and evaluations of bosses by their subordinates.

In one of the few empirical studies that has been conducted on secretaries' perceptions of their women bosses, Stratham (1985, 1986) found evidence suggesting that women like working for women at least as well, if not better, than they like working for men. For example, secretaries rated women supervisors as significantly more capable than men supervisors. Women were viewed as more considerate bosses who treated their secretaries as equals, inquired about their career goals, attempted to improve their positions, consulted them about decisions, and worked well as team members. In only one area, permitting time away from work, were men supervisors characterized as more lenient than women supervisors. Not surprisingly, the secretaries in Stratham's samples who had women supervisors rated women bosses more positively than those with men supervisors. Secretaries with women supervisors saw their bosses as more considerate, hardworking, thorough, and appreciative of subordinates than did secretaries to men. They were also less likely to see women supervisors as hard to work for, reluctant to delegate, and emotional. Interestingly, they were as likely, if not more so, to see women supervisors as more demanding.

These results were further corroborated in a second study by Stratham (1986b), based on interviews with the secretaries of women and men bosses, in which she found nearly unanimous positive acclaim for women bosses, who were depicted by their secretaries as more considerate and appreciative than men. Although secretaries of women enjoyed working for them, bosses' sex was not predictive of overall job satisfaction. Stratham found that secretaries were better off in some ways with bosses who were men, in other ways with bosses who were women. Secretaries of women reported less overload and stress and greater likelihood of being included in decision making and long-term planning. On the other hand, secretaries of men reported greater satisfaction with salary and fringe benefits and greater opportunity for advancement.

These differential satisfactions are easily explained when one considers that males still occupy positions of greater authority in the workplace than do females. The power and prestige of a male boss may in fact translate into better pay and benefits, or at least the perception that that is the case (Nieva & Gutek, 1981).

A study of 7500 secretaries, bosses, and other office workers was recently completed by *Working Woman* magazine (Kagan & Malvaux, 1986). They reported that, of the 51% of secretaries who had a preference regarding sex of boss (almost half expressed no preference), most preferred working for a man. Of secretaries who were currently working for women, the preference for a male boss held, although it was diminished.

As women come to occupy more important and powerful positions within various organizations, they may acquire the ability to distribute more and greater rewards. Secretaries' experiences, job conditions, and satisfactions with or preference for female versus male bosses may be altered as power shifts within the workplace. In fact, controlling for boss status has been found in one study (O'Leary & Ickovics, 1987) to result in greater job satisfaction for employees of women compared to employees of men.

O'Leary and Ickovics (1987) studied 20 secretaries of women and 20 secretaries of men in the D.C. metropolitan area. The women and men bosses were matched by general type and size of organization. Each of the secretaries worked for a boss who was high in status and thus capable of providing relatively equal organizational rewards, regardless of sex.

The overall pattern of results obtained clearly suggests that women who worked for women like both their bosses and their jobs. Indeed, it appears that women who work for women enjoy an advantage over women who work for men in that they are more likely to be provided the core job characteristics, such as task identify and task significance, that lead to experienced meaningfulness of work and result in job satisfaction. The fact that secretaries of women bosses viewed their jobs as more worthwhile and saw their suggestions as taken more seriously than secretaries of men indicates that women's process achievement orientation (Veroff & Sutherland, 1985) in the workplace may provide a structure that enhances task outcomes for their women subordinates.

The interpersonal concern of women that results in their behavioral commitment to maintaining positive interpersonal relations with their secretaries—as evidenced by women bringing their secretaries flowers, inquiring about their personal lives, expressing concern for them as individuals, treating them with consideration, and encouraging their best efforts—may culminate in a context congenial to the secretaries' enhanced performance. It is interesting to note that preliminary analyses of secretarial behaviors suggest that the interpersonal concern of their women bosses is reciprocated. Secretaries of women are more likely to report discussing their personal lives with their bosses, complimenting them, and acting sensitive to their needs than are secretaries of men. Furthermore, they are more likely than secretaries of men to describe themselves in stereotypically feminine terms, perhaps because their (women) bosses permit or encourage them to be cooperative, soothing, less tough, and less responsible.

To the extent that women bosses structure their secretaries' work in such a way as to recognize their individual significance in the work environment, it is not surprising that their secretaries report themselves to be satisfied with both their bosses and their jobs. Indeed, this structure appears to be independent of the specific behaviors that women bosses exhibit, as satisfaction with women bosses is independent of core job dimensions. In contrast, for secretaries of men, both boss and position satisfaction depend upon job characteristics.

Because the secretaries rated both themselves and their bosses on the same adjectival scales, it was possible to compare the self- and boss ratings made on the 28 scales. Interestingly, although the secretaries' mean self-ratings were actually slightly higher than their mean boss ratings, the characteristics on which they rated themselves most positively were different from those on which they rated their bosses most positively. These results may be interpreted to suggest that complementary strengths on the part of women secretaries and their women bosses may be important predictors of favorability of relationships.

The secretaries in O'Leary and Ickovics's study were asked to list the three things they liked best and least about their bosses. Although many of the secretaries did not chose to identify three things about their bosses that they liked least, those who did frequently cited criticism, unclear expectations for performance, and moodiness. It is important to note that the few secretaries who disliked their bosses were as extreme in their negative characterizations of them as those who liked their bosses were positive. It may be that the relationship between women working for women is characterized more by its affective extremity than that of women working for men.

Although only those who have women bosses may want them, increasing numbers of women and men are going to find that they have women bosses whether they want them or not. The results of this study clearly suggest that, contrary to the myth, working for a woman has some advantages as measured by satisfaction with position.

Overall, these results, coupled with those of Stratham, call into question the assumption that women who work for women are not satisfied with their jobs or their bosses. Indeed, it may be that the actuality of working for a woman is the best antidote to the expressed preference of subordinates for male bosses, a heartening possibility in a work world that will be increasingly populated by women working for and with women.

WORKING WITH WOMEN

Are Women Prejudiced Against Women?

Early studies of women's evaluation of the competence of other women indicated that women are prejudiced against women (Goldberg, 1968). For example, in Goldberg's classic study, college women were asked to evaluate six professional articles in terms of writing style, profundity, professional status, professional competence, and persuasiveness. Half of the women were led to believe that articles were written by John T. McKay; the other half were led to believe they were authored by Joan T. McKay. "John's" journalistic efforts were viewed more favorably than "Joan's" on all criteria measured regardless of the sex-role appropriateness of the content of the texts: law and city planning (masculine) versus dietetics and elementary education (feminine). Similar results have been obtained in studies requiring the evaluation of the artistic merit of paintings and the qualifications of student applicants for a study abroad program (Wallston & O'Leary, 1981).

Although Goldberg's finding is generally considered well established, one attempt to replicate it nine years later (Isaacs, 1981) was unsuccessful. Another study examining women's prejudice against their same-sex peers found that female respondents evaluated high-status women as more competent than high-status men, and low-status women as less competent then low-status men (Peck, 1978). The social desirability of such responses had certainly increased in the intervening years, although more recently there is evidence to suggest that considerable backsliding has occurred, and that responses that were considered inappropriately sexist in the mid- to late 1970s have become alarmingly common in the mid-1980s (O'Leary, 1986).

Abramson, Goldberg, Greenberg, and Abramson (1977) found that female attorneys and paralegal workers were evaluated as more competent by women than by men. They interpreted their findings as evidence of a "talking Platypus" phenomenon indicating that when success is unexpected it tends to be magnified. In fact, women are judged to be as competent as men when the criteria on which their performance is evaluated are explicit (Abramson et al., 1977; Ilgen, 1983; Jacobson & Effertz, 1974), or when the existence of such criteria may be inferred from the fact that its worth is acknowledged by an authoritative source (Nieva & Gutek, 1980; Wallston & O'Leary, 1981).

In a recent review of the literature relevant to the devaluation of women's competence, Lott (1985) concludes that the tendency to devalue competent women, although not invariable, is more the rule than the exception. Competent women are most likely to be devalued when judgments are made in serious, believable, and realistic contexts, and when there are potential consequences for the evaluator, and negative evaluations of competent women are least likely in situations where persons are judging someone they know well, or with whom they have worked or interacted. Nieva and Gutek (1981) have suggested that evaluators of a person's actual past performance are called upon to make fewer inferences, and as a result have less of an opportunity for bias than evaluators of the more ambiguous qualifications of unknown persons. Consistent with this suggestion is the finding that only those who have women bosses evaluate them positively.

It should be noted, however, that the differentials in salary, promotion, and other institutional rewards persist among women who are well known to their evaluators, that is, women workers in real work environments. Indeed, the least equivocal evidence for bias against women in the work force is obtained in studies in which evaluations are made by actual decision makers in work settings (Lott, 1985).

Not surprisingly, the findings demonstrating competency biases disadvantaging women have received considerable attention in the management literature (Heneman, 1977; Muchinsky & Harris, 1977). Generally, women do not evaluate women more stringently than do men in either laboratory or field settings (Bartol & Butterfield, 1976; Gupta, Jenkins, & Behr, 1983; Hammer, Kim, Baird, & Bigoness, 1974; Izraeli, Izraeli, & Eden, 1985; Lee & Avares, 1977; Rosen & Jerdee, 1973).

In one study, women's attitudes toward women in management were found to determine how the failure (but not success) of a female manager was interpreted (Garland, Hale, & Burnson, 1982). The more positive a woman's attitude toward women in management, the less likely she was to "excuse" a female manager's failure as due to bad luck. It may be that women are harsher critics of other women than men when they fail because they are cognizant of the likelihood that failure may be used to prevent women from obtaining the opportunity to succeed or fail on subsequent occasions.

Although women's actual performance is unlikely to be differentially evaluated by women, they are less likely to be perceived as leaders than men (see Porter & Geis, 1981). Offermann (1985) reports that subjects of both sexes rate the influence of female leaders on group productivity as less significant than that of male leaders. Many of the studies that have been conducted to examine the effects of supervisor sex on the reactions of subordinates have been based on the premise that evaluations of supervisory behavior depend on congruence between sex-role norms and supervisory style. Given that women are supposed to be sympathetic, humanitarian, and compassionate (Tyler, 1965), and concerned for others' welfare (Miner, 1974), female supervisors should be rated lower than their male counterparts when exhibiting initiating and structuring behaviors (Parsons & Bales, 1955). Indeed, Bartol and Butterfield (1976) and Rosen and Jerdee (1973) report that female managers depicted as utilizing masculine leadership styles (initiating behaviors) were judged by women (and men) as worse managers than male managers using the same leadership style. Similar results for the managerial styles—reward versus threat—have been obtained. Apparently, sex-role congruence can play a role in determining reactions to managerial behavior. Behavior high in initiation clashes with sex-role expectations when the manager is a woman (Nieva & Gutek, 1981), although this effect has been shown to be less pronounced when the subordinates are women (Petty & Lee, 1975).

Consistent with this finding were results obtained by Jago and Vroom (1982), who found that women are penalized for behaving autocratically. They asked 61 male and 22 females managers to judge the degree of participation of 5 to 10 other members of mixed-sex training groups and to describe their affective response to each person. Men and women perceived to be participative were rated equally favorably. Women perceived to be autocratic were negatively evaluated, however, in contrast to autocratic males, whose evaluations, although modest, were positive. The authors interpret these results to suggest that men as managers have substantially greater freedom than is afforded women managers to engage in either autocratic or participative managerial behaviors without risking negative evaluations among their peers. Consistent with this interpretation is Petty and Lee's (1975) observation of lower work satisfaction among subordinates with female supervisors perceived to be low in consideration. Jago and Vroom's failure to find sex of rater effects indicates that men and women agree about what constitutes "appropriate" managerial behavior on the part of women.

The differential evaluation of the performance of women and men in supervisory roles may be less a function of sex than of power (Golding, Resnick, & Crosby, 1983; Nieva & Gutek, 1981). For example, in a national sample survey, Hansen (1974) found that female supervisors have significantly less autonomy than their male counterparts. Paralleling this report of lower autonomy for women supervisors is the finding that women supervisors' behavior has less impact on their subordinates' job satisfaction than does men's. Nieva and Gutek (1981) suggest that women supervisors' lower levels of autonomy, compared to men, may account for the lower satisfaction found in all-female groups (Hansen, 1974; Roussel, 1974). To the extent that women supervisors exercise less organizational power than their male counterparts, their ability to mediate on behalf of their subordinates is diminished.

Consistent with this view are the results of a recent study by South, Bonjean, Corder, and Markham (1982), who reported that the women subordinates of women supervisors in a federal bureaucracy described their jobs as less satisfying and their morale as lower than the subordinates of men. In addition, they were more likely to describe their women supervisors as controlling and particularistic. Interestingly, when the authors controlled for sex differences in organizational power among supervisors, corresponding differences in subordinate satisfaction were reduced. Gutek (1985) reports a similar diminution of satisfaction among male subordinates of female supervisors when subordinate's income and supervisor's job prestige are controlled.

In a replication and extension of the classic study by Pheterson, Kiesler, and Goldberg (1971), Lisenmeir and Wortman (1979) obtained an interaction of leader expertise, leader sex, and subject sex. Women devalued the accomplishments of other women, relative to men, if the other women's competence had not been demonstrated. Men's evaluations were not similarly affected by the sex of the target, suggesting that women may be particularly sensitive to the differential power of same-sex others.

In at least one study (Golub & Canty, 1982), women subordinates evaluating women managers have been found to have unclear role expectations regarding their supervisors' behaviors (effective versus ineffective). As a result, they restrict their range of responses by using only the central portion of the rating scale, suggesting a lack of confidence. To the extent that the rater lacks confidence in the rating of dissimilar others, the ratings will be less varied. In the case of women rating women, the critical determinant of restricted range may not be similarity, but rather ambiguity of role expectation. When women's role expectations for the behavior of other women are clear, they have been found to rate women leaders more (not less) favorably (Lord, Phillips, & Rush, 1980; Offermann, 1985; O'Leary & Ickovics, 1987).

It has been suggested that, because women's roles are lower in status than men's, they are perceived as less capable of making worthwhile contributions in the marketplace and as less deserving of the opportunity to express themselves and exert leadership in groups (Berger, Rosenholtz, & Zeditch, 1980). Recently, Alagna and Reddy (1985) obtained evidence that dominant women in mixed-sex groups were seen as "too ambitious" and "too take charge," suggesting that, when women try to exert leadership, their behavior may be perceived as disruptive.

Sex Effects in the Laboratory
Versus the Field

Evidence from laboratory studies generally suggests that sex differences, although not insignificant, are small (Deaux, 1985). Such evidence has led many to argue that the case favoring sex similarities outweighs that favoring sex differences, a conclusion met with incredulity by those whose reference point is outside the laboratory. Differences between women and men are apparent in such arenas as occupation (Nieva & Gutek, 1981), division of household labor (Gilbert, 1985), child care (Bernard, 1981), and the distribution of power (Lipman-Blumen, 1984).

The difference between the laboratory and the field setting in the kinds of information they provide needs to be more clearly recognized. Within the laboratory, the sexes' ability to perform specific tasks may be assessed. In the field, observed differences between the sexes are less indicative of capability than of choice, situational factors, and structural considerations (Deaux, 1985). Further, given the frequent reliance on the "paper people paradigm" in the laboratory, the external validity of results obtained in studies using this paradigm must be questioned (Ilgen, 1983).

In a recent meta-analytic analysis (i.e., a quantitative review of the literature, Eagly, 1986), comparing the evaluations of "paper people," in which the subjects read a series of vignettes containing scaled behavior descriptions and then rated the performance of hypothetical ratees, with ratings based on direct observations, Murphy and his colleagues (Murphy, Herr, Lockhard, & Maguire, 1986) conclude that systematically different results are generated by these two approaches. The paper people approach leads to an overestimate of the effects of some variables such as performance level and purpose of rating, such as leniency. Many of the laboratory studies cited in support of the contention that women are evaluated differently than men utilize paper people paradigms. Research is needed to assess the extent to which these findings can be replicated in observational studies.

Further, as Deaux (1985) so aptly observes, recognition of the differences between what women *can* do and what they *do* do is essential to understanding the cause of discrepancies between capabilities and actualities. It is critically important to examine the social context in which their behavior occurs in order to understand why women "can't be more like men."

Female bonding. In *Men in Groups,* Tiger (1970) dealt with two controversial issues. First, he hypothesized that certain cultural and historical features are more simply explained in biological terms. Second, he was persuaded that there exists a biological predisposition among human groups to establish all-exclusive male collectives. Tiger speculated that the inclination to form all-male groups, a phenomenon he labeled "male-bonding," has its "roots in human evolutionary history." According to Tiger, male bonding led inevitably to inequity between the sexes and the eventual exclusion of women from the sources of power within the group.

Tiger's postulation of a male bond has been criticized on several counts, not the least of which was his overreliance on analyses of societies with highly visible male organizations, to the exclusion of those with well-established female groups (Doyle, 1983). Despite what some viewed as an intuitively appealing hypothesis, demonstrating the biological basis for the phenomenon that Tiger describes has proved difficult, and the notion is generally regarded to be of questionable validity.

Perhaps even more intuitively appealing is the postulation of an inclination on the part of women to bond together to preserve themselves and their offspring. Certainly, much of the recent revisionist feminist literature relevant to the female experience (see Bernard, 1981; French, 1985) suggests that women's bonds with women have historically provided them a foundation of psychological and social support. Although this view is counter to the popular twentieth-century belief that women have always competed against one another for scarce (male) resources, history attests to its accuracy (see Schlissel, 1982).

In an early test of Tiger's theory of male-bonding, Booth (1972) found women to be superior to men on measures of social participation. He also found evidence of stronger affective bonds between women than men. Women reported more same-sex friendships than did men, and women's friendships were "affectively richer" in that they were characterized by more spontaneous and frequent interactions and more shared confidences than men's friendships with men. Further, women reported greater kin-involvement than men. Wheeler and Nezlek (1977) attributed women's richer friendship patterns to their restricted mobility, suggesting that women are forced to focus on fewer (deeper) relationships. There is no evidence that women have fewer same-sex friends than men (Booth, 1972), however, as would be expected if the restricted mobility hypothesis obtained.

Rapidly accumulating research relevant to sex differences in the provision of social support (Belle, 1987) reveal that women do enjoy broader, and perhaps deeper, social networks than men. Often, these networks are populated primarily or exclusively by women (Brehm, 1985). There may, however, be differences in the value attached to these relationships as a function of age. Wright and Kemple (1981) found that girls who were juniors in high school reported that they valued their male and female friendships equally. By freshman year in college, Wheeler and Nezlek's women subjects reported more intimacy in and satisfaction with opposite-sex interactions. The extent to which this effect is limited to young women in competition with one another for male attention has not been assessed. There is, however, evidence suggesting that adult women's relationships are more emotional and more intimate than men's (Bell, 1981; Dickens & Perlman, 1981; Rubin, 1985) and that these relationships persist into old age (Fischer & Oliker, 1980).

Within the last ten years, there has been a dramatic increase in the writings by women about women (see Chodorow, 1978; Gilligan, 1982; Goldberg, Clinchy, Belenky, & Tarule, 1987; Gurin, 1978; Kaplan & Surrey, 1984). The predominant theme in all this new work emphasizes women's relational concerns. The extent to which these concerns affect their work-related behavior has yet to be determined.

It has been suggested that one of the prices professional women are forced to pay for their career success in male-dominated occupations is the sacrifice of their supportive relationships with same-sex friends. Goodenow (1986), however, obtained evidence that women in high-status occupations had richer same-sex friendships than lower-status women. They not only scored higher on measures of the instrumental value of their friendships with other women, they also viewed their women friends as higher in status value. Undoubtedly, women's relationships with women in the workplace are subject to the influence of their experiences with one another outside it. Indeed, the very characteristics that in one situation may promote understanding and cooperation may enhance competition in another. Of critical importance may be the structural position of women in relation to one another—superior, subordinate, or peer (Kanter, 1977).

IMPLICATIONS

Clearly, most of the research available on women's relationships with women in the workplace has focused on the vertical dimension of work. Although rarely explicitly addressed, all the research on this topic touches on questions of women and power. Empirical evidence for Queen Beeism has proved elusive, although anecdotal reports of the phenomenon are frequent. Preliminary analyses of the results of a study by O'Leary, Grossman, and Belle (1987) exploring the mentorship between women and men in academe suggest that men restrict their mentoring functions to those that are explicitly career related, that is, sponsorship, exposure-and-visibility, coaching, protection, and challenging assignments. In contrast, women mentors' relations with their mentees are much less likely to be restricted to career functions, but also include role modeling, acceptance and confirmation, counseling, and friendship (Kram, 1986). Indeed, one woman mentor told of accompanying her pregnant mentee to the labor room when she learned that there was no one else available to assist her. Apparently, women see mentoring responsibilities as encompassing the assumption of responsibilities for the emotional as well as the career-relevant well-being of their protégés. Several women mentors spoke of their increasing reluctance to get involved with younger women because they were no longer ready to give as much of themselves as these younger women demanded.

It has been demonstrated that effort acquires differential meaning when it is exerted by women versus men (O'Leary & Hansen, 1985). It may be that power also has differential meaning depending upon the sex of the person wielding it. Certainly there is ample evidence to suggest that identical behaviors performed by women versus men in the workplace are ascribed different labels (e.g., bitchy versus assertive). To the extent that these different labels elicit differential responses, it is important to begin to identify them and to examine the consequences of the responses they elicit.

The parameters of the stereotypes of the woman boss must be empirically demonstrated if we are to begin to understand the dynamics of the behavior that may follow from that stereotype. Recently, O'Leary (1987b) obtained evidence that men bosses were characterized as more competent, powerful, tough, and respected than women bosses by a sample of undergraduate students and secretaries-in-training. On the other hand, women bosses were depicted as more pleasant, friendly, accepting, helpful, close, supportive, soothing, open, permissive, emotional, and loyal than men. The generalizability of these findings should be explored in future studies.

The implications of the finding that negative attitudes toward women bosses decline with experience with such bosses should be addressed with an eye to determining whether women are more or less likely than men to change their attitudes toward working for women when they do. Preliminary results of an interview study conducted by O'Leary (1987c) with secretarial students suggest that the criteria women use to evaluate women bosses may be distinctly different from those used to evaluate men. For example, young women secretarial students in a cooperative program reported making immediate judgments about women supervisors to whom they were assigned for a week based on feelings of competition. In contrast, their evaluations of men supervisors took longer to make and were not based on competitive feelings about tangential issues such as mode of dress and grooming. One question of critical importance is the extent to which individuating information about a particular woman boss generalizes to others, especially when the subordinates are women.

The possibility that bosses' sex may actually mediate the relationship postulated by Hackman and Oldham (1976), in their job characteristics of work motivation model, between core job characteristics and critical psychological states is intriguing. To the extent this is so, bosses' sex, or perhaps more aptly, bosses' gender, becomes a significant structural variable in the organizational context. Certainly the available data are sufficiently suggestive to warrant further exploration along these lines.

Horizontal relations among women in the workplace have received little attention by researchers interested in women and work. Among the important questions that have not been addressed are the implications of women workers' identification with women in the work force (Gurin, 1987) on job satisfaction and productivity as well as on their relationship with women workers. In her forthcoming book, Briles (personal communication, March 1987) examines women professionals' views of their colleagues' ethical business behaviors. Based on a random sample survey of the individuals listed in *Who's Who of American Women* and *Who's Who in Business and Finance*, Briles found that women professionals were much more likely than men to report that they had suffered unethical treatment at the hands of another woman in business than they were to report unethical treatment in the hands of a man, by a 54% margin. In contrast, men professionals reported themselves to have experienced unethical treatment by women and men in business in relatively equal proportions (61% versus 68%, respectively, a margin of only 11%). Further, only 48% of the men viewed the unethical treatment they received at the hands of women to be intentional, as contrasted to 62% of the women who attributed intentionality to their women peers' unethical behavior. Even more dramatic was the finding that only 15% of the men thought that their unethical treatment by men was intentionally caused, as contrasted with 80% of the women who viewed it that way. These results led Briles to conclude that women may be less ethically inclined than men, particularly when dealing with other women, or at least more sensitive to perceived breeches of ethics by women versus men. The possibility that women's standards for the behavior of women versus men in the marketplace are more stringent should be explored in order to understand better the dynamics of the competition between women so frequently offered to explain why women do not get along with other women. In the workplace, this competition may be based on the reality of limited opportunities for women, or it may reflect affective reactions to the violation of expectations for women's behavior that are unrealistically high.

Women working for and with women is a contemporary reality. Research that enhances our understanding of the implications of that reality is needed.

REFERENCES

Abramson, P. R., Goldberg, P. A., Greenberg, J. H., & Abramson, L. M. (1977). The talking platypus phenomenon: Competency ratings as a function of sex and professional status. *Psychology of Women Quarterly, 2,* 114-124.

Agins, T. (1986, March 24). The uneasy office. *The Wall Street Journal.*

Alagna, S. W., & Reddy, D. M. (1985). Self and peer ratings and evaluations of group process in mixed sex and male medical training groups. *Journal of Applied Social Psychology, 15*(1), 31-45.

Albin, S. (1984, December). Female bosses: Can being too good be bad for business? *The Washington Woman,* pp. 29-31.

Aries, E. (1976). Interaction patterns and themes of male, female and mixed sex groups. *Small Group Behavior, 7,* 7-18.

Bardwick, J. M. (1977). Some notes about power relationships between women. In A. G. Sargent (Ed.), *Beyond sex roles.* St. Paul, MN: West.

Bartol, K. M., & Butterfield, D. A. (1976). Sex effects in evaluating leaders. *Journal of Applied Psychology, 61,* 446-454.

Bartol, K. M., & Martin, D. C. (1986). Men and women in task groups. In R. D. Ashmore & F. K. DelBoca (Eds.), *The social psychology of male-female relations* (pp. 259-301). New York: Academic Press.

Bern, P. (1987). *How to work for a woman boss.* New York: Dodd, Mead.

Bell, R. (1981). Friendships of women and men. *Psychology of Women Quarterly, 5*(3), 402-417.

Belle, D. (1987). Gender differences in social support. In R. Barnett, L. Biener, & G. Baruch (Eds.), *Women and stress.* New York: Free Press.

Berger, J., Rosenholtz, S. J., & Zelditch, M., Jr. (1980). Status organizing processes. In A. Inkles, N. J. Smelser, & R. H. Turner (Eds.), *Annual review of sociology* (Vol. 6, pp. 479-508). Palo Alto, CA: Annual Reviews, Inc.

Bernard, J. (1981). *The female world.* New York: Free Press.

Booth, T. (1972). Sex and social participation. *American Sociological Review, 37,* 183-192.

Bowman, G., Wortney, B. N., & Greyser, S. H. (1965). Are women executives people? *Harvard Business Review, 43,* 14-28, 154-178.

Brehm, S. (1985). *Intimate relationships.* New York: Random House.

Broverman, I. K., Vogel, R. S., Broverman, D. M., Clarkson, F. E., & Rosenkrantz, P. S. (1972). Sex-role stereotypes: A current reappraisal. *Journal of Social Issues, 28,* 59-78.

Brown, L. K. (1979). Women and business management. *Signs, 5*(2), 266-287.

Cann, C. H. (1984). Women, organizations and power: Structural and individual perspectives. In *Proceedings of Women and Work Conference.* Austin: University of Texas.

Chodorow, N. (1978). *The reproduction of mothering.* Berkeley: University of California Press.

Davidson, M. J., & Cooper, C. L. (1984). *Working women: An international survey.* New York: John Wiley.

Deaux, K. (1979). Self-evaluations of male and female managers. *Sex Roles, 5,* 570-580.

Deaux, K. (1985). Sex and gender. In L. Porter & M. Rosensweig (Eds.), *Annual review of psychology* (Vol. 36, pp. 49-81). Palo Alto, CA: Annual Review.

Dickens, W. J., & Perlman, D. (1981). Friendship over the life cycle. In S. Duck & R.

Gilmour (Eds.), *Personal relationships. Vol. 2: Developing personal relationships.* London: Academic Press.

Dion, K. L. (1985). Sex, gender, and groups: Selected issues. In V. E. O'Leary, R. K. Unger, & B. S. Wallston (Eds.), *Sex, gender, and social psychology.* Hillsdale, NJ: Erlbaum.

Dipboye, R. L., Fromkin, H. L., & Wiback, K. (1975). Relative importance of applicant sex, attractiveness, and scholastic standing in evaluations of job applicant resumes. *Journal of Applied Psychology, 60,* 39-43.

Dobbins, D., & Platz, S. J. (1986). Sex differences in leadership: How real are they? *Academy of Management Review, 11*(1), 118-127.

Doyle, J. (1983). *The male experience.* Dubuque, IA: William C Brown.

Eagly, A. H. (1983). Gender and social influence: A social psychological analysis. *American Psychologist, 38,* 971-981.

Eagly, A. H. (1986). *Sex differences in social behavior.* Hillsdale, NJ: Erlbaum.

Eagly, A. H., & Steffen, V. J. (1984). Gender stereotypes stem from the distribution of men and women into social roles. *Journal of Personality and Social Psychology, 43,* 915-928.

Eagly, A. H., & Wood, W. (1982). Inferred sex differences in status as a determinant of gender stereotypes about social influence. *Journal of Personality and Social Psychology, 43,* 915-928.

Falbo, T., Hazen, M. D., & Linimon, D. (1982). The costs of selecting power bases or messages associated with the opposite sex. *Sex Roles, 8,* 147-157.

Ferber, M., Huber, J., & Spitze, G. (1979). Preference for men as bosses and professionals. *Social Forces, 58,* 466-476.

Fischer, C. S., & Oliker, S. J. (1980). *Friendship, sex and the life cycle* (Working paper no. 318). Berkeley: University of California, Berkeley, Institute of Urban and Regional Development.

Freedman, A. M. (1986, March 24). How to do everything better. *The Wall Street Journal,* p. 27D.

French, M. (1985). *Beyond power: On women and men and morals.* New York: Summit Books.

Gallup, G. H. (1978). *The Gallup Poll: Public opinion 1972-1977.* Wilmington, DE: Scholarly Resources.

Garland, H., Hale, K. F., & Burnson, M. (1982). Attribution for the success and failure of female managers: A replication and extension. *Psychology of Women Quarterly, 7*(2), 155-162.

Gilbert, L. A. (1985). *The dual-career couple.* Hillsdale, NJ: Erlbaum.

Gilligan, C. (1982). *In a different voice.* Cambridge, MA: Harvard University Press.

Goldberg, N. R., Clinchy, B. M., Belenky, M. F., & Tarule, J. M. (1987). Women's ways of knowing: On gaining a voice. In P. Shaver & C. Hendricks (Eds.), *Review of personality and social psychology.* Beverly Hills, CA: Sage.

Goldberg, P. (1968). Are women prejudiced against women? *Trans Action, 5,* 28-30.

Golding, J., Resnick, A., & Crosby, F. (1983). Work satisfaction as a function of gender and job status. *Psychology of Women Quarterly, 7*(3), 286-290.

Golub, S., & Canty, E. M. (1982). Sex role expectations and the assumption of leadership by college women. *Journal of Social Psychology, 116,* 83-90.

Goodenow, C. (1986). Friendship patterns of adult women: Relationship to lifespan development and psychological well-being. (Doctoral dissertation, State University of New York at Buffalo, 1985). *Dissertation Abstracts International, 46,* 3582B.

Gupta, N., Jenkins, D., & Behr, T. A. (1983). Employees gender, gender similarity, and supervisors-subordinate cross evaluations. *Psychology of Women Quarterly, 8*(2), 174-184.

Gurin, P. (1987). The political implications of women's statuses. In F. J. Crosby (Ed.), *Spouse, parent, worker.* New Haven, CT: Yale University Press.

Gutek, B. A. (1985). *Sex in the workplace: Impact of sexual behavior and harassment on women and men.* San Francisco: Jossey-Bass.

Hackman, J. R., & Oldham, G. R. (1976). Motivation through the design of work; A test of a theory. *Organizational Behavior and Human Performance, 16,* 250-279.

Hall, R. H. (1985). *The dimensions of work.* Beverly Hills, CA: Sage.

Hammer, W. C., Kim, J. S., Baird, L., & Bigoness, W. J. (1974). Race and sex as determinants of ratings by potential employers in a simulated work sampling task. *Journal of Applied Psychology, 59,* 705-711.

Hansen, D. (1974). *Sex differences and supervision.* Paper presented at the 82nd Annual Meeting of the American Psychological Association, New Orleans.

Hansen, R. D., & O'Leary, V. E. (1983). Actresses and actors: The effects of sex on causal attributions. *Basic and Applied Social Psychology, 4,* 209-230.

Harlan, A., & Weiss, C. (1981). *Moving up: Women in managerial career ladders* (Working paper no. 86). Wellesley, MA: Wellesley College, Center for Research on Women.

Heneman, H. G. (1977). Impact of test information and applicant sex on applicant evaluations in a selection simulation. *Journal of Applied Psychology, 62,* 524-526.

Ilgen, D. R. (1983). Gender issues in performance appraisal: A discussion of O'Leary and Hansen. In F. Landy, S. Zedeck, & J. Cleveland (Eds.), *Performance measurement and theory* (pp. 219-230). Hillsdale, NJ: Erlbaum.

Isaacs, M. B. (1981). Sex role stereotyping and the evaluation of the performance of women: Changing trends. *Psychology of Women Quarterly, 5,* 187-195.

Izraeli, D. N., Izraeli, D., & Eden, D. (1985). Giving credit where credit is due: A case of no sex bias in attribution. *Journal of Applied Psychology, 15*(6), 516-530.

Jacobs, R. (1979). That was no lady that was my boss. *Savvy, 4,* 51-53.

Jacobson, M. B., & Effertz, J. (1974). Sex roles and leadership perceptions of the leaders and the led. *Organizational Behavior and Human Performance, 12,* 383-396.

Jago, A. G., & Vroom, V. H. (1982). Sex differences in the incidence and evaluation of participative leader behavior. *Journal of Applied Psychology, 67*(6), 776-783.

Kagan, J., & Malvaux, J. (1986, May). The uneasy alliance between boss and secretary. *Working Woman,* pp. 105-109, 134, 138.

Kahn, W. A., & Crosby, F. (1985). Discriminating between attitudes and discriminatory behaviors: Change and stasis. In L. Larwood, A. Stromberg, & B. A. Gutek (Eds.), *Women and work: An annual review* (Vol. 1). Beverly Hills, CA: Sage.

Kanter, R. M. (1977). *Men and women of the corporation.* New York: Basic Books.

Kanter, R. M. (1983). *The change masters: Innovation for productivity in the American corporation.* New York: Simon & Schuster.

Kaplan, A., & Surrey, J. L. (1984). The relational self in women: Developmental theory and public policy. In L. E. Walker (Ed.), *Women and mental health policy.* Beverly Hills, CA: Sage.

Kram, K. (1986). *Mentoring at Work: Developmental relationships in organizational life.* Glenview, IL: Scott, Foresman.

Larwood, L., Stromberg, A., & Gutek, B. A. (1985). *Women and work: An annual review* (Vol. 1). Beverly Hills, CA: Sage.

Laws, J. L. (1975). The psychology of tokenism: An analysis. *Sex Roles, 1*, 51-67.

Lee, D. M., & Avares, K. M. (1977). Effects of sex on descriptions and evaluations of supervisory behavior in a simulated industrial setting. *Journal of Applied Psychology, 65*, 176-182.

Lisenmeir, J. A., & Wortman, C. B. (1979). Attitudes toward workers and their work: More evidence that sex makes a difference. *Journal of Applied Social Psychology, 9*(4), 326-334.

Lipman-Blumen, J. (1984). *Gender roles and power.* Englewood Cliffs, NJ: Prentice-Hall.

Lord, R. G., Phillips, J. S., & Rush, M. C. (1980). Effects of sex and personality on perceptions of emergent leadership, influence and social power. *Journal of Applied Psychology, 65*, 176-182.

Lott, B. (1985). The devaluation of women's competence. *Journal of Social Issues, 41*(4), 43-60.

Maslow, A. (1962). *Toward a psychology of being.* New York: Van Nostrand.

Miner, J. B. (1974). The real crunch in managerial manpower. *Harvard Business Review, 51*(6), 146-158.

Moss, M. K., & Frieze, I. H. (1984, June). *College students perceptions of career success strategies for male and female occupations.* Paper presented at the annual meeting of the Pennsylvania Psychological Association, Lancaster.

Muchinsky, P. M., & Harris, S. L. (1977). The effect of applicant sex and scholastic standing on the evaluation of job applicant resumes in sex-typed occupations. *Journal of Vocational Behavior, 11*, 95-108.

Murphy, K. R., Herr, B. M., Lockhard, M. C., & Maguire, E. (1986). Evaluating the performance of paper people, *Journal of Applied Psychology, 71*(4), 555-559.

Nieva, V. F., & Gutek, B. A. (1980). Sex effects on evaluation. *Academy of Management Review, 5*, 269-276.

Nieva, V. F., & Gutek, B. A. (1981). *Women and work: A psychological perspective.* New York: Praeger.

Offermann, L. R. (1985). *Impact of sex composition on leader influence and perceptions of leadership.* Unpublished manuscript, George Washington University.

Offermann, L. R. (1986). Visibility and evaluation of female and male leaders. *Sex Roles, 14*(9/10), 533-543.

O'Leary, V. E. (1974). Some attitudinal barriers to occupational aspirations in women. *Psychological Bulletin, 81*, 809-826.

O'Leary, V. E. (1986). The case of eternal vigilance. *Division 35 Newsletter, 13*(4).

O'Leary, V. E. (1987a, March). *When reciprocity fails: Another look at Queen Bees.* Paper presented at the 12th Annual National Conference of AWP, Denver.

O'Leary, V. E. (1987b). [Stereotypes of women and men bosses]. Unpublished data, Boston University.

O'Leary, V. E. (1987c). [Secretarial students' perceptions of women and men bosses]. Unpublished data, Boston University.

O'Leary, V. E., Grossman, F., & Belle, D. (1987). [Mentors in academe]. Unpublished data, Boston University.

O'Leary, V. E., & Hansen, R. D. (1983). Performance evaluation: A social psychological perspective. In F. Landy, S. Zedeck, & J. Cleveland (Eds.), *Performance measurement and theory* (pp. 197-218). Hillsdale, NJ: Erlbaum.

O'Leary, V. E., & Hansen, R. D. (1985). Sex as an attributional fact. In T. Sonderegger (Ed.), *The Nebraska Symposium on Motivation* (Vol. 32). Lincoln: University of Nebraska Press.

O'Leary, V. E., & Ickovics, J. R. (1987, April). *Who wants a woman boss? Only those who have them.* Paper presented at the Eastern Psychological Association Meetings, Arlington, VA.

Parsons, T., & Bales, R. F. (1955). *Family socialization and interaction process.* Glencoe, IL: Free Press.

Peck, T. (1978). When women evaluate women, nothing succeeds like success: The differential effects of status upon evaluations of male and female professional ability. *Sex Roles, 5,* 205-214.

Petty, M. M., & Lee, G. (1975). Moderating effects of sex of supervisor and subordinate on relationships between supervisory behavior and subordinate satisfaction. *Journal of Personality and Social Psychology, 60*(5), 624-628.

Pheterson, G. I., Kiesler, S. G., & Goldberg, P. (1971). Evaluation of the performance of women as a function of their sex, achievement and personal history. *Journal of Personality and Social Psychology, 19,* 114-118.

Porter, N., & Geis, F. L. (1981). *Androgyny and leadership in mixed-sex discussion groups.* Unpublished manuscript, University of Delaware.

Powell, G., & Butterfield, D. A. (1979). The "good manager": Masculine or androgynous? *Academy of Management Journal, 22,* 395-403.

Riger, S., & Galligan, P. (1980). Women in management: An exploration of competing paradigms. *American Psychologist, 35,* 902-910.

Rosen, B., & Jerdee, T. H. (1973). The influence of sex-role stereotypes on evaluations of male and female supervisory behavior. *Journal of Applied Psychology, 57*(1), 44-48.

Rosen, B., & Jerdee, T. H. (1974). Influence of sex-role stereotypes on personnel decisions. *Journal of Applied Psychology, 59,* 9-14.

Rousel, C. (1974). Relationship of sex of department head to department climate. *Administrative Science Quarterly, 19,* 211-220.

Rubin, L. B. (1985). *Just friends: The role of friendship in our lives.* New York: Harper & Row.

Sargent, A. (1984). *The androgynous manager.* New York: MACOM.

Schein, V. E. (1973). The relationship between sex-role stereotypes and requisite management characteristics. *Journal of Applied Psychology, 57,* 95-100.

Schein, V. E. (1975). Relationships between sex role stereotypes and management characteristics among female managers. *Journal of Applied Psychology, 60,* 340-344.

Schlissel, L. (1982). *Women's diaries of the westward journey.* New York: Schocken.

Slade, M. (1984, October 15). Relationships: Women and their secretaries. *New York Times,* p. 15.

Smith, H. J., & Grenier, M. (1982). Sources of organizational power for women: Overcoming structural obstacles. *Sex Roles, 8*(7), 733-746.

Snodgrass, S. E. (1985). Women's intuition: The effect of subordinate role on interpersonal sensitivity. *Journal of Personality and Social Psychology, 49*(1), 146-155.

South, S. J., Bonjean, C. M., Corder, J., & Markham, W. T. (1982). Sex and power in the federal bureaucracy: A comparative analysis of male and female supervisors. *Work and Occupations, 9*(2), 233-254.

Staines, G., Travis, C., & Jayerante, T. E. (1973). The queen bee syndrome. *Psychology Today, 7*(8), 55-60.

Stratham, A. (1985). *The gender model revisited: Differences in the management styles of men and women.* Unpublished manuscript, University of Wisconsin, Parkside.

Stratham, A. (1986a, August). *Gender and management styles: Findings and implications.* Paper presented at the annual meeting of the American Sociological Association, New York.

Stratham, A. (1986b). *Women working for women: The manager and her secretary.* Unpublished manuscript, University of Wisconsin, Parkside.

Sutton, S. D., & Moore, K. K. (1985). Probing opinions: Executive women—20 years later. *Harvard Business Review, 85,* 5, 42-66.

Terborg, J. R. (1977). Women in management: A research review. *Journal of Applied Psychology, 62,* 642-664.

Tiger, L. (1970). *Men in groups.* New York: Vintage.

Tyler, L. (1965). *The psychology of human differences.* New York: Appleton-Century-Crofts.

Veroff, J., & Sutherland, E. (1985). Achievement motivation and sex roles. In V. E. O'Leary, R. K. Unger, & B. S. Wallston (Eds.), *Women, gender, and social psychology.* Hillsdale, NJ: Erlbaum.

Wallston, B. S., & O'Leary, V. E. (1981). Sex makes a difference: Differential perceptions of women and men. In L. Wheeler (Ed.), *Review of personality social psychology* (Vol. 2). Beverly Hills, CA: Sage.

WBZ-TV. (1986, June). *Evening Magazine.* Boston, MA.

West, C. (1982). Why can't a woman be more like a man? An interactional note on organizational gameplaying for managerial women. *Work and Occupations, 9*(1).

Wolman, C., & Frank, H. (1975). The solo woman in a professional peer group. *American Journal of Orthopsychiatry, 45,* 164-171.

Wheeler, L., & Nezlek, J. (1977). Sex differences in social participation. *Journal of Personality and Social Psychology, 35,* 742-754.

Wright, P. H., & Kemple, T. W. (1981). Friends and parents of a sample of high school juniors: An exploratory study of relationship intensity and interpersonal rewards. *Journal of Marriage and the Family, 43,* 559-570.

9

Trade Union Stewards

HANDLING UNION, FAMILY, AND EMPLOYMENT RESPONSIBILITIES

PAMELA ROBY
LYNET UTTAL

As paid employment has assumed increasing importance for an ever expanding proportion of women, women's admission to the labor force, the quality of their working conditions, and their remuneration have taken on a significance paralleling that for men. Because unions play an important role in addressing these issues, union participation is important to employed women and their families. In this chapter, we examine three major questions: How have family responsibilities affected the ways women as compared with men handle union responsibilities? How do these women and men, all of whom are full-time employees, manage union responsibilities in addition to family and employment responsibilities? How do unions assist stewards in integrating their family and union responsibilities?

This chapter reports on one part of a larger study on female and male trade union stewards. The larger study examines gender similarities and differences in

AUTHORS' NOTE: This is a revised version of a paper presented to the 36th Annual Meeting of the Society for the Study of Social Problems, New York, August 28, 1986. We thank the trade union stewards whom we interviewed for their perspectives and time. We also thank the Academic Senate, the Feminist Studies ORA, the Graduate Opportunity Mentorship Program, and the Social Science Division of the University of California, Santa Cruz, and the Women and Work Research Center of the University of Texas—Arlington, for financial assistance. We appreciate the generous advice and other assistance of Anne Burke, Alice Cook, Arlene Daniels, Evelyn Nakano Glenn, Barbara Gutek, Jane Hood, Marcy Howe, John Kitsuse, Chalsa Loo, Joyce Miller, Martha Moorehouse, James Mulherin, Jim Potterton, Carol Ray, Jan Robinson, Patricia Sexton, George Strauss, Mike Webber, Barbara Wertheimer, Norma Wikler, and the principle officers of the union locals where we did our research.

relation to four major sets of questions about trade union stewards' leadership. First, how do women as compared with men come to be union stewards? Second, how does women stewards' leadership experience compare with that of men? Third, what goals, if any, do women and men stewards have for themselves, for their families, their workplaces, their unions, their nation, and the world; and to what extent and how do they see their union work helping them achieve these goals? Fourth, how do social structural factors such as industry, union, family, race, and age effect each of the above?

With women's increasing awareness of the political and economic problems they confront, scholars concerned with these conditions have begun to examine gender similarities and differences regarding the definition of, attitudes toward, and the practice of leadership and power (see *Asian Women's Journal* Editors, 1975; Bunch, 1980; Denmark, 1977; Dumas, 1980; Gillett, 1984; Gilligan, 1982; Hartsock, 1981; Henley, 1975; Jacobson & Effertz, 1974; Lockheed & Hall, 1976; Mamola, 1979; Miller, 1983; Russ, 1982; Wexley & Hunt, 1974). To date, most literature concerning the relationship of gender to attitudes about leadership and patterns in the exercise of leadership and power has been limited to small group laboratory research or to feminist theorizing. Our larger study allows us to examine gender similarities and differences in attitudes toward and the practice of leadership in a natural environment and with a nonstudent, nonprofessional population as has been called for by small group laboratory researchers and others (Denmark, 1977; Lockheed & Hall, 1976; Zinn, 1983). Elsewhere, one of us has reported on women's paths to rank and file trade union leadership and their experience as rank and file leaders as well as on union stewards' goals for the world, and on methodological issues related to the study of trade unions and working people (Roby, 1986, 1987a, 1987b, 1987c, 1987d).

In this chapter, we will present background information concerning women and unions and then examine three major questions concerning the relationship of family and union responsibilities: How have family responsibilities affected women's as compared with men's handling of union responsibilities? How do these women and men, all of whom are full-time employees, manage union responsibilities in addition to family and employment responsibilities? How do unions assist stewards in integrating their family and union responsibilities?

WOMEN, UNIONS, AND UNION LEADERSHIP

Since 1940, an ever larger proportion of employed women have been employed mothers (U.S. Department of Labor, 1986a, p. 1). In 1986, 62.8% of all women with children under age 18 were in the U.S. labor force; and 54.4% of mothers with children under 6 years were in the labor force (U.S. Department of Labor, 1986a, Table 3). Women are also assuming even more financial responsibility for their families. In addition to the growing percentage of households headed by women, women's wages are accounting for a large proportion of two-earner families' earnings. In 1986, 64.2% of U.S. wives with employed husbands were in the labor force, up from 57.8% in 1981 (U.S. Department of Labor, 1982, Table 9, p. 157; 1987, Table 8, p. 166). In 1986, wives employed full-time contributed 39.5% and those employed part-time contributed 28.3% to the earnings of dual-earner couples, up from 38.3% and 24.7% in 1981 (U.S. Department of Labor, 1979b, p. 4; 1981; 1986b, p. 3).

The growing importance of paid employment to women and their families is occurring within the context of broad changes in the economic structure of the United States and the world. The increasing movement of capital between regions of the nation and the world and between industries, the centralization of ownership and managerial control of capital in multinational corporations, and the growing global competition and underutilization of human and material resources are affecting women and workers throughout the world. In the United States, declining economic growth, deindustrialization, rapidly rising military expenditures, and the attempt by corporations and the Reagan administration to restore profitability to big capital by restructuring the economy have disproportionately affected workers, especially women and people of color (see Bluestone & Harrison, 1982; Miller & Tomaskovic-Devey, 1983; O'Connor, 1984; Piven & Cloward, 1982; Power, 1984; Rosen, 1982; Sweezy, 1985). The gap between rich and poor was wider in 1984 than at any time since the U.S. Bureau of the Census began collecting statistics on the distribution of income in 1947 (U.S. Bureau of the Census, 1985, p. 49). At the same time, the percentage of poor who were women and children also increased (Pearce, 1978; R. Sidel, 1986, pp. 11, 15). The Reagan administration's cuts in child care, Aid to Families with Dependent Children, and job training programs have particularly affected low-paid working women (see Erie & Rein, 1982; Schafran, 1982; R. Sidel, 1982; V. Sidel, 1982). Corporate and governmental actions have simultaneously made the organizing efforts of trade unions' and increasing or maintaining worker compensation more difficult (Mercury News Wire Services, 1984; Wrenn, 1985).

Within this context, union participation is important to both working women and their families. Organized labor has unique powers and potential for maintaining and improving workers' employment conditions and remuneration. Workers' participation in unions makes possible and affects the outcome of unions' daily handling of workers' grievances and enforcement of contracts and laws relating to workers' rights. Workers' participation in unions also affects unions' collective bargaining efforts, which directly determine workers' wages and working conditions. In addition, the very fate of unions is important to women and all workers in the United States and throughout the world. In the United States, no other institution, as Alice Cook (1984, p. 12) points out, is "prepared or authorized to represent workers in collective bargaining for wages and working conditions." Despite union setbacks, organized women workers in all industries continue to earn more and have more substantial health care, retirement, vacation, and other fringe benefits than their female counterparts who are not covered by union contracts (U.S. Department of Labor, 1987, Table 61, p. 221). Furthermore, this union/nonunion advantage of union women is greater than that of union men. Full-time female wage and salary workers who were union members earned 25% more than their female counterparts who were not covered by a union contract in 1986. The median usual weekly earnings of the former were $368 as compared with $274 for the latter. Men who were union members earned an average of 18% more than their male counterparts who were not covered by a union contract in 1986. The median usual weekly wage or salary of the former was $482; the latter earned a median wage of $394 (see Raphael, 1974, p. 27; U.S. Department of Labor, 1979, pp. 2-4).

In the United States, nearly six million women were union members in 1986 and another million working women were covered by union contracts (U.S. Department of Labor, 1987, p. 219). These female employees are obviously affected most directly by the health of unions and the nature of union leadership, policies, and practices, but the conditions of unorganized women are also influenced by the state of unions. Gains that unionized workers attain in wages, benefits, and working conditions affect those of unorganized workers in the surrounding area (Freeman & Medoff, 1984; Kahn, 1978). In addition, the healthier unions are, and the greater the role women play within them, the more reason unorganized women will have to join unions, and the greater their reward will be when they do.

Unions have had an uneven history with regard to their treatment of women. Ruth Milkman has provided the most detailed historical analysis of how unions have excluded or ignored women as well as fought for their rights over the last 100 years (Milkman, 1980, pp. 95-149; see Balser, 1987; Milkman, 1985, 1986; Strom, 1983). Especially when labor has been under attack, male unionists have often viewed female members with suspicion, have discouraged woman-centered organizational forms within unions, and have excluded women from the inner circles of leadership (Kessler-Harris, 1985; Milkman, 1987, pp. 27-48). In addition, many unions have at one time or another shown little interest in organizing women, particularly Black women, or have paid little attention to the special needs of women workers (Cerullo & Feldberg, 1984; Meyerowitz, 1985; Terborg-Penn, 1985).

Since the 1974 founding meeting of the Coalition of Labor Union Women (CLUW), which was attended by 3500 women unionists from all parts of the country, many changes have occurred within the trade union movement (Wertheimer, 1984b, p. 295). In 1980, Joyce Miller, president of CLUW and vice president of the Amalgamated Clothing and Textile Workers Union, became the first woman to be appointed to the AFL-CIO executive council. The following year, Barbara Hutchinson of the American Federation of Government Employees (AFGE) was the second woman and the first Black woman elected to the Executive Council. In 1987, Lenore Miller, President of the Retail, Wholesale and Department Store Union, was elected as a vice president of the AFL-CIO's 35-member Executive Council. Many unions have established departments for women, and a number have filed court cases concerning pay equity, pregnancy disability, wage discrimination, and other issues of concern to women (Bell,

1985; Gabin, 1985; Milkman, 1985, pp. 301-303, 307-314; Wertheimer, 1984a, p. 301). Beginning with the International Union of Electrical Workers (IUE) in 1967, the United Automobile, Aerospace and Agricultural Implement Workers of America (UAW), Communication Workers of America (CWA), the American Federation of State, County and Municipal Employees (AFSCME), the Service Employees Industrial Union (SEIU), and other unions have regularly held regional and/or national conferences for female members on women's issues and leadership skills (Wertheimer, 1984b, pp. 290-292, 297-301). Several hundred women generally attend each conference. At the micropolitical level, many old-time union women have commented that members attending union meetings are now addressed as "sisters and brothers" rather than "you guys" and that union letters are generally signed "in unity" rather than "fraternally yours" (Nelson, 1984; see Henley, 1975).

These micro- and macro-structural changes in unions' relationship to women have been facilitated and buttressed by worker education for women. The major labor education programs for women in existence today include the extensive, year-round offerings at the Institute for Women and Work at the New York City Extension Division of Cornell University's New York State School of Industrial and Labor Relations and the Program on Women and Work at the University of Michigan's Institute for Labor and Industrial Relations (Kornbluh & Kornbluh, 1981; Wertheimer, 1984b, pp. 292-293), and four annual regional trade union women's summer institutes cosponsored by the AFL-CIO, CLUW, and university labor studies programs in the region (there are the West Coast, East Coast, Midwest, and Southern Trade Union Women's Institutes; Wertheimer, 1984b, p. 303). Although these programs have been part of and influenced by the modern-day labor union women's movement, their goals are similar to those of the Women's Trade Union League's Training School for Women Organizers founded in 1914 (Jacoby, 1984) and the Bryn Mawr Summer School for Women, which ran from 1921 to 1938 and included a broad-based feminist vision for social change (summer schools for women workers were later instituted at Wisconsin, Barnard, and elsewhere; Heller, 1984; Roydhouse, 1981; Wertheimer, 1981) as well as education programs of the International Ladies' Garment Workers' Union (ILGWU), the IUE, the UAW, and other individual unions (Johnson & Komer, 1981; Wong, 1984).

These recent changes in unions have accompanied a shift in union membership. The percentage of union members who are women nearly doubled between 1960 and 1986 (from 18% to 34.2%; U.S. Department of Labor, 1987, Table 59, p. 219). Nevertheless, the percentage of union members who are women remains considerably lower than women's representation in the labor force (44.5% in 1986; U.S. Department of Labor, 1987, Tables 1-2, pp. 156-157). Women also remain underrepresented among union officers and staff (Bergquist, 1974; Dewey, 1971; Hartman, 1976; Koziara & Pearson, 1980; LeGrande, 1978; Raphael, 1974; Wertheimer & Nelson, 1975).

When we began to study women's leadership in unions, we decided for several reasons to focus on the conditions and perspectives of trade union stewards. Over the past decade, women have constituted an increasing proportion of most unions' stewards.[1] Trade union stewards occupy an influential position in the workplace. Stewards are union members and employees of private enterprises or government agencies who are elected by union members in their unit (office or shop) or appointed by the union to represent their coworkers and the union (for descriptions of the historical roots of the union steward, see Nash, 1983; Peck, 1963). In many unions, a steward's primary role is to handle the initial step or steps of worker grievances. In most unions, stewards also have political, educational, and organizational responsibilities. In some unions, the steward watches for company violations of the contract but a business agent or higher-level union staff member rather than the steward actually handles the grievances. A grievance is a complaint made by a worker to a union steward or representative about her or his employer's violating the contract or a law, acting unfairly, or jeopardizing the workers' health or safety (see Cook, 1962; Miller & Form, 1951; Nash, 1983; Peck, 1963). Working side by side with others in the steno pool, warehouse, or factory, stewards represent their coworkers before management, communicate between the members and the union, serve as relatively independent leaders of their constituents, and, in handling grievances, interpret and extend the negotiating process and contract (Cook, 1962).

Stewards' understanding of workers' problems, their decisions to act or not act, and their ability to represent workers effectively significantly affect women's everyday employment experiences. A good steward can make a big difference in areas of particular interest to female employees such as termination practices related to workers' absences involving the care of sick children, the distribution of overtime, the allocation of promotions and special job assignments, the scheduling of workdays, and sexual harassment. In addition to the importance of women serving effectively as stewards to their constituents (who are generally women given the sex-segregated labor force), service as a steward is a step toward higher-level positions in unions and workplaces (Cook, 1984, p. 16; Koziara, Bradley, & Pearson, 1982, p. 45; Wertheimer & Nelson, 1975, p. 130). Furthermore, by working as stewards, women gain leadership skills, which they may use in reshaping their workplaces and unions, developing new workplace organizations, and attaining other employment goals of their choosing.

Little attention has been devoted to the study of union stewards in the United States since the important research of 25, 30, and 35 years ago (Mills, 1948; Peck, 1963; Sayles & Strauss, 1967). This lack of attention of the study of trade union stewards in the United States stands in marked contrast to the considerable research and writing on stewards in Great Britain over the last 20 years (Batstone, Boraston, & Frankel, 1977; Goodman & Whittingham, 1969; Marsh, 1973; McCarthy, 1966; Nicholson, 1978; Nicholson, Ursell, & Blyton, 1981; Robertson & Schuller, 1982; Schuller & Robertson, 1983; Terry, 1982; Ursell, Clegg, Lubbock, Blyton, & Nicholson, 1979). Women were largely ignored by the earlier U.S. studies because, to quote the title of a chapter of Sidney Peck's (1963) book, which was a direct quote from a male steward, "A Woman's Place Is with Her Kids." Even in the more recent British research on union stewards, gender issues have been largely neglected. Now both changing labor market and union conditions call for new studies of the leadership and attitudes of trade union stewards in the United States.

UNION LIFE AND FAMILY LIFE

Since a large and increasing percentage of working women are working mothers, if the underrepresentation of women among union officers and staff is to be overcome, the question of how women and husbands of working women are to handle both family and union responsibilities in addition to full-time jobs must be addressed. Previous research on women's union participation has begun to explore how family life affects the extent of women's union participation. Various studies show how women's family life, culture, and family commitments increase (Benson, 1978, p. 48; Frankel, 1984, p. 58; Lamphere, 1984, pp. 256-258; Sacks, 1984, pp. 33, 183; Turbin, 1984, pp. 1-13) or decrease (Creighton, 1982) their propensity to organize their workplaces and to assume leadership (Wertheimer & Nelson, 1975, pp. 136-138).

This is the first systematic study of how women and men in the United States handle union, family, and employment responsibilities. It builds on and adds to the research literature concerning the interface of work and family life. This literature raises a number of important points that deserve consideration in relation to union leadership. Others who have carefully reviewed this literature (Berheide, 1984; Berk & Shih, 1980; Ferree, 1976, 1984; Gutek, Larwood, & Stromberg, 1986; Gutek, Nakamura, & Nieva, 1981; Nieva, 1985; Piotrkowski & Repetti, 1984; Pleck, 1985; Pleck, Staines, & Lang, 1980; Stein, 1984; Wilkinson, 1984; Zavella, in press) report five major findings that relate to our study. First, a variety of family factors affect women's decisions to seek or continue employment (Mortimer, Hall, & Hill, 1978; Nieva, 1985; Nieva & Gutek, 1981). Second, men and women assume different household tasks (Berk, 1985; Berk & Shih, 1980; Holmstrom, 1973; Hood, 1983; Kanter, 1977; E. Pleck, 1976; J. Pleck, 1977, 1985; Rapoport & Rapoport, 1965, 1971, 1980; Szalai et al., 1972). Third, men's contribution to household work increases only minimally when their wives increase their employment and contribution to the family income (Meissner et al., 1975; Walker & Woods, 1976). Fourth, a husband and/or children generally impede women's careers and political activity (Laws, 1979; Lipman-Blumen, 1984, pp. 108-109; Lipman-Blumen & Bernard, 1979; Mortimer, Hall, & Hill, 1978). Fifth, women with demanding professional or managerial careers marry later and less frequently, divorce more often, and have fewer children than their male counterparts (Carroll, 1987; Epstein, 1983, pp. 329-379; Freeman, 1977, pp. 165-188; Gutek, Larwood, & Stromberg, 1986, p. 225; Lorber, 1984, p. 80; Rosow & Rose, 1972, pp. 587-598; Simeone, 1987, pp.

121-122). Our study allows us to examine whether and how these findings apply to trade union stewards.

Because of historical and normative assignments of responsibility, and because of current ideological assumptions, the literature has generally explicitly assumed that women have created the employment/family conflict through their increasing participation in the labor force. The solutions studied have also been women-focused, that is, they focus on how women resolve the employment/family conflict that *they* (women) are experiencing. Because men's participation in the home has been documented to show only minimal alterations in participation in household tasks by men in response to their wives' increasing employment and cosharing of the traditionally male provider role (Meissner et al., 1975; Walker, 1970; Walker & Woods, 1976), focusing on how women have been affected is not an unreasonable place to start studying the problem of employment/family conflicts. Therefore, most of the research we have on the employment/family topic so far examines how women are affected and have strategized and coped in response to employment/work conflicts rather than on how male spouses or employers, unions, and other public institutions adapt or might adapt to families. This chapter examines how both men and women union stewards experience and cope with the triad of family, union, and employment responsibilities. It includes stewards' reports on ways their spouses effectively assist them and ways their unions support and might support their handling of family as well as union responsibilities.

METHODS

Observation and Participant Observation

Prior to and during the early stages of this study, Pamela Roby familiarized herself with issues of concern to trade union women by participant observation at the first New York State Trade Union Women's Conference, which 600 attended in the midst of a heavy snowstorm in 1973; at the founding meeting of the Coalition of Labor Union Women to which 3500 women came largely at their own expense from all parts of the nation in 1974; at a UAW Detroit Area Women's Chapter Christmas party in 1974; and at meetings of the San Jose chapter of the Coalition of Labor Union Women in 1976 and the San Mateo CLUW chapter in 1985. She also did participant observation at the second and third West Coast Trade Union Women's Summer Institutes in 1983 and 1984, at meetings of Union W.A.G.E. (Union Women's Alliance to Gain Equality), at San Jose City College Labor Studies classes, and at the ILGWU's and the Machinists' trade union stewards meetings. She toured workplaces, observed the 1985 CWA national convention and an Executive Board meeting of one union local, and interviewed one or more principal officers of each local in which stewards were interviewed as well as national female officers and/or heads of women's departments of these unions concerning the role of stewards and the history of women in their unions. As a union member, Lynet Uttal in 1982 dealt with a personal grievance, attended general grievance meetings, and worked with a steward in resolving her grievance case.

The Sample

This chapter is based on 124 in-depth structured interviews conducted between July 1985 and August 1986, with a stratified sample of women and men shop stewards from ten major trade unions that represent wage-earning industrial and service workers, that is, nonprofessional employees. The unions from which the sample was drawn have over 100,000 female members internationally and are major northern California unions. The sample was drawn from union locals in the larger San Jose, San Francisco, and Oakland metropolitan areas. It was stratified by (a) type of union: those with members in predominantly manual and nonmanual, public, and private work; those with predominantly male, predominantly female, and with mixed-gender union memberships; those with predominantly Euro-American memberships and those with predominantly Afro-American, Asian American, and/or Hispanic memberships; and those with predominantly progressive or conservative reputations; (b) gender: 47% of the sample is female; and (c) race: 43% of the sample is Asian American, Black, or Hispanic. In this article, we examine only the issue of gender.

The ten unions from which the sample is drawn are the AFGE; the CWA; the Hotel Employees, Restaurant Employees International Union (HERE); the International Association of Machinists and Aerospace Workers (IAM); the International Brotherhood of Electrical Workers (IBEW); the International Brotherhood of Teamsters, Chauffeurs, Warehousemen and Helpers of America (the Teamsters); the ILGWU; the SEIU; the UAW; and the United Food and Commercial Workers International Union (UFCW).

The inclusion of both women and men in the sample enables us to examine similarities and differences in the ways in which the social construction of gender affects family and union responsibilities for women and men. The sample is distinguished from those of most previous work-and-family studies in that the respondents are union leaders as well as full-time employees, in that they work in wage-earning rather than professional jobs, and in that the women and men work within the same corporations or government agencies and belong to the same unions. The fact that the men and women within the sample are from the same workplaces and the same unions enables us to hold constant at least some of the variables (e.g., full-time employment, workplace) that might otherwise confound the study of gender similarities and differences.

The San Francisco, Oakland, and San Jose metropolitan areas from which we drew our sample are particularly appropriate settings for the study of rank and file labor leaders because (a) most studies of unions, including most recent studies, have been centered in the East (especially New York) or the Midwest and have neglected the rapidly growing West Coast; (b) these areas are highly unionized; (c) they are characterized by many of the new and growing areas of work including clerical and public sector employment, high-technology manufacturing, and new forms of automobile manufacture (the NUMMI-New United Motors Manufacturing plant) as well as traditional garment, retail, and communications industries; and (d) their work forces comprise many different ethnic and racial groups.

The female stewards in our sample had been employed 17 years on the average, or slightly less than the average of 20 years for male stewards. The female stewards' lengthy employment records demonstrate that they are not intermittent or temporary employees as often is assumed for women. Both female and male stewards reported working on the job over 40 hours a week on the average, but the men worked about 4 more hours of overtime than their female counterparts.[2] Our sample population's full-time employment was taken as a constant and was not examined in this study.

The Interviews and Interview Schedule

The authors and two sociology students (one male and one female in their midtwenties) conducted the 124 final in-depth interviews. The interviewers were each trained in interviewing skills, writing summaries of the interviewees' responses on the interview schedule, and tape-recording all interviews. All four interviewers were familiar with unions and able to communicate effectively with working people.

The interviews, which were conducted in locations of the respondents' choosing, generally in the home or union hall, averaged just over three hours in length. Interviews conducted in respondents' homes frequently gave us the opportunity to meet members of their families and to observe aspects of their family life, which often related to questions in the interview schedule. Our interview schedule consisted of approximately half closed-ended and half open-ended questions. We conducted two waves of pretest interviews in the process of developing the final interview, bringing the total number of interviews with rank and file trade union leaders to 158.

FINDINGS AND ANALYSIS

The Influence of Family Responsibilities on Stewards' Union Participation[3]

Women workers have long been described as hard to organize and, once organized, less likely to participate in their unions than men (Sacks, 1984, p. 1; Sayles & Strauss, 1967, p. 124; Wertheimer & Nelson, 1975, p. 134). Their lack of participation has been attributed to their primary responsibilities being in the home. Recently, feminist scholars have challenged this characterization of

TABLE 9.1
Distribution of Stewards by Domestic Living Status and by Gender

Gender	Domestic Living Status				
	Living with Partner & Children %	Living Only with Children %	Living Only with Partner %	Single %	Total %
Male	66 (n = 40)	5 (n = 3)	11 (n = 7)	18 (n = 11)	100 (n = 61)*
Female	25 (n = 14)	27 (n = 15)	21 (n = 12)	27 (n = 15)	100 (n = 56)

*The total n is based on 117 couples. Five homosexual cohabitating couples and two male stewards whose domestic living status information is missing data are not included.

working women (Katz & Kemnitzer, 1984, pp. 216, 218; Lamphere, 1984, pp. 248, 262-263; Sacks, 1984, p. 1). In this section, we compare the level of union activity of the female stewards with that of the male stewards. In addition, we contrast the effect of family responsibilities on women's and men's performance of union responsibilities.

In comparing female and male stewards' levels of union activity, we used four different measures of current participation in union activities: (a) the proportion of union meetings that stewards attended, (b) whether the stewards currently held other union positions, (c) whether the stewards participated in other union activities, and (d) whether the stewards reported doing steward work outside of working hours. When simply comparing female and male stewards' levels of union activity, we found that the women whom we interviewed had similar rates of participation as the men on the first three indicators and a significantly lower rate on the fourth indicator.

Because we also wanted to learn how family responsibilities affected these stewards' levels of union activity, we divided stewards according to four categories of domestic living situations. We categorized stewards as (a) living with a partner and children; (b) living with children; (c) living with only a partner; or (d) single (never married, divorced, separated, or widowed persons without children).[4] When we did this, we found that men and women stewards were not similarly distributed among these four different domestic living categories. Instead, we found that male stewards were much more likely than female stewards to be living with a partner and children (66% as compared with 25%); 5% of the male stewards lived only with children, 11% lived only with a partner, and 18% were single. In contrast, female stewards were evenly distributed among the four different domestic living patterns: 25% of the female stewards were living with a partner and children, 27% were living only with children, 21% were living only with partners, and 27% were single (see Table 9.1).[5]

When we examined the relationship of stewards' domestic living situations to gender and union activity, we found clear variations. After creating a summary measure of the above four indicators, we found that single female stewards had higher rates of participation than female stewards with partners and children. Single female stewards also had higher participation rates than single male stewards, and similar rates to male stewards with partners and children. Male stewards with partners and children had higher participation rates than either single male or female stewards with partners and/or children (see Uttal, 1987).

These findings show in sum that the presence of a partner and children affect stewards' levels of participation in union activities, but do so inversely for men and women. For women, the presence of a partner and/or children lowers their level of participation in union activities. For men, the presence of a partner and children boosts their level of union participation.

ADJUSTING FAMILY LIFE TO UNION NEEDS

How do these women and men, all of whom are full-time employees, adjust their family lives so as to handle union responsibilities in addition to family and full-time employment responsibilities? Clearly, not all of the female or male stewards in this sample have to handle traditional family responsibilities such a raising and caring for children or managing households for families. More women than men did not have such responsibilities: 56% of the female stewards and 23% of the male stewards reported living without partners. Female stewards were also less likely than male stewards to be living with children of any age (49% as compared with 69%) and less likely than male stewards to be living with children under age 12 (29% as compared with 42%). In all, 27% of the female stewards and 18% of the male stewards resided with neither partners nor children.

The finding that a relatively small percentage of female stewards lived with partners and/or children does not mean that our question concerning how they adjusted their family lives so as to handle union responsibilities does not apply to them. Rather, female stewards, in particular, reported that living without partners or children was one of the ways that they had adjusted their personal lives so as to be able to handle union responsibilities in addition to their employment and personal responsibilities.

Carole, a 31-year-old gas company serviceperson, was especially aware of these competing demands and struggled with her competing desires to work for her union and still have time for her personal life.[6]

For a long time, it was a big conflict to me how often I could see family, friends or lover when I was involved in the union. A constant source of stress—when will I get out to see mom? I always made the union meeting and worried about others later. I was always explaining to my lover why I had meetings four nights a week. I eventually got involved in a relationship with someone in the union. Ultimately, I became less involved in the union. But then I'm always cutting away big stressful parts. Like the conflict with my lover about time. [The solution was] I just don't be in the relationship. I created space for myself by not being so active in the union and that entered into my being angry at the union. . . . I couldn't figure out a way to be involved and not too involved. [Note: R is currently on two committees and attended 40 steward meetings in the last 12 months plus 8 general union meetings. This represents a very high activity rate. She no longer lives with her lover, and lives alone]. (R154)[7]

Joyce, a 36-year-old billing specialist divorced from her husband, reported that independent living was the best strategy to allow her to continue her level of union activity:

[My boyfriend and I] would probably be living together if it weren't for the union. But because I need the time in the evening to do phone calls and paperwork, I've hesitated to set up that arrangement. I need my solitude. (R106)

Another way of reducing family-union conflicts in order to handle union responsibilities was to dissolve traditional marital arrangements. Of the female stewards, 34% were partnerless because of divorce or separation. An additional 14% of the female stewards were divorced and remarried. In comparison, fewer male stewards reported currently being partnerless because of divorce or separation (13%) or remarried (11%). A number of currently divorced, separated, and remarried female stewards reported that they had resolved conflicting union and family responsibilities by divorcing or separating from their partners.

Dorothy, who had been a steward for over eight years, reported:

The union is not the only reason our marriage broke up, but when I told [my husband] that I was thinking about running for vice-president [of the union], he said, "I thought you might be . . . well, let me tell you something now. If you decide to run for vice-president, you also decide to terminate our marriage."

It was not an easy decision. . . . It was three months of hard soul-searching. I finally said, I'm running. It didn't matter whether I won or lost. I have to live, and I have to live myself as a person. (PT-1B)

Several other women who were divorced also volunteered that not only was their spouse's lack of support for their union work a factor in their decision to divorce, but that if they were not involved in the union, they would be involved in "something else." Rosemarie recalled that her ex-husband had asked her "Who comes first—me or the union?" and that she replied, "It's something I enjoy and need. If I wasn't active in the union, I'd be active in the PTA or something else" (PT).

None of the women we interviewed is a passive victim within the institution of marriage. Rather, each works in her own unique way to shape marriage to fit her needs. Some who divorced later found partners who now effectively support their union work and goals. Dale, who was divorced, said of her present partner, who is also a member of her local,

> My man's not only my total support but the recipient of all my anxieties when I come home. He's a little jealous when I go out of town [on union business], but he never tries to talk me out of it. If he did, it would destroy our relationship. (PT)

Patricia, one of the remarried respondents, reported:

> [My first husband] was very jealous of any outside interest. My present husband gives me drive. I pull him in and ask for his input. We were married when I ran for office. After I was nominated, I had some doubts as to whether I could perform the duties and thought of dropping out of the race. He was the one who kept encouraging me. He told me, "You're ready for it."

Several female stewards explained how they were able to do union activities by reducing their domestic responsibilities by having their children live with other people. Mary, a 34-year-old supply clerk, is in her second marriage. After she left her first husband, she altered her life in two ways in order to do union work:

> I let my youngest daughter stay with my sister and my son stayed with my older sister. I stopped seeing the guy I was seeing. (R210)

Currently, Mary's two children live with her six months a year and live the rest of the year with her mother. Gloria, a 47-year-old food service worker, reported that she did not have to change her personal life in any way in order to do union work in addition to her family life, because "I didn't have a family. My two children lived with their dad from 15 years old on" (R222).

The addition of union activities to employment and family responsibilities was not conflict-free for either men or women who were living with a partner and children in traditional family living situations. Both men and women reported that they had experienced conflicts in the last 12 months. In fact, more male stewards (58%) than female stewards (43%) reported that they had experienced a family-union conflict in the last 12 months.

Men and women, however, reported qualitatively different types of union-family conflicts and resolutions of these conflicts. The central type of conflict that male stewards experienced revolved around issues of absence or attendance at family events due to simultaneous union responsibilities. Usually, they reported that they gave priority to the union responsibility and missed the family event. Women, on the other hand, reported that their main conflict issue was how to keep union responsibilities from interfering with or subtracting from family time. Their resolutions involved keeping union responsibilities from impinging on or invading their family time.

Rebecca, a 47-year-old health insurance specialist, reported that she helped her husband with his business in the evenings. She felt that union meetings once a month cut into this family responsibility. Her solution was to do her union work only during work hours and while riding public transportation home so that she was available to help him in the evenings (R110). Other women reported that they kept their union responsibilities out of their family time by cutting back on their own personal needs, such as sleep (Rs 110, 123, 153).

Several female stewards, regardless of their own domestic living status, reported that the lack of recognition of women's domestic responsibilities was evidenced by the organization of union activities (and not their own interest levels) and this hindered their own and other women's participation (Rs 105, 110, 141, 152, 153, 154, 173, 174). It was especially difficult for women to integrate their domestic responsibilities with the nature, timing, and location of union meetings. Pamela, a 26-year-old customer service representative, is married and lives with her 7-year-old son; her second husband's 6-year-old daughter stays with them every other month for a weekend:

> Things are not set up for working women. Meetings last a long time with everyone [telling their] complaints so I don't go. If they were only a few hours . . . but they're too long to be away from the family. If I leave early I feel embarrassed because people want to know why [I'm leaving early]. (R153)

Cheryl, a 41-year-old customer representative, married but with no children, also had problems with the way the union scheduled its meetings:

> The majority, but not all, in charge of the union are men. They don't worry about holidays. Invariably they schedule workshops the weekend before Thanksgiving. Some of this planning is off kilter. But more women are getting involved. I [guess they] figure if you're dedicated enough you'll make other arrangements. (R152)

Male stewards, on the other hand, did not report that the organization of union meetings was problematic for them because of competing family responsibilities. Women reported that when they confronted union-family scheduling conflicts, they were faced with the likelihood that the family activity would not be taken care of at all if they did not do it or if they did not do preparatory work ahead of time for someone else to carry it out. Women either skipped union meetings or made arrangements ahead of time so that things could be easily taken care of by others at home in their absence. Rose Marie, who is 48 years old, reported:

> If I know ahead of time that I have a meeting, I leave some food that my husband can heat up. (R143)

On the other hand, men could be late to or absent from family events and their absence did not jeopardize the occurrence of the event. Several male stewards with partners and children reported that missing family events was a common solution to their family-union conflicts. The events simply went on without them. Jack, a 50-year-old truck driver, said:

> There was a union meeting and one of the kid's birthdays. We had [the kids] over. I went to the meeting. (R464)

Mike, a 46-year-old business systems technician, reported that he had missed a unique, once-in-a-lifetime family event:

> During a strike, my youngest daughter was born and I was out picketing. [My wife] was in the hospital and . . . she wanted me to be there and I went to picket duty. (R303)

Hurt feelings of the family members who had to adjust to unexpected absences were justified by male stewards by explaining the seriousness of union responsibilities. Ralph, a 46-year-old truck driver, recalled:

> An employee was going to be discharged on my daughter's birthday last year. I stuck around to circumvent termination. I got chewed out. There were hurt feelings from my little girl. I explained the price of a job to a family if I hadn't taken the time. (R462)

In addition, male stewards seemed comfortable with using non-employment time to do union work. Several male stewards reported:

> I go out in the evening and Saturdays to union functions. (R462)

> On occasion [I would spend] longer hours at the office and dinner would be late. The family and house are flexible. It's not a major disruption [if] I stay late. I don't throw others' routines off if I spend time with the union. I've given up occasional free Saturdays for the union, but I did that for overtime before I was a steward. (R410)

Male stewards' coming home late for dinner and other schedule changes made other people adjust their plans to accommodate the stewards' union responsibilities. Male stewards, however, did not perceive this as problematic or inconvenient for others. Adjustments that involved others were reported without any suggestion that others were adversely affected in any way:

> I had a dinner engagement and I was ready to leave but I got involved in a situation which I had to check out as a steward. I had to postpone prior [dinner] plans even though it ended up not being worth the time. (R361)

> I adopt family routines to meetings. (R423)

> I've rescheduled family activities, sometimes on short notice. (R466)

> There is no clash between my family life and job. I just have to tell them, "Tonight I have a meeting," so they know when to start dinner. (R342)

Male stewards' option to miss family functions by prioritizing family responsibilities below union responsibilities and adapting family routines to their union responsibilities was possible because the partners of male stewards provided the services that fulfilled male stewards' needs for their children to be fed, clothed, and cared for on a daily basis even when the male stewards were not available to perform these tasks themselves. Male stewards with partners and children reported that they did 21% of the cooking, 21% of meal cleanup, 29% of grocery shopping, 19% of general housecleaning, 20% of the laundry, and 56% of bill paying as compared to 61%, 51%, 67%, 51%, 61%, 78%, respectively, reported by female stewards with partners and children. This happened in spite of the fact that 65% of the male stewards with partners and children had partners who were employed.

Although, on the average, female stewards do a much higher percentage of household chores than male stewards, there is great variation around this average. A few women reported having fully employed spouses who did the majority of the household's tasks. For several, this division of labor occurred because their partners arrive home from work several hours earlier than they do. Others reported that "discussion and struggle" shifted their family's housework ratio. Janice, an SEIU steward, reported, "We had a lot of family meetings for awhile about how everything is to be divided. Hopefully they are over" (R142). The husband of another, a Teamster steward who had been married for 21 years, does half the grocery shopping, most of the housecleaning, and 99% of the cooking. She said that this arrangement came about "he's a better housekeeper than I am. I don't do it. He does it, and I'm glad. I think it's great" (R161). Although a few female stewards had spouses who assumed considerably more than the housework, the majority of the married and cohabiting women did nearly all the housework themselves.

Spouses also helped stewards handle family, union, and employment responsibilities by directly assisting them with their union work. A small minority of female and male stewards reported that their partners did not support their union work. The majority of both male and female married stewards stated that their spouses supported their union work and cited concrete ways in which they felt supported by their partners. The type of support both female and male stewards reported most frequently was their spouses' encouragement, lack of complaints about the amount of time they spent doing union work, and help with thinking through problems. They reported that their partners were good listeners and helped them figure out union issues. Rick's description of his wife's assistance summarizes what several male stewards reported:

> When she recognizes that I really need to talk about something that happened on the job with an employee, she'll sit and listen. She may never offer a plan of action, but she'll be a sounding board and she's a cheering section. (R344)

Cherise, an IBEW steward, told us:

> He dialogues with me about [my steward work]. . . . He asks me questions. He's excited when I'm excited! (R155)

Sharon, a UAW steward, noted, "He's understanding when I attend classes or meetings for the union, and he takes care of our son" (R291). Another UAW steward related that her husband is "real glad I'm there doing some good" (R292).

Female stewards with partners but no children reported that their partners did not object to the amount of time they spent doing union work.

If I say I'm going to be late, he says, "Fine, no problem." (R110)

He doesn't object to the time and energy I expend or the late-night calls. (R181)

He tolerated the fact that I'm gone so much and do so much union work when I'm home. (R104)

He's told me it's up to me how much work I put into it. He's not put any stipulations on my having to be home at a certain time for dinner or what we have for dinner. If I'm late due to union work or if I were to run for a higher union office, that's fine. His feeling is probably every woman should do so something like this. (R111)

There was, however, an additional qualitative difference in the type of support that male stewards received from their partners as compared to what female stewards received from their partners. More male than female stewards reported receiving concrete services from their partners for the doing of union tasks. A few more women than men reported that their spouses taxied them to meetings, but a sizable number of a male stewards and no female stewards reported that their partners provided secretarial and editorial support:17

She's a good editor. She translates from my jargon to standard English. (R410)

She types stuff for me. She gives me emotional support. (R404)

When I have meetings, she puts the dates on the calendar. She reads my union paper when it comes and asks me questions. (R371)

My wife is a secretary and she types things for me which saves me time. (R421q212)

... she's an excellent writer and will edit what I write and suggests ways of saying something I may not have thought of. (R344)

She types some of my work. (R454)

We discuss problems at work. She gives input. We go over [the union] literature. She helps me do research. (R481)

And they reported that their partners freed them from domestic concerns so that they could participate in union activities: "She'll assume total responsibility for child care to free me to attend meetings" (R441). In addition to these concrete services, some men also felt supported by their partners' joining in their union activities with them. Jack noted, for example, "She goes to picnics, labor parades, joins along with me" (R464).

When female stewards did report getting concrete support services from others, the service was usually help with domestic rather than union responsibilities. In addition, this support generally did not come from their partners, but from their older children or their mothers. Claudine, a 34-year-old account clerk, reported that she maintained the responsibility for household work, but that she was able to shift the actual performance of domestic responsibilities to her daughter. She observed:

> During negotiations, I was gone constantly. My family and I talked a lot on the phone. This was discussed with my family before I started. I said, "This is what I want to do," and they said "Go for it!" Luckily, I have a 13-year-old daughter who can cook and do laundry. (R142)

Jenny, who lives with her 13-year-old son and her mother, reports, "My mother is a live-in baby-sitter, cook, and housekeeper." (R121) Janet, a 32-year-old single mother, manages by swapping child-care time with her mother who also has young children (R202).

Other female stewards in nontraditional living arrangements but no male stewards said they handled the combined load of union, family, and employment responsibilities by cutting back on housework and/or organizing their time better. Several pointed out that they had long needed to be better organized and that additional union work was the catalyst they needed:

> I don't clean house as much as I used to. (R101)

> I buy more convenience foods, fast foods. (R106)

> I don't clean as well as I used to around the house. Also, I don't sleep as much as I used to. (R123)

> I decided some of [the housework] wasn't that important. I'm at my best if I have a million things to do. I'm real happy. (R152)

> I organize my personal time and work time differently than before. I used to be pretty lazy. Now I'm more organized. My housework and personal life are more organized due to my scheduling time. Too bad it took the union involvement to do that. It helps. (R156)

On the other hand, a number of the male stewards but no female stewards mentioned that they cut back on recreational activities in order to take on additional union responsibilities:

> I quit being in Knights of Columbus. (R329)

> Yeah. My union work has probably taken quite a bit of time. Primarily instead of watching TV for two hours, . . . [I work] on union stuff. (R454)

> It changes your life, and you wonder sometimes how much. . . . I used to run a lot, about 30 minutes every night. (R465)

In summary, both male and female stewards had to make decisions about how to prioritize domestic and union responsibilities. Female stewards with partners and children prioritized family responsibilities over union responsibilities. Single female stewards, like most male stewards, prioritized union responsibilities over personal responsibilities. This was, however, accomplished by conscious and unconscious decisions to limit and/or eliminate their involvement in families. Men placed union responsibilities over family responsibilities in spite of having families to whom they answered. When male stewards had conflicting responsibilities, they reported asking their families to excuse their absences, apologized to their children for missing their birthday parties, and told their wives not to delay dinner for them. When women had conflicting personal and union responsibilities, they were less likely than men to even have partners or children to whom they made these excuses. If they had partners and children, they took special care to keep union responsibilities from impinging upon family time. Unlike men who depended heavily on their partners for all types of support services, female stewards generally either handled matters by themselves or relied upon people other than their spouses for support.

WAYS UNIONS SUPPORT STEWARDS' HANDLING UNION-FAMILY AND EMPLOYMENT RESPONSIBILITIES

The stewards whom we interviewed reported that unions provide four major types of support for their handling of family and union responsibilities: (a) a variety of family-respecting practices; (b) released time; (c) services including recreational activities; and (d) repayment of out-of-pocket expenses. Some of the ways in which unions accommodate families are a matter of union policy. Others are a matter of individual decision and practice on the part of union business agents and officers. While some unions are more supportive of stewards' family responsibilities than are others, no single union offers all of the supports mentioned below (see American Federation of Labor-Congress of Industrial Organizations, 1986; Donahue, 1987; Lerner, 1986, pp. ix, 317-329).

Family-Respecting Practices

When asked, "Has the union done anything that has made it easier for you to participate or be active in the union?" stewards most frequently cited factors related to the scheduling or location of meetings or other practices that facilitate their combining family life and union life. Some union locals schedule membership and steward meetings at times and places that are especially convenient for the stewards (R234, 241, 329, 451, 454). Sometimes the time that was considered "especially convenient" was right after work; sometimes it was in the evening. Other stewards said that their unions schedule meetings at rotating times and locations so that members with families can attend at least some meetings that fit in well with their family and work schedules (R182, 467). CWA and UFCW stewards appreciated that fact that their locals held their monthly membership meetings at two different times on the same day so that they could choose the time that best fit their family and work schedules. The scheduling of meetings some distance in the future was also cited as helpful, for it allowed stewards to plan family activities around meetings rather than making them confront the choice of canceling family plans or missing union meetings. Delores, an SEIU steward who was actively involved in union negotiations and was the mother of three teenagers, noted the importance of an additional consideration, the inclusion of breaks:

> We had breaks of an hour or two during negotiations when I could run home and check with the kids on surprise visits. (R242)

Other busy parents, who sometimes had difficulty keeping track of meetings themselves, appreciated union staff for making "sure I know when the meetings are, especially the important ones" (R141, 213, 481).

In a few cases, union staff made special provisions for stewards with special family responsibilities. Chuck, a HERE steward, who had full responsibility for his 5- and 18-month-old daughters when his wife was away at work, told us that he was only able to be a steward because a business agent had given him special on-the-job training for his steward work, thus making it unnecessary for him to attend the steward training classes that were held during his parenting time (R381). Union staff gave him "their home phone numbers" so he could call them whenever he found he needed more information. Other stewards reported that the understanding that business agents and union officers showed them and the care with which they filled them in on activities they missed when their family members were in the hospital or having difficulties made a big difference to them (R343).

Stewards often took the initiative in integrating their families into their union activities. Many told us about taking their children to union meetings (R201, 292, 301, 30). When union officers and business agents were receptive to young people attending their meetings and allowed for mild disruptions, stewards found this practice to be a good solution for handling a potential union-family conflict. They also felt good about the union officers' understanding concerning their children and liked having other union stewards and officers come to know their children and having their children come to feel a part of their union. Others reported that they think it is important for their children to see them taking on union responsibilities and to learn about union and national affairs covered in the meetings. Ruth, a CWA steward, said that she felt that the San Francisco Central Labor Council-sponsored lectures by Chicago's late Mayor Washington and Jessie Jackson provided her children with valuable Black role models, education, and perspectives that they were unable to receive through their schools (PT-CW). Another 42-year-old CWA mother of three observed:

> I've involved my family in what I do. Every time I get a chance to take them with me, like the two picket lines and the 1984 campaign, I do. . . . My kids are like partners. (R30)

Now her oldest daughter is also employed with the telephone company and, not surprisingly, is a CWA steward too.

Released Time

The second most frequently cited union family accommodative policy was union activity (UA) time (R 30, 101, 103, 104, 291, 403). Offered by CWA and UAW, UA time enables stewards to take time off from their employment to do steward work. Stewards are paid their regular wages for this time either by their union or by their employer, depending on the terms of their contract. The UAW union coordinators at the New United Motors Manufacturing (NUMMI) plant have two hours a week of company-provided time for their union coordination work.[8] The CWA stewards' UA time is paid for by the union itself. Although the Machinists did not have UA time, Claudia, an IAM steward who was also an officer of the local CLUW chapter, reported, "Whenever I need time off for a CLUW function, if the company will let me off, the union will pay for my lost time, hotels, travel and other expenses" (R122). The provisions of such time means that these stewards have to do less or none of their steward or related work on family time.

Services Including Recreational Activities

Union family picnics and softball games are popular with some stewards. Others appreciate the union's arranging transportation to meetings for them (a number do not own cars), and/or providing meals at steward meetings so that they did not have to depend on other family members for these services. The meals provided at the ILGWU and IAM steward meetings that we observed also give stewards a chance to socialize, to learn informally from one another's experiences, and to get well enough acquainted to feel comfortable calling on one another when they have questions about steward issues.

Repayment of Out-of-Pocket Expenses

The money stewards spend while fulfilling their steward responsibilities is often significant when considered in relation to their salaries. The expenses stewards incur are often taken for granted by unions. Some unions, however, reimburse stewards for these expenses so that they do not place a burden on family budgets. Dennis, a Teamster who has served as a steward intermittently for 13 years, said that it helps when the union pays his phone bills for union calls so that this expense does not have to come out of the family budget (R 466). Margaret, a 60-year-old ILGWU steward, who earns under $5000 a year as a buttonholer in the depressed garment industry, told us, "Sometimes they pay for my gas for coming over there for meetings because I have to go 25 miles both ways" (R233). Shirley, an IBEW steward, noted that, when there is a "joint grievance, we meet for breakfast and they buy breakfast. They pay mileage and buy lunch for stewards' conferences too" (R151).

What Could Unions Do?

When asked, "What could your union do to make your participation easier?" stewards responded by suggesting many of the ways, described above, that some unions already help stewards. Stewards' most frequently cited request, like the support noted above that they most frequently appreciated, was for their union to schedule meetings at more convenient times (R 111, 141, 241, 291, 456, 464). A number also wanted more advanced warning for steward meetings (R 110, 181, 243, 371, 393). Carl, a 53-year-old UAW union coordinator, suggested:

> Maybe they could schedule things two or three weeks ahead of time. Then I could plan my family time better. (R393)

Others wanted more convenient meeting sites (R 143, 174, 181, 375). Of course, what a convenient meeting place and a convenient meeting time mean vary from family to family. Therefore, surveys might be used to determine the best time for union meetings. Members of other unions noted that meetings should be shorter and/or kept to the length of time promised. Ann winced and said, if they would "keep to their schedule, then I'd consider staying on [as a steward]. I could understand a few exceptions" but not going over the promised time at every meeting (R131). Steve, a member of another union, observed, they could "save time by not having so much confusion at meetings. [They could] put out written information that would be beneficial to stewards" (R 361).

Union activity time for steward work and meetings was the stewards' second most frequently cited request (R104, 105, 123, 151, 202, 242, 403, 405, 452, 457). The third most frequently proposed suggestion was the provision of child care and hot meals for members and their children during union meetings. George responded promptly to our question:

> Have a baby-sitting service! It would be a help if you could bring children and put them in a room while you're in the meeting instead of having them in the meeting. (R303)

Interestingly, more men than women with young children requested child-care services. Perhaps this finding reflects the facts, noted above, that more male than female stewards have young children. Sam wants this child care to be more than just baby-sitting:

> Provide meaningful child care with activities for meetings. Have classes for parents and kids, activities, baseball games, that kind of thing. (R404)

Renee was not concerned with child care during union meetings for she felt that her children were well cared by their father, who worked a different shift than hers, when she was not home. But she did want more family-centered union activities.

> They do have Easter parties for the children, but no husbands want to come. We need something for the whole family. (R31)

Finally, several stewards, whose unions do not reimburse their expenses, thought that they should. Marcy noted,

> I have to pay for parking and the baby-sitter [when I have a union meeting]. The union should pay something when stewards have families. (R183)

Stuart observed,

> Financially I experience a lot of expenses like phone bills. They could waive our
> monthly dues [to help with these].

In summary, unions assist stewards with family responsibilities in numerous
and varied ways. No one union offers all of the varied types of support, described
above. Rather, we gathered these examples of union policies and practices that
help stewards carry out their family responsibilities from our interviews with
stewards from 16 locals of 10 major international unions. Except for the
provision of meaningful child care during steward and membership meetings, all
the forms of support that stewards suggested for families are already being
offered by at least one union local. This finding would suggest that it would be
possible for other unions to implement these forms of support as well.

CONCLUSIONS, IMPLICATIONS, AND
SUGGESTIONS FOR FUTURE RESEARCH

Unions and other worker organizations have become increasingly important
to women as more and more women have entered the labor force and as women
have assumed increasing financial responsibilities for their families. As union
stewards, women shape the quality of their own and others' working conditions
by carrying out formal grievance procedures and informally handling daily
problems. Stewards may also affect workers' take-home wages by educating
coworkers about collective bargaining and unions, and by uniting workers in
seeking better wages. As growing numbers of workers, union members, and
stewards have considerable family responsibilities, union practices that enable
members and rank and file leaders to integrate their families into union activities
and otherwise assist them in integrating union and family activities have become
increasingly important to the health and survival of unions and to the condition
of workers. In this study, we have examined and compared how family
responsibilities have affected female and male stewards' handling of union
responsibilities, the ways stewards have managed union responsibilities in
addition to family and employment responsibilities, and the ways in which
unions have and might assist rank and file leaders in integrating union, family,
and work responsibilities.

One of the most striking findings of this study is the considerable gender
difference in the personal living arrangements of female and male stewards. The
concentration of male stewards in households with both partners and children as
compared with the even distribution of female stewards in households with and
without partners, and with and without children, suggests that the combination
of employment, public activity, and home life is experienced differently by men
and women and results in different family organizations.

The second major finding of our study is that, although both women and men experience union-family conflicts, they have qualitatively different types of conflicts with and resolutions for these conflicts. When male stewards had such conflicts, they generally prioritized the union over the family activity and relied on their wives to take of the family event. In contrast, female stewards with partners and children generally prioritized family activities over union activities and found that the family event such as children's birthdays simply did not happen without them. In this study, controlling for occupational differences and external activities, we found that the unequal division of housework and parenting persists. Male stewards, whether their spouses are employed or not, do considerably less housework than female stewards. Female stewards, if living with partners, are more likely to be living with an employed spouse and do much more housework than their male coworkers. This finding has been documented in previous studies for various workers.

Past studies have documented how women have reorganized their personal lives, especially the division of housework with spouses, in order to combine family and other activities. These studies demonstrate how the family accommodates to the needs of the public sphere. A third important set of findings in our study demonstrates how the public sphere can also be responsive to the needs of the family. This findings suggests that workplaces and union organizations, and not just families, can be altered in order to allow for the smoother integration of family and public activities of women and men.

Given the present-day crisis of unions coupled with the growing proportion of the labor force constituted by mothers with children under the age of 16 and a smaller but seemingly growing proportion of actively parenting fathers, unions would benefit from expanding activities and arrangements that accommodate members with families. An additional benefit of such efforts, evidenced in another portion of our study, is that people who begin their involvement with unions as children often become union activists as adults.

Of course, many of the strategies workers have suggested in this study for unions apply generally to their places of employment as well. Indeed, many corporations that are successfully resisting unionization currently offer family-oriented activities, child care, and other arrangements to accommodate families.

The first and foremost implication of this research is that, in order to understand how people combined family and public aspects of their lives (e.g., employment, union activism), we need to examine and compare men and women in all forms of personal living arrangements. In this study, most of the women stewards were not in a traditional living situation with both a partner and children, whereas most of the men were. If the larger employed population reflects this gender difference, we need to understand how and why some employed women have chosen or have been forced to reduce or eliminate the traditional family living arrangement from their lives. In general, we need to account for the integration of family and employment in family forms other than just dual-work and nuclear families.

Second, we need to look further at the types of changes organizations are making in response to the increasing numbers of workers who have serious commitments to family life and/or parenting. We need to understand why married men's participation in the household has not dramatically changed with the increasing employment of wives. We also need to understand why businesses and workers' organizations persist to the degree that they do in perceiving their employees as unencumbered by family responsibilities.

Third, because individuals evolved into their present life-styles over time, we need to understand how large groups of men and women arrive at such dissimilar domestic living patterns in spite of similar occupations and commitments to union activism. While a simple answer is that gender operates differently for men and women, we need to understand exactly how this process operates and what form it takes at any specific historical moment.

A fourth issue that needs further research is why female stewards with partners and children reported fewer union-family conflicts than male stewards with partners and children. Initially, this does not seen to make sense. How women and men develop these different definitions was not, however, explored in this study. Through longitudinal research, one could determine whether, over time, female stewards actually experience fewer conflicts, or whether they have simply worked out resolutions to many of the types of conflicts that press on women.

We hope that the research that we have reported here and future research will enable women workers to participate more fully in unions and other worker organizations. Women's fuller participation in such organizations could have deep implications for the organization of their workplaces as well as for their homes.

NOTES

1. Since 1983, the data on union membership have been derived from U.S. Bureau of the Census Current Population Household Surveys. Data have never been gathered on the numbers of women who hold local union posts across the country, and union locals do not calculate the percentage of their members or stewards who are female. With computerization, union locals are increasingly developing up-to-date, unified lists of stewards. It is generally agreed that, over the past decade, women have constituted an increasing proportion of most unions' stewards. For those northern California locals from which we have obtained lists of stewards, we have found that female members continue to be underrepresented among stewards (in one local, women were approximately 2% of the stewards and 7% of the membership; in a second local, women were 55% of the stewards and 68% of the membership; and, in a third local, 86% of the stewards and about 92% of the membership were female).

2. The average number of hours women worked at their place of employment excludes one woman who was on temporary disability and worked zero hours; 29% of the women as compared with 53% of the men reported working over 40 hours the week prior to their interview.

3. The data in this section on the influence of family responsibilities on stewards' union participation are examined in greater detail in Lynet Uttal's (1987) unpublished master's essay, "I Took My Daughter to the Union Meeting: Gendered Domestic Responsibilities and Union Steward Activity."

4. The importance of examining the relationship of the public and private spheres by comparing heterosexual couples and homosexual couples cannot be overstated (see Blumstein & Schwartz, (1983). Five homosexual couples were omitted in this analysis because of the small number of respondents in this category.

5. The distribution of workers in the total U.S. population among household types was similar to that among stewards: 52% of the full-time year-round male workers in the total U.S. population were in traditional families with a spouse and children under age 18, as compared with 32% of full-time, year-round female workers (U.S. Bureau of the Census, 1980, table 275).

6. All names have been changed to protect the anonymity of those whom we interviewed.

7. The code numbers refer to individual respondents.

8. Stewards in UAW local 2244 have been called "union coordinators" since the opening of the NUMMI plant.

REFERENCES

American Federation of Labor-Congress of Industrial Organizations Executive Council. (1986). Work and family: Who is really "pro-family"? In *AFL-CIO reviews the issues* (Report no. 3). Washington, DC: Author.

Asian Women's Journal Editors. (1975). Asian women as leaders. In *Asian Women* (pp. 102-102). Los Angeles: University of California, Asian Studies Center.

Balser, D. (1987). *Sisterhood and solidarity.* Boston: South End Press.

Batstone, E., Boraston, I., & Frankel, S. (1977). *Shop stewards in action.* Oxford: Basil Blackwell.

Bell, D. E. (1985). Unionized women in state and local government. In R. Milkman (Ed.), *Women, work and protest: A century of US women's labor history* (pp. 280-299). Boston: Routledge & Kegan Paul.

Benson, S. P. (1978). "The clerking sisterhood": Rationalization and the work culture of saleswomen in American department stores, 1890-1960. *Radical America, 12*(2).

Bergquist, V. A. (1974). Women's participation in labor organizations. *Monthly Labor Review, 97,* 3-9.

Berheide, C. W. (1984). Women's work in the home. *Marriage and Family Review,* 7(3/4), 37-55.

Berk, S. F. (1985). *The gender factory: The apportionment of work in American households.* New York: Plenum.

Berk, S. F., & Shih, A. (1980). Contributions to household labor: Comparing wives' and husbands' reports. In S. F. Berk (Ed.), *Women and household labor* (pp. 191-228). Beverly Hills, CA: Sage.

Bluestone, B., & Harrison, B. (1982). *The deindustrialization of America: Plant closings, community abandonment, and the dismantling of basic industries.* New York: Basic Books.

Blumstein, P., & Schwartz, P. (1983). *American couples: Money, work, sex.* New York: William Morrow.

Bunch, C. (1980). Woman power: The courage to lead, the strength to follow and the sense to know the difference. *Ms., 9*(1).

Carroll, S. J. (1987, April 23-26). *Gender difference and the contemporary leadership crisis.* Paper presented at the Wingspread Seminar on Leadership Research, Racine, WI. (Available from the Center for the American Woman and Politics, Eagleton Institute of Politics, Rutgers University).

Cerullo, M., & Feldberg, R. (1984). Women workers, feminism and the unions. *Radical America, 18*(5).

Cockburn, C. (Ed.). (1984, April). Trade unions and the radicalizing of socialist feminism. *Feminist Review, 16.*

Cook, A. (1962). Dual government in unions: A tool for analysis. *Industrial and Labor Relations Review, 15.*

Cook, A. (1984). Introduction. In A. H. Cook, V. R. Lorwin, & A. K. Daniels (Eds.), *Women and trade unions in eleven industrialized countries* (pp. 3-36). Philadelphia: Temple University Press.

Creighton, H. (1982). Tied by the double apron strings: Female work culture and organization in a restaurant. *The Insurgent Sociologist, 11*(3), 59-63.

Denmark, F. L. (1977). Styles of leadership. *Psychology of Women Quarterly, 2*(2), 99-113.

Denmark, F. L., & Diggory, J. C. (1966). Sex differences in attitudes toward leaders' display of authoritarian behavior. *Psychological Reports, 18,* 863-872.

Dewey, L. (1971, February). Women in labor unions. *Monthly Labor Review.*

Donahue, T. R. (1987, March 30). Remarks to the National Conference on Work and Family Life. In *AFL-CIO News.* Washington, DC: AFL-CIO, Department of Information.

Dumas, R. G. (1980). Dilemmas of Black females in leadership. In L. Rodgers-Rose (Ed.), *The Black woman.* Beverly Hills, CA: Sage.

Epstein, C. F. (1983). *Women in law.* Garden City, NY: Anchor Press/Doubleday.

Erie, S., & Rein, M. (1982). Welfare: The new poor laws. In A. Gartner, C. Greer, & F. Riessman (Eds.), *What Reagan is doing to us.* New York: Harper & Row.

Ferree, M. M. (1976). Paid work and housework as sources of satisfaction. *Social Problems, 23*(4), 431-441.

Ferree, M. M. (1984). The view from below: Women's employment and gender equality in working class families. *Marriage and Family Review, 7*(3/4), 57-77.

Frankel, L. (1984). Southern textile women: Generations of survival and struggle. In K. Sacks & D. Remy (Eds.), *My troubles are going to have trouble with me: Everyday trials and triumphs of women workers.* New Brunswick, NJ: Rutgers University Press.

Freeman, B. C. (1977). Faculty women in the American university: Up the down staircase. *Higher Education, 6,* 165-188.

Freeman, R. B., & Medoff, J. L. (1984). What unionism does to nonorganized labor. In R. B. Freeman & J. L. Medoff, *What do unions do?* New York: Basic Books.

Gabin, N. (1985). Women and the United Automobile Workers' Union in the 1950s. In R. Milkman (Ed.), *Women, work and protest: A century of US women's labor history* (pp. 259-279). Boston: Routledge & Kegan Paul.

Gillett, M. (1984, April). *Strategies for power.* Keynote address presented at the Second International Interdisciplinary Congress on Women, Groningen, The Netherlands.

Gilligan, C. (1982). *In a different voice: Psychological theory and women's development.* Cambridge, MA: Harvard University Press.

Goodman, J.F.B., & Whittingham, T. G. (1969). *Shop stewards in British industry*. London: McGraw-Hill.

Gutek, B. A., Larwood, L., & Stromberg, A. (1986). Women at work. In C. L. Cooper & I. Robertson (Eds.), *Review of industrial and organizational psychology* (pp. 217-234). New York: John Wiley.

Gutek, B. A., Nakamura, C. Y., & Nieva, V. F. (1981). The interdependence of work and family roles. *Journal of Occupational Behavior, 2*, 1-16.

Hartman, H. (1976). Capitalism, patriarchy, and job segregation by sex. In M. Blaxall & B. Reagon (Eds.), *Women and the workplace: The implications of occupational segregation*. Chicago: University of Chicago Press.

Hartsock, N. (1981). Political change: Two perspectives on power. In *Quest* Staff (Eds.), *Building feminist theory*. New York: Longman.

Heller, R. (1984). Blue collars and bluestockings: The Bryn Mawr Summer School for Women Workers, 1921-1938. In J. L. Kornbluh & M. Frederickson (Eds.), *Sisterhood and solidarity: Workers' education for women, 1914-1984* (pp. 107-147). Philadelphia: Temple University Press.

Henley, N. (1975). Power, sex and nonverbal communication. In B. Thorne & N. Henley (Eds.), *Language and sex: Difference and dominance* (pp. 184-199). Rowley, MA: Newbury.

Holmstrom, L. L. (1973). *The two-career family*. Cambridge, MA: Schenkman.

Hood, J. (1983). *Becoming a two job family*. New York: Praeger.

Jacobson, M. B., & Effertz, J. (1974). Sex roles and leadership: Perceptions of the leaders and the led. *Organizational Behavior and Human Performance, 12*, 383-396.

Jacoby, R. M. (1984). The Women's Trade Union League Training School for women organizers, 1914-1926. In J. L. Kornbluh & M. Frederickson (Eds.), *Sisterhood and solidarity: Workers' education for women, 1914-1984*. Philadelphia: Temple University Press.

Johnson, G. T., & Komer, O. (1981). Education for affirmative action: Two union approaches. In B. M. Wertheimer (Ed.), *Labor education for women workers*. Philadelphia: Temple University Press.

Kahn, L. (1978). The effect of unions on the earnings of nonunion workers. *Industrial and Labor Relations Review, 32*, 21-54.

Kanter, R. M. (1977). *Work and family in the United States: A critical review and agenda for research and policy*. New York: Russell Sage.

Katz, N., & Kemnitzer, D. S. (1984). Women and work in Silicon Valley: Options and futures. In K. B. Sacks & D. Remy (Eds.), *My troubles are going to have trouble with me: Everyday trials and triumphs of women workers* (pp. 209-218). New Brunswick, NJ: Rutgers University Press.

Kelly, J. (1979). The doubled vision of feminist theory: A postscript to the "Women and Power" Conference. *Feminist Studies, 5*(1), 216-227.

Kessler-Harris, A. (1985). Problems of coalition-building: Women and trade unions in the 1920s. In R. Milkman (Ed.), *Women, work and protest: A century of US women's labor history* (pp. 110-138). Boston: Routledge & Kegan Paul.

Kornbluh, J. L., & Kornbluh, H. (1981). Conferences: The one-day model. In B. M. Wertheimer (Ed.), *Labor education for women* (pp. 54-61). Philadelphia: Temple University Press.

Koziara, K. S., M. I. Bradley, & Pearson, D. A. (1982). Becoming a union leader: The path to local office. *Monthly Labor Review, 105*(2).

Koziara, K. S., & Pearson, D. A. (1980). Barriers to women becoming union leaders. In *Industrial Relations Research Association Proceedings* (33rd Annual Meeting).

Lamphere, L. (1984). On the shop floor: Multi-ethnic unity against the conglomerate. In K. Sacks & D. Remy (Eds.), *My troubles are going to have trouble with me: Everyday trials and triumphs of women workers* (pp. 247-263). New Brunswick, NJ: Rutgers University Press.

Laws, J. L. (1979). *The second X: Sex role and social role.* New York: Elsevier.

LeGrande, L. H. (1978). Women in labor organizations: Their ranks are increasing. *Monthly Labor Review, 101*(8).

Lerner, M. (1986). *Surplus powerlessness.* Oakland, CA: Institute for Labor and Mental Health.

Lipman-Blumen, J. (1984). *Gender roles and power.* Englewood Cliffs, NJ: Prentice-Hall.

Lipman-Blumen, J., & Bernard, J. (Eds.). (1979). *Sex roles and social policy.* Beverly Hills, CA: Sage.

Lockheed, M. E., & Hall, K. P. (1976). Conceptualizing sex as a status characteristic: Applications to leadership training strategies. *Journal of Social Issues, 32*(3), 111-124.

Lorber, J. (1984). *Women physicians: Careers, status, and power.* New York: Tavistock.

Mamola, C. (1979). Women in mixed groups: Some research findings. *Small Group Behavior, 20*(3), 431-440.

Marsh, A. (1973). *Managers and shop stewards shop floor revolution.* London: Institute of Personnel Management.

McCarthy, W.E.J. (1966). *The role of shop stewards in British industrial relations.* London: Royal Commission on Trade Unions and Employers' Associations.

Meissner, M., Humphreys, E. W., Meis, S. M., & Scheu, W. J. (1975). No exit for wives: Sexual division of labor and the cumulation of household demands. *Canadian Review of Sociology and Anthropology, 12,* 424-439.

Mercury News Wire Services. (1984, February 23). Court helps ailing firms break union contracts. *San Jose Mercury,* p. 1A.

Meyerowitz, R. (1985). Organizing the United Automobile Workers: Women workers at the Ternstedt General Motors Parts Plant. In R. Milkman (Ed.), *Women, work and protest: A century of US women's labor history* (pp. 259-279). Boston: Routledge & Kegan Paul.

Milkman, R. (1980). Organizing the sexual division of labor: Historical perspectives on "women's work" and the American labor movement. *Socialist Review, 49,* 95-150.

Milkman, R. (1985). Women workers, feminism and the labor movement since the 1960s. In R. Milkman (Ed.), *Women, work and protest: A century of US women's labor history* (pp. 300-322). Boston: Routledge & Kegan Paul.

Milkman, R. (1986, August 18-22). *Woman's place in the labor movement: Historical perspectives.* Paper presented at the 11th World Congress of Sociology, New Delhi, India.

Milkman, R. (1987). *Gender at work: The dynamics of job segregation by sex during World War II.* Urbana: University of Illinois Press.

Miller, D. C., & Form, W. H. (1951). *Industrial sociology.* New York: Harper.

Miller, J. B. (1983). Women and power. *Social Policy, 13*(4).

Miller, S. M., & Tomaskovic-Devey, D. (1983). *Recapitalizing America: Alternatives to the corporate distortion of national policy.* Boston: Routledge & Kegan Paul.

Mills, C. W. (1948). *The new men of power: America's labor leaders.* New York: Harcourt, Brace.

Mortimer, J., Hall, R., & Hill, R. (1978). Husbands' occupational attributes as constraints on wives' employment. *Sociology of Work and Occupations, 5*, 285-313.

Nash, A. (1983). *The union steward: Duties, rights and status.* Ithaca, NY: ILR Press.

National Commission on Working Women. (1986). Working mothers and their families: A fact sheet. In *Women at work.* Washington, DC: Author.

Nelson, A. (1984, August). *Women in high-level union offices.* Paper presented at the 3rd Women and Organizations Conference, Boston, MA.

Nicholson, N. (1978). The role of the shop steward: An empirical case study. *Industrial Relations Journal, 9*, 32-41.

Nicholson, N., Ursell, G., & Blyton, P. (1981). White collar stewards: Attitudes and performance. In *The dynamics of white collar unionism: A study of local union participation.* London: Academic Press.

Nieva, V. F. (1985). Work and family linkages. In L. Larwood, A. H. Stromberg, & B. Gutek (Eds.), *Women and work: An annual review* (Vol. 1). Beverly Hills, CA: Sage.

Nieva, V. F., & Gutek, B. (1981). *Women and work: A psychological perspective.* New York: Praeger.

O'Connor, J. (1984). *Accumulation crisis.* New York: Basil Blackwell.

Pearce, D. (1978). The feminization of poverty: Women, work and welfare. *Urban and Social Change Review, 11.*

Peck, S. M. (1963). *The rank-and-file leader.* New Haven, CT: College and University Press.

Piotrkowski, C. S., & Repetti, R. L. (1984). Dual-earner families. *Marriage and Family Review, 7*(3/4), 99-124.

Piven, F. F., & Cloward, R. A. (1982). *The new class war: Reagan's attack on the welfare state and its consequences.* New York: Pantheon.

Pleck, E. H. (1976). Two worlds in one: Work and family. *Journal of Social History, 10*(2), 178-193.

Pleck, J. H. (1977). The work-family role system. *Social Problems, 24*, 417-427.

Pleck, J. H. (1985). *Working wives/working husbands.* Beverly Hills, CA: Sage.

Pleck, J. H., Staines, G. L., & Lang, L. (1980). Conflicts between work and family life. *Monthly Labor Review, 103*(3), 29-32.

Power, M. (1984). Falling through the "safety net": Women, economic crisis, and reagonomics. *Feminist Studies, 10*(1).

Raphael, E. E. (1974). Working women and their membership in labor unions. *Monthly Labor Review, 97.*

Rapoport, R., & Rapoport, R. N. (1965). Work and family in contemporary society. *American Sociological Review, 30*, 381-394.

Rapoport, R., & Rapoport, R. N. (1971). Dual-career families. Harmondsworth, England: Penguin.

Rapoport, R., & Rapoport, R. N. (1976). Dual career families re-examined. New York: Harper & Row.

Rapoport, R., & Rapoport, R. N. (1980). Three generations of dual-career family research. In F. Pepitone-Rockwell (Ed.), *Dual-career couples.* Beverly Hills, CA: Sage.

Robertson, D., & Schuller, T. (1982). *Stewards, members and trade union training.* Glasgow: Glasgow University, Centre for Research in Industrial Democracy and Participation.

Roby, P. (1986, August). *Paths to rank-and-file trade union leadership: Gender similarities and differences.* Paper presented at the 11th World Congress of Sociology, New Delhi, India.

Roby, P. (1987a). Union stewards and women's employment conditions. In C. Bose & G. Spitze (Eds.), *Ingredients for women's employment policy.* Albany, NY: State University of New York Press.

Roby, P. (1987b, July). *The experience of leadership: Gender similarities and differences among trade union stewards.* Paper presented at the 3rd International Interdisciplinary Congress on Women, Dublin, Ireland.

Roby, P. (1987c, August). *Trade unions and peace.* Paper presented at the Society for the Study of Social Problems, Chicago.

Roby, P. (1987d, August). *Sociology, trade unions and working people: Methodological and ethical issues.* Paper presented at the annual meeting of the American Sociological Association, Chicago.

Rosen, S. M. (1982). Labor: A movement at risk? In A. Gartner, C. Greer, & F. Riessman (Eds.), *What Reagan is doing to us.* New York: Harper & Row.

Rosow, I., & Rose, K. D. (1972). Divorce among doctors. *Journal of Marriage and the Family, 34,* 587-98.

Roydhouse, M. W. (1981). Partners in progress: The affiliated schools for women workers, 1928-1939. In B. M. Wertheimer (Ed.), *Labor education for women workers.* Philadelphia: Temple University Press.

Russ, J. (1982). Power and helplessness in the women's movement. *Women's Studies Quarterly, 10*(1).

Sacks, K. (1984). Generations of working-class families and computers, ward secretaries, and a walkout in a Southern hospital. In K. Sacks & D. Remy (Eds.), *My troubles are going to have trouble with me: Everyday trials and triumphs of women workers.* New Brunswick, NJ: Rutgers University Press.

Sayles, L. R., & Strauss, G. (1967). *The local union.* New York: Harcourt, Brace and World.

Schafran, L. H. (1982). Women: Reversing a decade of progress. In A. Gartner, C. Greer, & F. Riessman (Eds.), *What Reagan is doing to us.* New York: Harper & Row.

Schuller, T., & Robertson, D. (1983). How representatives allocate their time: Shop steward activity and membership contact. *British Journal of Industrial Relations, 21*(3), 330-342.

Sidel, R. (1982). The family: A dream deferred. In A. Gartner, C. Greer, & F. Riessman (Eds.), *What Reagan is doing to us.* New York: Harper & Row.

Sidel, R. (1986). *Women and children last: The plight of poor women in affluent America.* New York: Penguin.

Sidel, V. W. (1982). Health care: Privatization, privilege, pollution, and profit. In A. Gartner, C. Greer, & F. Riessman (Eds.), *What Reagan is doing to us.* New York: Harper & Row.

Simeone, A. (1987). *Academic women: Working towards equality* (pp. 121-122). South Hadley, MA: Bergin & Garvey.

Staines, G. L., & Pleck, J. H. (1983). *The impact of work schedules on the family.* Ann Arbor, MI: Survey Research Center, Institute for Social Research.

Stein, P. J. (1984). Men in families. *Marriage and Family Review, 7*(3/4), 143-162.

Strom, S. H. (1983, summer). Challenging "woman's place": Feminism, the Left and industrial unionism in the 1930s. *Feminist Studies, 9,* 359-386.

Sweezy, P. M. (1985, May). What's wrong with the American economy? *Monthly Review, 36*(1), 1-10.

Szalai, A., Converse, P. E., Felheim, P., Scheuch, E. K., & Stone, P. F. (Eds.). (1972). *The use of time: Daily activities of urban and suburban populations in twelve countries.* The Hague: Mouton.

Terborg-Penn, R. (1985). Survival strategies among African-American women workers: A continuing process. In R. Milkman (Ed.), *Women, work and protest: A century of US women's labor history* (pp. 139-155). Boston: Routledge & Kegan Paul.

Terry, M. (1982). Organizing a fragmented workforce: Shop stewards in local government. *British Journal of Industrial Relations, 20*(1), 1-19.

Turbin, C. (1984). Reconceptualizing family, work and labor organizing: Working women in Troy, 1860-1890. *Review of Radical Political Economics, 16*(1), 1-16.

U.S. Bureau of the Census. (1980). *1980 census of population, detailed population characteristics* (Section A, United States). Washington, DC: Government Printing Office.

U.S. Bureau of the Census. (1985, April). *Current population reports* (P-60 Series, No. 146). Washington, DC: Government Printing Office.

U.S. Department of Labor, Bureau of Labor Statistics. (1979a). *Earnings and other characteristics of organized workers, May 1977* (Report no. 556). Washington, DC:.

U.S. Department of Labor, Bureau of Labor Statistics, Women's Bureau. (1979b). *Economic responsibilities of working women.* Washington, DC: Government Printing Office.

U.S. Department of Labor, Bureau of Labor Statistics. (1981). [Unpublished data from the March supplement of the *Current population survey*].

U.S. Department of Labor, Bureau of Labor Statistics. (1982, January). *Employment and earnings (Vol. 29).* Washington, DC: Government Printing Office.

U.S. Department of Labor, Bureau of Labor Statistics. (1986a, August 20). *Half of mothers with children under three now in labor force* (Press release 86-345). Washington, DC: Author.

U.S. Department of Labor, Bureau of Labor Statistics. (1986b). [Unpublished data from the March supplement of the *Current population survey*].

U.S. Department of Labor, Bureau of Labor Statistics. (1987, January). *Employment and earnings* (Vol. 34). Washington, DC: Government Printing Office.

Ursell, G.D.M., Clegg, T. D., Lubbock, C. W., Blyton, P. R., & Nicholson, N. (1979). Shop stewards' attitudes to industrial democracy. *Industrial Relations Journal, 10.*

Uttal, L. (1987). *I took my daughter to the union meeting: Gendered domestic responsibilities and union steward activity.* Unpublished master's essay, University of California, Santa Cruz, Board of Studies in Sociology.

Walker, K., & Woods, M. E. (1976). *Time use: A measure of household production of family goods and services.* Washington, DC: American Home Economics Association.

Wertheimer, B. M. (1981). Residential schools. In B. M. Wertheimer (Ed.), *Labor education for women workers* (pp. 83-97). Philadelphia: Temple University Press.

Wertheimer, B. M. (1984a). The United States of America. In A. Cook, V. R. Lorwin, & A. K. Daniels (Eds.), *Women and trade unions. In Eleven industrialized countries* (pp. 286-311). Philadelphia: Temple University Press.

Wertheimer, B. M. (1984b). To rekindle the spirit: Current education programs for women workers. In J. L. Kornbluh & M. Frederickson (Eds.), *Sisterhood and solidarity: Workers' education for women, 1914-1984* (pp. 285-323). Philadelphia: Temple University Press.

Wertheimer, B. M., & Nelson, A. H. (1975). *Trade union women: A study of their participation in New York City locals.* New York: Praeger.

Wexley, K. N., & Hunt, P. J. (1974). Male and female leaders: Comparison of performance and behavior patterns. *Psychological Reports, 35,* 867-872.

Wilkinson, D. Y. (1984). Afro-American women and their families. *Marriage and Family Review, 7*(3/4), 125-142.

Wong, S. S. (1984). From soul to strawberries: The international ladies' garment workers' union and workers' education, 1914-1950. In J. L. Kornbluh & M. Frederickson (Eds.), *Sisterhood and solidarity: Workers' education for women, 1914-1984* (pp. 37-74). Philadelphia: Temple University Press.

Wrenn, R. (1985). The decline of American labor. In *Socialist Review, 82.*

Zavella, P. (in press). *Women's work and Chicano families: Cannery workers of the Santa Clara Valley.* Ithaca: Cornell University Press.

Zinn, M. B. (1983, November). [Review of *In a different voice: Psychological theory and women's development,* by Carol Gilligan]. *Newsletter, 2*(1) (Memphis State University, Center for Research on Women).

10

Women's and Men's Commitment to Paid Work and Family

THEORIES, MODELS, AND HYPOTHESES

DENISE D. BIELBY
WILLIAM T. BIELBY

By the end of the 1970s, combining paid work and family was clearly a viable life-style for American women (Komarovsky, 1982; U.S. Department of Labor, 1979). In the 1980s, women *and* men are confronted with the "balancing act" that follows a dual commitment to paid work and family (Baruch, Barnett, & Rivers, 1983; Regan & Roland, 1982). Although allocation of time and division of labor between paid work and family has been well documented, how adults form and distribute subjective attachments across these roles has received little attention. The research reviewed here addresses the ways men and women become committed to their paid work and family roles. Synthesizing existing literature, we consider how those roles become sources of identity, how individuals develop preferences for a particular balance of paid work and family activities, and how commitments are affected by work experiences. We identify three alternative perspectives on the commitment process to account for those preferences. Finally, we explore the contributions that different models of commitment can make to understanding the linkages between the work and family spheres of both women and men.

As the labor force participation of married women has increased over the past two decades, so has social scientists' concern with the linkages between paid

AUTHORS' NOTE: Support for this project was provided by the Sociology Division of the National Science Foundation and by the Academic Senate Committee on Research, University of California, Santa Barbara. We gratefully acknowledge the bibliographic assistance of Melissa R. Partin.

work and family spheres. Investigators have recently documented the impact of one sphere on the other, after decades of research that treated work and family as separate institutions (Gutek, Nakamura, & Nieva, 1981; Mortimer & London, 1984; Nieva, 1985). The findings organize around three areas: (a) the impact of women's dual roles on socioeconomic resources and conditions within the family (Komarovsky, 1964; Sennett & Cobb, 1972); (b) the division of household and market labor between spouses within the two spheres (Stafford, 1980; Walker & Woods, 1976); and (c) the psychological impact of multiple roles, job structure, job satisfaction, and employment constraints and opportunities upon family members (Kohn & Schooler, 1983; Miller, Schooler, Kohn, & Miller, 1979; Staines, Pleck, Shepard, & O'Connor, 1978; Staines, Pottick, & Fudge, 1985; Voydanoff, 1983).

Some current research emphasizes another theme, the changing demography of the work-family context (i.e., delay of first marriage, lower fertility, and increase in single-parent households) and its impact upon institutional arrangements between paid work and family, including child care, relocation, job availability and advancement, and scheduling and transportion (England & Farkas, 1986; Gutek, Nakamura, & Nieva, 1981; Michelson, 1985). Research also shows persistence of the unequal contribution by males and females to the division of labor in household labor and child care. Males still spend more time than females in work outside the home and make a far smaller contribution than their spouses to child care and household labor (Coverman, 1985; Ericksen et al., 1979; Lein, 1979). Yet the distribution of subjective commitments by both sexes across work and family spheres is more complex than is apparent from behavioral measures of time use. Recent research, discussed below, specifically calls attention to the fact that the scientific literature makes assumptions about the presence or absence of subjective role attachment that are based solely upon behavioral measures of market or household labor.

COMMITMENT TO
WORK AND FAMILY

Women are committed to multiple roles and expend a great deal of effort fulfilling dual role obligations (Bielby & Bielby, 1988; Gerson, 1985). Relative to male employment patterns, female employment patterns are marked by career interruption and a greater likelihood of part-time, part-year employment (although the differences between men and women are decreasing, Blau & Ferber, 1985). Using information on female employment patterns to infer women's commitment to employment, however, may be misleading. Research on women's work commitment indicates that their labor force behaviors should be treated as empirically distinct and not as indicative of their social psychological attachments to employment (Angrist & Almquist, 1975; Bielby & Bielby, 1984). Female work commitment encompasses a complex life-style in which both occupational and family attachments are embedded. Consequently,

Denise D. Bielby and William T. Bielby 251

inferences about women's job commitment or effort devoted to paid work based solely upon family responsibilities may be misleading.

The same process of attribution applies to men, who are presumed to be more psychologically invested in the work role because of specialization in work outside the home. Examination of male commitments, however, has revealed the relative importance of family over work as a role with which they are involved. In a series of articles, Pleck (Pleck, 1978, 1983; Pleck & Lang, 1978; Staines & Pleck, 1983) examined the extent to which males are subjectively committed to and satisfied with the family role and its responsibilities, relative to their commitment to the work role. Within national samples of males representing all occupational groups, males' self-ratings of interest and satisfaction with the family role suggest that they are more committed to family than to work (see also Kessler & McRae, 1982; Staines, Pottick, & Fudge, 1985).

Although role specialization differentiates men's and women's relative *behavioral* attachments to work and family, *subjective* attachments are distinctly different indicators of commitment. Subjective attachments cannot be inferred from behavioral indicators alone, as Pleck and others have shown. Actual (and expected) behavioral role obligations may define not only how individuals allocate time to paid work and family, but they may form the basis for attributions made by others (notably employers) about subjective attachments of men and women to those roles. Furthermore, the connection between role behavior and subjective attachment may be different for women than it is for men. Moreover, the distributions of subjective investments men and women make to work and family may exhibit patterns that either conform to or contradict prevailing sex-role norms. Understanding how men and women form commitments to paid work and family requires a conceptual scheme for posing meaningful questions. Below, we contrast theoretical approaches for studying women's and men's commitment to work and family.

MEN'S AND WOMEN'S WORK COMMITMENT: DEFINITIONS, MODELS, AND HYPOTHESES

Commitment has been defined as the binding of an individual to behavioral acts (Kiesler, 1971; Salancik, 1977). It involves (a) the degree to which those acts become a source of meaning or *identity* (Spenner & Rosenfeld, 1986), and (b) *intentions* regarding those behavioral acts. These two dimensions—sometimes referred to as "attitudinal" and "behavioral" commitment—are explicitly recognized in most research (e.g., Kiesler, 1971). Also implied in the definition is (c) a *distributional* dimension. Individuals distribute or trade off commitments among alternative activities. Consequently, activities differ in their relative importance as sources of identity, and intentions regarding behavior are formed with respect to an allocation of time and effort across activities.

Understanding commitment to work and family requires attention to all three dimensions. Work and family roles are two important sources of *identity* in adulthood and activities for which individuals form *intentions* regarding their *distribution* of time and effort. We emphasize commitment to paid work, recognizing that the family is more important for most adults. The three dimensions of identity, intentions, and distribution are elements of each of the three theories reviewed below, although some formulations emphasize one dimension over the others.

Below, we discuss separately each of three theoretical approaches to commitment, identifying the factors specified by each theory as determinants of commitment. After specifying each of the theories, we contrast them in terms of the factors they emphasize and the assumed magnitude and direction of effects of those factors. A generic model of an individual's current paid work commitment, C_t, can be viewed as a function of current assessments of net rewards from work, R_t; the attractiveness of alternative activities, A_t; current investments in work activities (i.e., costs of reallocating activities), I_t; current job behaviors, B_t; prior behaviors, B_p; and prior commitments, C_p. The three theories differ, however, in the importance they place on the determinants R_t, A_t, I_t, P_t, B_p, and C_p.

Retrospective Rationality and Commitment to Work

Commitment can be viewed as a process of *retrospection*. Individuals adjust their preferences and subjective investments to conform to past behaviors and become bound to those behaviors to the extent that they are explicit, irrevocable, public, and volitional (Salancik, 1977).[1] Commitment makes subsequent behavior less changeable, thereby accounting for stability in behavior.

Applied mostly to the study of organizational commitment (e.g., O'Reilly & Caldwell, 1981; Pfeffer & Lawler, 1980), the perspective is equally applicable to commitment to paid work and family roles. As individuals find themselves constrained by a particular pattern of employment and family responsibilities, this perspective predicts that individuals change their subjective attachments to the roles so that they are consistent with those constraints.

A similar notion of the commitment process has been offered by Becker (1960). According to him, investments or "side bets" in an activity, insignificant in themselves, have a cumulative impact over the life course in committing a person to the activity. Becoming committed entails increasing obligations to an act such that abandonment of the line of activity becomes personally costly. Recognition of "sunk" costs, forgone alternatives, and one's own role in creating the situation are often retrospective (Angle & Perry, 1983). In this view, commitments to paid work and family roles are not determined by rational calculation based on expected costs and benefits of current and future activities. Rather, a history of prior work and family experiences determines one's balance of future commitments.

According to the retrospective perspective, commitment to paid work originates from prior work behaviors that bind individuals to those behaviors, stabilizing subsequent behaviors and commitment. A stylized expression for this view would be

$$C_t = f_1(B_p, C_p); \quad B_t = f_2(B_p, C_p); \quad C_p = f_3(B_p)$$

If men and women differ in their commitments toward paid work, it is because of differences in the cumulative impact of prior committing behaviors, *not* because of differences in the current balance of costs and benefits of work and family roles. Thus, during the courses of their careers, different "side bets" (Becker, 1960) may be made by (and for) men and women, in terms of familial constraints, job and employer shifts, decisions to acquire or not to acquire certain skills, and so on. By accounting for these prior commitments and behaviors, we should be able to explain current differences between men and women in their commitments to work.

Prospective Rationality: An Exchange Perspective on Work and Family Roles

According to exchange perspective, individuals contribute to an association as long as it provides resources for them to meet their own needs and values. Commitment to an activity is a function of the net rewards from the activity, the costs of leaving the activity, and the net rewards available from alternative activities. The exchange perspective provides the major alternative to the retrospective rationality approach to the study of organizational commitment (Angle & Perry, 1983; Farrell & Rusbult, 1981; March & Simon, 1958; Marks, 1977; Mowday, Porter, & Steers, 1982), and we believe that it provides a viable alternative for understanding work commitment as well. In a *prospective* model of rational choice, sunk costs are irrelevant, and alternatives forgone affect commitment only if they increase the current cost of leaving the work role. According to the prospective view, individuals adjust their commitments to paid work and family solely on the basis of their current assessments of the net costs and benefits of performance in the two roles and the costs of changing the distribution of their efforts at home and at work. In contrast to the retrospective view, commitment is not a process that stabilizes behavior. If commitments and behaviors are stable, it is only because the balance of net costs and benefits is stable over time as well.

According to the prospective view, commitment to an activity is determined by the current balance of rewards, investments, and alternatives to the activity, that is,

$$C_t = f(R_t, A_t, I_t)$$

If the expected net balance of expected costs and benefits from alternative activities differs for men and women, then their commitments should differ accordingly. In contrast to the retrospective view, perceptions of current and future opportunities should be more decisive than past behaviors in determining commitment to adult roles.

Noncognitive Approaches: Taking Commitments for Granted

Both the retrospective and the prospective approaches emphasize conscious, deliberate processing of information. The former considers individuals' interpretations of prior actions, while the latter emphasizes the weighing of costs and benefits of future actions. In this sense, both are "cognitive" approaches. We use the term *noncognitive* to refer to approaches that reject the notion that commitments result from conscious deliberation over the meaning of past behavior or the expected net benefits of future activities. Instead, *noncognitive* approaches emphasize the degree to which subjective orientations and intentions regarding behavior are habitual, rulelike, or taken for granted (Pfeffer, 1982, chaps. 6-7).

For example, some social behaviors seem to be governed by "scripts"—sequences of activities triggered by cues in the environment—not by rational (or irrational) decisions of individuals (Abelson, 1976; Laws & Schwartz, 1977; Schank & Abelson, 1977). Thus it may be that certain family and work activities are habitual, rather than the result of intentions. Collins (1981) has argued that stable patterns of behavior persist because of the affect produced in social interaction. For example, an individual may derive feelings of membership from work or family activities. Those activities are neither recognized as binding, nor evaluated with respect to the net benefit to be derived from them. Instead, there is an *emotional* basis for the persistence of a particular mix of work and family roles that is taken for granted.

From a different perspective, there is a growing body of research showing how acts in organizations "are continued and transmitted without question" (Pfeffer, 1982, p. 239) and "take on a rulelike status in social thought and action" (Meyer & Rowan, 1977, p. 341). It may be that similar "institutionalization processes" (Zucker, 1981) shape individual commitments to paid work and family. If widely shared norms exist concerning appropriate orientations toward paid work and family on the part of males and females, individuals may conform to those expectations without reflecting upon other options available to them.

In short, research on the role of scripts in micro-level action, theories of the affective basis of social interaction, and studies of institutionalization processes all suggest ways in which identification with and intentions toward work and family become taken for granted in adult life. Noncognitive approaches suggest that commitments remain stable despite changing behaviors, investments, rewards, and costs associated with activities; that is,

$$C_i = f(C_p).$$

Due to early socialization, men and women develop different notions of how they should balance paid work and family roles. A *symbolic* meaning is attached to one's orientation toward adult roles, and the affect associated with one's orientations accounts for the stability of commitment, regardless of patterns of labor force participation, family responsibilities, job opportunities, and the like.

Combining Three Perspectives on Commitment: An Explanatory Model

Our overview of three perspectives generates a generic model of the commitment process:

$$C_t = f(R_t, I_t, A_t, B_t, C_p, B_p)$$

that subsumes the mechanisms of the various perspectives. It expresses work commitment as a function of prior commitment, current and prior paid work rewards, job and family investments and alternatives, family constraints, and employment experiences. Models corresponding to the specific perspectives are nested within the generic model, so the relative impact of alternative mechanisms allows us to assess the adequacy of each of the perspectives. Hypotheses about specific effects on work commitment are reported in Table 10.1. Translating the simple equations presented above into an empirically testable *operational* model requires careful attention to issues of research design and measurement that need to be addressed in any actual empirical study of commitment. We have presented a stylized version here to emphasize the substantive content of the model, showing how empirical research can address alternative perspectives on commitment.

Table 10.1 does not distinguish between differential effects on the three dimensions of commitment—identity, intentions, and distribution. Where we expect such differences, however, we describe them below. Distinguishing among the theories rests primarily on two sorts of variables: variables having strong effects and those having no effect. According to the prospective or exchange view, current rewards, investments, and alternatives should have the strongest effects on work commitment, and aspects of the respondent's prior work and family situation should have no effect. From the retrospective perspective, almost all attributes are hypothesized to have small effects on work commitment, but the largest effects should be due to the cumulative impact of prior work experiences (e.g., as measured by years of work experience, job tenure, and organizational tenure). In contrast, we have argued that a noncognitive approach implies that only prior work commitment influences present orientation toward work. As we noted above, the three approaches differ accordingly in their explanations for sex differences in work commitment: attributing any "commitment gap" to differences in current costs and benefits of work versus family activities, to differences in prior committing work and family

TABLE 10.1
An Explanatory Model of Commitment to Paid Work:
Hypothesized Relationships Under Alternative Perspectives
on the Commitment Process

| | Perspective on Commitment to Paid Work | | |
Determinants of Commitment	Retrospective	Prospective	Noncognitive
Current employment situation			
job rewards	−	++	0
job investments	+	++	0
job alternatives	?	?	0
employment experiences	+	0	0
Current family situation			
investments	−	− −	0
alternatives	−	− −	0
constraints	−	?	0
Prior employment situation			
job rewards	−	0	0
job investments	+	0	0
job alternatives	?	0	0
employment experiences	++	0	0
Prior family situation			
investments	−	0	0
alternatives	−	0	0
constraints	−	0	0
Prior work commitment	+	0	++

NOTE: 0 = no effect; +, − = modest effect; ++, − − = strong effect; and ? = ambiguous, no hypothesis.

experiences, or to differences in commitments developed in early adulthood and taken for granted later in life.

The explanatory model does not simply *combine* the three theoretical perspectives into a single explanatory scheme. Depending on the pattern of relationships detected when this model is empirically tested, it can indeed distinguish among various theoretical approaches. According to Table 10.1, distinctive patterns of relationships would allow us to rule out specific theories. If *prior behaviors* have strong effects, then both prospective and noncognitive theories would be undermined. If *prior work commitment* is the only factor having a strong effect, then both prospective and retrospective approaches can be dismissed as explanations. If *prior behaviors* and *prior commitment* have no effect, we can rule out the retrospective theory. If both past and current rewards and investments have large effects, however, then the situation is more ambiguous, calling for some reconciliation of prospective and retrospective rationality theories.

There are several relationships in Table 10.1 for which we were unable to formulate specific hypotheses. One concerns the impact of current and prior job alternatives. Organizational commitment has been shown to be negatively related to alternative employment prospects, consistent with the exchange or prospective view (Farrell & Rusbult, 1981; Pfeffer & Lawler, 1980). That is, commitment to one's current employer declines with prospects for employment elsewhere. Nevertheless, we do not expect that finding to generalize to work commitment. Indeed, ease of changing employers is characteristic of many craft and professional occupations, and is likely to be most common among individuals who identify with their occupational roles instead of their places of employment. Thus we suspect that the extent of job alternatives is positively related to work commitment, especially with respect to the identity dimension. The mechanism has more to do with occupational socialization than with either retrospective or prospective rationality, however, so we show no specific hypothesis in Table 10.1.

Another source of ambiguity is the effect of family constraints on work commitment. The retrospective perspective offers a clear hypothesis: As individuals find themselves constrained by their family activities, they will shift their commitments away from work and toward family.[2] It is more difficult to form a hypothesis from the prospective approach. On the one hand, family constraints might be viewed as a cost of engaging in family activities, and as a cost associated with an alternative to work, it should lead to increased commitments to the work role. Depending on how they are measured, however, family constraints may reflect *sunk* costs, that is, costs of dealing with family matters that one must bear regardless of how one distributes commitments to work and family. Consequently, we pose no hypothesis for the effect of current family constraints from the prospective perspective.

Alternatively, it could be argued that, from an exchange perspective, one must consider the resources that an individual has available to bring to a potential activity. Presumably, the greater the resources one can contribute to an activity, the more one receives in exchange, leading to greater commitment. According to this argument, individuals burdened with heavy family constraints have less time and effort to devote to paid work activities and therefore are less committed to them. Note that this leads to the same hypothesis that we have posed for the retrospective perspective.

Finally, we have posed one seemingly counterintuitive hypothesis derived from the retrospective perspective: Prior and current work rewards should have a *negative* effect on work commitment. Pay, promotion opportunities, and job security are each external justifications for participating in the work role. The retrospective rationality perspective suggests that individuals are less likely to internalize attitudes about acts for which they receive a high level of external justification (Aronson, 1980). Applied to the process of commitment to work, we should find that high levels of job rewards lead to a lower level of identification with the work role and thus a lower level of commitment on the identity dimension. The external justification hypothesis has received partial support in studies of organizational commitment (O'Reilly & Caldwell, 1981; Pfeffer & Lawler, 1980), and detection of a negative effect of work rewards on the identity dimension of work commitment would provide strong support for the retrospective over the prospective approach.

SUMMARY AND CONCLUSION

Do men and women differ in their commitments to paid work and family? If so, is it because of different experiences, rewards, and costs associated with paid work and family roles that influence those commitments, or is it because of differences in early socialization to adult roles? Answers to these questions require an understanding of the mechanisms that produce commitments to adult roles. In this chapter, we have summarized three theoretical perspectives that pose alternative mechanisms for the commitment process, and we have derived a model that allows hypotheses from these perspectives to be tested empirically. Research guided by the model we propose can tell us the extent to which women's and men's commitments to work are influenced by (a) contemporaneous assessments of the expected costs and benefits of paid work versus alternative activities; (b) prior experiences that commit one retrospectively to paid work or family; and (c) orientations toward paid work and family that are the product of early socialization and remain stable and "taken for granted" throughout adulthood.

We have no strong prior expectations about which of the three perspectives on commitment will receive the most empirical support. We suspect, however, that the same set of mechanisms operate for men and women. That is, if men and women do differ considerably in their commitments to work and family, researchers will be able to account for those differences by examining some combination of (a) the cumulative impact of experiences, investments, and "side bets" in paid work and family spheres; (b) the rewards and opportunities available to men and women through paid work and at home; and (c) the ways young men and women internalize and retain normative prescriptions for adult life.

Distinguishing among various mechanisms of the commitment process allows us to choose among differing social theories, but it has wider implications as well. First, it helps us understand *trends* in adults' commitments to and attitudes about work and family. For example, support for the noncognitive approach would suggest that changing commitments lag behind changes in sex-role attitudes. It implies that commitments change only after the prevailing normative climate produces new patterns of socialization to adult roles. In contrast, the retrospective perspective suggests that changing commitments may lead changes in sex-role attitudes. Economic forces may pull women with children into the labor force, committing them to the dual role regardless of prior socialization or contemporary normative climate. Finally, the prospective view suggests that women's commitments are more likely to follow changes in career *opportunities* (which changes the balance of net costs and benefits from work and family roles). According to that perspective, neither changing attitudes about working women nor labor force participation per se should influence identity with and intentions toward the work role.

The model we have proposed prescribes longitudinal research with data on work and family role behaviors, rewards, investments, and alternatives, and measures of commitment that capture the identity, behavioral, and distributional dimensions of the construct. Past research on work commitment provides limited insight into the mechanisms of the commitment process, because it has not been guided by a comprehensive theoretical approach. Nevertheless, some of that research is suggestive of what studies guided by our model might reveal. For example, job conditions have been shown to influence a variety of subjective orientations, from psychological functioning to job satisfaction, and the causal mechanisms appear to be similar for men and women (Kohn & Schooler, 1978; Miller 1980; Miller, Schooler, Kohn, & Miller, 1979). Studies with the Quality of Employment Surveys (Quinn, Mangione, & Seashore, 1975; Quinn & Staines, 1979a, 1979b) show that extrinsic job rewards have little impact on job involvement and work effort, and that job autonomy is the strongest predictor of these dimensions related to work commitment (Bielby & Bielby, 1988; Lorence, in press-a). These studies showed that, compared to men in jobs with similar amounts of job autonomy, women exhibit higher job involvement and devote greater effort to their jobs. Findings such as these underscore the importance of avoiding the assumption that women have weaker social psychological attachments to work than men simply because they have less continuous patterns of labor force participation (e.g., Polachek, 1979).

In contrast to research showing modest to strong effects of work context on social psychological attachment to work, there is some evidence that work commitment is a more stable subjective orientation, less influenced by workplace experiences than are other subjective attachments. In our earlier work (Bielby & Bielby, 1984), we found that work commitment among a cohort of female college graduates remained remarkably stable in the years following graduation, despite changing family and work contingencies. That research, however, was based on a rather homogeneous population studied over a relatively short phase of the adult life course. Further research is needed to determine whether the stability of commitment shows up in a representative sample of the work force, or whether it is as susceptible to situational factors as are psychological functioning, job satisfaction, organizational commitment, and the like.

Another recent study by Lorence (in press-b) examines trends in commitment to work over the past decade, using a measure in the General Social Survey of intentions regarding behavior (i.e., Would the respondent continue to work if he or she had enough money to live on comfortably?). His analysis of a series of cross-sectional surveys shows increasing work commitment among women over the period 1973 to 1985, with no significant difference in the level of work commitment among men and women by 1985. Consistent with the retrospective perspective on commitment, Lorence finds no effect of extrinsic job rewards on commitment. He finds increasing commitment within age cohorts of women and speculates that this may be due to retrospective commitments made by these women to prior career behaviors.

There is less research on commitment to family roles, especially men's commitment to family roles. As noted above, increased involvement with family activities increases men's sense of overall well-being and suggests that perhaps men's commitments to family roles follow their behaviors, as implied by retrospective theories of commitment. In any event, in understanding how men and women become committed to paid work and family roles, it is important to keep separate the distinction between behavior in a role and commitment to that role, for both men and women, both paid work and family spheres. In this chapter, we have proposed three alternative theories for understanding the link between behavior and commitment to work and family and a model for empirically distinguishing among the possible mechanisms that account for the relationship between behavior and commitment. In our view, our limited knowledge from past research on the topic in part reflects an inadequate conceptualization of the underlying mechanisms. Our aim is to provide a better conceptual grounding of future research on women's and men's commitments to adult roles, as well as to formulate an empirically testable model that will allow for more definitive conclusions from future research.

NOTES

1. Although Kiesler (1971) and Salancik (1977, pp. 7-8) emphasize the behavioral aspect of the retrospective rationality approach, subjective orientations figure in as well. Their emphasis is on the consequences of past behavior for consistency in future behavior. The process is mediated, however, by an internalization of the meaning of past behavior. Their perspective disputes the notion of one-way causality between subjective orientations (preferences and attitudes) on the one hand and behavior on the other, but they do not ignore the role of subjective orientations.

2. Accordingly, we expect the negative effects hypothesized in the middle column of Table 10.1 to be strongest on the preference for work versus family dimension and weakest on the intentions dimension.

REFERENCES

Abelson, R. P. (1976). Script processing in attitude formation and decision making. In J. S. Carroll & J. W. Payne (Eds.), *Cognition and social behavior* (pp. 33-45). Hillsdale, NJ: Lawrence Erlbaum.

Angle, H. L., & Perry, J. L. (1983). Organizational commitment: Individual and organizational influences. *Work and Occupations, 10,* 123-146.

Angrist, S., & Almquist, E. (1975). *Careers and contingencies: How college women juggle with gender.* New York: Dunellen.

Aronson, E. (1980). *The social animal* (3rd ed.). San Francisco: W. H. Freeman.

Baruch, G., Barnett, R., & Rivers, C. (1983). *Lifeprints.* New York: McGraw-Hill.

Becker, H. S. (1960). Notes on the concept of commitment. *American Journal of Sociology, 66,* 32-40.

Bielby, D. D., & Bielby, W. T. (1984). Work commitment, sex role attitudes, and women's employment. *American Sociological Review, 49,* 234-247.

Bielby, D. D., & Bielby, W. T. (1988). She works hard for the money: Household responsibilities and the allocation of work effort. *American Journal of Sociology, 93,* 1031-1059.

Blau, F., & Ferber, M. (1985). Women in the labor market: The last twenty years. In L. Larwood, A. Stromberg, & B. A. Gutek (Eds.), *Women and work: An annual review* (Vol. 1, pp. 19-49). Newbury Park, CA: Sage.

Collins, R. (1981). On the microfoundations of macrosociology. *American Journal of Sociology, 86,* 984-1014.

Coverman, S. (1985). Explaining husbands' participation in domestic labor. *Sociological Quarterly, 26,* 81-97.

Dubin, R., Champoux, J. E., & Porter, L. W. (1975). Central life interests and organizational commitment of blue collar and clerical workers. *Administrative Science Quarterly, 20,* 411-421.

England, P., & Farkas, G. (1986). *Households, employment, and gender.* New York: Aldine.

Eriksen, J. A., Yancey, W. L., & Eriksen, E. P. (1979, May). The division of family roles. *Journal of Marriage and the Family,* pp. 301-313.

Farrell, D., & Rusbult, C. E. (1981). Exchange variables as predictors of job satisfaction, job commitment, and turnover: The impact of rewards, costs, alternatives, and investments. *Organizational Behavior and Human Performance, 27*(28), 78-95.

Gerson, K. (1985). *Hard choices.* Berkeley: University of California Press.

Gutek, B., Nakamura, C. Y., & Nieva, V. (1981). The interdependence of work and family roles. *Journal of Occupational Behavior, 2,* 1-16.

Hartmann, H. (1981). The family as the locus of gender, class, and political struggle: The example of housework. *Signs, 6,* 365-394.

Kessler, R. C., & McRae, J. A. (1982). The effect of wives' employment on the mental health of married men and women. *American Sociological Review, 47,* 216-227.

Kiesler, C. A. (1971). *The psychology of commitment.* New York: Academic Press.

Kohn, M. L., & Schooler, C. (1978). The reciprocal effects of the substantive complexity of work and intellectual flexibility: A longitudinal assessment. *American Journal of Sociology, 38,* 97-118.

Kohn, M., & Schooler, C. (1983). *Work and personality.* Norwood, NJ: Ablex.

Komarovsky, M. (1964). *Blue-collar marriages.* New York: Random House.

Komarovsky, M. (1982). Female freshmen view their future: Career salience and its correlates. *Sex Roles, 8,* 299-314.

Lein, L. (1979, October). Male participation in home life: Impact of social supports and breadwinner responsibility on the allocation of tasks. *Family Coordinator*, pp. 489-494.

Lorence, J. (in press-a). Age and gender differences in work involvement.

Lorence, J. (in press-b). Subjective labor force commitment of U.S. men and women: 1973-1985. *Social Science Quarterly*.

Laws, J. L., & Schwartz, P. (1977). *Sexual scripts*. New York: Dryden.

March, J. G., & Simon, H. A. (1958). *Organizations*. New York: John Wiley.

Marks, S. R. (1977). Multiple roles and role strain: Some notes on human energy, time, and commitment. *American Sociological Review, 42*, 921-936.

Meyer, J. W., & Rowan, B. (1977). Institutionalized organizations: Formal structure as myth and ceremony. *American Journal of Sociology, 83*, 340-363.

Michelson, W. (1985). *From sun to sun*. Totowa, NJ: Rowman & Allanheld.

Miller, J. (1980). Individual and occupational determinants of job satisfaction: A focus on gender differences. *Sociology of Work and Occupations, 7*, 337-366.

Miller, J., Schooler, C., Kohn, M. L., & Miller, K. A. (1979). Women and work: The psychological effects of occupational conditions. *American Journal of Sociology, 85*, 66-94.

Mortimer, J. T., & London, J. (1984). The varying linkages of work and family. In P. Voydanoff (Ed.), *Work and family*. Palo Alto, CA: Mayfield.

Mowday, R. T., Porter, L., & Steers, R. M. (1982). *Employee-organization linkages: The psychology of commitment, absenteeism, and turnover*. New York: Academic Press.

Nieva, V. F. (1985). Work and family linkages. In L. Larwood, A. Stromberg, & B. Gutek (Eds.), *Women and work* (Vol. 1, pp. 162-190). Beverly Hills, CA: Sage.

O'Reilly, C. A., III, & Caldwell, D. F. (1981). The commitment and tenure of new employees: Some evidence of postdecisional justification. *Administrative Science Quarterly, 26*, 597-616.

Pfeffer, J. (1982). *Organizations and organization theory*. Boston: Pitman.

Pfeffer, J., & Lawler, J. (1980). Effects of job alternatives, extrinsic rewards, and behavioral commitment on attitude toward the organization: A field test of the insufficient justification paradigm. *Administrative Science Quarterly, 25*, 38-56.

Pleck, J. (1978). Males' traditional attitudes toward women: Conceptual issues in research. In J. Sherman & F. Denmark (Eds.), *The psychology of women*. New York: Psychological Dimensions.

Pleck, J. (1983). Husbands' paid work and family roles: Current research issues. In H. Lopata & J. Pleck (Eds.), *Research on the interweave of social roles* (Vol. 3). Greenwich, CT: JAI Press.

Pleck, J., & Lang, L. (1978). *Men's family role: Its nature and consequences* (Working paper). Wellesley, MA: Wellesley College Center for Research on Women.

Polachek, S. W. (1979). Occupational segregation among women: Theory, evidence, and a prognosis. In C. B. Lloyd, E. S. Andrews, & C. L. Gilroy (Eds.), *Women in the labor market* (pp. 137-157). New York: Columbia University Press.

Quinn, R. P., Mangione, T. M., & Seashore, S. E. (1975). *The 1972-73 Quality of Employment Survey*. Ann Arbor, MI: Institute for Social Research.

Quinn, R. P., & Staines, G. (1979a). *Quality of Employment Survey, 1977: Cross section*. Ann Arbor, MI: Inter-University Consortium for Political and Social Research.

Quinn, R. P., & Staines, G. (1979b). *Quality of Employment Survey, 1973-1977 Panel Study*. Ann Arbor, MI: Inter-University Consortium for Political and Social Research.

Regan, M. C., & Roland, H. E. (1982). University students: A change in expectations and aspirations over the decade. *Sociology of Education, 55*, 223-228.

Salancik, G. R. (1977). Commitment and the control of organizational behavior and belief. In B. Staw & G. Salancik (Eds.), *New directions in organizational behavior* (pp. 1-54). Chicago: St. Clair.

Schank, R. C., & Abelson, R. P. (1977). *Scripts, plans, goals and understanding: An inquiry into human knowledge structures.* Hillside, NJ: Lawrence Erlbaum.

Sennett, R., & Cobb, J. (1972). *The hidden injuries of class.* New York: Knopf.

Spenner, K., & Rosenfeld, R. (1986). *Women, work and identities: An event history analysis.* Paper presented at the 11th World Congress of Sociology, International Sociological Association, New Dehli, India.

Stafford, F. (1980). Women's use of time converging with men's. *Monthly Labor Review, 103*, 57-59.

Staines, G., & Pleck, J. (1983). *The impact of work schedules on the family.* Ann Arbor, MI: Institute for Social Research.

Staines, G., Pleck, J., Shepard, L., & O'Connor, P. (1978). Wives' employment status and marital adjustment: Yet another look. *Psychology of Women Quarterly, 3*, 90-120.

Staines, G., Pottick, K., & Fudge, D. (1985). The effects of wives' employment on husbands' job and life satisfaction. *Psychology of Women Quarterly, 9*, 419-424.

U.S. Department of Labor. (1979). *1979 employment and training report of the president.* Washington, DC: Government Printing Office.

Voydanoff, P. (1983). Unemployment and stress. In H. Lopata & J. Pleck (Eds.), *Research on the interweave of social roles* (Vol. 3). Greenwich, CT: JAI Press.

Walker, K., & Woods, M. E. (1976). *Time use: A measure of household production of family goods and services.* Washington, DC: American Home Economics Association.

Zucker, L. G. (1981). Organizations as institutions. In S. B. Bacharach (Ed.), *Perspectives in organizational sociology: Theory and research.* Greenwich, CT: JAI Press.

11

When Discrimination Makes "Sense"

THE RATIONAL BIAS THEORY

LAURIE LARWOOD
EUGENE SZWAJKOWSKI
SUZANNA ROSE

Rational bias theory conceives of discrimination as the consequence of self-interested managers making personnel decisions concerning subordinates based on the managers' own careers rather than on the abilities of their subordinates. The theory is situational and perceptual in nature and is additive to other social science approaches to discrimination rather than conflicting with them. This chapter reviews three studies offering preliminary support for rational bias in organizations. The findings suggest explanations as to why organizational discrimination has proven difficult to eradicate, and practical implications as to how discrimination might be overcome.

Women accounted for 44% of the civilian labor force in 1986; yet only 37% of executive, administrative, and managerial positions were filled by women (U.S. Bureau of Labor Statistics, 1986, p. 30). Median earnings for men in these positions exceeded those for women by nearly $11,000 per year (U.S. Department of Labor, 1985). In part, the difference in income reflects differences in position: by and large, women are absent from upper levels of major administrative hierarchies. For example, just 2% of 1362 top executives in a major 1985 survey were women; only one chief executive among the 500 largest U.S. industrial firms is a woman—and she acknowledges that she obtained the position through family control of the firm (Hymowitz & Schellhardt, 1986). One might argue that any influx of women into lower-level positions (U.S. Bureau of Labor Statistics, 1986) will eventually force organizations to move women up and to pay them equally with men. Nonetheless, inequality between males and females in opportunity and organizational outcomes (for example, salary and advancement decisions) has been well documented (see Larwood & Gattiker, 1987; Rosenbaum, 1984, pp. 217-222), and continues despite both federal and state antidiscrimination legislation and three decades of feminist and civil rights activism.

Both the patterns of workplace discrimination and some of the major economic, sociological, and psychological theories dealing with it have been examined in earlier volumes of *Women and Work* (see Madden, 1985) and will not be critiqued here. Instead, this article summarizes the work to date on a new line of research examining *rational bias theory*—a theory of discrimination recently proposed by Larwood, Gutek, and Gattiker (1984). Rational bias theory takes no issue with the usefulness of established social science-based theories. Instead, the new theory aims to explain and combat discrimination in some types of managerial personnel actions. In particular, rational bias theory holds that discrimination toward subordinates may be influenced by situational factors irrespective of any personal preference on a manager's part, of official antidiscrimination standards, or of known subordinates' abilities. In this theory, discrimination is the predictable outcome of a "rational" or self-interested response to perceptions of the attitudes of others in superior power positions. When a manager assumes that powerholders have discriminatory preferences, discrimination makes "sense" because engaging in it seems likely to help the manager's own career. It is important to understand that the rationality spoken of in rational bias theory is purely subjective, as seen from the standpoint of the manager in a position to discriminate.

The following section of this article discusses the basis for rational bias theory. Later sections describe the early research results supporting it, and the implications of those results.

THE MANAGERIAL
CHOICE TO DISCRIMINATE

Although there are alternative ways to categorize theories of discrimination in organizations (see Larwood, Gutek, & Gattiker, 1984), one of the simplest is by the level of the discriminator's attention to self-interest. Given a social climate interpreted as biased, there are at least three different levels on which theories can operate. In organizations, discrimination is ultimately the result of a decision made by some individual to select, promote, or train a particular person, or to authorize a particular rate of pay. At the first, or least self-interested, level, we accept that the managerial decision maker is unconcerned with social pressures on him or her to discriminate, that he or she seeks only the most ideal skills for the organization and is willing to pay accordingly. Differences in pay or opportunities for men or women as a group can arise when members of one group are correctly perceived as bringing different factors such as higher education to the labor market. Human capital theory, advanced primarily by economists, predicts this result (Becker, 1975; O'Neill, 1985).

Alternatively, discrimination might occur through unintentionally misperceiving the skills or interests of the victim of discrimination—consistent with notions of stereotyping from sociological and psychological theory (Nieva & Gutek, 1981; Shepela & Viviano, 1984; Terborg & Ilgen, 1975). For example, if women are incorrectly stereotyped as less qualified at production work, they are less likely to be enthusiastically recruited for a production engineering position.

At the second level, of increased self-interested behavior, a decision maker might be assumed to favor the group of which he or she is a part or to favor another pressure group. Thus the decision maker might routinely defend the organization's status structure by matching consensually high-status people with high-status positions and higher pay—consistent with some sociological research (Kanter, 1977, pp. 164-205; Lockheed & Hall, 1976). Alternatively, he or she might prejudicially favor one group over another and preferentially pay members of some groups more or more readily hire and promote them—as in economic discrimination theory (Madden, 1985) or in the psychological and sociological study of in-group/out-group relations (Dye & Renick, 1981; Larwood & Blackmore, 1978; Mai-Dalton & Sullivan, 1981).

At the third level of behavior, directed by substantial concern with self-interest, a different picture emerges that is not entirely explicable through prior theories. Here, individual decision makers operate as free agents *solely to their own advantage* rather than to that of the organization or group. Because managerial decision makers at this level are self-interested, they are very sensitive to what will help or hinder their own careers. The managers actively seek out normative information that may suggest what decisions are expected of them and which are most personally advantageous. Sometimes decisions aiding oneself are consistent with defending status hierarchies, and at times they result in obtaining the best employees and helping them succeed. Nonetheless, the managers make such decisions without reference to these concerns—unless they are themselves likely to be affected. Rational bias theory proposes that this type of behavior explains much of the discrimination taking place in organizations: Self-interested decision makers find personal advantage in it even though they may not care for discrimination personally, may be conversant with the laws against it, may understand that the people being discriminated against are as capable as anyone else, or may even be themselves a member of the disadvantaged group. This picture of instrumental discrimination offers both new solutions to discrimination and an explanation for the partial ineffectiveness of some existing solutions.

How realistic is this depiction? We have drawn it as sharply as possible and certainly do not believe that those in business or other organizations behave without regard for ethics. The self-interested manager—one who behaves as though coolly and rationally weighing the personal advantage of alternatives—is, however, well-recognized in organizational motivation theory. For example, expectancy, or VIE (valence-instrumentality-expectancy), theory suggests that managers prefer alternatives yielding the highest subjective expected value on the basis of a conscious or unconscious calculation. Expectancy theory has been repeatedly applied in predicting decision outcomes (Campbell & Pritchard, 1976; DeCotiis & LeLouarn, 1981; Matsui, Kagawa, Nagamatsu, & Ohtsuka, 1977; Vroom, 1964). Of course, awareness of the legal penalty for discrimination and the likelihood of being discovered would play a role in a manager's consideration of alternatives according to the expectancy approach.

If self-interest is accepted as a determinant of behavior, how does the managerial decision maker infer that it is in his or her self-interest to discriminate or refrain from discriminating? Correspondent inference theory, a form of attribution theory developed to examine the manner in which an alert perceiver infers the beliefs of others, suggests that such inferences may readily be made from the statements and behaviors of others in the working environment (see Jones & Davis, 1965; Jones & McGillis, 1976; Ross & Fletcher, 1985, pp. 75-79). Earlier research indicates that such inferences and a resulting show of solidarity with the opinions attributed to more powerful others may be particularly likely when the manager is ambitious (Porter & Roberts, 1976, p. 1575; Webber, 1970), and may occur even though the powerful others will not be affected directly by the decision (Baskett, 1973).

Predictions of Rational Bias Theory

It follows then that discrimination might be anticipated to occur whenever potential discriminators feel that they are served by paying attention to the norms of the situation within which they work, and whenever those norms appear to favor discrimination. Under these conditions, a combination examined in Study 1 below, discrimination "makes sense." The conditions further give rise to several specific hypotheses offered by Larwood, Gutek, and Gattiker (1984). Although these hypotheses seemed consistent with the theory, common sense, and limited social science research, they had not been tested within the management arena. The hypotheses were intended to predict biased behavior resulting from the importance of the situation (Hypothesis 1, below), perception of social signals (Hypotheses 2 to 4), relative power (Hypotheses 5 to 7), status (Hypotheses 8 and 9), and stereotyping and competence (Hypotheses 10 and 11). The specific hypotheses provided below were operationalized and tested in Studies 2 and 3.

> *Hypothesis 1:* A manager is likely to ignore pressures for discrimination when less is at stake, and to pay more attention to them when more is at stake.

Other than situational importance (Hypothesis 1), the extent of rational biases might also vary with the social signals provided by those holding power over the managerial decision maker. If the norm favors discrimination, then discrimination is the usual, or default, behavior. On the contrary, however, individuals who send differing social signals—such as by themselves being members of discriminated-against groups—or who engage in counternormative behavior attract attention and may allow the inference that their preferences oppose the norms (Jones & McGillis, 1976, p. 391; Ross & Fletcher, 1985, p. 77). Such counternormative signals may suggest that the manager risks punishment for discrimination. Those who are sensitive to such signals might then decrease discrimination or even overcompensate for it.

Hypothesis 2: If someone holding power over the manager is a member of a discriminated-against group, then the manager is less likely to discriminate.

Hypothesis 3: If a member of a discriminated-against group made the initial contact with the manager on behalf of the powerholder, the manager is less likely to discriminate.

Hypothesis 4: If the powerholder has gone to an unusual length to state the unacceptability of discrimination, the manager is less likely to discriminate.

The rational bias phenomenon is based on seeking advantage under conditions of relative insecurity. Thus it seems reasonable for managers who are in particularly weak positions to pay more attention to the apparent preferences of those having power over them in order better to maintain or to improve their positions (Bass, 1981, p. 431-429; Hollander, 1964).

Hypothesis 5: A manager inexperienced in any position is more likely to discriminate.

Hypothesis 6: If the powerholder indicates that prior interactions with the manager were unsatisfactory, the manager is more likely to discriminate.

Hypothesis 7: If the relationship between the manager's and the powerholder's organization is not well established, the manager is more likely to discriminate.

Because rational bias is based on beliefs concerning the opinions of powerholders, managers are likely to be more sensitive if their subordinates are in close contact with the powerholders, or if they seem to be operating independently, than if the subordinates are out of sight or clearly controlled. Contact between a subordinate and the powerholder immediately increases the salience of sex and race differences (Larwood, Zalkind, & Legault, 1975). The manager then can be seen as intentionally and fully responsible for any unusual behavior by the subordinate (Ross & Fletcher, 1985); at the same time, the manager calls the powerholder's beliefs into question if the subordinate does not have the anticipated characteristics (Moscovici, 1985). Finally, sex and race have status values—with women and minorities having lower status than males and Whites—and performance is often assumed to be consistent with status (Allen, 1979; Eagly & Wood, 1982; Lockheed & Hall, 1976). Any affront to the beliefs or status of the powerholder might be partly mitigated, however, by assuring that the unexpected subordinates are operating under close supervision.

Hypothesis 8: Discrimination increases with the subordinate's expected increasing external contact with the powerholder.

Hypothesis 9: Discrimination is greater against those seen by the powerholder to be operating independently than against those who are closely supervised.

A final pair of predictions concerns credibility. There is a great deal of literature in psychology and sociology to the effect that men and women are each preferred on tasks that are socially stereotyped as appropriate for them (see Hansen & O'Leary, 1984; Nieva & Gutek, 1981, pp. 76-79; Shepela & Viviano, 1984). Although the supporting (and frequently erroneous) assumption might be made that men and women have different backgrounds (Geis, 1983), in the context of testing rational bias theory, we specified the backgrounds and work histories of the subordinates as identical. Nonetheless, a client might still be concerned with the assignment of someone who does not fit a stereotypic role. On the other hand, we anticipated that objective evidence known to the client that the subordinate is truly extraordinarily qualified would overwhelm discrimination because it would eliminate any suspicion that inappropriate assignments are made or that the person assigned is competent (Taynor & Deaux, 1973).

> *Hypothesis 10:* Discrimination is greater if subordinates are associated with projects stereotyped as inappropriate than with projects stereotyped as appropriate to them.
>
> *Hypothesis 11:* Discrimination is overridden by recognized irrefutable evidence that the individual is consistently superior in performance.

TESTING RATIONAL BIAS THEORY

As noted above, many of the components of rational bias theory—power, perceptional and motivational processes—are already well established in the management and social science literatures. There seems no need to reexamine these phenomena in order to test the resulting theory. What has largely been missing, however, is a set of observations as to whether the components perform together in the manner anticipated.

Field studies have reported some indirect evidence corroborating the notion of rational bias. One early study reported that managers were more likely to discriminate against Jewish male subordinates when they were expected to work with potentially biased customers (Quinn, Tabor, & Gordon, 1968; see also Dexter, 1979, 1985). Compared with managers who fail to comply with affirmative action guidelines, those following the guidelines may believe they risk losing prestige in the eyes of others (Barnhill/Hayes, Inc., 1979).

In directly testing rational bias theory, one would ideally develop a field experiment in which managers gave their views on the organization's support for discrimination and then were observed to make personnel decisions in response to their situation. As a practical matter, this research is exceptionally difficult for two reasons: most medium and large U.S. organizations have become "gun-shy" concerning research that might expose them to discrimination litigation (as this would if it demonstrated the theory), and discrimination may be difficult to observe if the managers making discriminatory decisions are also aware of the legal implications.

Although ruling out the most direct tests, we were able to design two types of indirect examinations of the theory. In one (Study 1), we surveyed the views of executives employing outside management consulting firms. Although actual discrimination was not examined, the results could be matched with an earlier study of the management consulting industry to show whether pressures from the client firm might reasonably be a source of observed statistical discrimination in consulting firms. Thus Study 1 might provide an overall confirmation that the conditions for rational bias do exist and can be used to explain actual discrimination. It may be argued that the executives we surveyed had no reason to respond honestly; however, studies of self-report of illegal behavior suggested that the responses would be reliable (see Hollinger & Clark, 1983, pp. 21-22).

The operation of rational bias theory allows a series of more detailed predictions to be made concerning when discrimination will, or will not, occur (Hypotheses 1 to 11, described in the preceding section). The specific predictions are tested in the section below, describing Studies 2 and 3. Because of the need for precision, these more complex studies applied a different technique from Study 1, examining the preferences of business students during a series of experimental scenarios in which they were asked to select between a male and a female subordinate. Surveys and laboratory experiments with students used as surrogates for managers have sometimes been attacked as providing an invalid portrait of the world drawn from those not yet experienced in it. We disagree with this criticism for three reasons. Most of the students surveyed in our research worked, and many had substantial experience. Second, consensual biases are often unexpressed and the students are likely to have information as accurate concerning the consensual norms of business as the managers potentially making decisions to discriminate. Finally, the meta-analyses (statistical summarizations of the effects found in earlier studies) of Kraiger and Ford (1985) and Olian (1986) indicate that, for personnel decisions, sex and race discrimination are more difficult to find in laboratory conditions than in the field. Thus any finding of discrimination seems likely to be generalizable to actual business conditions.

Study 1: Can Discrimination Result from Rational Bias?

In a study of 61 California management consulting firms, Gealy, Larwood, and Elliott (1979) found that the proportion of women decreased with increasing hierarchical level from 91% of support personnel to just 4% of consulting partners. Explaining the reasons for this decrease, the owners of the consulting firms said that clients were less likely to accept women consultants, that the types of problems to which they could be applied were limited, and that women had a more difficult time than men in establishing contacts and client-consultant rapport. The owners also reported that women consultants had the owners' confidence, suggesting that any problems experienced by women stemmed either from the women's consulting techniques or from the owners' fears of the reaction of clients to women consultants. Potential sex differences in consulting technique were ruled out in another phase of the Gealy et al. study, which compared the consulting strategies of female with male consultants.

The following question was asked by the present Study 1 (Larwood & Gattiker, 1985): Do *client* firms really prefer male consultants over female consultants, and, if so, why? Could the consulting firm owners in the Gealy et al. findings be reacting to pressure to discriminate on the part of their clients? This would be consistent with rational bias theory's overall prediction of decisions favoring one's own career. If there were no pressure from consulting firm clients, then the consulting firm owners might be assumed to be using client-consultant interaction as a convenient way to hide their own discriminatory preferences or to be reacting only to incorrectly perceived client expectations.

In order to determine the appropriate explanation, Study 1 surveyed 52 consulting *client* firms in the southwestern United States in 1982. The firms averaged over 4000 employees each and had business specialties paralleling those of the consulting firms in Gealy, Larwood, and Elliott (1979). All but three of the surveys were completed by men, generally the chief executive or a vice-president.

In response to direct questions, officers of the client firms evaluated their preferences for male or female consultants on a scale from 1 (definitely the male) to 7 (definitely the female) with 4 being the neutral scale midpoint. The client firm executives stated that they would prefer to work with a male consultant (mean 3.69), believed that a man would provide better advice (3.61), felt a man would be more credible to others (3.28), and felt that the male consultant would more readily gain rapport with their staffs (3.39). The clients also preferred male consultants for problems of a technical or planning and policy nature, but were more willing to consider women for marketing and personnel. Each of the findings was statistically significant (beyond .05) and corroborated the beliefs of consulting firm owners in the Gealy et al. study that women consultants were more likely to have difficulty with clients and might be restricted to particular problems.

As suggested by rational bias theory, a self-interested consulting firm owner would respond to the biases of clients by discriminating against women consultants if the views of clients could not be changed. This would occur despite information that the women consultants were as good as men. With consequently restricted experience and limited demand for their skills, one would expect to see fewer women at the top in the management consulting business—as found earlier by Gealy et al.

On the basis of Study 1, the antecedents (discriminatory client attitudes) and consequences (sex discrimination by those serving the clients) predicted by rational bias theory were empirically supported. Nonetheless, the link between the antecedents and the consequences, as well as the conditions under which bias—or even reverse discrimination—might take place, still had to be examined.

Studies 2 and 3: Are the Specific Hypotheses of Rational Bias Supported?

Two studies were undertaken using students of business administration at a major urban (nonresidential) university in order to fill these gaps. Of 374 participants in Study 2 (Szwajkowski & Larwood, 1986), 43% were female, 76% were White, 96% had work experience, and 80% were currently employed; the mean age was 24. Of the 293 respondents in Study 3 (Larwood, Szwajkowski, & Rose, 1988), 51% were female, 74% were White, 94% had been employed, and 78% were currently employed; the average age was 22. As we pointed out earlier, any discriminatory results based on these samples seemed readily generalizable to business practice (see Olian, 1986).

In addition to the hypotheses described above, Studies 2 and 3 were together designed to determine whether rational bias can successfully predict racial discrimination. Study 2 examined the first seven predictions while specifying only subordinate and, where appropriate, powerholder sex. Study 3 reexamined Hypotheses 2 to 4, providing both sex and race information, thereby allowing the effect of the double specification to be examined. Study 3 alone investigated Hypotheses 8 to 11.

Why add the race variable? At least one study (Schmitt & Lappin, 1980) found that White females were more consistently discriminated against in performance ratings than other sex/race groups; thus race might be a confounding factor. It was of substantial interest to know whether Black women would be treated relative to Black men in the same manner as White women relative to White men and whether sex and race considered together would produce different effects than sex separately. Because the primary issue of concern in this review is sex discrimination, comparisons between Black and White subordinates of the same sex will not be discussed.

While there is little managerial literature examining the position of Blacks in personnel decisions (see, however, Kraiger & Ford, 1985), and less concerning Black women (see Nkomo, in press; Olian, 1986), field studies have demonstrated that the earnings levels and occupational prestige of samples of Black workers with college degrees are lower than comparably educated Whites (Parcel, 1979). Although Blacks constituted 11% of the labor force in 1985, only 6% of executives, administrators, and managers were Black (U.S. Department of Labor, 1986). A slower rate of salary increase and promotion has been documented for minority MBAs as compared with White MBAs (Brown & Ford, 1977). Blacks averaged a salary increase of 23% over a five-year period, compared to 54% for Whites in that study; just 31% of Black but 73% of White MBAs who had been out of school for four or more years had reached middle management or higher positions.

In Studies 2 and 3, the participants volunteered for a computerized experiment. The computer presented a hypothetical situation placing the participant in the role of a middle-level manager in a firm dependent on obtaining contracts from other firms. The participant was given two sub-ordinates, both of whom had been hired by the participant from the top 10% of a Big Ten MBA graduating class on the same recruiting trip. These stipulations were unequal in any material way. The two subordinates were depicted as a male and a female in Study 2, while both their sex and race (Black or White) were varied in Study 3. A series of questions followed, asking participants either (Study 2 only) how likely their firm was to receive a contract from the outside organization under a series of hypothesis-related conditions if it sent the female rather than the male subordinate to negotiate with the customer, or (both Studies 2 and 3) which subordinate they would personally select to help them negotiate the contract. Respondents were assigned to independent conditions at random by the computer. For both studies, final information was gathered concerning the perceived values of business and whether the participants felt they could influence those values. All research questions used a seven-point scale response format, such that a 4.0 indicated neutral or no preference.

Results

Hypothesis 1 (Study 2). Is sex discrimination by managers greater for more important tasks? Participants were presented with a situation in which one of their assistants was to join the negotiations with a client for either a major or a minor contract. As expected, they felt that their firm would be less likely to succeed with a larger contract if the female subordinate was sent to the negotiations than with a smaller contract, and they were more likely to send a male themselves for the larger than for the smaller contract. These differences are depicted for Study 2 in Figure 11.1; for convenience in interpretation, the results in that figure are shown as differences from the scale midpoint (means below 4.0 indicate belief that a male is more likely to succeed or indicate a preference for a male, while the reverse is true for means above 4.0). All differences discussed are statistically significant at .05 or better unless indicated.

Hypotheses 2 to 4 (Study 2). The next three hypotheses asked whether information concerning a client's preferences would influence discrimination. For each of these hypotheses, study participants were presented with a situation having either the circumstances signaling counternormative conditions (a woman making the final contract decision for the client, contact between the firms made through a woman, or the client firm's president "speaking out against discrimination" and writing "a book on the importance of not discriminating"), or the opposite (a man making the client's decision, contact through a man, or the client's president known "as an expert on all aspects of business management" and writing "a book on how to be an effective manager"). It should be noted that effective management cannot be construed as directly encouraging discrimination—but it was expected to allow the default norm to operate. Supporting the predictions, participants reported that their firm would be more likely to obtain the contract if it sent a woman in each of the counternormative circumstances than in the opposite conditions. Likewise, they

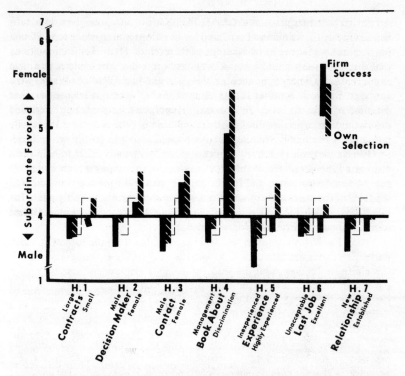

NOTE: Differences are shown from the scale midpoint (4.0) on a seven-point scale for each hypothesis. "Firm Success" indicates the participant's belief that a firm would be helped or hurt by the female subordinate. "Own Selection" refers to the subordinate the study participant would prefer. Using Hypothesis 4 as an example, the figure shows that males are modestly seen as more helpful for contact with a firm whose president has written on effective management and are somewhat more preferred by our study participants. In contrast, women are viewed as substantially more helpful for contact with a firm whose president has written against discrimination and are strongly preferred by our participants.

Figure 11.1 Rational Bias: Sex

were significantly more willing to select the female subordinate to accompany themselves in the counternormative conditions.

Hypotheses 5 to 7 (Study 2). The final three hypotheses of Study 2 suggested that a manager's discrimination is more likely when he or she appears to be in a position of weakness or insecurity than when he or she is in a position of strength. Managers were depicted as having either weak situations (the manager was inexperienced and new on the job, previous work had been unacceptable and a warning had been issued, the firm had never before worked with the client) or stronger ones (the manager was experienced, previous work had been excellent and a commendation had been issued, the firm has an established relationship with the client). The individual experience hypothesis (5) was supported both for questions asking the likelihood of obtaining the contract if a woman rather than a man was sent, and for questions asking which subordinate participants would prefer to accompany themselves. Hypothesis 6, predicting that discrimination would increase with less successful prior interaction, was supported only when respondents considered the likelihood of obtaining the contract if a woman rather than a man were sent—but not for the personal decision of who to send. In contrast, Hypothesis 7, predicting increased discrimination when dealing with a new client, was supported only by participants personally deciding whether to send a male or female subordinate.

Overall, the results for Study 2 agree quite well with theory *both* for questions estimating the likelihood of the firm's success when sending a male or female subordinate to the client, and for the participant's willingness as a manager to send one or the other subordinate. Because respondents received only one of the two forms of each question, results of the two question formats are independent of and provide confirmation for one another.

Study 3 added subordinate race as a variable. The question format in which participants were asked to choose between two subordinates was retained, while the alternate format inquiring into the firm's likelihood of success with a particular subordinate was dropped in the third study. In order to be certain that the results of Study 3 were consistent with those of Study 2, the studies were overlapped, with the signaling hypotheses (2 to 4) being tested a second time. Thereafter, Hypotheses 8 through 11 were examined.

Hypotheses 2 to 4 (Study 3). In Study 3, the two subordinates had a different sex and race combination. Consequently, the client decision maker (for Hypothesis 2) or the contact person (for Hypothesis 3) was identical to one of the subordinate combinations. The particular combination was varied at random by the computer program, and any respondent saw only one form of each question. Our reexamination statistically confirmed the earlier results. Looking just at the two conditions comparing male and female subordinates of the same race (White male with White female subordinate, or Black male with Black female subordinate), respondents said they preferred to send someone matching the sex of the client decision maker, and that they preferred to be accompanied by someone of the same sex as the original contact within their own firm. Hypothesis 4 was also reconfirmed: They preferred to send a woman when the client's president had spoken out and written a book against discrimination more often than when the speaking and writing was merely about management. Figure 11.2 shows these results against the scale midpoint (4.0 on the seven-point scale) for each subordinate comparison. Again, all differences described are statistically significant unless noted.

For cross sex x race comparisons (White female with Black male or White male with Black female subordinate), participants again preferred to be accompanied by the subordinate matching the client or the contact person. Similarly, they preferred the Black female over the White male if the client's president had written against discrimination. These results confirm the Study 2 findings and provide strong support of rational bias theory. Interestingly, in the

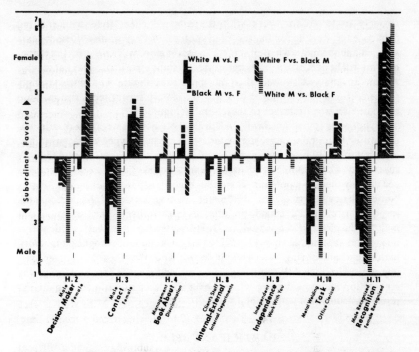

NOTE: Differences are shown from the scale midpoint (4.0) on a seven-point scale for each hypothesis. Study participants indicated the extent of their preference for one of the subordinates over the other in a comparison between two of them. Using Hypothesis 4 as an example, the figure shows that our study participants, asked to select someone to accompany them to a firm whose president has written a book on effective management, select a White male over a White female, a White female over a Black male, and a White male over a Black female. Selecting someone to accompany them to a client who had written against discrimination, they preferred a Black female over a Black male, a Black male over a White female, and (most strongly) a Black female over a White male.

Figure 11.2 Rational Bias: Sex x Race

ambiguous comparison between a White female and a Black male subordinate, participants preferred that the Black male accompany them if the client had written against discrimination, but that the White female do so if the client wrote about good management practice. The analyses for Study 3 found no other inversions of sex effect.

Hypotheses 8 and 9 (Study 3). These hypotheses predict that discrimination is stronger when subordinates have more outside contact, or when the subordinates are more independent of supervision. In order to examine Hypothesis 8, respondents were asked to select a subordinate to work out final details on a potential contract either with the client's staff or with other departments in their own firm. As anticipated, the male subordinate was more strongly preferred for work with the external client than with internal departments. Results for the test of Hypothesis 9 were similar. Respondents selected a subordinate when either "the assistant alone will work with the client" or "you will be completely in charge of the assistant's work with the client firm." Again, an analysis showed that the male subordinate was more strongly preferred for the independent than for the closely supervised position. Subordinate race was irrelevant to these results (Figure 11.2).

Hypotheses 10 and 11 (Study 3). Our final predictions were that discrimination would be found to be greater on tasks that are stereotyped as inappropriate, but that it would be overcome by objective evidence of an individual's superiority. For Hypothesis 10, participants were asked to select an assistant to accompany them to a potential client that needed help in modernizing either its "office clerical services" or its "metal welding services." As anticipated, respondents preferred female subordinates in the office clerical situation, but males in the metal welding situation. Questions testing Hypothesis 11 identified one of the assistants as having "quickly become nationally recognized for work in this field" and having "won a major award" while the other had "not received any unusual notice." Without regard to sex or race, the person winning the recognition and award was preferred over the other subordinate. Again, the result was consistent with theory.

PARTICIPANT BELIEFS

Discrimination in rational bias theory results from the external pressures perceived by the manager. Thus it was important in Studies 2 and 3 to establish that respondents believed that the norm of business supported discrimination and that they were forced to accept that norm. These beliefs would lead to the assumption that clients of the hypothetical firm around which the hypotheses above were built would support the prevailing norms (Ross & Fletcher, 1985, p. 76) and might pressure them to do likewise. A final series of questions in both studies assessed perceived business attitudes toward discrimination and beliefs that the participants could influence those attitudes. These questions were asked *last*, so that awareness of them could not affect earlier results. The participants indicated that they strongly believe both that business discriminates and that there is little they can do to alter the discrimination, at least by the clients (Table 11.1).

Of course, the beliefs concerning a preference for discrimination shown in Table 11.1 may be quite wrong and may not reflect actual preferences or intended practice of top executives. Nonetheless, if a manager *believes* that those having power maintain discriminatory preferences, or is even unsure, he or she may feel that it is advantageous to discriminate. In order to establish the link between the values ascribed to business and discrimination, the beliefs were entered as multiple regression predictors of the results for Study 3. In each of the tests relating the beliefs to the hypotheses predicting bias (Hypotheses 1 to 10),

TABLE 11.1
Assumed Bias in Business and Ability to Influence It

Question	Study 2 Mean	Study 3 (Overall) Mean
1. What proportion of business people have a predisposition that results in discrimination? (1 [all] −7 [none])	3.69	3.51
2. Business people believe (men/Whites) are (more) capable than (women/Blacks) at making important decisions. (1 [definitely more] −7 [definitely less])	2.37	2.76
3. Business people believe (men/Whites) are (more) capable than (women/Blacks) at impressing clients. (1 [definitely more] −7 [definitely less])	3.08	3.10
4. People at the top of organizations are (more) biased against (women/Blacks) than people at the bottom. (1 [much more] −7 [much less])	3.12	3.18
5. In working with a client, business people subordinate their own preferences to those of the client. (1 [always] −7 [never])	2.90	2.92
6. Clients are influenced by their feelings, desires, and emotions. (1 [completely] −7 [not at all])	3.03	3.10
7. If a client is biased against (women/Blacks), there is little that someone trying to sell to the client can do aside from go along. (1 [strongly agree] −7 [strongly disagree])	3.29	3.54

NOTE: Study 2 examined only sex comparisons, while Study 3 data include sex x race comparisons. Actual sex and race terms were assigned randomly by computer in the study. The sex and race terms and scale directions in parentheses indicate the outcome directions shown by means. Means below 4.0 indicate greater bias against women or Blacks on a seven-point scale. All means differ significantly from the scale midpoint at .05 or better by a two-tail t-test.

the relationships were statistically reliable (beyond .05), accounting for an average of 46% of the adjusted variance in the personal selections respondents had made. Plainly, those who thought business was more biased were themselves more willing to discriminate. This would, of course, be expected if the attribution of bias led to later discrimination as predicted by rational bias theory. In contrast, the results for Hypothesis 11, which correctly predicted that discrimination would be overridden by obvious ability, were not reliably related to the beliefs concerning business values. Because the situation testing the hypothesis was intended as one in which pressures toward bias can be ignored, the lack of a significant relationship here also fits rational bias theory.

Finally, it would be easy to assume that men are more biased against women than women, or that Whites are more biased against minorities than minorities. Similarly, those with longer work experience might have learned that discrimination is not an acceptable way to behave or might have perceived that discrimination is not the norm. Thus the results might be artifactual to our particular sample. Multiple regression analyses of the relationships between demographic background and results for the hypotheses produced neither consistent nor meaningful findings. Said differently, women as well as men and Blacks as well as Whites were equally likely to engage in the discriminatory preferences we have described.

CONCLUSIONS FOR THE THEORY

Rational bias theory suggests that some (but not all) discrimination results from the activities of self-interested managers. The managers assess the apparent biases in their environment before making personnel decisions themselves. In order to gain the greatest advantage, they make personnel decisions consistent with perceived environmental demands. In a climate supporting discrimination, decisions sensitive to discrimination follow. Although one may readily argue that bias is not objectively rational for a firm or work group interested in productivity, bias nonetheless may be perceived as politically advantageous or even requisite of organizations and individuals in situations subordinate to powerholders who are thought to prefer discrimination.

The three studies reviewed here each support rational bias theory. The first study found that rational bias is a viable explanation of the Gealy, Larwood, and Elliott (1979) findings of discrimination in management consulting. The original research found that consultants discriminated against women, while the research discussed here found a counterpart in the biased preferences of consulting; however, it was not certain that the consultants surveyed by Gealy et al. were actually responding to the client preferences uncovered in Study 1.

The following two studies placing management students in the position of making personnel decisions were designed in order to assess simultaneously presumed preferences for discrimination by business people and the counterpart reactions to those preferences. Study 2 used alternative questions to determine whether the business students felt their firms would be benefited or hurt by selecting a woman for a particular assignment, and whether they personally would select a man or a woman to accompany them on the assignment. Study 3 asked participants to select one from among two subordinates differing in sex and race to accompany them to the assignment.

For both studies, the results supported hypotheses associated with rational bias theory. Overall, these hypotheses proposed that participants would predict outcomes to be influenced by subordinate sex, and would themselves select subordinates in a sex-conscious manner. The results indicated that participants felt that discrimination is a workplace norm, and the biases of clients and customers are difficult to change.

Given those conditions, Studies 2 and 3 found evidence that men were preferred on more important assignments, on assignments dealing with men or obtained through men, on assignments in which the client's biases are not known, on riskier or less-well-established assignments, on assignments involving more external or independent action, on assignments in which tasks are stereotyped as appropriate for men, or when they have been independently recognized as good in their field. Discrimination is overridden, and in some cases women are preferred, when the assignments are less important, when women are being dealt with or assignments have been obtained through women, when the client is known to be against discrimination (not necessarily supportive of women), on less risky and better-established assignments, on assignments involving more internal or less independent action, on those stereotyped as appropriate to women, or when the women have been independently recognized as good.

As a general rule, the results we found were robust across changes in the research design and in the participants' characteristics. Thus Study 2 found that participants' decisions for their subordinates largely paralleled results on the alternate questionnaire form asking for the firm's likelihood of obtaining a contract by sending a woman to negotiate with the client (Figure 11.1). Study 3 found that all subordinate race combinations generally produced results in the same direction favoring either a female or a male subordinate irrespective of the race of either one (Figure 11.2). Although not elaborated upon in this summary, we also found that neither participant sex, race, age, nor work experience played a consistent role in the results.

Three studies do not, of course, "prove" a theory. They can demonstrate only that, under some limited sets of circumstances, the theory has performed successfully. At least two types of further research are needed. First, more research needs to explore the current predictions of rational bias. Field studies would be particularly welcome, perhaps pairing archival analyses of personnel records with the surveyed perceptions of biases in the particular organization. Our work has focused on discrimination occurring when an individual attempts to match the presumed biases of an external powerholder in a second organization. Rational bias theory should also be useful in describing interactions within a *single* organization—perhaps working under a biased superior predictably evokes this phenomenon. Research to date has examined situations in which a discriminator's self-interest coincides with the firm's interest in obtaining a contract; it would be of interest to examine situations in which the two instead diverge.

Research is also necessary to develop rational bias theory further. Any situation in which a manager's self-interest is at stake and values concerning women are related may have the potential to arouse discrimination. Thus hypotheses might explore the extent to which variations in the manager's personal concern with self-interest affects subsequent discrimination. Perhaps, for instance, some measure of altruism as a personality dimension can be found to predict resistance to discrimination. Similarly, rather than consider only the assignments given to personnel, it would be fair to ask how rational bias translates to income. For example, is there a trade-off in salary at which a manager is willing to employ a woman despite awareness of a prevailing atmosphere of bias? Must powerholders be informed of the bargain in order for the rational manager to feel secure? Or does their knowledge that the woman has been hired cheaply undermine her credibility on counterstereotypic assignments?

IMPLICATIONS FOR CAREER
DEVELOPMENT AND POLICY

Although it overlaps in prediction with other views of discrimination, rational bias theory comes from a different perspective. Consequently, one might anticipate that its predictions, if they continue to be supported, would lead to somewhat different emphases for policy and career development. This section discusses some of the implications of rational bias theory for individuals, managers and organizations, and policymakers intending to diminish the impact of discrimination and to utilize better human resources.

The Problem and the Basis for Change

Most striking, but not surprising, we found that our study participants held the view that business prefers to use men over women in the most frequently encountered operations. Although this dark view may be incorrect, it is certainly supported by labor market statistics; other research indicates that the perception of discrimination correlates highly with such statistics (Turner & Turner, 1981). It is against this backdrop that managers believe they cannot afford the risk of employing a woman on major projects (Hypothesis 1) and that they respond to a chief executive who desires good management practice by discriminating (i.e., selecting a man over a presumably equally qualified woman—Hypothesis 4). Although Study 1 found that the employers of management consultants did prefer discrimination among consultants, it is not necessarily true that a particular client, or even broad groups of clients, prefer to discriminate. The point, however, is that discrimination based on rational bias may continue irrespective of the actual preferences of powerholders. Unless powerholders who dislike discrimination effectively communicate their preference (Hypotheses 2 to 4), they are assumed to support that norm.

Affirmative action and the statement that one is an "equal opportunity/ af- firmative action employer" seem now to be a part of the general landscape among medium- and large-sized organizations. Because affirmative action is widely required by government regulation, the announcement of it alone can no longer provide the signal that the organization really does not support discrimination. Instead, it signals only that the organization understands the regulatory environment (see Hitt, Zikmund, & Pickens, 1982). Thus rational bias is likely to be unaffected by such policies unless they are administered in an extraordinary manner that makes them credible as a preference.

Nothing that we have said should be taken to indicate that equal opportunity is a lost cause; far from it. With each hypothesis, we have striven to show that although one alternative leads to discrimination, another reverses or eliminates bias. Without exception, everything examined here suggests that rational bias provides a keen two-edged sword. The following sections provide some specific ideas on how that sword might be put to use.

Suggestions for Organizational and Governmental Policymakers

Organizations are interlocked, and many managers are not in a position to practice complete equal opportunity unless they are assured that those holding power over them prefer that policy. Those attempting to influence policy will ideally start at the top of this chain. It follows that the chain of reactive discrimination can most readily be broken by the intervention of either of two types of organizations (or situations). In one ideal type, the organization should be independent of important individual powerholders and capable of influencing those beholden to it further down the chain. Such organizations include the U.S. government (which instead continues to support discrimination in many areas such as the military, procurement, high government service-level positions, and cabinet appointments), but also those firmly in control of critical resources such as organizations holding unique technology, solid market positions, or im- portant natural resources. A second organization type with the potential to break the chain of discrimination is an organization associated with a female- dominated profession, such as retailing (in which women have traditionally been welcome to work but not to become executives), or an essential profession in which women have a solid representation and to which negative stereotypes do not apply.

Equal opportunity pressure groups are likely to have the greatest success in making their case to these types of organizations because of the position and nature of the firms and government organizations. Nonetheless, for the organizations to influence others, we emphasize that they must provide a credible (visible, unavoidable, impressive, and continuing) signal (Hypothesis 4). While a single woman in the President's Cabinet is likely to signal only that the government is aware of women, turning over several of the more important cabinet positions (Defense, Commerce, Treasury) to women and announcing that they have a mandate to assure that both government employees and suppliers cease discrimination would send a message that change is essential and inevitable. It seems likely that if the chairmen of IBM, Hewlitt-Packard, Unisys, and Digital Equipment were to provide firm signals both within their firms and to suppliers that bias is hurting their firms and will no longer be tolerated, the reverberations would be felt throughout the electronics and office technology industries, if not societywide. Firms can accomplish a great deal by appointing women as line vice-presidents in powerful areas such as production and marketing and instructing them that bias will not be necessary nor tolerated.

Suggestions for Managers and Organizations

Can anything be done by the many (perhaps even the majority) individual lower-level managers who would prefer to make personnel decisions on the basis of ability rather than politics? Is it necessary for them to ignore self-interest or to go out on a limb? We are aware of the adage that revolutionary change can only be enjoyed by those who survive the revolution. Fortunately, there are some ways that have been suggested by our findings for managers both to prosper and to make bias-free decisions. Probably the most obvious is to ensure objective recognition of the abilities of subordinates (Hypothesis 11). Rather than leaving this valuable strategy to chance, the manager should encourage women subordinates to obtain that recognition from professional or other sources that is likely to be accepted by those to whom the manager is responsible. Having obtained the recognition, women should be further encouraged to publicize their unusual activities. This not only takes pressure off the manager for explaining his or her personnel decisions, but may greatly enhance the women's value to the firm.

Women can also be "safely" placed in either of two positions. They can be started in the less exposed areas of any operation—those that are well established (Hypothesis 7), internal (Hypothesis 8), highly supervised (Hypothesis 9), or stereotypically appropriate (Hypothesis 10). Alternatively, they can be asked to operate entrepreneurially, for instance, as project managers on low-risk projects (Hypothesis 1). If, in any situation, the women prove themselves or acquire the credentials accepted in the business, then this evidence can be used as the means to move them elsewhere quickly, just as with any other form of objective recognition. We are suggesting that a deliberate effort be made to help women acquire and take advantage of the credibility that society does not automatically accord them.

Suggestions for Individual Career Development

It would be tempting to recommend that women intent on developing their own careers begin with the leading firms and government organizations. If they are fortunate enough as to begin in a bias-free organization or to join a boss who is aware of and willing to resist pressure for discrimination, the leading organizations are in fact helpful. While lower levels in many larger and successful organizations are open to women and provide a way to obtain experience, upper and more meaningful positions, however, are still closed. We suspect that the type of organization or situation that can provide a major career push for most women is, ironically, the "secondary sector" or "niche player" firm. These are relatively weak firms and entrepreneurial ventures, often in commodity or cyclical industries, or nonessential suppliers. Because of their weakness, they must be careful to take advantage of the best available human resources. Although they might prefer to avoid upsetting their powerholders, they are often forced to take that risk, and certainly cannot afford to discriminate elsewhere. These firms have traditionally been most likely to put women at the top of seemingly safer and less demanding staff operations such as personnel (Hypothesis 10), to use women internally or when they seem to be closely supervised (Hypotheses 8 and 9), or to apply women in "safe" situations (Hypotheses 6 and 7), and are statistically more willing to move them into critical top line positions. Application of women in these roles will provide some with the experience to move into comparable positions with primary sector employers, or with the objective evidence of their ability needed to counter discrimination and to obtain more influence with their present employers (Hypothesis 11). Over the long run, we expect that the success of women in these positions will also gradually allay the fear of those managers who discriminate on the basis of unfounded rational bias.

REFERENCES

Allen, W. R. (1979). Family roles, occupational statuses, and achievement orientations among Black women in the United States. *Signs, 4*, 670-686.

Barnhill-Hayes, Inc. (1979). *Employer attitudes toward affirmative action.* Milwaukee: Author.

Baskett, G. D. (1973). Interview decisions as determined by competency and attitude similarity. *Journal of Applied Psychology, 57*, 343-345.

Bass, B. M. (1981). *Stogdill's handbook of leadership.* New York: Free Press.

Becker, G. S. (1975). *Human capital.* New York: Columbia University Press.

Brown, H. A., & Ford, D. L., Jr. (1977). An exploratory analysis of discrimination in the employment of Black MBA graduates. *Journal of Applied Psychology, 62*, 50-56.

Campbell, J. P., & Pritchard, R. D. (1976). Motivation theory in industrial and organizational psychology. In M. D. Dunnette (Ed.), *Handbook of industrial and organizational psychology* (pp. 63-130). Chicago: Rand McNally.

DeCotiis, T. A., & LeLouarn, J.-Y. (1981). A predictive study of voting behavior in a representative election using union instrumentality and work perceptions. *Organizational Behavior and Human Performance, 27,* 103-118.

Dexter, C. R. (1979). Organizational determinants of occupational discrimination: Women managers in business. *Academy of Management Proceedings,* pp. 386-390.

Dexter, C. R. (1985). Women and the exercise of power in organizations: From ascribed to achieved status. In L. Larwood, A. H. Stromberg, & B.A. Gutek (Eds.), *Women and work* (Vol. 1, pp. 239-258). Beverly Hills, CA: Sage.

Dye, T. R., & Renick, J. (1981). Political power and city jobs: Determinants of minority employment. *Social Science Quarterly, 62,* 475-486.

Eagly, A. H., & Wood, W. (1982). Inferred sex differences in status as a determinant of gender stereotypes about social influence. *Journal of Personality and Social Psychology, 43,* 915-928.

Gealy, J., Larwood, L., & Elliott, M. P. (1979). Where sex counts: Effects of consultant and client gender in management consulting. *Group and Organization Studies, 4,* 201-211.

Geis, F. L. (1983, April). *Women, sex-roles and achievement: The self-fulfilling prophecy.* Paper presented at the annual meeting of the Eastern Psychological Association, Philadelphia.

Hansen, R. D., & O'Leary, V. E. (1984). Sex-determined attributions. In V. E. O'Leary, R. K. Unger, & B. S. Wallston (Eds.), *Women, gender, and social psychology.* Hillsdale, NJ: Lawrence Erlbaum.

Hitt, M. A., Zikmund, W. G., & Pickens, B. A. (1982). Discrimination in industrial employment: An investigation of race and sex bias among professionals. *Work and Occupations, 9,* 217-231.

Hollander, E. P. (1964). *Leaders, groups, and influence.* New York: Oxford University Press.

Hollinger, R. C., & Clark, J. P. (1983). *Theft by employees.* Lexington, MA: Lexington Books.

Hymowitz, C., & Schellhardt, T. D. (1986, March 24). The glass ceiling: Why women can't seem to break the invisible barrier that blocks them from the top jobs. *The Wall Street Journal, 4,* 1D-5D.

Jones, E. E., & Davis, K. E. (1965). From acts to dispositions: The attribution process in person perception. In L. Berkowitz (Ed.), *Advances in experimental social psychology* (Vol. 2). New York: Academic Press.

Jones, E. E., & McGillis, D. (1976). Correspondent inferences and the attribution cube: A comparative reappraisal. In J. H. Harvey, W. J. Ikes, & R. F. Kidd (Eds.), *New directions in attribution research* (Vol. 1). Hillsdale, NJ: Lawrence Erlbaum.

Kanter, R. M. (1977). *Men and women of the corporation.* New York: Basic Books.

Kraiger, K., & Ford, J. K. (1985). A meta-analysis of ratee race effects in performance ratings. *Journal of Applied Psychology, 70,* 56-65.

Larwood, L., & Blackmore, J. (1978). Sex discrimination in managerial selection: Testing predictions of the vertical dyad linkage model. *Sex Roles, 4,* 359-368.

Larwood, L., & Gattiker, U. E. (1985). Rational bias and interorganizational power in the employment of management consultants. *Group and Organization Studies, 10,* 3-17.

Larwood, L., & Gattiker, U. E. (1987). A comparison of the career paths used by successful men and women. In B. A. Gutek & L. Larwood (Eds.), *Women's career development* (pp. 129-156). Beverly Hills, CA: Sage.

Larwood, L., Gutek, B., & Gattiker, U. E. (1984). Perspectives on institutional discrimination and resistance to change. *Group and Organization Studies, 9,* 333-352.

Larwood, L., Szwajkowski, E., & Rose, S. (1988). Sex and race discrimination resulting from manager-client relationships: Applying the rational bias theory of managerial discrimination. *Sex Roles, 18,* 9-29.

Larwood, L., Zalkind, D., & Legault, J. (1975). The bank job: A field study of sexually discriminatory performance on a neutral role task. *Journal of Applied Social Psychology, 5,* 68-74.

Lockheed, M. E., & Hall, K. P. (1976). Conceptualizing sex as a status characteristic: Applications to leadership training strategies. *Journal of Social Issues, 32*(3), 111-124.

Madden, J. F. (1985). The persistence of pay differentials: The economics of sex discrimination. In L. Larwood, A. H. Stromberg, & B. A. Gutek (Eds.), *Women and work* (Vol. 1, pp. 76-114). Beverly Hills, CA: Sage.

Mai-Dalton, R. R., & Sullivan, J. J. (1981). The effects of manager's sex on the assignment to a challenging or a dull task and reasons for the choice. *Academy of Management Journal, 24,* 603-612.

Matsui, T., Kagawa, M., Nagamatsu, J., & Ohtsuka, Y. (1977). Validity of expectancy theory as a within-person behavioral choice model for sales activities. *Journal of Applied Psychology, 62,* 764-767.

Moscovici, S. (1985). Social influence and conformity. In G. Lindzey & E. Aronson (Eds.), *Handbook of social psychology* (3rd ed., pp. 73-122). New York: Random House.

Nieva, V. F., & Gutek, B. A. (1981). *Women and work: A psychological perspective.* New York: Praeger.

Nkomo, S. (in press). Race and sex: The forgotten case of the Black female manager. In S. Rose & L. Larwood (Eds.), *Women's careers: Pathways and pitfalls.* New York: Praeger.

Olian, J. D. (1986). Staffing. In E. A. Locke (Ed.), *Generalizing from laboratory to field settings* (pp. 13-42). Boston: Lexington Books.

O'Neill, J. (1985). Role differentiation and the gender gap in wage rates. In L. Larwood, A. H. Stromberg, & B. A. Gutek (Eds.), *Women and work* (Vol. 1, pp. 76-114). Beverly Hills, CA: Sage.

Parcel, T. L. (1979). Race, regional labor markets and earnings. *American Sociological Review, 44,* 262-279.

Porter, L. W., & Roberts, K. H. (1976). Communication in organizations. In M. D. Dunnette (Ed.), *Handbook of industrial and organizational psychology* (pp. 1553-1589). Chicago: Rand McNally.

Quinn, R. P., Tabor, J. M., & Gordon, L. K. (1968). *The decision to discriminate.* Ann Arbor, MI: Institute for Social Research.

Rosenbaum, J. E. (1984). *Career mobility in a corporate hierarchy.* Orlando, FL: Academic Press.

Ross, M., & Fletcher, G.J.O. (1985). Attribution in social perception. In G. Lindzey & E. Aronson (Eds.), *Handbook of social psychology* (3rd ed., pp. 73-122). New York: Random House.

Schmitt, N., & Lappin, M. (1980). Race and sex as determinants of the mean and variance of performance ratings. *Journal of Applied Psychology, 65,* 428-435.

Shepela, S. T., & Viviano, A. T. (1984). Some psychological factors affecting job segregation and wages. In H. Remick (Ed.), *Comparable worth and wage discrimination* (pp. 47-58). Philadelphia: Temple University Press.

Szwajkowski, E., & Larwood, L. (1986). *Discrimination resulting from manager-client relationships: A test of the rational bias theory of managerial discrimination.* Paper presented at the annual meeting of the Academy of Management, Chicago.

Taynor, J., & Deaux, K. (1973). When women are more deserving than men: Equity, attribution, and perceived sex differences. *Journal of Personality and Social Psychology, 28,* 474-486.

Terborg, J. R., & Ilgen, D. R. (1975). A theoretical approach to sex discrimination in traditionally masculine occupations. *Organizational Behavior and Human Performance, 13,* 352-376.

Turner, C. B., & Turner, B. F. (1981). Racial discrimination in occupations: Perceived and actual. *Phylon, 42,* 322-334.

U.S. Bureau of Labor Statistics, Department of Labor. (1986, July). *Employment and earnings.* Washington, DC: Government Printing Office.

U.S. Department of Labor. (1986). *The United Nations decade for women, 1976-1985: Employment in the United States.* Washington, DC: Government Printing Office.

Vroom, V. H. (1964). *Work and motivation.* New York: John Wiley.

Webber, R. A. (1970). Perceptions of interactions between superiors and subordinates. *Human Relations, 23,* 235-248.

ABOUT THE AUTHORS

DENISE D. BIELBY is Associate Research Sociologist in the Department of Sociology at the University of California, Santa Barbara. Her current research examines gender issues in work commitment and sex differences in employment patterns in the entertainment industry. In 1986, she received, with William Bielby, the Kathleen Gregory Klein Award for Excellence in Feminist Studies from the Popular and American Culture Associations. She holds a Ph.D. from the University of Wisconsin—Madison.

WILLIAM T. BIELBY is Professor of Sociology at the University of California, Santa Barbara. His recent research examines sex segregation in the workplace and the relationship among organizational practices, technology, and the organization of work. He holds a Ph.D. from the University of Wisconsin—Madison.

CARY L. COOPER is Professor of Organizational Psychology at the University of Manchester in England. He is the only American to hold a Chair in a British university. He is the President of the British Academy of Management (1987-1988), the editor of the international scholarly journal *The Journal of Occupational Behavior,* the author of over 45 books and 250 scholarly articles, and, in 1986, was awarded the prestigious applied psychologist Myers Lecture by the British Psychological Society. He has also been an adviser to the World Health Organization and the International Labour Office (U.N. agencies) on stress in the workplace.

MARÍA PATRICIA FERNÁNDEZ KELLY is Research Scientist at the Institute for Policy Studies and Assistant Professor of Sociology at the Johns Hopkins University. She is the author of *For We Are Sold, I and My People: Women and Industry in Mexico's Frontier* (Albany: State University of New York Press, 1983). With filmmaker Lorraine Gray, she coproduced *The Global Assembly Line,* an award-winning documentary explaining the effects of economic internationalization in the Philippines, the U.S.-Mexican border, and the United States, which has been nominated for an Emmy.

ANNA M. GARCÍA is Research Associate at the Center for U.S.-Mexican Studies at the University of California, San Diego. She has participated in several projects focusing on health delivery and access to public services on the part of Mexican immigrants. Her current work is part of the "Collaborative Study of Hispanic Women in Garment and Electronics Industries in Southern California." With María Patricia Fernández Kelly, she is coauthor of "Informalization at the Core: Hispanic Women, Homework and the Advanced Capitalist State" in the volume, *The Comparative Study of the Informal Sectors,* edited by Alejandro Portes, Manuel Castells, and Lauren Bentan (in press).

PATRICIA A. GWARTNEY-GIBBS is Assistant Professor of Sociology and Research Associate at the Center for the Study of Women in Society, both at the University of Oregon. Her research interests and publications include life span and social-demographic approaches to the study of work, occupational segregation, and earnings, as well as marital and premarital events. She is embarking on a new study of nonpecuniary forms of inequality, specifically, sex differences in workplace jurisprudence.

ELINA HAAVIO-MANNILA is Associate Professor of Sociology at the University of Helsinki. Her research work covers gender roles, family, work, politics, and immigration. She is the first author of *Unfinished Democracy: Women in Nordic Politics* (Oxford: Pergamon Press, 1985), and has published books and articles in Finnish and English. She was the editor of the Finnish *Journal of Sociology* and President of the Westermarck Society, and is currently on the editorial boards of several scientific journals.

IRJA KANDOLIN is a social scientist at the Institute of Occupational Health, Helsinki, Finland.

KAISA KAUPPINEN-TOROPAINEN is a social scientist at the Institute of Occupational Health, Helsinki, Finland. For the 1987 academic year, she served as a Visiting Scholar at the Center for Continuing Education for Women (CEW) at the University of Michigan in Ann Arbor.

GAIL WARSHOFSKY LAPIDUS is Professor of Political Science at the University of California at Berkeley. She holds a Ph.D. from Harvard University and is the author of numerous studies of Soviet politics, society, and foreign policy. Her works on women's roles in the U.S.S.R. include *Women in Soviet Society: Equality, Development and Social Change* (University of California Press, 1979), the conference volume *Women in Russia,* coedited with Dorothy Atkinson and Alexander Dallin (Stanford University Press, 1977), and a collection of Soviet writings in translation titled *Women, Work and Family in the USSR* (M.E. Sharpe, 1982).

LAURIE LARWOOD is Dean of the School of Business, State University of New York at Albany. She is one of the founding editors of *Women and Work,* and is also editor of *Group and Organization Studies* and *Journal of Management Case Studies;* she is currently a member of the editorial boards of *Sex Roles* and *Journal of Occupational Behavior.* Her books include *Women in Management* (with Marion Wood), *Women's Career Development* (with Barbara Gutek), *Women's Careers: Pathways and Pitfalls* (with Suzanna Rose), and *Organizational Behavior and Management.* She obtained her Ph.D. in Psychology from Tulane University and previously headed a California manufacturing firm.

SUZAN N.C. LEWIS is Senior Lecturer in Psychology in the Department of Psychology and Speech Pathology at Manchester Polytechnic. She gained her Ph.D. from the University of Manchester, Institute of Science and Technology, in 1986. Her research interests include stress and the transition to parenthood in dual-earner couples.

JUNE NASH is Professor of Anthropology at City College and the Graduate Center of the City University of New York. She has worked with the Maya of Chiapas in Mexico, with Bolivian tin miners, and, most recently, electrical workers in the United States. She has written *In the Eyes of the Ancestors, Belief and Behavior in a Maya Village; We Eat the*

Mines and the Mines Eat Us; Dependency and Exploitation in a Bolivian Tin Mine, and *From Tank Town to High Tech; The Restructuring of Industry in America.*

VIRGINIA E. O'LEARY received her Ph.D. in social psychology from Wayne State University in 1969. She was on the faculty of Oakland University in Rochester, Michigan, from 1970 to 1980. She spent six years in full-time administration with the American Psychological Association, where she served as Deputy Executive Officer for Public Affairs from 1981 to 1984. She is author of *Toward Understanding Women* (Brooks/Cole, 1977) and coeditor of *Women, Gender, and Social Psychology* (Erlbaum, 1985) with Barbara Strudler Wallston and Rhoda K. Unger. A two-time recipient of the Association for Women in Psychology's Distinguished Publication Award, she is Past President of the Division of Psychology of Women of the American Psychological Association. She if currently a Visiting Scholar at Radcliffe College.

PAMELA ROBY is Professor of Sociology and Women's Studies at the University of California at Santa Cruz. She has authored *Women in the Workplace,* coauthored *The Future of Inequality* with S. M. Miller, and edited *The Poverty Establishment* and *Child Care—Who Cares? Foreign and Domestic Infant and Early Childhood Development Policies* as well as having published extensively on the subjects of education, prostitution laws, and income policies. She is Past President of Sociologists for Women in Society and Past Chair of the American Sociological Association's Section on Sex and Gender.

SUZANNA ROSE is Associate Professor of Psychology and Women's Studies at the University of Missouri—St. Louis. She holds a Ph.D. in psychology from the University of Pittsburgh. Her research is on women's friendships and professional networks. She is editor of the recently released *Career Guide for Women Scholars* and coeditor with Laurie Larwood of *Women's Careers: Pathways and Pitfalls* (in press).

EUGENE SZWAJKOWSKI is Assistant Professor in the Department of Management at the University of Illinois at Chicago. He received his Ph.D. in organizational behavior at the University of Illinois at Urbana—Champaign, where he returned as a Visiting Assistant Professor for 1986-1987. His major specialty is the study of factors contributing to illegal and unethical organizational behavior.

LYNET UTTAL is a Ph.D. candidate in the Sociology Board of Studies at the University of California, Santa Cruz. Her interests include the integration of public and private lives and women of color in the United States.

KATHRYN B. WARD is Associate Professor of Sociology at Southern Illinois University at Carbondale. Her current research includes the international debt crisis, the contemporary U.S. women's movement, and the feminist critique of sociology. She is author of the book *Women in the World-System* and articles in *Review, Social Science Quarterly, Work and Occupations,* and *The Sociological Quarterly.*

Women and Work: An Annual Review

The Sage series **Women and Work: An Annual Review** brings together research, critical analysis, and proposals for change in a dynamic and developing field—the world of women and work. Cutting across traditional academic boundaries, the series approaches subjects from a multidisciplinary perspective. Historians, anthropologists, economists, sociologists, managers, psychologists, educators, policymakers, and legal scholars share insights and findings—giving readers access to a scattered literature in a single comprehensive yearly volume.

Women and Work will examine differences among women—as well as differences between men and women—related to nationality, ethnicity, social class, and sexual preference. The series will explore demographic and legal trends, international and multinational comparisons, and theoretical and methodological developments.

Series Editors

Laurie Larwood
State University of New York, Albany

Barbara A. Gutek
Claremont Graduate School

Ann H. Stromberg
Pitzer College

VOLUMES IN THIS SERIES

WOMEN AND WORK
An Annual Review, Volume 1
edited by LAURIE LARWOOD, *State University of New York, Albany*
ANN H. STROMBERG, *Pitzer College*
& BARBARA A. GUTEK, *Claremont Graduate School*

WOMEN AND WORK
An Annual Review, Volume 2
edited by ANN H. STROMBERG, *Pitzer College*
LAURIE LARWOOD, *State University of New York, Albany*
& BARBARA A. GUTEK, *Claremont Graduate School*

WOMEN AND WORK
An Annual Review, Volume 3
edited by BARBARA A. GUTEK, *Claremont Graduate School*
ANN H. STROMBERG, *Pitzer College*
& LAURIE LARWOOD, *State University of New York, Albany*

NOTES